PEARSON
mywritinglab™

If practice makes perfect, imagine what *better* practice can do . . .

MyWritingLab is an online learning system that provides better writing practice through progressive exercises. These exercises move students from literal comprehension to critical application to demonstration of their ability to write properly. With this better practice model, students develop the skills needed to become better writers!

When asked if they agreed with the following statements, students responded favorably.

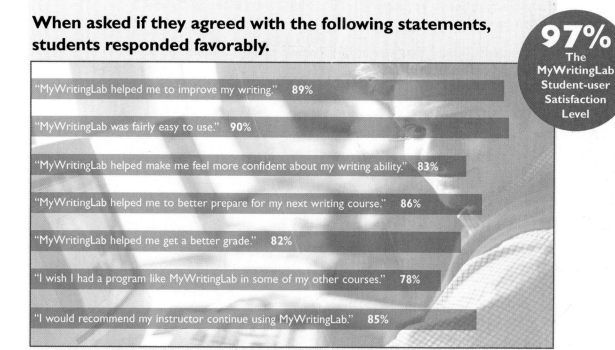

"MyWritingLab helped me to improve my writing." **89%**

"MyWritingLab was fairly easy to use." **90%**

"MyWritingLab helped make me feel more confident about my writing ability." **83%**

"MyWritingLab helped me to better prepare for my next writing course." **86%**

"MyWritingLab helped me get a better grade." **82%**

"I wish I had a program like MyWritingLab in some of my other courses." **78%**

"I would recommend my instructor continue using MyWritingLab." **85%**

97%
The MyWritingLab Student-user Satisfaction Level

Student Success Story

"The first few weeks of my English class, my grades were at approximately 78%. Then I was introduced to MyWritingLab. I couldn't believe the increase in my test scores. My test scores had jumped from that low score of 78 all the way up to 100% (and every now and then a 99)."

—Exetta Windfield, *College of the Sequoias* (MyWritingLab student user)

If your book did not come with an access code, you may purchase an access code at www.mywritinglab.com

www.mywritinglab.com

Registering for MyWritingLab™...

It is easy to get started! Simply follow these steps to get into your MyWritingLab course.

1) **Find Your Access Code** (it is either packaged with your textbook, or you purchased it separately). You will need this access code and your course ID to join your MyWritingLab course. Your instructor has your course ID number, so make sure you have that before logging in.

2) **Click on "Students"** under "Register or Buy Access." Here you will be prompted to enter your access code, enter your e-mail address, and choose your own login name and password. After you register, you can **login under "Returning Users"** to use your new login name and password every time you go back into MyWritingLab.

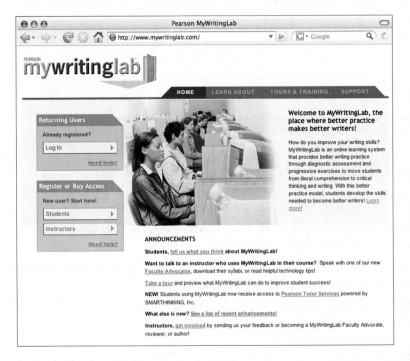

After logging in, you will see all the ways MyWritingLab can help you become a better writer.

www.mywritinglab.com

The Homepage ...

Here is your MyWritingLab HomePage.
You get a bird's eye view of where you are in your course every time you log in.

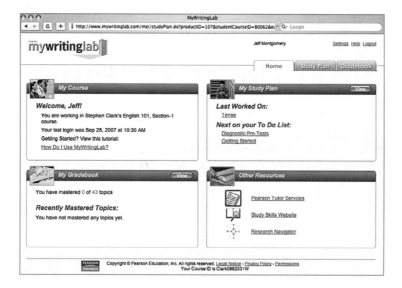

Your **Course** box shows your class details.

Your **Study Plan** box shows what you last completed and what is next on your **To Do** list.

Your **Gradebook** box shows you a snapshot of how you are doing in the class.

Your **Other Resources** box supplies you with amazing tools such as:

- **Pearson Tutor Services**—click here to see how you can get help on your papers by qualified tutors . . . before handing them in!

- **Research Navigator**—click here to see how this resembles your library with access to online journals for research paper assignments.

- **Study Skills**—extra help that includes tips and quizzes on how to improve your study skills

Now, let's start practicing to become better writers. Click on the Study Plan tab. This is where you will do all your course work.

The Study Plan . . .

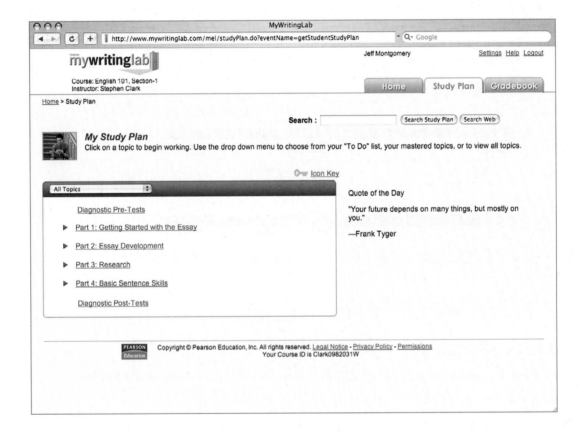

MyWritingLab provides you with a simple Study Plan of the writing skills that you need to master. You start from the top of the list and work your way down. You can start with the Diagnostic Pre-Tests.

The Diagnostic Pre-Tests contain five exercises on each of the grammar, punctuation, and usage topics. You can achieve mastery of the topic in the Diagnostic Pre-Test by getting four of five or five of five correct within each topic.

After completing the Diagnostic Pre-Test, you can return to your Study Plan and enter any of the topics you have yet to master.

www.mywritinglab.com

Watch, Recall, Apply, Write . . .

Here is an example of a MyWritinglab Activity set that you will see once you enter into a topic. Take the time to briefly read the introductory paragraph, and then watch the engaging video clip by clicking on "Watch: Tense."

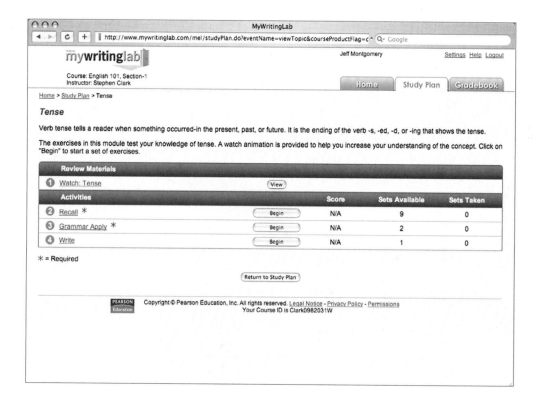

The video clip provides you with a helpful review.
Now you are ready to start the exercises. There are three types:

- Recall—activities that help you *recall* the rules of grammar
- Apply—activities that help you *apply* these rules to brief paragraphs or essays
- Write—activities that ask you to demonstrate these rules of grammar in your own writing

www.mywritinglab.com

Helping Students Succeed . . .

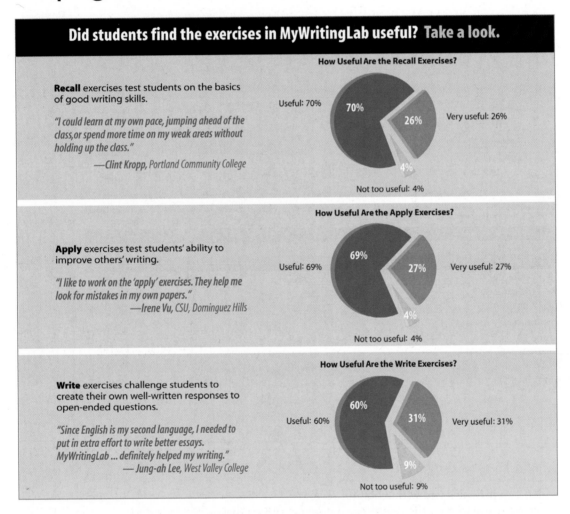

Did students find the exercises in MyWritingLab useful? Take a look.

How Useful Are the Recall Exercises?

Recall exercises test students on the basics of good writing skills.

"I could learn at my own pace, jumping ahead of the class, or spend more time on my weak areas without holding up the class."

—*Clint Kropp, Portland Community College*

Useful: 70%
70%
26%
Very useful: 26%
4%
Not too useful: 4%

How Useful Are the Apply Exercises?

Apply exercises test students' ability to improve others' writing.

"I like to work on the 'apply' exercises. They help me look for mistakes in my own papers."

—*Irene Vu, CSU, Dominguez Hills*

Useful: 69%
69%
27%
Very useful: 27%
4%
Not too useful: 4%

How Useful Are the Write Exercises?

Write exercises challenge students to create their own well-written responses to open-ended questions.

"Since English is my second language, I needed to put in extra effort to write better essays. MyWritingLab ... definitely helped my writing."

— *Jung-ah Lee, West Valley College*

Useful: 60%
60%
31%
Very useful: 31%
9%
Not too useful: 9%

Students just like you are finding MyWritingLab's Recall, Apply, and Write exercises useful in their learning.

Here to Help You ...

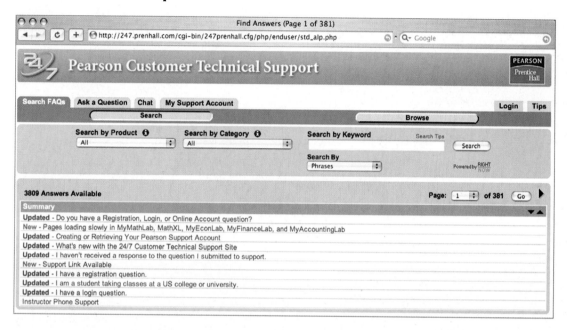

Our goal is to provide answers to your MyWritingLab questions as quickly as possible and deliver the highest level of support. By visiting **www.mywritinglab.com/help.html**, many questions can be resolved in just a few minutes. Here you will find help on the following:

- ☑ System Requirements
- ☑ How to Register for MyWritingLab
- ☑ How to Use MyWritingLab

For student support, we also invite you to contact Pearson Customer Technical Support (shown above). In addition, you can reach our Support Representatives online at **http://247.pearsoned.com**. Here you can do the following:

- ☑ Search Frequently Asked Questions about MyWritingLab
- ☑ E-mail a Question to Our Support Team
- ☑ Chat with a Support Representative

Along These Lines
Writing Sentences and Paragraphs

Why Do You Need This New Edition?

If you're wondering why you should buy this new edition of *Along These Lines: Writing Sentences and Paragraphs*, here are ten good reasons:

❶ A new bright, visually appealing design helps you find key concepts easily as you become an active learner.

❷ New and lively writing topics draw on your work, home, and school experiences so that you can write about what you know well.

❸ "Jumping In," a new feature that opens every writing chapter, links an eye-catching photograph to the chapter's focus and initiates thinking, encourages discussion, and sparks your writing.

❹ "One Quick Question," a new feature at the beginning of every grammar chapter, includes a photo of students engaged in a college activity. One grammar question related to the subject of the chapter engages you in the prereading stage of reading effectively.

❺ New and varied exercises in every writing chapter help you navigate easily through each stage of the writing process.

❻ New editing exercises in every grammar chapter connect grammar principles to real-world writing.

❼ More photo-related writing topics will sharpen your perception and challenge your creativity.

❽ An expanded appendix, "Grammar Practice for Nonnative Speakers," reinforces the essentials of basic grammar.

❾ New and timely readings on such thought-provoking topics as the price of fame, a mother's search for her addicted son, and a daughter's struggle for a father's respect will gain your attention and prompt ideas for your own writing.

❿ And now—use *Along These Lines: Writing Sentences and Paragraphs* alongside Pearson's unique MyWritingLab (www.mywritinglab.com) and find a world of resources specifically for you!

Along These Lines

Writing Sentences and Paragraphs

Fourth Edition

John Sheridan Biays, professor emeritus of English
Broward College

Carol Wershoven, professor emerita of English
Palm Beach Community College

Prentice Hall

Upper Saddle River   London   Singapore
Toronto   Tokyo   Sydney   Hong Kong   Mexico City

Senior VP/Publisher: Joe Opiela
Editor in Chief: Craig Campanella
Editorial Project Manager: Jessica A. Kupetz
Editorial Assistant: Gina Aloe
VP/Director of Marketing: Tim Stookesbury
Executive Marketing Manager: Megan Galvin-Fak
Marketing Manager: Tom DeMarco
Marketing Assistant: Jean-Pierre Dufresne
Senior Operations Supervisor: Sherry Lewis
Operations Specialist: Christina Amato
Senior Art Director: Nancy Wells
Art Director: Suzanne Duda
Interior and Cover Designer: Ximena Tamvakopoulos
Manager, Visual Research: Beth Brenzel
Photo Researcher: Kathy Ringrose
Manager, Rights & Permissions: Zina Arabia
Image Permission Coordinator: Joanne Dippel
Manager, Cover Visual Research & Permissions: Karen Sanatar
Cover Art: Shutter Stock
Full-Service Project Management & Composition: Black Dot Group
Printer/Binder: Webcrafters, Inc.
Cover Printer: Lehigh-Phoenix Color Corporation
Text Font: 11/13 ITC Century Book

Credits and acknowledgments for material borrowed from other sources and reproduced, with permission, in this textbook appear on page 495.

Library of Congress Cataloging-in-Publication Data
Biays, John Sheridan.
    Along these lines : writing sentences and paragraphs / John Sheridan Biays, Carol
      Wershoven.—4th ed.
    p. cm.
  ISBN-13: 978-0-205-64893-1
  ISBN-10: 0-205-64893-2
    1. English language—Sentences. 2. English language—Paragraphs. 3. English
      language—Rhetoric. I. Wershoven, Carol. II. Title.
  PE1441 .B53 2009
  808'.042—dc22   2009012760

10 9 8 7 6 5 4 3 2 1

Prentice Hall
is an imprint of

www.pearsonhighered.com

ISBN 10: 0-205-64893-2
ISBN 13: 978-0-205-64893-1

Contents

 CHAPTER 29 Writing from
Reading   441

Appendix A: Readings for
Writers   465

Appendix B: Grammar Practice for Nonnative Speakers   487

Photo Assignments to Accompany the Writing Chapters

Preface

TO INSTRUCTORS

We know from our many years of working with beginning writers that students will view writing as a natural process if they engage in various instructional activities (e.g., individual, collaborative, creative, computer-related) that recognize different learning styles. The *Along These Lines* series is based on this premise, and we are indebted to literally hundreds of instructors who have offered invaluable suggestions for refining our work.

Striking a balance between teaching creatively and meeting statewide or departmental "exit-test" objectives can be challenging for any composition instructor. On a positive note, however, we are constantly amazed by the tireless efforts of so many educators across the country who remain committed to quality developmental instruction despite severe budget restraints and ever-increasing class sizes. Such dedicated instructors simply want their students to succeed, and when these professionals offer advice, we know we should pay close attention.

As you preview this new edition, you may notice several improvements and unique features. Many changes in this edition reflect the collective wisdom of developmental instructors nationwide, and we believe that *Along These Lines: Writing Sentences and Paragraphs*, Fourth Edition, is the most comprehensive, user-friendly, and visually appealing text to date. Thanks for your continued interest in our work and for supporting developmental education along *all* lines.

UNIQUE FEATURES AND IMPROVEMENTS FOR THE FOURTH EDITION

Extensive Visual Enhancements

- Each grammar chapter opens with a "Quick Question" feature and includes an engaging photograph of students thinking, reading, studying, or interacting. Each quick question is related to the grammar principle covered in the chapter and provides an incentive to preview the content.
- A new feature, "Jumping In," opens each writing chapter and links an eye-catching, full-color photograph to the chapter's focus and initiates thinking, encourages discussion, and sparks prewriting about a particular rhetorical pattern.

Expanded Grammar Coverage

- New editing exercises in each chapter require students to apply the relevant grammar principle to sample writing assignments.
- An expanded appendix, "Grammar Practice for Nonnative Speakers," reinforces the essentials of basic grammar.

Enhanced Writing Instruction and Topic Choices

- New and varied writing assignments draw on work, home, and school experiences to help sharpen students' focus and generate specific details.
- New exercises throughout the writing chapters emphasize the importance of revising and proofreading, skills essential for subsequent writing courses.
- More photo-related writing topics will sharpen students' perceptions and challenge their creativity.

POPULAR FEATURES RETAINED

In response to suggestions from current users and new reviewers, we have retained these distinctive and popular features:

The Grammar Section

- Three types of grammar exercises—*Practice* (simple reinforcement), *Collaborate* (partner or group work), and *Connect* (application of the grammar principal to paragraphs) exercises.
- Grammar concepts taught step-by-step, as in "Two Steps to Check for Fragments."
- A Chapter Test at the end of most grammar chapters, ideal for class review or quick quizzes.

The Writing Section

- Visually appealing checklists, charts, and "Info Boxes."
- A lively conversational tone, including question-and-answer formats and dialogues.
- Framed examples of an outline, draft, and final version of a writing assignment in each chapter.
- A "Walk-Through" writing assignment at the end of each chapter that guides students, step-by-step, through the stages of the writing process.
- A Peer Review Form in most chapters so students can benefit from a classmate's reaction to their drafts.

The Readings

- Professional reading selections grouped in a special appendix for easy reference.
- Vocabulary definitions based on the specific context of the writer's intent.
- Writing options sparked by a selection's content and designed to elicit thinking, not merely rote replication of a model.

OUR PHILOSOPHY

We believe that an effective text should respect each student's individuality and innate desire to learn and succeed. We trust that the *Along These Lines* series will continue to help students flourish within a framework of respect, encouragement, and meaningful interaction as they work through the writing process.

ACKNOWLEDGMENTS

We have been gratified and encouraged by the positive reception the *Along These Lines* series has generated over the years. We are indebted to the following professionals for their frank, comprehensive reviews, which helped us immensely during our revision process:

Jeremy Abad	Chaffey College
Nancy Alexander	Methodist University
Kina Burkett	Jefferson Davis Community College
Beverly Dile	Elizabethtown Community and Technical College
James Fields	Iowa Western Community College
Leona Fisher	Chaffey College
Anita Griffin	Hinds Community College
Carin Halper	Fresno City College
Curtis Harrell	Northwest Arkansas Community College
Aleyenne Johnson-Jonas	Art Institute of California
Billy Jones	Miami Dade College–Kendall Campus
Peter Kearly	Henry Ford Community College
Tracy Lassiter	Eastern Arizona College
Teri Maddox	Jackson State Community College
Jennifer Olds	Chaffey College
Ann Schlumberger	Pima Community College–West Campus
Margaret Wanning	Piedmont Technical College
Tammy White	Forsyth Technical Community College
Brian Wren	Gwinnett Technical College

Dave Nitti and Gina Aloe, editorial assistants, kept us in the loop on reviews and communicated with us often. Somehow, they even managed to keep the business-related red tape and paperwork at bay so we could concentrate on our rounds of revisions.

We are indebted to Craig Campanella, editor in chief of Developmental English, and Matt Wright, acquisitions editor for Developmental English. Craig is still adept at allaying authors' fears while overseeing Pearson's entire English list. His enthusiasm for his work and his knack for fostering collegiality is both admirable and inspiring. Matt's commitment to Developmental English is also obvious, and we know we'll be in good hands for subsequent editions.

We were most fortunate to work with Sandy Reinhard and her associates at Black Dot Group. Throughout the copyediting, proofing, and production phases, Sandy kept us intact and relatively sane. She resolved scheduling snags, fixed design problems, met page count mandates, and commiserated with authors. We know we couldn't have been in better—or kinder—hands.

Additionally, we extend thanks to Maureen Benicasa, production editor, whose calm and confident assurance during the series' production process always boosted our morale. Kudos also to Kathleen Karcher, permissions editor; Edith Bicknell, copy editor; Ximena Tamvakopoulos, designer; Suzanne Duda, art director; Leslie Osher, creative design director; Becky Dodson, proofreader; and Leoni McVey, indexer. We are also very grateful to Tom DeMarco, marketing manager, for his enthusiastic support of our series.

Finally, and most importantly, we thank the many students and colleagues who, for over three decades, intrigued, impressed, and inspired us. You made our journey extraordinary along *all* lines.

John Sheridan Biays
Carol Wershoven

CHAPTER 1

Quick Question

True or False: The subject of a sentence always starts the sentence.

(After you study this chapter, you will be confident of your answer.)

The Simple Sentence

Identifying the crucial parts of a sentence is the first step in many writing decisions: how to punctuate, how to avoid sentence fragments, and how to be sure that subjects and verbs *agree* (match). Moving forward to these decisions requires a few steps backward—to basics.

RECOGNIZING A SENTENCE

Let's start with a few definitions. A basic unit of language is a **word.**

> **examples:** cap, desk, tree

A group of related words can be a **phrase.**

> **examples:** battered baseball cap, on the desk, tall palm tree

When a group of words contains a subject and a verb, it is called a **clause.** When the word group has a subject and a verb and makes sense by itself, it is called a **sentence** or an independent clause.

> If you want to check whether you have written a sentence and not just a group of related words, you first have to check for a subject and a verb. Locating the verbs first can be easier.

RECOGNIZING VERBS

Verbs are words that express some kind of action or being. **Action verbs** tell what somebody or something does.

action verbs:
Computers *hold* an amazing amount of information.
We *call* our parents once a month.
The boxer *exercises* at my local gym.
You *missed* the bus yesterday.
David *dented* the back of my car.
He *drives* like a maniac.
They *study* together on weekends.
I *believe* her story.

Sometimes a verb tells what something or somebody is. Such verbs are called **being verbs**. Words like *feels, looks, seems, smells, sounds,* and *tastes* are part of the group called being verbs. Look at some examples of being verbs and their functions in the following sentences:

being verbs:
The computer *is* a great invention.
The boxer *looks* tired today.
You *sound* happy.
David *is* a good candidate for traffic school.
He *seems* unaware of traffic lights.
They *are* the best students in my class.
I *feel* confident about her story.
Gossip *is* nasty and mean.

Exercise 1   **Recognizing Action Verbs**

Underline the action verbs in the following sentences.

1. The frog jumped into the bushes.

2. Sometimes, Mike brings me coffee.

3. My bedroom needs new curtains.

4. Photographs remind us of happy times.

5. Ruben arrived at the airport on time.

6. Your friends appreciate your honest advice.

7. A daily walk reduces my stress levels.

8. A leaky pen smeared my new shirt.

9. Ashley takes her daughter to school on weekdays.

10. An old joke delighted the children.

Exercise 2   **Recognizing Being Verbs**

Underline the being verbs in the following sentences.

1. College students are usually sleep-deprived.

2. My new shirt feels like silk against my skin.

3. On Sunday nights, I am worried about Monday's demands.

4. Last night, Peter sounded enthusiastic and hopeful.

5. My cousins were my rivals in high school.

6. Professor Duvall is a well-known jazz musician.

7. The salesperson seemed rude and bad-tempered.

8. Your house looks beautiful today.

9. The salad greens taste bitter.

10. Recess was my favorite part of elementary school.

Exercise 3   **Writing Sentences with Specific Verbs**

Collaborate

With a partner or group, write two sentences using each of the verbs listed below. Each sentence must have at least five words. When you have completed the exercise, share your answers with another group or with the class. The first one is done for you.

1. verb: dragged

   sentence 1: *I dragged the heavy bag across the floor.*

   sentence 2: *Lori dragged herself out of a warm bed.*

2. verb: smells

   sentence 1: _____

   sentence 2: _____

3. verb: argues

   sentence 1: _____

   sentence 2: _____

4. verb: seem

   sentence 1: _____

   sentence 2: _____

5. verb: slapped

   sentence 1: _____

   sentence 2: _____

6. verb: wins

   sentence 1: _____

   sentence 2: _____

7. verb: was

   sentence 1: _____

   sentence 2: _____

8. verb: were

   sentence 1: _____

   sentence 2: _____

   9. verb: smiled

   sentence 1: _____

   sentence 2: _____

   10. verb: annoys

   sentence 1: _____

   sentence 2: _____

Helping Verbs

The verb in a sentence can be more than one word. There can be **helping verbs** in front of the main verb (the action verb or being verb). Here is a list of some frequently used helping verbs:

INFO BOX: **Common Helping Verbs**

am	had	might	were
can	has	must	will
could	have	shall	would
did	is	should	
do	may	was	

Here are some examples of sentences with main and helping verbs:

main and helping verbs:
You *should have answered* the question. (The helping verbs are *should* and *have*.)
Laurie *will notify* the lottery winner. (The helping verb is *will*.)
Babies *can recognize* their mothers' voices. (The helping verb is *can*.)
I *am thinking* about a career in medicine. (The helping verb is *am*.)

Exercise 4 **Recognizing the Complete Verb: Main and Helping Verbs**

Underline the complete verb (both main and helping verbs) in each of the following sentences.

   1. Tim may have borrowed my leather jacket.

   2. My mother should have been more careful with her money.

   3. By 3:00 p.m., I was checking my watch impatiently.

   4. Over the weekend, we must clean the kitchen and the bathroom.

   5. Isabella's parrot can say ten different phrases.

   6. You and Adam are spreading rumors about me.

   7. Lynette could have been injured in the car accident.

   8. I will be seeing my stepbrother next month.

   9. Two of the salespeople were considering a transfer to another store.

   10. On Sunday, Leah and I did expect better weather for the cookout.

Exercise 5   **Writing Sentences with Helping Verbs**

Complete this exercise with a partner or group. First, ask one person to add at least one helping verb to the verb given. Then work together to write two sentences using the main verb and the helping verb(s). Appoint one spokesperson for your group to read all your sentences to the class. Notice how many combinations of main and helping verbs you hear. The first one is done for you.

1. **verb:** complained

   verb with helping verb(s): *must have complained*

   sentence 1: *My supervisor must have complained about me.*

   sentence 2: *She must have complained twenty times yesterday.*

2. **verb:** denying

   verb with helping verb(s): _____

   sentence 1: _____

   sentence 2: _____

3. **verb:** forgive

   verb with helping verb(s): _____

   sentence 1: They should forgive you.

   sentence 2: The mother must forgive her daughter for the mess,

4. **verb:** said

   verb with helping verb(s): _____

   sentence 1: _____

   sentence 2: _____

5. **verb:** given

   verb with helping verb(s): _____

   sentence 1: _____

   sentence 2: _____

6. **verb:** expecting

   verb with helping verb(s): _____

   sentence 1: We have been expecting you.

   sentence 2: _____

7. **verb:** broken

   verb with helping verb(s): _____

   sentence 1: He must have broken the vase.

   sentence 2: _____

8. **verb:** encourage

   verb with helping verb(s): _____

   sentence 1: _____

   sentence 2: _____

9. **verb:** growing

verb with helping verb(s): _____

sentence 1: _____

sentence 2: _____

10. **verb:** caused

verb with helping verb(s): _____

sentence 1: _____

sentence 2: _____

More Than One Main Verb

Helping verbs can make the verb in a sentence longer than one word, but there can also be more than one main verb.

more than one main verb:
Antonio *begged* and *pleaded* for mercy.
I *ran* to the car, *tossed* my books on the backseat, and *jammed* the key in the ignition.
My dog *steals* my shoes and *chews* on them.

Exercise 6   **Recognizing Main Verbs**

Some of the sentences below have one main verb; some have more than one main verb. Underline all the main verbs in each sentence.

1. Every night, my brother drives to his girlfriend's house, honks his car horn, and waits for her in his car.

2. Edward Kansky and Nick Stamos sell silver jewelry and leather belts at the flea market.

3. Alicia borrowed my clothes but rarely returned them.

4. My favorite place for breakfast is a pancake house with seven kinds of pancakes and eight flavors of syrup.

5. Your mother called and invited us to dinner tomorrow night.

6. A drunk driver shattered one car's taillight, smashed another's front end, and skidded into a trash can.

7. Felice ordered a salad for lunch and cut the lettuce into tiny pieces.

8. Some of the animals in his paintings look like dragons or other fantastic creatures from an imaginary world.

9. My oldest friend understands my problems, accepts my weaknesses, and believes in my strengths.

10. Marty is close to his sister and talks to her at least once a week.

Connect

Exercise 7   **Recognizing Verbs in a Selection from "The Tell-Tale Heart"**

This selection is from "The Tell-Tale Heart," a horror story by Edgar Allan Poe. In it, an insane murderer has killed an old man and buried him under the floor.

When the police arrive, they find nothing, but the murderer is convinced that he—and the police—can hear the old man's heart beating under the floor. In this selection, the murderer describes what he feels as he hears the heart beat louder and louder.

Underline all the verbs in the selection. Notice how a careful choice of verbs can make writing exciting and suspenseful.

The officers were satisfied. My manner had convinced them. I was singularly at ease. They sat, and while I answered cheerfully, they chatted of familiar things. But, ere* long, I felt myself getting pale and wished them gone. My head ached, and I fancied* a ringing in my ears: but still they sat and still chatted. The ringing became more distinct: —it continued and became more distinct: I talked more freely to get rid of the feeling: but it continued and gained definitiveness—until, at length,* I found that the noise was not within my ears.

No doubt I now grew very pale; —but I talked more fluently, and with a heightened voice. Yet the sound increased—and what could I do? . . . I gasped for breath—and yet the officers heard it not. I talked more quickly, more vehemently;* but the noise steadily increased. I arose and argued about trifles, in a high key and with violent gesticulations,* but the noise steadily increased. Why would they not be gone? I paced the floor to and fro with heavy strides, as if excited to fury by the observation of the men—but the noise steadily increased. Oh God! What could I do? I foamed—I raved—I swore! . . . It grew louder—louder—louder! And still the men chatted pleasantly, and smiled. Was it possible they heard not? Almighty God! —no, no! They heard! —they suspected! —they knew!

*ere: before
*fancied: imagined
*at length: after a time
*vehemently: furiously
*gesticulations: gestures

RECOGNIZING SUBJECTS

After you learn to recognize verbs, you can easily find the subjects of sentences because subjects and verbs are linked. If the verb is an action verb, for example, the **subject** will be the word or words that answer the question "Who or what is doing that action?" Follow these steps to identify the subject:

sentence with an action verb:
The cat slept on my bed.

Step 1: Identify the verb: *slept*

Step 2: Ask, "Who or what slept?"

Step 3: The answer is the subject: The *cat* slept on my bed. The *cat* is the subject.

If the verb is a being verb, the same steps apply to finding the subject.

sentence with a being verb:

Clarice is his girlfriend.

Step 1: Identify the verb: *is*

Step 2: Ask, "Who or what is his girlfriend?"

Step 3: The answer is the subject: *Clarice* is his girlfriend. *Clarice* is the subject.

Just as there can be more than one verb, there can be more than one subject.

examples: *Coffee* and a *doughnut* are a typical breakfast for me.

His *father* and *grandfather* own a landscaping service.

Exercise 8 **Recognizing Subjects in Sentences**

Underline the subjects in the following sentences.

1. The pudding tastes like caramel and cream.

2. Sylvia Jong might have left a message on my cell phone.

3. Grease and dirt stuck to the surface of the stove.

4. Something woke me in the middle of the night.

5. Lorraine and Pierre have family members in Haiti.

6. Smoking is becoming an expensive and socially unacceptable habit.

7. Greed and arrogance led William to a series of bad decisions.

8. Peanuts can cause dangerous allergic reactions in some people.

9. They brought their cousin to our engagement party.

10. A quilt can be a valuable piece of family history.

Collaborate

Exercise 9 **Adding Subjects to Sentences**

Working with a partner or group, complete the paragraph below by adding subjects to the blank lines. Before you fill in the blanks, discuss your answers and try to come to an agreement about the worst movie, the worst music video, and so on. When you have completed the paragraph, share your answers with another group or with the class.

This year has seen many achievements in the arts and entertainment, but it has also

seen many creative disasters. On movie screens, there have been some terrible

movies. Without a doubt, _____ was the worst movie of the year. It should never have been made. On television, _____ was the worst and also the

most irritating show. Every time I see it, I want to turn it off or kick in the television

screen. _____ and _____ take the prize for the worst actor and

actress of the year. They should consider other careers. In the field of music,

_____ ranks as the least successful music video of the year.

_____ is the most annoying song because the radio played it far too often.

Last, _____ is the most annoying singer.

MORE ABOUT RECOGNIZING SUBJECTS AND VERBS

Recognizing the Core Subject

When you look for the subject of a sentence, look for the core word or words;
do not include descriptive words around the subject. Look for the subject, not
for the words that describe it.

> **the core subject:**
> Light blue *paint* will brighten these walls.
> Cracked *sidewalks* and rusty *railings* made the old school dangerous for
>   children.

Prepositions and Prepositional Phrases

Prepositions are usually short words that often signal a kind of position or
possession, as shown in the following list:

INFO BOX: Some Common Prepositions

about	before	by	inside	on	under
above	behind	during	into	onto	up
across	below	except	like	over	upon
after	beneath	for	near	through	with
among	beside	from	of	to	within
around	between	in	off	toward	without
at	beyond				

A **prepositional phrase** is made up of a preposition and its object. Here are
some prepositional phrases. In each one, the first word is the preposition; the
other words are the object of the preposition.

> **prepositional phrases:**
> about the movie   of mice and men
> around the corner   off the wall
> between two lanes   on the mark
> during recess   up the chimney
> near my house   with my sister and brother

An old memory trick can help you remember prepositions. Think of a chair. Now, think of a series of words you can put in front of the chair:

around the chair	*with* the chair
by the chair	*to* the chair
behind the chair	*near* the chair
between the chairs	*under* the chair
of the chair	*on* the chair
off the chair	*from* the chair

These words are prepositions.

You need to know about prepositions because they can help you identify the subject of a sentence. Here is an important grammar rule about prepositions:

Nothing in a prepositional phrase can ever be the subject of a sentence.

Prepositional phrases describe people, places, or things. They may also describe the subject of a sentence, but they never *include* the subject. Whenever you are looking for the subject of a sentence, begin by putting parentheses around all the prepositional phrases:

parentheses and prepositional phrases:
The park (behind my apartment) has a playground (with swings and slides).

Nothing in the prepositional phrase can be the subject. Once you have eliminated these phrases, you can follow the steps to find the subject of the sentence.

Step 1: Identify the verb: *has*

Step 2: Ask, "Who or what has?"

Step 3: The answer is the subject: The *park*. The *park* is the subject.

By marking off the prepositional phrases, you are left with the core of the sentence. There is less to look at.

(Across the street) a *child* (with a teddy bear) sat (among the flowers).
subject: *child*

The *student* (from Jamaica) won the contest (with ease).
subject: *student*

Exercise 10 **Recognizing Prepositional Phrases, Subjects, and Verbs**

Put parentheses around the prepositional phrases in the following sentences. Then underline the subjects and verbs, putting *S* above the subject and *V* above the verb.

1. Two (of my friends) graduated (from Western High School) (in 2004).

2. My puppy raced (down the stairs) and skidded (across the wet floor) (into my arms.)

3. A bunch (of flowers) and a card lay (on the kitchen counter.)

4. The girl (with the long black hair) was the most attractive stranger (at

   my brother's party.)

5. The mud (on the side (of my car) came from a deep puddle (at the end) of

   the street.)

6. Nothing except a sincere apology from that man can soothe the anger

   in my heart.

7. The children climbed over a crumbling wall (onto the decaying

   property) (with the haunted cabin) behind the tall trees.

8. At one point, the troops were driving through dangerous territory

   without clear directions.

9. Near the end of class, I looked (under my desk) and saw a mouse

   (among the books (on the floor.)

10. One of my friends completes his reading assignments between

    classes, writes his papers around midnight, and studies for his tests

    on the weekends.

Exercise 11 **Writing Sentences with Prepositional Phrases**

Collaborate

Do this exercise with a partner. First, add one prepositional phrase to the core sentence. Then ask your partner to add a second prepositional phrase to the same sentence. For the next sentence, switch places. Let your partner add the first phrase; you add the second. Keep switching places throughout the exercise. When you have completed the exercise, share your sentences (the ones with two prepositional phrases) with the class. The first one is done for you.

1. **core sentence:** Employees are concerned.

   Add one prepositional phrase: _Employees are concerned about their_
   paychecks.

   Add another prepositional phrase: _Employees at the central plant are_
   concerned about their paychecks.

2. **core sentence:** Eduardo ran.

   Add one prepositional phrase: _____

   Add another prepositional phrase: _____

   _____

3. **core sentence:** A huge truck skidded.

   Add one prepositional phrase: _____

   _____

   Add another prepositional phrase: _____

   _____

4. **core sentence:** Kelly called me.

   Add one prepositional phrase: _____

   Add another prepositional phrase: _____

   _____

5. **core sentence:** Young adults should be ready.

   Add one prepositional phrase: _____

   _____

   Add another prepositional phrase: _____

   _____

6. **core sentence:** A man in black appeared.

   Add one prepositional phrase: _____

   _____

   Add another prepositional phrase: _____

   _____

Word Order

When we speak, we often use a very simple word order: first, the subject; then the verb. For example, someone would say, "He lost the key." *He* is the subject that begins the sentence; *lost* is the verb that comes after the subject.

However, not all sentences use such a simple word order. Prepositional phrases, for example, can change the word order. To identify the subject and verb, follow these steps:

prepositional phrase and changed subject-verb order:
Behind the cabinet was a box of coins.

Step 1: Mark off the prepositional phrases with parentheses: (Behind the cabinet) was a box (of coins). Remember that nothing in a prepositional phrase can be the subject of a sentence.

Step 2: Find the verb: *was*

Step 3: Who or what was? A box was. The subject of the sentence is *box*.

After you change the word order of this sentence, you can see the subject (S) and the verb (V) more easily.

A *box* of coins *was* behind the cabinet.

(Even though *coins* is a plural word, you must use the singular verb *was* because *box* is the singular subject.)

Exercise 12 Finding Prepositional Phrases, Subjects, and Verbs in
Complicated Word Order

Put parentheses around the prepositional phrases in the following sentences.
Then underline the subjects and verbs, putting an *S* above each subject and a *V*
above each verb.

1. (Across the street)(from my grandmother's) apartment is an empty lot
                                              S   V
   (with cracked cement.)

2. By a border of white roses stood a small dog without a collar.

3. (Behind all Mario's) bragging and bluster hid a shy man with a longing
                                          V   S   V
   for approval.

4. Inside the crumpled envelope lay a rusty key on a thin gold chain.

5. From the back of the auditorium came the loud sound (of someone)
                        S   V
   snoring happily.

6. Among the items in the old wooden chest is a faded photograph
   of my grandparents on their wedding day.

7. Through the halls echoed the sound (of excited schoolchildren
                 S   V
   (on their way to the lunchroom.)

8. Down the snow-covered street raced two boys on shiny new sleds.

9. (Under the pile of leaves) slithered a thin silver snake with black
                                  V   S
   markings.

10. Within walking distance of my house stands a famous monument
    to the soldiers of World War II.

More on Word Order

The expected word order of a subject followed by a verb will change when a
sentence starts with *There is/are*, *There was/were*, *Here is/are*, or *Here
was/were*. In such cases, look for the subject after the verb:

S-V order with There is/are, Here is/are:

There *are* a *supermarket* and a *laundromat* near my apartment.

Here *is* my best *friend.*

To understand this pattern, you can change the word order:

A *supermarket* and a *laundromat are* there, near my apartment.

My best *friend is* here.

You should also note that even when the subject comes after the verb, the verb has to *match* the subject. For instance, if the subject refers to more than one thing, the verb must refer to more than one thing:

There are a *supermarket* and a *laundromat* near my apartment. (Two things, a supermarket and a laundromat, *are* near my apartment.)

Word Order in Questions

Questions may have a different word order. The main verb and the helping verb may not be next to each other.

Word order in questions:

question: Did you study for the test?
subject: *you*
verbs: *did, study*

To understand this concept, you can think about answering the question. If someone accused you of not studying for the test, you might say, "I *did study* for it." You would use two words as verbs.

question: Will she call her mother?
subject: *she*
verbs: *will, call*

question: Is Charles making the coffee?
subject: *Charles*
verbs: *is, making*

> **Exercise 13** **Recognizing Subjects and Verbs in Questions and *Here is/are, There is/are* Word Order**

Underline the subjects and verbs in the following sentences, putting an *S* above each subject and a *V* above each verb.

1. There is somebody with a package at the front door.

2. Have we driven off the main road and missed the right exit?

3. Do you expect an answer to your letter?

4. Here is our chance for a family vacation.

5. Would Mrs. Sung like a gift card for her birthday?

6. On the left side of the street there are a barbershop and an

   electronics store.

7. There was a long line at the college bookstore today.

8. Can Amber take me to the doctor's office on Friday?

9. Has your new boss told you the rules for overtime pay?

10. Here are George's old photograph album and Marisol's first crayon drawings.

Words That Cannot Be Verbs

Sometimes there are words that look like verbs in a sentence but are not verbs. Such words include *adverbs* (words like *always, often, nearly, never, ever*) that are placed close to the verb but are not verbs. Another word that is placed between a helping verb and a main verb is *not*. *Not* is not a verb. When you are looking for verbs in a sentence, be careful to eliminate words like *often* and *not*.

> They will not accept his apology. (The complete verb is *will accept.*)
> Matthew can often repair his truck by himself. (The complete verb is *can repair.*)

Be careful with *contractions.*

> He hasn't called me in a long time. (The complete verb is *has called. Not* is not a part of the verb, even in contractions.)
> Don't you speak Spanish? (The complete verb is *do speak.*)
> Won't you come inside? (The complete verb is *will come. Won't* is a contraction for *will not.*)

Recognizing Main Verbs

If you are checking to see if a word is a main verb, try the pronoun test. Combine your word with this simple list of pronouns: *I, you, he, she, it, we, they.* A main verb is a word such as *look* or *pulled* that can be combined with the words on this list. Now try the pronoun test.

> For the word *look:* I look, you look, he looks, she looks, it looks, we look, they look
> For the word *pulled:* I pulled, you pulled, he pulled, she pulled, it pulled, we pulled, they pulled
> But the word *never* can't be used alone with the pronouns:
> ~~I never, you never, he never, she never, it never, we never, they never~~ (Never did what?)
> *Never* is not a verb. *Not* is not a verb, either, as the pronoun test indicates: ~~I not, you not, he not, she not, it not, we not, they not~~ (These combinations don't make sense because *not* is not a verb.)

Verb Forms That Cannot Be Main Verbs

There are forms of verbs that can't be main verbs by themselves, either. An *-ing* verb by itself cannot be the main verb, as the pronoun test shows.

> For the word taking: ~~I taking, you taking, he taking, she taking, it taking, we taking, they taking~~

If you see an *-ing* verb by itself, correct the sentence by adding a helping verb.

He ~~taking~~ his time. (*Taking*, by itself, cannot be a main verb.)
correction: He *is taking* his time.

Another verb form, called an *infinitive*, also cannot be a main verb. An infinitive is the form of the verb that has *to* placed in front of it.

INFO BOX: Some Common Infinitives

to call	to eat	to live	to smile
to care	to fall	to make	to talk
to drive	to give	to run	to work

Try the pronoun test and you'll see that infinitives can't be main verbs:
For the infinitive *to live:* ~~I to live, you to live, he to live, she to live, we to live, they to live~~

So if you see an infinitive being used as a verb, correct the sentence by adding a main verb.

He ~~to live~~ in a better house.
correction: He *wants* to live in a better house.

The infinitives and the *-ing* verbs just don't work as main verbs. You must put a verb with them to make a correct sentence.

Exercise 14   **Correcting Problems with Infinitive or *-ing* Verb Forms**

Most—but not all—of the following sentences are faulty; an *-ing* verb or an infinitive may be taking the place of a main verb. Rewrite the sentences that have errors.

1. A red-haired woman eagerly sorting through the dresses on the sale rack at the store.

2. Demanding managers, rude diners, and cheap tippers all giving me a headache at my restaurant job.

3. A girl in my math class asked to study with me before the next test.

4. My aunt and uncle to visit their son in Jamaica sometime in November.

5. At the beginning of the year, Sammy expecting a promotion and a raise at his workplace.

6. One of the most successful music producers in the country to judge a local talent contest at the River Center tomorrow.

7. With his college diploma in his hand, Carl thinking about a move to a city with more opportunities for employment and a better quality of life.

8. Laura's fears about meeting new people are keeping her from enjoying the social activities of most people in her age group.

9. A bad cold making me sneeze, reach for a tissue, and rely on cough drops for a few minutes of relief.

10. Somebody in this house leaving the refrigerator door open and spoiling all the food.

Exercise 15   Finding Subjects and Verbs: A Comprehensive Exercise

Underline the subjects and verbs in the following sentences, putting an *S* above each subject and a *V* above each verb.

1. On the front seat of the car is a roll of paper towels.

2. Christopher could have bought his brother a gift with more meaning behind it.

3. Here are the winner of the tournament and her coach.

4. Courtesy and cooperation can often ease the tension between opposing sides in a conflict.

5. After a long day at work, I can never find a place to sit on the bus.

6. Haven't you reported the burglary to the police?

7. Ron wanted to take a nap before dinner.

8. Under all the glamour of Tina's job are endless hours of hard work and of constant stress.

9. Did you ever think about running away from home?

10. Elaine and George won't ask Hannah for a favor like borrowing money.

Exercise 16   Finding Subjects and Verbs: A Comprehensive Exercise

Underline the subjects and verbs in the following sentences, putting an *S* above each subject and a *V* above each verb.

1. Beneath the pile of dirty clothes was a pair of old leather boots in terrible condition.

2. In the summer, Wallace drives to the mountains and hikes on trails at McLendon Park.

3. The Cuban coffee and pastries at Sylvia's restaurant attracted customers from miles away.

4. Without Peter's help, Jamie might never have gotten the chance to start a new career.

5. Below street level is an underground mall with fifty shops and restaurants.

6. Paul's love for his children has made him into a generous and com-passionate man.

7. There was a gold border around the rim of the blue vase.

8. Isaac's cat leaped into my lap and became a blissful ball of orange fur.

9. Haven't you ever seen the view from the top of Randall Hill?

10. Without a ticket for the evening show, you don't have a chance of getting into the club.

Collaborate

Exercise 17 **Creating Your Own Text**

Do this exercise with a partner or a group. Following is a list of rules you have just studied. Write two examples for each rule. When your group has completed the examples for each rule, trade your group's completed exercise with another group's and check their examples while they check yours. The first rule has been done for you.

Rule 1: The verb in a sentence can express some kind of action.

example 1: *My cousin studies biology in college.*

example 2: *Yesterday the rain destroyed the rose bushes.*

Rule 2: The verb in a sentence can express some state of being.

example 1: _____

example 2: _____

Rule 3: The verb in a sentence can consist of more than one word.

example 1: _____

example 2: _____

Rule 4: There can be more than one subject in a sentence.

example 1: _____

example 2: _____

Rule 5: If you take out the prepositional phrases, it is easier to identify the subject of a sentence because nothing in a prepositional phrase can be the subject of a sentence. (Write sentences containing at least one prepositional phrase. Put parentheses around the prepositional phrases.)

example 1:_____

example 2:_____

Rule 6: Not all sentences have the simple word order of first subject, then verb. (Give examples of sentences with more complicated word order.)

example 1:_____

example 2:_____

Rule 7: Words like *not, never, often, always,* and *ever* are not verbs. (Write sentences using one of those words, putting a *V* above the correct verb.)

example 1:_____

example 2:_____

Rule 8: An *-ing* verb form by itself or an infinitive (*to* preceding the verb) cannot be a main verb. (Write sentences with *-ing* verb forms or infinitives, putting a *V* above the main verb.)

example 1:_____

example 2:_____

Exercise 18 Recognizing Subjects and Verbs in a Paragraph

Connect

Underline the subjects and verbs in the following paragraph, putting an *S* above each subject and a *V* above each verb.

My grandparents live in a wonderful place. They are not rich and do not have a car, a computer, or cable television. They have the good fortune to live on an island in the Caribbean. A mile from their house is the ocean with its blue-green waves. On my visits to my grandparents, I love to run on the rocky shore with the sea at my feet. Between my grandparents' house and the ocean is a small market. One man at the market sells fresh fish and conch. Conch is the creature inside the big conch shells. You can hold these big shells to your ears and hear the ocean. Conch can be used to make conch salad, conch chowder, and delicious conch fritters. Another stall at the market sells mangoes, bananas, and limes. Around the corner from the market stands my grandparents' small wood house. It rests on concrete blocks and has no air-conditioning. The breeze blows through the open windows and cools the tiny

rooms. To me, that house is part of paradise.

Connect

Exercise 19 Recognizing Subjects and Verbs in a Paragraph

Underline the subjects and verbs in the following paragraph, putting an *S* above each subject and a *V* above each verb.

My brother has an irritating habit of removing all the change from his pockets at the

end of each day. He saves this change for a rainy day. On that day, he will take all the

change to the bank and come home with paper money in the same amount. That rainy

day has never arrived. For years, mounds of nickels, dimes, pennies, and quarters

have appeared in every part of the house. These piles fill every container in the house,

from a huge coffee mug in the kitchen to a plastic drinking glass in the bathroom.

Inside the kitchen cabinets are freezer storage bowls with heavy piles of coins under

their plastic lids. My brother's stash of spare change is filling our home with heavy

deposits of coins. He should sort and exchange the heavy metal for some lighter,

paper cash.

Chapter Test: The Simple Sentence

Underline the subjects and verbs in the following sentences, putting an *S* above each subject and a *V* above each verb.

1. Lucy and Brian have always been interested in tracing their family's roots in Korea.

2. In a matter of minutes, two friends from my childhood would leave for a journey into enemy territory.

3. On rainy days, the plaster around the windows in my house smells musty and looks damp.

4. Can't Brianna and Jennifer ask their father to lend them some money for the security deposit on an apartment?

5. Under the old bridge on River Road is the perfect spot for fishing and enjoying a sunny day.

6. Tony has been giving me some good advice about applying for a job at the deli.

7. From the tracks near my house came the sound of a train whistle and the blare of a horn.

8. Without any signs of nervousness, Zachary walked across the stage and faced the huge audience.

9. Didn't you call me on Saturday and ask me about a good place to buy a bicycle?

10. Without the help of good friends, I could never have adjusted to my new life in a strange country.

Beyond the Simple Sentence: Coordination

A group of words containing a subject and a verb is called a **clause.** When that group makes sense by itself, it is called a sentence or an independent clause. A sentence that has one independent clause is called a **simple sentence.** If you rely too heavily on a sentence pattern of simple sentences, you risk writing paragraphs like this:

> My father never got a chance to go to college. He had to struggle all his life. He struggled to make a good living. He dreamed of sending his children to college. He saved his money for their education. Today, all three of his children are in college. Two of them are working toward degrees in business. My father is very proud of them. His third child has pleased my father the most. The third child, my brother, is majoring in education. My father will be proud of his son the teacher. He thinks a teacher in the family is a great gift.

instead of

> My father never got a chance to go to college, and he had to struggle all his life to make a good living. He dreamed of sending his children to

college, so he saved his money for their education. Today, all three of his children are in college. Two of them are working toward degrees in business. My father is very proud of them, yet his third child has pleased my father the most. The third child, my brother, is majoring in education. My father will be proud of his son the teacher, for he thinks a teacher in the family is a great gift.

If you read the two paragraphs aloud, you'll notice how choppy the first one sounds. The second one is smoother. The first one is made up of simple sentences, while the second one combines some simple sentences for a more flowing style.

OPTIONS FOR COMBINING SIMPLE SENTENCES

Good writing involves **sentence variety.** This means mixing a simple sentence with a more complicated one and using both short and long sentences. Sentence variety is easier to achieve if you can combine related, short sentences into one.

Some students avoid such combining because they're not sure how to do it. They don't know how to punctuate the new combinations. It's true that punctuating involves memorizing a few rules, but once you know them, you'll be able to use them automatically and write with more confidence. Here are three options for combining simple sentences followed by the punctuation rules you need to use in each case.

OPTION 1: USING A COMMA WITH A COORDINATING CONJUNCTION

You can combine two simple sentences with a comma and a coordinating conjunction. The coordinating conjunctions are *for, and, nor, but, or, yet,* and *so.*

To **coordinate** means to *join equals.* When you join two simple sentences with a comma and a coordinating conjunction, each half of the combination remains an **independent clause,** with its own subject (S) and verb (V).

Here are two simple sentences:

    S   V   S   V
Joanne drove the car. *Richard studied* the map.

Here are two simple sentences combined with a comma and with the word *and,* a coordinating conjunction (CC).

    S   V   , CC   S   V
Joanne drove the car, *and Richard studied* the map.

The combined sentences keep the form they had as separate sentences; that is, they are still both independent clauses, with a subject and verb and with the ability to stand alone.

The word that joins them is the **coordinating conjunction.** It is used to join *equals.* Look at some more examples. These examples use a variety of coordinating conjunctions to join two simple sentences (also called independent clauses).

sentences combined with *for:*

     S   V   , CC   S   V
My *mother was* furious, *for* the *doctor was* two hours late. (Notice that
   for means *because.*)

sentences combined with *nor:*

S   V   V   , CC   V   S   V

*We could*n't *see* the stage, *nor could we hear* the music. (Notice what happens to the word order when you use *nor.*)

sentences combined with *but:*

S   V   , CC   S   V

She brought a cake, *but she forgot* a cake slicer.

sentences combined with *or:*

S   V   , CC S   V

Mr. Chung can call my office, *or he can write* me.

sentences combined with *yet:*

S   V   , CC S   V

I loved botany, *yet I* never *got* a good grade in it. (Notice that *yet* means *but* or *nevertheless.*)

sentences combined with *so:*

S   V   , CC S   V

Marshall brought her flowers, *so she forgave* him for his rudeness. (Notice that *so* means *therefore* or *as a result.*)

Note: One easy way to remember the coordinating conjunctions is to call them, as a group, **fanboys** (**f**or, **a**nd, **n**or, **b**ut, **o**r, **y**et, **s**o).

Where Does the Comma Go?

The comma goes *before* the coordinating conjunction (*for, and, nor, but, or, yet, so*). It comes before the new idea—the second independent clause. It goes where the first independent clause ends. Try this punctuation check. After you've placed the comma, look at the combined sentences. For example,

> John saved his money, and he bought a new car.

Now split it into two sentences at the comma:

> John saved his money. And he bought a new car.

If you put the comma in the wrong place, after the coordinating conjunction, like this:

comma in wrong place:

> ~~John saved his money and, he bought a new car.~~

Your split sentences would look like this:

> John saved his money and. He bought a new car. (The split doesn't make sense.)

This test helps you see whether the comma has been placed correctly—where the first independent clause ends. (Notice that, in addition to starting a sentence with *and*, you can also begin a sentence with *for, nor, but, or, yet,* or *so*—as long as you've written a complete sentence.)

Caution: Do *not* use a comma every time you use the words *for, and, nor, but, or, yet, so;* use one only when the coordinating conjunction joins independent clauses. Do not use a comma when the coordinating conjunction joins words:

> tea or coffee
> exhausted but relieved
> love and happiness

Do not use a comma when the coordinating conjunction joins phrases:

> on the patio or in the garden
> in the glove compartment and under the seats
> with harsh words but without anger

A comma is used when the coordinating conjunction joins two independent clauses. Another way to say the same rule is to say that a comma is used when the coordinating conjunction joins two simple sentences.

Placing the Comma by Using S-V Patterns

An independent clause, or simple sentence, follows this basic pattern:

> S (subject)   V (verb)

Here is an example:

> S V
> *He ran.*

You can add to the basic pattern in several ways:

> S   S V
> *He* and *I ran.*

> S   V   V
> *He ran* and *swam.*

> S   S V   V
> *He* and *I ran* and *swam.*

Study all the examples above, and you'll notice that you can draw a line separating the subjects on one side and the verbs on the other:

S	V
SS	V
S	VV
SS	VV

So whether the simple sentence has one subject (or more than one), the pattern is subject(s) followed by verb(s).

Compound Sentences

When you combine two simple sentences, the pattern changes:

two simple sentences:

> S V
> *He swam.*

> S V
> *I ran.*

two simple sentences combined:

> S V   S V
> *He swam,* but *I ran.*

In the new pattern, SVSV, you can't draw a line separating all the subjects on one side and all the verbs on the other. The new pattern is called a **compound sentence**: two simple sentences, or independent clauses, combined into one.

Learning the Coordinating Conjunctions

You've just studied one way to combine simple sentences. If you are going to take advantage of this method, you need to memorize the coordinating conjunctions—*for, and, nor, but, or, yet, so*—so that your use of them, with the correct punctuation, will become automatic.

Exercise 1 **Recognizing Compound Sentences and Adding Commas**

Add commas only where they are needed in the following sentences.

1. I need to stop at the supermarket, or I won't have anything for dinner tomorrow.

2. The motel in Springfield was not the most luxurious place in the world, nor was it the most recently renovated.

3. Rudy was eager to find a better job, for he wanted to get his own apartment.

4. I took a trip to New York last summer, but couldn't squeeze in a trip to the Empire State Building.

5. Valerie spends most of her money on fashionable clothes, yet the latest styles don't always look good on her.

6. It snowed on Sunday, so I couldn't take a long walk with my dog.

7. Two of my friends from high school are getting married next month, and moving to a small town in Pennsylvania.

8. Once a week, my father washes his car, and he uses a special kind of wax to polish it.

9. Someone at the office bought me a Valentine's Day card, and sent it to my house.

10. All my brothers have black hair, but I decided to be a redhead.

Exercise 2 **More on Recognizing Compound Sentences and Adding Commas**

Add commas only where they are needed in the following sentences.

1. Mr. Mendoza and Mr. Polsky arranged the transportation, and provided the refreshments for the children's field trip to the science museum.

2. My next door neighbor has neither a sense of humor, nor a tolerance for young people's parties.

3. Coffee gets me started in the morning, but too much caffeine leaves me with a bad headache.

4. Ricky's sister can take Ricky to work on Tuesday, or he can get a ride with me.

5. The tea kettle was screeching so Miriam ran to turn off the heat on the stove.

6. My four-year-old dropped his bowl of oatmeal on the floor and I reached for the roll of paper towels.

7. I will never speak to Frank again for he betrayed my trust in him.

8. Patrick loves to watch NASCAR events on television so I got him tickets to a live race for his birthday.

9. Alan's presentation at the city council was a nervous yet moving appeal for a homeless shelter in our town.

10. My history teacher is thinking about giving our class a take-home final examination or assigning a final paper.

Collaborate

Exercise 3 Writing and Punctuating Compound Sentences

Working with a partner or a group, write the compound sentences described below. Be sure to punctuate them correctly. When you have completed the exercise, share your answers with another group or with the class.

1. Write a compound sentence using the coordinating conjunction *for.*

   I had to use an umbrella for it was raining.

2. Write a compound sentence using the coordinating conjunction *and.*

   _____

3. Write a compound sentence using the coordinating conjunction *nor.*

   _____

4. Write a compound sentence using the coordinating conjunction *but.*

   _____

5. Write a compound sentence using the coordinating conjunction *or.*

   _____

6. Write a compound sentence using the coordinating conjunction *yet.*

   _____

7. Write a compound sentence using the coordinating conjunction *so.*

   _____

OPTION 2: USING A SEMICOLON BETWEEN TWO SIMPLE SENTENCES

Sometimes you want to combine two simple sentences (independent clauses) without using a coordinating conjunction. If you want to join two simple sentences that are related in their ideas and you do not want to use a coordinating conjunction, you can combine them with a semicolon.

two simple sentences:

S   V   S   V
I washed the floor. *He dusted* the furniture.

two simple sentences combined with a semicolon:

S   V   ; S   V
I washed the floor; *he dusted* the furniture.

Here are more examples of this option in use:

S   V   ; S   V
He swam; I ran.

S   V   V ; S   V   V
Jacy couldn't sleep; she was thinking about her job.

S   V   ; S   V
Skindiving is expensive; *you need* money for equipment.

Notice that when you join two simple sentences with a semicolon, the second sentence begins with a lowercase letter, not a capital letter.

Exercise 4 Recognizing Compound Sentences and Adding Semicolons

Add semicolons only where they are needed in the following sentences.

1. Eating fruits and vegetables can be good for your health and lead to weight loss.

2. One winter morning, I was late getting to work my car wouldn't start.

3. Gloria left town yesterday her family called and invited her to go to San Juan with them.

4. Dr. Kerensky examined my little boy's throat but couldn't find any signs of an infection.

5. You can borrow my accounting book I don't need it this week.

6. The movie was a waste of money the plot confused me and put me to sleep.

7. Roger's knowledge of Spanish and Portugese makes him a good candidate for a sales job in Latin America and gives him an advantage in applying for work in the travel industry.

8. Everything is ready the dinner is on the table.

9. Sean can feed Aunt Sandra's parakeets I will take the dog for a walk.

10. Andrew drove me home from the hospital and made me a cup of tea and some toast.

Exercise 5 More on Recognizing Compound Sentences and Adding Semicolons

Add semicolons only where they are needed in the following sentences.

1. Sammy gossips about all his friends I can never trust him with a secret.

2. Tamara sometimes changes the oil in the car Phil never does.

3. Jessica or her cousin could invite their aunt to dinner and pay a little attention to the elderly woman.

4. Everything in our bedroom is dusty or dirty we really need to clean.

5. My clothes don't fit me anymore and are not worth giving away to a charity.

6. Bill won't marry again he is afraid of getting hurt and wants to protect himself from rejection.

7. A kind little man with a huge heart and a tough-talking lady guided me through some terrible times and inspired me to change.

8. It's raining hard we need our umbrellas.

9. Marrying young can satisfy your immediate needs it can also lead you to a whole new set of needs.

10. My psychology class introduced me to different ways to understand other people's behavior and taught me how to recognize my own motives.

OPTION 3: USING A SEMICOLON AND A CONJUNCTIVE ADVERB

Sometimes you may want to join two simple sentences (independent clauses) with a connecting word called a **conjunctive adverb.** This word points out or clarifies a relationship between the sentences.

INFO BOX: Some Common Conjunctive Adverbs

also	furthermore	likewise	otherwise
anyway	however	meanwhile	similarly
as a result	in addition	moreover	still
besides	incidentally	nevertheless	then
certainly	indeed	next	therefore
consequently	in fact	now	thus
finally	instead	on the other hand	undoubtedly

You can put a conjunctive adverb (CA) between simple sentences, but when you do, you still need a semicolon in front of the adverb.

two simple sentences:

S V   S V
I got a tutor for College Algebra. *I improved* my grade.

two simple sentences joined by a conjunctive adverb and a semicolon:

S V   ; CA S   V
I got a tutor for College Algebra; *then I improved* my grade.

S V   ;   CC   S   V
I got a tutor for College Algebra; *consequently, I improved* my grade.

Punctuating after a Conjunctive Adverb

Notice the comma after the conjunctive adverb in the sentence, *I got a tutor for college algebra; consequently, I improved my grade.* Here's the generally accepted rule:

> Put a comma after the conjunctive adverb if the conjunctive adverb is more than one syllable long.

For example, if the conjunctive adverb is a word like *consequently, furthermore,* or *moreover,* you use a comma. If the conjunctive adverb is one syllable, you do not have to add a comma after it. One-syllable conjunctive adverbs are words like *then* or *thus.*

punctuating with conjunctive adverbs:

Every month, I paid my whole credit card debt; *thus* I avoided paying interest.

Every month, I paid my whole credit card debt; *consequently,* I avoided paying interest.

Exercise 6 **Recognizing and Punctuating Compound Sentences with Conjunctive Adverbs**

Add semicolons and commas only where they are needed in the following sentences.

1. Professor Choo is a dynamic teacher on the other hand he gives quizzes every week.

2. Professor Choo is a dynamic teacher but gives quizzes every week.

3. My baby was crying for her breakfast meanwhile the doorbell began to ring.

4. Lamont always tells silly jokes undoubtedly he will have a couple of new ones to tell at my party.

5. That property used to be a cow pasture now it is being turned into a strip mall.

6. Nick usually gets up at 7:00 a.m. however he has to wake up at 5:00 a.m. tomorrow and take his father to the airport.

7. You can sign up for classes during the early registration period and avoid the long lines of late registration.

8. Emily and Kate eat lunch in the student center on Mondays but never seem to mix with other students much.

9. My father hates to watch television in fact he hasn't watched an hour of television in years.

10. The weather had been dangerously dry finally a heavy rain saved the trees.

More on Recognizing and Punctuating Compound Sentences with Conjunctive Adverbs

Add semicolons and commas only where they are needed in the following sentences.

1. Jim has always been a loyal friend to Adam certainly he will come to Adam's wedding.

2. Jonetta's love of animals certainly played a role in her choice of a college major.

3. Greg might work in his father's landscaping business and even study accounting at night.

4. I'll wash my clothes on Saturday morning next I'll treat myself to breakfast at the Pancake Palace.

5. Keira begged and pleaded with her father still he would not lend her the money for a tattoo.

6. Al never seems to have any money on him yet always wears expensive clothes.

7. We'll go shopping then we can meet your brother at the mall.

8. Tina is not interested in me besides she already has a boyfriend.

9. Steve lived at home and worked at a full-time job for a year as a result he saved enough money for college tuition.

10. Jerry was the best of all the contestants in the hip-hop contest incidentally he is my cousin.

Selecting the Right Conjunctive Adverb

In the sentences below, circle the conjunctive adverb that expresses the meaning given in the hint. The first one is done for you.

1. Hint: Select the word that means *at last*.

   The concert lasted for hours; (in fact, finally), we were free to leave our seats.

2. Hint: Select the word that means *as a result*.

   Dinner at the restaurant was expensive; (consequently, otherwise), I had no money left for a movie afterward.

3. Hint: Select the word that means *in addition*.

   Howard stood by me in bad times; (on the other hand, moreover), he gave me financial help.

4. Hint: Select the word that means *at this moment*.

   Last year, I was struggling to finish high school; (next, now) I am earning Bs and Cs in college.

5. Hint: Select the word that means *in spite of that.*

    Carrie hated seafood; (nevertheless, certainly), she pretended to enjoy Leo's homemade fish casserole.

6. Hint: Select the word that means *for that reason.*

    My mother wants to find a job in an office; (therefore, undoubtedly), she is taking a class in basic computer skills.

7. Hint: Select the word that means *at the same time.*

    Alice checked every corner of the house for the missing cat; (otherwise, meanwhile), Simon searched the neighborhood.

8. Hint: Select the word that means *in the same way or manner.*

    My boyfriend loves to play basketball; (similarly, anyway) I have been playing basketball for years.

9. Hint: Select the word that means *as a substitute.*

    I can't afford to buy movie tickets for my four children; (undoubtedly, instead), I rent movie DVDs.

10. Hint: Select the word that means *yet.*

    Walter can be impatient and pushy; (moreover, however), he's a good man in a crisis.

Collaborate

Exercise 9 **Writing Sentences with Conjunctive Adverbs**

Working with a partner or group, write one sentence for each of the conjunctive adverbs below. When you have completed this exercise, share your answers with another group or with the class. The first one is done for you.

1. Write a compound sentence using *instead.*

    She couldn't find her notes for her speech to the jury; instead, she

    relied on her memory.

2. Write a compound sentence using *then.*

    _____

    _____

3. Write a compound sentence using *furthermore.*

    _____

    _____

4. Write a compound sentence using *on the other hand.*

    _____

    _____

5. Write a compound sentence using *otherwise.*

    _____

    _____

6. Write a compound sentence using *therefore.*

_____

_____

7. Write a compound sentence using *thus.*

_____

_____

8. Write a compound sentence using *in addition.*

_____

_____

9. Write a compound sentence using *undoubtedly.*

_____

_____

10. Write a compound sentence using *certainly.*

_____

_____

Exercise 10   Combining Simple Sentences Three Ways

Add (1) a comma, or (2) a semicolon, or (3) a semicolon and a comma to the following sentences. Do not add, change, or delete any words. Just add the correct punctuation.

1. Lee Anne cannot afford to buy a new computer nor can she keep relying on her roommate's computer.

2. The refrigerator has been making a strange noise all day I hope nothing is wrong with it.

3. Frank gets bored at home so he drives aimlessly around town.

4. I don't want this hamburger you can eat it.

5. My closet is full of clothes however none of them fit me right.

6. Matthew is supportive and positive in dealing with his employees in fact he is the best boss in the company.

7. The expensive and complicated coffeemaker was a waste of money, for nobody in the family ever learned how to use it.

8. My aunt collects Elvis Presley figurines moreover she is a member of an Elvis fan club.

9. Manuel is my oldest brother but I don't know him well.

10. Ask the teacher to postpone the math test then plead with her to review all the material on the test for another week.

Exercise 11 **More on Combining Simple Sentences Three Ways**

Add (1) a comma, or (2) a semicolon, or (3) a semicolon and a comma to the following sentences. Do not add, change, or delete any words. Just add the correct punctuation.

1. Sandra might have run into bad weather on the highway, or she might have gotten a late start.

2. Eli called every paint store in town; finally, he found a place with the right color of latex paint.

3. My mother never pays attention to family gossip; thus she remains friends with everyone in our large family.

4. I am tired of getting up early in the morning; in fact, I would like to sleep until noon every day for a year.

5. The new shoe store is in a great location, yet it hasn't attracted many customers.

6. Yesterday, Shareena was flirting with me; now she walks by without talking to me.

7. Lionel was hungry, so he made some toast with strawberry jelly.

8. My husband and his brother cleaned out our garage on Saturday, and I sorted through the boxes in the basement.

9. My grandfather walks two miles every day; in addition, he belongs to a bicycle club and rides on weekends.

10. I took my sister to her favorite restaurant; then I asked her for a big favor.

Collaborate

Exercise 12 **Combining Simple Sentences**

Following are pairs of simple sentences. Working with a partner or group, combine each pair into one sentence. Remember the three options for combining sentences: (1) a comma and a coordinating conjunction, (2) a semicolon, (3) a semicolon and a conjunctive adverb. When you have combined each pair into one sentence, exchange your exercise with another group. Write a new sentence below each sentence prepared by the other group. The first is done for you.

1. Take-out pizza for a family of six is expensive.

   My children and I make our own pizza at home.

   combination 1: *Take-out pizza for a family of six is expensive, so my children and I make our own pizza at home.*

   combination 2: *Take-out pizza for a family of six is expensive; instead, my children and I make our own pizza at home.*

2. Alicia recently earned her G.E.D.

   She is thinking about taking some college courses.

   combination 1: _____

combination 2: _____

_____

3. You never kept your friends' secrets.

   Most people no longer trust you.

   combination 1: _____

   _____

   combination 2: _____

   _____

4. Mrs. Garcia's house was always a mess.

   Everyone loved the warmth and happiness in her home.

   combination 1: _____

   _____

   combination 2: _____

   _____

5. My parents were divorced after four years of marriage.

   I never knew my father well.

   combination 1: _____

   _____

   combination 2: _____

   _____

6. Andrea never complained about being poor.

   She did not want sympathy from others.

   combination 1: _____

   _____

   combination 2: _____

   _____

7. The community center has been closed for three years.

   Teens have nowhere to go after school.

   combination 1: _____

   _____

   combination 2: _____

   _____

8. We can go to a movie at the multiplex.

   We can play games at the arcade.

   combination 1: _____

   _____

combination 2: _____

_____

9. Charlotte Ling is a great chess player.

She started playing chess in elementary school.

combination 1: _____

_____

combination 2: _____

_____

10. We have run out of sugar.

I can put honey in my tea.

combination 1: _____

_____

combination 2: _____

_____

Connect

Exercise 13 **Punctuating Compound Sentences in a Paragraph**

Add commas and semicolons only where they are needed in the paragraph below.

Long car trips can be fun; however, they can also be stressful. My happiest memories of long journeys are of trips with Jamie, my girlfriend. We always had something to talk about, so we were never bored. The hours seemed to fly by; besides, we were happy to be alone together on the open road. We amused each other with stories of our childhood, or our high school pranks then we sang along with the radio. Traveling with my sister's two children was different; certainly, it was not fun. Five-year-old Annie and four-year old Jesse shared the backseat, and they used the space to smack, kick, and push each other. After an hour of combat, the children joined forces, but their new enemies were my sister and I. They made demands; they complained loudly. First, they wanted to stop, and get a snack. At our stop, the children ate sugary snacks; as a result, they were full of energy for more fighting and screaming. The car trip with these children seemed endless, for every minute brought more conflicts, and new demands to stop for a bathroom break, to go faster, or to go home.

Exercise 14   **Punctuating Compound Sentences in a Paragraph**

Connect

Add commas and semicolons only when they are needed in the paragraph below.

A habitually late friend or family member can be irritating however certain strategies can reduce the stress that others suffer in dealing with the latecomer. One such strategy is the lie. A punctual person can lie about the time of a movie or party as a result the habitually late person may actually show up on time. Unfortunately, the latecomer could soon discover this trick so it may not work for long. Another strategy is more dramatic but more exhausting for the punctual person. In this strategy, the punctual person shouts or screams at the late person. In some cases, the punctual person may also threaten the late person. Unfortunately, dramatic scenes may frighten the latecomer but they will not lead to a change in or his or her behavior. Finally, the most useful strategy is a type of surrender. A punctual person can simply arrive late, too.

Chapter Test: Beyond the Simple Sentence: Coordination

Add a comma, a semicolon, or a semicolon and a comma to the following sentences. Do not add, change, or delete any words; just add the correct punctuation.

1. Joel has no interest in team sports similarly his son chooses solitary activities like running and weightlifting.

2. I have to find a place to store my comic book collection or the boxes of comics will invade every space in my room.

3. The stretch of turnpike near my house is under construction now it takes me an extra thirty minutes to get to work.

4. Everything on the menu at Ricci's Restaurant is expensive a bowl of onion soup costs five dollars.

5. I can finish my social science project by Monday anyway I can try.

6. People have stopped going to the movies at the Mountain Theater for ten cars in the parking lot were vandalized last week.

7. Peter needs to send in his job application by next week otherwise he might miss the deadline for new hiring.

8. Rebecca rarely spoke about her family nor did she ever mention any details about her years in Chile.

9. I called Brian three times finally he picked up the phone.

10. Nicole is satisfied with her B in Art Appreciation still she would rather have an A.

CHAPTER 3

Quick Question

True or False: A comma splice is an error that occurs when a writer uses a comma when a semicolon is necessary.

(After you study this chapter, you will be confident of your answer.)

Avoiding Run-on Sentences and Comma Splices

RUN-ON SENTENCES

If you run two independent clauses together without the necessary punctuation, you make an error called a **run-on sentence.** This error is also called a **fused sentence.**

> **run-on sentence error:**
> I worked hard in the class I earned a good grade.

> **run-on sentence error corrected:**
> I worked hard in the class, and I earned a good grade. (To correct this error, you need a comma before the coordinating conjunction *and.*)

> **run-on sentence error:**
> I worked hard in the class I earned a good grade.

> **run-on sentence error corrected:**
> I worked hard in the class; I earned a good grade. (To correct this error, you need a semicolon between the two independent clauses.)

run-on sentence error:
I worked hard in the class I earned a good grade.

run-on sentence error corrected:
I worked hard in the class. I earned a good grade. (To correct this error, you need to create two sentences with a period after "class" and a capital letter to begin the second sentence.)

Steps for Correcting Run-on Sentences

When you edit your writing, you can correct run-on sentences by following these steps:

Step 1: Check for two independent clauses.

Step 2: Check that the clauses are separated by either a coordinating conjunction (*for, and, nor, but, or, yet, so*) and a comma, or by a semicolon.

Follow the steps in checking this sentence:

Spaghetti is cheap I buy it often.

Step 1: Check for two independent clauses. You can do this by checking for the subject-verb, subject-verb pattern that indicates two independent clauses.

    S   V   S V
Spaghetti is cheap *I buy* it often.

The pattern indicates that you have two independent clauses.

Step 2: Check that the clauses are separated by either a coordinating conjunction (*for, and, nor, but, or, yet, so*) and a comma, or by a semicolon.

There is no punctuation between the independent clauses, and there is no coordinating conjunction. You therefore have a run-on sentence. You can correct it three ways:

run-on sentence corrected with a coordinating conjunction and a comma:
Spaghetti is cheap, *so* I buy it often.

run-on sentence corrected with a semicolon:
Spaghetti is cheap; I buy it often.

run-on sentence corrected with a period and a capital letter:
Spaghetti is cheap. I buy it often.

Follow the steps once more, checking this sentence:

I bought a new computer it is too complicated for me.

Step 1: Check for two independent clauses. Do this by checking the subject-verb, subject-verb pattern.

S V   S V
I bought a new computer *it is* too complicated for me.

Step 2: Check that the clauses are separated by either a coordinating conjunction (*for, and, nor, but, or, yet, so*) and a comma, or by a semicolon.

There is no punctuation between the independent clauses. There is no coordinating conjunction, either. Without the proper punctuation, this is a run-on sentence. Correct it three ways:

> **run-on sentence corrected with a coordinating conjunction and a comma:**
> I bought a new computer, *but* it is too complicated for me.

> **run-on sentence error corrected with a semicolon:**
> I bought a new computer; it is too complicated for me.

> **run-on sentence error corrected with a period and a capital letter:**
> I bought a new computer. It is too complicated for me.

Using the steps to check for run-on sentences can also help you avoid unnecessary punctuation. Consider this sentence:

> Alan stuffed the papers into the trash and carried the trash bag to the curb.

> Check for two independent clauses. Do this by checking the subject-verb, subject-verb pattern.

> S   V   V
> *Alan stuffed* the papers into the trash and *carried* the trash bag to the curb.

> The pattern is SVV, not SV, SV. You have one independent clause, not two. The sentence is not a run-on sentence.

Following the steps in correcting run-on sentences can help you avoid a major grammar error.

Exercise 1   Correcting Run-on Sentences

Some of the sentences below are correctly punctuated. Some are run-on (fused) sentences—two simple sentences run together without any punctuation. If a sentence is correctly punctuated, write *OK* in the space provided. If it is a run-on sentence, put an *X* in the space provided and correct the sentence above the lines.

1. __X__ Lawrence loves to work with numbers he is studying accounting.

2. __OK__ My beagle puppy likes big dogs but is afraid of the cats in our neighborhood.

3. __X__ Mrs. Dorismond borrowed my umbrella she had left hers at home.

4. __OK__ Vincent gets plenty of exercise at his job with the power company and takes a martial arts class once a week.

5. __X__ My younger brother failed his driving test he is going to retake it in a few weeks.

6. __OK__ People in my neighborhood sit outside on summer evenings and chat with the neighbors about sports, scandals, or the weather.

7. __X__ My sister has a small child at home she needs a job with flexible hours.

8. ___X___ Dinner at the cafeteria was terrible the microwaved chicken patty had slivers of ice in it.

9. ___OK___ I sensed Phil's insincerity and began to suspect his motives from the first words of our conversation.

10. ___OK___ The furniture in my parents' living room looks expensive but is a combination of thrift shop treasures and my father's carpentry.

Exercise 2   **More on Correcting Run-on Sentences**

Some of the following sentences are correctly punctuated. Some are run-on (fused) sentences—two simple sentences run together without any punctuation. If the sentence is correctly punctuated, write *OK* in the space provided. If it is a run-on sentence, put an *X* in the space provided and correct the sentence above the lines.

1. ___X___ Water was coming in through a leak in the window frame it was dripping down the newly painted wall.

2. ___X___ I'm going to get my hair cut tomorrow I want to look good for Emily's party.

3. ___OK___ The store detective looked at me with suspicion and asked to see the contents of my bag.

4. ___X___ My car radio is not working right I can get only two radio stations.

5. ___X___ Tom complained about his brother Rick's clothes Rick wears Tom's clothes now.

6. ___X___ Sabrina still thinks about her first love she sighs over old photographs of the two of them together and listens to their special songs.

7. ___OK___ I studied my psychology notes for an hour then I fell asleep in my chair.

8. ___OK___ Waiting in line to register for classes and standing in line at the financial aid office can take several hours.

9. ___OK___ My sister is shy thus some people mistakenly believe she is snobbish.

10. ___OK___ Coffee and iced tea contain caffeine and can keep me awake at night.

COMMA SPLICES

A **comma splice** is an error that occurs when you punctuate with a comma but should use a semicolon instead. If you are joining two independent clauses without a coordinating conjunction, you *must use* a semicolon. A comma isn't enough.

comma splice error:
The rain fell steadily, the valley filled with water.

comma splice error corrected:
The rain fell steadily; the valley filled with water.

comma splice error:
I lost my umbrella, now I have to buy a new one.

comma splice error corrected:
I lost my umbrella; now I have to buy a new one.

Correcting Comma Splices

When you edit your writing, you can correct comma splices by following these steps:

Step 1: Check for two independent clauses.

Step 2: Check that the clauses are separated by a coordinating conjunction (*for, and, nor, but, or, yet, so*). If they are, then a comma in front of the coordinating conjunction is sufficient. If they are not separated by a coordinating conjunction, you have a comma splice. Correct it by changing the comma to a semicolon.

Follow the steps to check for a comma splice in this sentence:

The puppy jumped up, he licked my face.

Step 1: Check for two independent clauses. You can do this by checking for the subject-verb, subject-verb pattern that indicates two independent clauses.

               S   V   S   V
The *puppy jumped* up, *he licked* my face.

Step 2: Check that the clauses are separated by a coordinating conjunction.

There is no coordinating conjunction. To correct the comma splice error, you must use a semicolon instead of a comma:

comma splice error corrected:
The puppy jumped up; he licked my face.

Be careful not to mistake a short word like *then* or *thus* for a coordinating conjunction. Only the seven coordinating conjunctions (*for, and, nor, but, or, yet, so*) with a comma in front of them can join independent clauses.

comma splice error:
Suzanne opened the letter, then she screamed with joy.

comma splice error corrected:
Suzanne opened the letter; then she screamed with joy.

Then is not a coordinating conjunction; it is a conjunctive adverb. When it joins two independent clauses, it needs a semicolon in front of it.

Also remember that conjunctive adverbs that are two or more syllables long (like *consequently, however, therefore*) need a comma after them *as well as* a semicolon in front of them when they join independent clauses.

Anthony passed the placement test; consequently, he can take Advanced Mathematics.

(For a list of some common conjunctive adverbs, see Chapter 2).

Sometimes writers use commas before and after a conjunctive adverb and think the commas are sufficient. Check this sentence for a comma splice by following the steps:

The van held all my tools, however, it used too much gas.

Step 1: Check for two independent clauses by checking for the subject-verb, subject-verb pattern.

     S   V   S V

The *van held* all my tools, however, *it used* too much gas.

Step 2: Check for a coordinating conjunction.

There is no coordinating conjunction. *However* is a conjunctive adverb, not a coordinating conjunction. Without a coordinating conjunction, a semicolon is needed between the two independent clauses.

comma splice corrected:
The van held all my tools; however, it used too much gas.

Following the steps in correcting comma splices can help you avoid a major grammar error.

Exercise 3   Correcting Comma Splices

Some of the following sentences are correctly punctuated. Some contain comma splices. If the sentence is correctly punctuated, write *OK* in the space provided. If it contains a comma splice, put an *X* in the space provided and correct the sentence. To correct the sentence, you do not need to add words; just correct the punctuation.

1. __X__ One of my brothers lives in a small apartment in Miami, the other one has a house in the hills of South Dakota.

2. __X__ I have to get some help with my algebra assignments; otherwise, I might fail the class.

3. __X__ Ray asked his uncle for advice about getting a job, then Ray applied for work at three places in town.

4. __OK__ Good childcare costs about half of my salary, but my little boy deserves a warm and caring environment.

5. __X__ Pete has a bad cold and a cough, nevertheless, he insists on shoveling the snow outside our house.

6. __OK__ The pizza place is across the street from the campus, so it gets most of its business from college students.

7. __X__ I know the manager at the McLean Auditorium, thus I was able to get tickets for the sold-out show.

8. __X__ Mr. O'Neill is afraid to fly, also, he doesn't like to drive long distances.

9. __X__ The cable television company put me on hold for fifteen minutes, finally, a human voice spoke to me.

10. __OK__ Ethan won't answer my questions about his living arrangements, nor will he explain his strange schedule.

Exercise 4   More on Correcting Comma Splices

Some of the following sentences are correctly punctuated. Some contain comma splices. If the sentence is correctly punctuated, write *OK* in the space provided. If it contains a comma splice, put an *X* in the space provided and correct the sentence. To correct the sentence, you do not need to add words; just correct the punctuation.

1. ___ok___ My two-year-old has a cold, so I can't drop him off at his preschool today.

2. ___X___ Mr. Scheindlin enjoys Greek food, he comes to the annual Greek festival every year.

3. ___X___ Patrick and Claudia have three cats, moreover, they have a large Doberman.

4. ___X___ Jeans with status labels cost too much, I buy my jeans at a discount store.

5. ___X___ Someone broke into my parents' house, as a result, my parents have to get all their locks changed.

6. ___ok___ I have been seeing Lisa for six months, yet I sometimes think about my former girlfriend.

7. ___X___ Pete wouldn't go to the fair with me, however, he promised he would meet me for breakfast next week.

8. ___ok___ André always borrowed money from me and my sister, then he found a good job and paid us back.

9. ___X___ Eric handed me a small velvet box, it contained a pair of sparkling earrings.

10. ___ok___ I'll call you tomorrow after school, or you can e-mail me any time.

Collaborate

Exercise 5 Completing Sentences

With a partner or group, write the first part of each of the following incomplete sentences. Make your addition an independent clause. Be sure to punctuate your completed sentences correctly. The first one is done for you.

1. *My candle suddenly blew out;* _____ then I saw the ghost.

2. _____ meanwhile, someone screamed.

3. _____ yet he kept smiling at me.

4. _____ next we'll plan a wedding.

5. _____ now I can't sleep.

6. _____ consequently, he won't speak to me.

7. _____ for I'm really hungry.

8. _____ but the shadowy figure followed us.

9. _____ instead, you can be honest.

10. _____ and a swarm of bees appeared.

Connect

Exercise 6 Editing a Paragraph for Run-on Sentences and Comma Splices

Edit the following paragraph for run-on sentences and comma splices. There are six errors.

Umbrellas are a great invention; however, they do not solve all my problems with rainy days. I am sure to carry my umbrella on a rainy morning, yet I am not sure to stay dry. My umbrellas have a habit of blowing backwards in the wind; then they look like huge cones pointing away from my head. I tend to buy cheap umbrellas; as a result, the cloth tends to slip off many of the metal tips at the ends of the spokes. Many of my cheap umbrellas fall or blow into pieces; thus I am always buying more umbrellas. These replacements cost money; consequently, I never have enough money to buy a more expensive, better quality umbrella. Another bad habit of mine contributes to my umbrella predicament. I keep losing umbrellas; therefore, I can start the day with an umbrella and end the day without one. Buying a strong, sturdy, high-priced umbrella and hanging on to it appears to be the only way out of my umbrella dilemma.

Exercise 7 **Editing a Paragraph for Run-on Sentences and Comma Splices**
Edit the following paragraph for run-on sentences and comma splices. There are five errors.

Connect

Working on the weekends can be a great fit for one person's schedule and a terrible strain on another person's time. My experiences have shown both the advantages and disadvantages of such a schedule. I was quite happy working long weekend hours last semester, at that time, I had a light course load at college. I was able to do my assigned reading and studying during the week then I could put in many weekend hours as a pizza delivery person. The money was good, and I managed to get fairly good grades for the term. This semester is a much more difficult one, I am taking an advanced math class and a chemistry class. Both of these classes demand hours of study soon the extra study time stretched well into the weekend. First, I had to reduce my hours at the pizza shop later, I had to quit the job. Next semester, I have to take another chemistry class and a challenging physics class. During that semester, I will look for part-time work on weeknights and save my weekends for hours of study.

Chapter Test: Avoiding Run-on Sentences and Comma Splices

Some of the sentences below are correctly punctuated. Some are run-on sentences, and some contain comma splices. If a sentence is correctly punctuated, write *OK* in the space provided. If it is a run-on sentence or contains a comma splice, put an *X* in the space provided and correct the sentence above the lines. To correct a sentence, add the necessary punctuation. Do not add any words.

1. __X__ My father fought a bad cold for a week finally he felt better on Monday evening.

2. __OK__ Cherie can take classes in early childhood education at the college, or she can volunteer at a daycare facility for some experience in the field.

3. __X__ I don't like science classes, nevertheless, I have to take them as part of the requirements for my degree.

4. __OK__ Lenny took a second job; thus he managed to pay off his credit card debt.

5. __X__ That car is a good buy, in fact, it's the highest-rated car in its class for auto safety and fuel economy.

6. __OK__ It's a cold night, so let's have some cocoa.

7. __X__ You need a haircut, you look like a shaggy dog.

8. __X__ Our house is fifty years old, consequently, it often needs little repairs and improvements to the inside and the outside.

9. __OK__ Charlyce took a chance on a recent graduate with little experience in sales and hired him for the Boston office.

10. __X__ The two men have been friends since high school they are both in their forties.

CHAPTER 4

Beyond the Simple Sentence: Subordination

Quick Question

Which sentence(s) is/are correct?

A. Whenever I eat spicy food, I feel sick.
B. I feel sick whenever I eat spicy food.

(After you study this chapter, you will be confident of your answer.)

MORE ON COMBINING SIMPLE SENTENCES

You may remember these principles of grammar:

- A clause has a subject and a verb.
- An independent clause is a simple sentence; it is a group of words, with a subject and a verb, that makes sense by itself.

Chapter 2 described three options for combining simple sentences (independent clauses). There is another kind of clause called a **dependent clause.** It has a subject and a verb, but it does not make sense by itself. It cannot stand alone because it is not complete by itself. That is, it *depends* on the rest of the sentence to give it meaning. You can use a dependent clause in another option for combining simple sentences.

47

OPTION 4: USING A DEPENDENT CLAUSE TO BEGIN A SENTENCE

Often, you can combine simple sentences by changing an independent clause into a dependent clause and placing it at the beginning of the new sentence.

two simple sentences:

S   V   S   V
I missed my bus. *I slept* through my alarm.

changing one simple sentence into a beginning dependent clause:

S   V   S   V
Because *I slept* through my alarm, *I missed* my bus.

OPTION 5: USING A DEPENDENT CLAUSE TO END A SENTENCE

You can also combine simple sentences by changing an independent clause into a dependent clause and placing it at the end of the new sentence:

S   V   S   V
I missed my bus because *I slept* through my alarm.

Notice how one simple sentence can be changed into a dependent clause in two ways:

two simple sentences:

S   V   S   V
Nicholas played his guitar. *Jared sang* an old song.

changing one simple sentence into a dependent clause:

S   V   S   V
Nicholas played his guitar while *Jared sang* an old song.

or

S   V   S   V
While *Jared sang* an old song, *Nicholas played* his guitar.

Using Subordinating Words: Subordinating Conjunctions

Changing an independent clause to a dependent one is called **subordinating.** How do you do it? You add a subordinating word, called a **subordinating conjunction,** to an independent clause, which makes it dependent—less "important"—or subordinate, in the new sentence.

Keep in mind that the subordinate clause is still a clause; it has a subject and verb, but it doesn't make sense by itself. For example, here is an independent clause:

S   V
David cooks.

Somebody (David) does something (cooks). The statement makes sense by itself. But if you add a subordinating conjunction to the independent clause, the clause becomes dependent—incomplete, unfinished—like this:

When David cooks (When he cooks, what happens?)
Unless David cooks (Unless he cooks, what will happen?)
If David cooks (If he cooks, what will happen?)

Now, each dependent clause needs an independent clause to finish the idea:

dependent clause   independent clause
When David cooks, he makes wonderful meals.

dependent clause   independent clause
Unless David cooks, you will not get a decent dinner.

dependent clause   independent clause
If David cooks, dinner will be delicious.

There are many subordinating conjunctions. When you put any of these words in front of an independent clause, you make that clause dependent. Here is a list of some subordinating conjunctions.

INFO BOX: **Subordinating Conjunctions**

after	before	so that	whenever
although	even though	though	where
as	if	unless	whereas
as if	in order that	until	whether
because	since	when	while

If you pick the right subordinating conjunction, you can effectively combine simple sentences (independent clauses) into a more sophisticated sentence pattern. Such combining helps you add sentence variety to your writing and helps to explain relationships between ideas.

simple sentences:
  S   V   V   S   V
Emily had never *studied* art. *She was* a gifted painter.

new combination:
dependent clause   independent clause
Although Emily had never studied art, she was a gifted painter.

simple sentences:
S   V   S   V
I bought a new leash last night. My *puppy chewed* up his old one.

new combination:
independent clause   dependent clause
I bought a new leash last night because my puppy chewed up his
     old one.

Punctuating Complex Sentences

The new combination, which has one independent clause and one or more dependent clauses, is called a **complex sentence.** Complex sentences are very easy to punctuate. See if you can figure out the rule for punctuating by yourself. Look at the following examples. All are punctuated correctly:

dependent clause   independent clause
Whenever I visit my mother, I bring flowers.

independent clause   dependent clause
I bring flowers whenever I visit my mother.

> dependent clause   independent clause
> While he was talking, I was daydreaming.
> independent clause   dependent clause
> I was daydreaming while he was talking.

In the examples above, look at the sentences that have a comma. Now look at the ones that don't have a comma. Both kinds of sentences are punctuated correctly. Do you see the rule?

When a dependent clause comes at the beginning of the sentence, the clause is followed by a comma. When a dependent clause comes at the end of a sentence, the clause does not need a comma.

Here are some correctly punctuated complex sentences:

> Although he studied hard, he failed the test.
> He failed the test although he studied hard.

> Until I started running, I was out of shape.
> I was out of shape until I started running.

Exercise 1   Punctuating Complex Sentences

All of the following sentences are complex sentences—they have one independent and one or more dependent clauses. Add a comma to each sentence that needs one.

1. Life in Hamilton Heights has been dull since you left town.

2. As I told you before there are no exceptions to this rule.

3. I ran through the streets as I held my jacket over my head in an attempt to protect myself from the pounding rain.

4. Before Elaine married Lance Rosicky she lived in an apartment at the corner of Maple Street and Fourth Avenue.

5. Whenever my dog sees a squirrel she goes into a frenzy of racing around and leaping at the trees.

6. Ron wants to get a part-time job after he finishes his first semester of college.

7. When I stay up late on a weeknight I am groggy and irritable the next day.

8. After John got a new car he struggled to find the money for the hefty car payments and the insurance bills.

9. Call your mother when you get home from work.

10. Unless somebody changes his mind Dave and Steve will paint my house over the weekend.

Exercise 2   More on Punctuating Complex Sentences

All of the following sentences are complex sentences—they have one independent and one or more dependent clauses. Add a comma to each sentence that needs one.

1. Although the area once had a reputation for criminal activity and urban decay it is slowly renewing itself and emerging as an attractive neighborhood.

2. Lewis is taking care of his two nephews while his sister is in the hospital.

3. Maybe Marcie can tell me where Leonard put the box of envelopes.

4. Toby smiled at me as if he had a wonderful secret.

5. Since there's nothing I want to watch on television I'm going to listen to some music.

6. Even if Laura can't find the perfect job she can earn money and learn about her field in a less attractive job.

7. Ardese called me last night because she is worried about her father's health.

8. Tom will drive me to Tulsa next week unless he has to fill in for someone at the station.

9. Because my parents spoke Spanish at home I grew up knowing two languages.

10. I want to research used cars on the Internet before I visit any car dealerships.

Exercise 3   Combining Sentences

Combine each pair of sentences below into one smooth, clear sentence. The new combination should include one independent and one dependent clause and an appropriate subordinating word.

1. The utilities room smelled like smoke. An electrical fire had broken out there a week earlier.

   combined: _____

   _____

2. Pronto Spaghetti Sauce in a jar is tasty. It is no substitute for home-made sauce.

   combined: _____

   _____

3. Brendan drove slowly down the streets of the city. I checked the map for directions to the courthouse.

   combined: _____

   _____

4. I am enjoying a hot shower. The doorbell rings.

   combined: _____

   _____

5. It starts to rain. We can move the party indoors.

   combined: _____

   _____

6. You always give me some ridiculous story. You tell me the truth.

   combined: _____

   _____

7. Claudia had never wanted to go out dancing. She met a man who liked nightclubs.

   combined: _____

   _____

8. I got a job at a hotel. I could afford to buy some furniture.

   combined: _____

   _____

9. Andrew doesn't need his truck tomorrow. You can borrow it.

   combined: _____

   _____

10. Tonya wants to finish all her assignments by Friday. She can have the weekend free for relaxing.

    combined: _____

    _____

Exercise 4 **Creating Complex Sentences**

Do this exercise with a partner or group. Each item below lists a dependent clause. Write two different sentences that include the dependent clause. One sentence should begin with the dependent clause; the other sentence should end with the dependent clause. The first one is done for you.

1. dependent clause: whenever I visit my grandmother

   sentence 1: *Whenever I visit my grandmother, she tells me stories about life in Havana.*

   sentence 2: *I bring a box of chocolates whenever I visit my grandmother.*

2. dependent clause: even if Kevin apologizes

   sentence 1: _____

   _____

   sentence 2: _____

   _____

3. dependent clause: as shots were fired at the soldiers

   sentence 1: _____

   _____

   sentence 2: _____

   _____

4. dependent clause: before our baby is born

   sentence 1: _____

   _____

   sentence 2: _____

   _____

5. dependent clause: since I have to work overtime this weekend

   sentence 1: _____

   _____

   sentence 2: _____

   _____

6. dependent clause: after he spent a year in prison

   sentence 1: _____

   _____

   sentence 2: _____

   _____

7. dependent clause: while the family slept

   sentence 1: _____

   _____

   sentence 2: _____

   _____

8. dependent clause: unless you can think of a better place

   sentence 1: _____

   _____

   sentence 2: _____

   _____

9. dependent clause: although my room is a mess

   sentence 1: _____

   _____

   sentence 2: _____

   _____

10. dependent clause: because my boss was a kind person

    sentence 1: _____

    _____

    sentence 2: _____

    _____

Exercise 5   Editing a Paragraph with Complex Sentences

Edit this paragraph by adding or omitting commas. There are eight places that contain errors.

Meeting people in a new place can be difficult. When I first came to Crestwood I was thirteen years old. Thirteen is a tough age to be, because it is a time of physical and emotional changes. Worse, I was thirteen in a strange place where the customs and the language were new. My first challenge was to learn English so that I could function in school. Whenever I could respond to a classmate's greeting I felt proud. I seemed to learn more slang than good English, but the slang helped me to fit into the new environment. As I became more comfortable with the language I faced my next challenge. I had to figure out the latest fads and fashions. Unless I could look like the other students I would always be an outsider. Whenever I grasped the importance of one style of clothing or hair the style changed. Looking like a Crestwood boy was not easy. Although the transformation of a thirteen-year-old Latino boy into a young American took time it eventually happened. After I completed my first year in my new place I felt comfortable with my new friends.

Exercise 6   Editing a Paragraph with Complex Sentences

Edit this paragraph by adding commas or omitting commas. There are six places that contain errors.

When long hair looks good on a man he should not think about cutting it. Russell had always been known for his attractive head of long, sleek brown hair with its red, sunburnt glints. Russell began to think about cutting his hair, when a few of his friends teased him about looking like a girl. They encouraged him to follow the latest styles and get rid of his extra hair. These friends had recently shaved their heads and did not look very attractive after their style change. Although Russell would not agree to join them in their bald state he did consent to a haircut. His friends cheered him, while the stylist clipped, shaped, and snipped Russell's hair. The result was a short cut. After the session at the hair salon was complete Russell looked stylish. Unfortunately, he looked like hundreds of men with the same haircut. Russell will not be the real Russell, until he lets his hair grow again.

Chapter Test: Beyond the Simple Sentence: Subordination

All of the following sentences are complex sentences, but some are not correctly punctuated. Write *OK* next to the ones that are correctly punctuated and *X* next to the ones that are not.

1. ___X___ Whether Julie comes to my birthday party or stays home, we will have a good time.

2. ___OK___ Liam is glad he entered the contest even though he didn't win a big prize.

3. ___X___ Give me a call, when you arrive at the train station.

4. ___OK___ After our baby was born, my husband and I stopped going out on the weekends.

5. ___OK___ My two sisters and I packed the dishes into boxes, while my father began painting the empty kitchen cabinets.

6. ___OK___ Since my parents live three hundred miles away, I visit them only on long weekends or holidays.

7. ___OK___ Don't get married until you are ready to handle the financial responsibilities of committing to another person for life.

8. ___OK___ My best friend was looking at me as if he had never seen me before.

9. ___X___ When Harry comes over, he stays for hours.

10. ___OK___ My mother knew Michael, before he became a basketball legend.

relative pronouns
that
which

Quick Question

Which sentence(s)
is/are correct?

A. I took a long hike
   in the woods
   yesterday, for it
   was a beautiful
   day.
B. Because it was a
   beautiful day, I
   took a long hike in
   the woods
   yesterday.

(After you study this
chapter, you will be
confident of your
answer.)

CHAPTER 5

Combining Sentences: A Review of Your Options

Combining sentences helps you to avoid a choppy writing style in which all your sentences are short. The pattern of one short sentence after another makes your writing repetitive and boring. When you mix the length of sentences, using some long ones and some short ones, you use a strategy called **sentence variety.**

You can develop a style that includes sentence variety by combining short, related sentences clearly and smoothly. There are several ways to combine sentences. The following chart helps you to see them all at a glance. It also includes the punctuation necessary for each combination.

INFO BOX: **Options for Combining Sentences**

Coordination

Option 1
Independent clause

, for
, and
, nor
, but
, or
, yet
, so

independent clause.

Option 2
Independent clause

{ ; (semicolon only) }

independent clause.

Option 3
Independent clause

; also,
; anyway,
; as a result,
; besides,
; certainly,
; consequently,
; finally,
; furthermore,
; however,
; incidentally,
; in addition,
; in fact,
; indeed,
; instead,
; likewise,
; meanwhile,
; moreover,
; nevertheless,
; next
; now
; on the other hand,
; otherwise,
; similarly,
; still
; then
; therefore,
; thus
; undoubtedly,

independent clause.

Subordination

Option 4	After Although As As if Because Before Even though If In order that Since So that Though Unless Until When Whenever Where Whereas Whether While	dependent clause, independent clause. (When you begin with a dependent clause, put a comma at the end of the dependent clause.)
Option 5 Independent clause	after although as as if because before even though if in order that since so that though unless until when whenever where whereas whether while	dependent clause

Note: In Option 4, words are capitalized because the dependent clause will begin your complete sentence.

Exercise 1   **Combining Simple Sentences**

Following are pairs of simple sentences. Combine each pair of sentences into one clear, smooth sentence. Create two new combinations for each pairing. The first one is done for you.

1. My car wouldn't start yesterday.

    The car battery was dead.

    combination 1: *My car wouldn't start yesterday because the battery was dead.*

    combination 2: *The car battery was dead; as a result, my car wouldn't start yesterday.*

2. Allison was afraid to be alone.

    She tolerated her boyfriend's selfish behavior.

    combination 1: _____

    _____

    combination 2: _____

    _____

3. My brother has to get up early to go to work every day.

    He feels lucky to have a little job security.

    combination 1: _____

    _____

    combination 2: _____

    _____

4. Professor Montand is friendly and understanding.

    He demands his students' best work.

    combination 1: _____

    _____

    combination 2: _____

    _____

5. My brother and his friends get together on Sunday afternoons.

    They talk about sports for hours.

    combination 1: _____

    _____

    combination 2: _____

    _____

6. I cooked some fish last night.

   My cat started circling the kitchen.

   combination 1: _____

   _____

   combination 2: _____

   _____

7. You can go to the new action film.

   You won't like it much.

   combination 1: _____

   _____

   combination 2: _____

   _____

8. My four-year-old nephew found the salt shaker.

   He sprinkled the entire living room carpet with salt.

   combination 1: _____

   _____

   combination 2: _____

   _____

9. Sam's grandmother is a cranky woman.

   He visits her regularly.

   combination 1: _____

   _____

   combination 2: _____

   _____

10. I am sleeping on my sister's couch.

    I was evicted from my apartment.

    combination 1: _____

    _____

    combination 2: _____

    _____

Collaborate

Exercise 2 **Create Your Own Text**

Following is a list of rules for sentence combining through coordinating and subordinating sentences. Working with a group, create two examples of each rule and write those sentences on the lines provided. After your group has completed this exercise, share your examples with another group.

Option 1: You can join two simple sentences (two independent clauses) into a compound sentence with a coordinating conjunction and a comma in front of it. (The coordinating conjunctions are *for, and, nor, but, or, yet, so.*)

example 1: _____

_____

example 2: _____

_____

Option 2: You can combine two simple sentences (two independent clauses) into a compound sentence with a semicolon between independent clauses.

example 1: _____

_____

example 2: _____

_____

Option 3: You can combine two simple sentences (two independent clauses) into a compound sentence with a semicolon and a conjunctive adverb between independent clauses. (Some common conjunctive adverbs are *also, anyway, as a result, besides, certainly, consequently, finally, furthermore, however, in addition, incidentally, indeed, in fact, instead, likewise, meanwhile, moreover, nevertheless, next, now, on the other hand, otherwise, similarly, still, then, therefore, thus,* and *undoubtedly.*)

example 1: _____

_____

example 2: _____

_____

Option 4: You can combine two simple sentences (two independent clauses) into a complex sentence by making one clause dependent. The dependent clause starts with a subordinating conjunction. If the dependent clause begins the sentence, the clause ends with a comma. (Some common subordinating conjunctions are *after, although, as, because, before, even though, if, in order that, since, though, unless, until, when, whenever, where, whereas, whether, while.*)

example 1: _____

_____

example 2: _____

_____

Option 5: You can combine two simple sentences (two independent clauses) into a complex sentence by making one clause dependent. If the dependent clause comes after the independent clause, no comma is needed.

example 1: _____

_____

example 2: _____

_____

Connect

Exercise 3 **Combining Sentences in a Paragraph**

In the following paragraph, combine each pair of underlined sentences into one clear, smooth sentence. Write your combination in the space above the old sentences.

I made my choice of careers years ago. I was a child. My parents gave me a puppy for my seventh birthday, and I fell in love. Most children love puppies instantly. Most children lose interest in the dogs or take them for granted. I was not like most children. My dog became my best friend. I took responsibility for his care. I loved to walk him, feed him, and brush him. Soon I wanted my dog to have a little brother or sister. I brought home a stray dog. At age ten, I had three dogs, two cats, and three hamsters. My parents accepted all these new members of the family. They could see my love for animals. At fourteen, I volunteered to walk the dogs at the animal shelter. I saw the kindness of the staff. I recognized the needs of the helpless animals. I wanted to do more than walk the dogs. From my first puppy to my teen work at the shelter, I had been moving toward one goal. Today, I am closer to that goal. I am studying veterinary science.

Connect

Exercise 4 **Editing a Paragraph with Compound and Complex Sentences**

Edit the following paragraph, adding commas and semicolons where they are necessary and taking out unnecessary commas. There are ten errors.

Because I am twenty-nine and single, people seem eager for me to marry. My aunts constantly ask if I am seeing anyone. If I say yes they want to know more details. They ask me whether the relationship is serious. They want to know where the romance is headed. I know they have good intentions but I hate these regular quizzes. My parents are more tactful however they frequently mention their desire for grandchildren. Even my coworkers are interested in my love life. My boss asks me about my plans for the weekend meanwhile two of the ladies in the office try to fix me up with their relatives.

The worst attempts at matchmaking come from the security guard at the building,

where I work. He brings me articles about online dating services and singles clubs

until I am ready to scream. All these people have good intentions yet they cannot

push me into marriage. Although I would like to make my family and friends happy I

have to please myself first.

Exercise 5   Editing a Paragraph with Compound and Complex Sentences

Edit the following paragraph, adding semicolons and commas where they are
necessary and taking out unnecessary commas. There are nine errors.

I have recently started to notice the size and weight of women's bags I am amazed

at and horrified by these monstrous accessories. My sister carries a huge canvas

shoulder bag whenever she leaves the house. I tried to pick it up the other day after

she dropped it on the couch. It weighed about twenty pounds. It must have been full

of rocks undoubtedly, she uses it as a weapon against muggers. I feel sorry for any

purse snatcher with a plan to rob my sister for he or she would wind up with a severe

injury. In fact, I think my sister's shoulder is sinking under the weight of her bag. My

girlfriend is another woman burdened by her bag. Unlike my sister, she carries a

handbag however, it bulges with electronics, cell phone accessories, and even a tiny

umbrella. It weighs about as much and my sister's bag and seems to be dragging my

girlfriend's arm down. Since I've become more conscious of women's bags I've

noticed many women struggling under the weight of huge, bulky handbags and shoul-

der bags. Observing this trend has made me feel sympathy for women but it has

also made me glad to leave home with only keys, a wallet, and a cell phone in my

pockets.

Chapter Test: Combining Sentences: A Review of Your Options

All of the following sentences are compound or complex sentences, but some are not correctly punctuated. Write *OK* next to the ones that are correctly punctuated and *X* next to the ones that are not.

1. OK   Maggie seldom asks a question in class, nor does she talk to other students at the end of class.

2. OK   Charlie just started a new job; next he wants to save some money for a car.

3. X   My bedroom was too hot, I got up and opened a window.

4. X   While the traffic crawled down the main road; I took a shortcut.

5. X   The house was too small for my family because, my grandparents came to live with us.

6. OK   You can keep resenting your brother's bad behavior; on the other hand, you can confront him about it.

7. OK   Unless Jackie feels better, she won't go out tomorrow.

8. OK   The house at the top of the hill was the most expensive one in the neighborhood, for it had an enormous backyard with a heated pool.

9. X   Give me ten more minutes to sleep, then I'll get up.

10. X   The movie held my interest, although it could have been a half hour shorter.

CHAPTER 6

Quick Question

True or False: There is more than one way to correct a sentence fragment.

(After you study this chapter, you will be confident of your answer.)

Avoiding Sentence Fragments

A **sentence fragment** is a group of words that looks like a sentence, is punctuated like a sentence, but is not a sentence. Writing a sentence fragment is a major error in grammar because it reveals that the writer is not sure what a sentence is. The following groups of words are all fragments:

fragments:
Because parents with small children want a car with room for a car seat, stroller, diaper bags, and toys.
Her father being an open-minded individual.
For example, the controversy over the safety of air bags.

There are two simple steps that can help you check your writing for sentence fragments.

INFO BOX: **Two Steps in Recognizing Sentence Fragments**

Step 1: Check each group of words punctuated like a sentence; look for a subject and a verb.

Step 2: If you find a subject and a verb, check that the group of words makes a complete statement.

RECOGNIZING FRAGMENTS: STEP 1

Check for a subject and a verb. Some groups of words that look like sentences may actually have a subject but no verb, or they may have a verb but no subject, or they may have no subject *or* verb.

fragments:

The bowl with the bright gold rim. (*Bowl* could be the subject of the sentence, but there is no verb.)

Can't be a friend of mine from college. (There is a verb, *Can be*, but there is no subject.)

On the tip of my tongue. (There are two prepositional phrases, *On the tip* and *of my tongue*, but there is no subject or verb.)

Remember that an *-ing* verb by itself cannot be the main verb in a sentence. Therefore, groups of words like the following ones may look like sentences but are missing a verb and are really fragments.

fragments:

The man cooking the Texas chili for the barbecue contest.

A few brave souls taking the plunge into the icy lake in mid-March.

My friend Cynthia being loyal to her selfish and manipulative sister.

An infinitive (*to* plus a verb) cannot be a main verb in a sentence, either. The following groups of words, which contain infinitives, are also fragments.

fragments:

Next week a representative of the airlines to meet with travel agents from across the country.

My hope to help the children of the war-torn nation.

Something nutritious to eat for supper.

Groups of words beginning with words like *also, especially, except, for example, for instance, in addition,* and *such as* need subjects and verbs. Without subjects and verbs, these groups can be fragments, like the ones below:

fragments:

Also a dangerous neighborhood in the late hours of the evening.

Especially a house with a large basement.

For example, a box of high-priced chocolates.

Checking for subjects and verbs is the first step in recognizing the major sentence errors called fragments.

| Exercise 1 | **Checking Groups of Words for Subjects and Verbs** |

Some of the following groups of words have subjects and verbs; these are sentences. Some groups are missing subjects, verbs, or both; these are fragments. Put an *S* next to each sentence; put an *F* next to each fragment.

1. _F_ Todd taking his time about selecting a meeting place for the conference next week.

2. _S_ In addition, the weather made traveling a pleasure.

3. _F_ The lieutenant's strategy being to motivate the soldiers by creating a bond of loyalty.

4. _F_   From the rushing waters of Niagara Falls to the desert stillness of the Arizona desert.

5. _S_   Her plan for renovating the old house seems practical.

6. _F_   Except for a small dent in the right rear fender of the Dodge truck.

7. _F_   The dark gray cat jumping onto the chair and curling up in my lap, purring with happiness.

8. _F_   For example, a suspicious-looking person on a dark, uninhabited city street.

9. _S_   For instance, divorced parents maintain friendly relations for the sake of their children.

10. _S_   Certainly wouldn't consider a job at a place with a reputation for paying low wages and offering few benefits.

Exercise 2   **More on Checking Groups of Words for Subjects and Verbs**

Some of the following groups of words have subjects and verbs; these are sentences. Some groups are missing subjects, verbs, or both; these are fragments. Put an *S* next to each sentence; put an *F* next to each fragment.

1. _S_   Learning a language takes practice.

2. _S_   A hint of sadness appeared in his paintings.

3. _F_   Needs a used car with low mileage and a good safety record.

4. _S_   Mr. Sabatino's explanation for the fire being an electrical problem in the basement.

5. _S_   Especially a woman with a good education and excellent references from previous employers.

6. _S_   From the end of the line came a loud voice.

7. _F_   Might have chosen a partner with more common sense.

8. _F_   One conflict with little chance of a resolution in the next few months.

9. _S_   Linda is spreading a rumor around the neighborhood.

10. _S_   Except for my mother, no one likes cornbread.

RECOGNIZING FRAGMENTS: STEP 2

If you are checking a group of words to see if it is a sentence, the first step is to look for a subject and verb. If you find a subject and a verb, Step 2 is to check that the group of words makes a complete statement. Many groups of words have both a subject and a verb but don't make sense by themselves. They are **dependent clauses.**

How can you tell if a clause is dependent? After you've checked each group of words for a subject and verb, check to see if it begins with one of the subordinating conjunctions that start dependent clauses.

INFO BOX: Subordinating Conjunctions			
after	before	so that	whenever
although	even though	though	where
as	if	unless	whereas
as if	in order that	until	whether
because	since	when	while

A clause that begins with a subordinating conjunction is a dependent clause. When you punctuate a dependent clause as if it were a sentence, you have a kind of fragment called a **dependent-clause fragment.** These fragments do not make a complete statement.

dependent-clause fragments:
After she gave him a kiss. (What happened after she gave him a kiss?)
Because lemonade tastes better than limeade. (What will happen because lemonade tastes better than limeade?)
Unless you leave for the movie right now. (What will happen unless you leave for the movie right now?)

It is important to remember both steps in checking for fragments:

Step 1: Check for a subject and a verb.

Step 2: If you find a subject and verb, check that the group of words makes a complete statement.

Exercise 3 **Checking for Dependent-Clause Fragments**

Some of the following groups of words are sentences. Some are dependent clauses punctuated like sentences; these are sentence fragments. Put an *S* next to each sentence and an *F* by each fragment.

1. _F_ Because I often see Dean at the coin laundry on Saturday afternoons.

2. _F_ Although Wesley is eligible for a student loan and can get some financial help from his father.

3. _F_ Before the movie theater opened down the street from my apartment.

4. _S_ Behind my friend's bragging is a fear of rejection.

5. _F_ If I can afford new tires for my car and have the brakes checked.

6. _S_ On Sundays my mother starts to think about the coming week at work.

7. _S_ Acting silly is typical of preteen girls.

8. _F_ Whether my mother will approve of my new girlfriend.

9. _S_ At the bottom of the garbage bag was Mia's lost engagement ring.

10. _F_ Whenever Harris gets hungry for some fried catfish and hush puppies.

Exercise 4 **More on Checking for Dependent-Clause Fragments**

Some of the following groups of words are sentences. Some are dependent clauses punctuated like sentences; these are sentence fragments. Put an *S* next to each sentence and an *F* by each fragment.

1. _F_ Then the kitten licked the sleeping child.

2. _F_ Unless Claudia asks for a transfer to another department.

3. _S_ From my grandfather I inherited a love of fishing.

4. _F_ Even though the prices at Classic Style can be high.

5. _F_ Because somebody complained about the broken traffic light at the intersection of River Road and Carson Boulevard.

6. _S_ Without Darrell there wouldn't be a party.

7. _F_ Since Pete signed up for a class in electrical engineering.

8. _S_ After Tower College opened a branch campus near Westburg and started offering weekend classes.

9. _S_ When the price of nearly everything rises and my salary stays at the same low figure.

10. _S_ Inside your heart is a warm spot for your first love.

Exercise 5 **Using Two Steps to Recognize Sentence Fragments**

Some of the following are complete sentences; some are sentence fragments. To recognize the fragments, check each group of words by using the two-step process:

Step 1: Check for a subject and a verb.

Step 2: If you find a subject and a verb, check that the group of words makes a complete statement.

Then put an *S* next to each sentence and an *F* next to each fragment.

1. _S_ Two of the cashiers at Food Depot want to try for a supervisor's position.

2. _S_ A change in the schedule of the softball games to be discussed at the meeting next week.

3. _F_ As if he had been asking my friends about me and investigating my background.

4. _F_ For instance, an aggressive driver weaving in and out of traffic lanes at high speeds.

5. _F_ One person making all the decisions for a large and diverse family.

6. _F_ Without a thought for the dangers of the mission or for her own safety.

7. _S_ On top of the hill, blue and yellow wildflowers bloomed in the summer.

8. _S_ When you get around to fixing the broken hinge on the cabinet door.

9. _S_ Making cookies is fun for small children and their parents.

10. _F_ One of Justin's strongest traits being his strong loyalty to his family and old friends.

Exercise 6 **More on Using Two Steps to Recognize Sentence Fragments**

Some of the following are complete sentences; some are sentence fragments. To recognize the fragments, check each group of words by using the two-step process:

Step 1: Check for a subject and a verb.

Step 2: If you find a subject and a verb, check that the group of words makes a complete statement.

Then put an *S* next to each sentence and an *F* next to each fragment.

1. _S_ Some of the most distinguished heart surgeons in the country to meet in San Francisco next month and study new ways to prevent heart disease.

2. _S_ In the middle of the crowd stood a man in a bumblebee costume and another man dressed as the team mascot.

3. _F_ The reason being a lack of interest in participating in a talent show.

4. _S_ Bargaining over the price of a car can be stressful.

5. _S_ At times Christopher can be annoying or rude.

6. _F_ Whenever my grandparents bring out the old photographs of the Jamaican branch of the family.

7. _S_ Out of the drawer jumped a small green lizard.

8. _F_ Because half the clothes in my closet are hand-me-downs from my two sisters.

9. _F_ Has to get a doctor to examine the bruise on his leg.

10. _F_ Turning into an argument over the responsibilities of a son to a distant and demanding father.

CORRECTING FRAGMENTS

You can correct fragments easily if you follow the two steps for identifying them.

Step 1: Check for a subject and a verb. If a group of words is a fragment because it lacks a subject or a verb, or both, *add what is missing.*

fragment: Jonette giving ten percent of her salary. (This fragment lacks a main verb.)

corrected: Jonette gave ten percent of her salary. (The verb *gave* replaces *giving,* which is not a main verb.)

fragment: Can't study with the television on. (This fragment lacks a subject.)

corrected: Salvatore can't study with the television on. (A subject, *Salvatore,* is added.)

fragment: Especially at the end of the day. (This fragment has neither a subject nor a verb.)

corrected: I often feel stressed, especially at the end of the day. (A subject, *I*, and a verb, *feel*, are added.)

Step 2: If you find a subject and a verb, check that the group of words makes a complete statement. To correct the fragment, you can turn a dependent clause into an independent one by removing the subordinating conjunction, *or* you can add an independent clause to the dependent one to create a statement that makes sense by itself.

fragment: When Mrs. Diaz offered him a job. (This statement does not make sense by itself. The subordinating conjunction *when* leads the reader to ask, "What happened when Mrs. Diaz offered him a job?" The subordinating conjunction makes this a dependent clause, not a sentence.)

corrected: Mrs. Diaz offered him a job. (Removing the subordinating conjunction makes this an independent clause—a sentence.)

corrected: When Mrs. Diaz offered him a job, he was very happy. (Adding an independent clause to the end of the sentence turns this into a statement that makes sense by itself.)

corrected: He was very happy when Mrs. Diaz offered him a job. (Adding an independent clause to the beginning of the sentence turns this into a statement that makes sense by itself.)

> **Note:** Sometimes you can correct a fragment by adding it to the sentence before or after it.

fragment (in italics): *Even if he lowers the price.* I can't afford that car.
corrected: Even if he lowers the price, I can't afford that car.

fragment (in italics): Yvonne hates large parties. *Like the one at Matthew's house.*
corrected: Yvonne hates large parties like the one at Matthew's house.

You have several choices for correcting fragments: you can add words, phrases, or clauses; you can take words out or combine independent and dependent clauses. You can change fragments into simple sentences or create compound or complex sentences. If you create compound or complex sentences, be sure to use correct punctuation.

Exercise 7 Correcting Fragments

Correct each sentence fragment below in the most appropriate way.

1. A few of the women in my child development class campaigning for a childcare facility on campus.

   corrected: _____

   _____

2. (A siren began to scream behind me.) As I stopped at a red light on Thompson Drive,

   corrected: As I stopped at a red light on Thompson Drive, a siren began to cream behind me.

3. Sarah wants to finish college. To find a good job and move out of her parents' house.

corrected: _____

_____

4. A beautiful woman in a red Corvette stealing the last parking space in the lot.

corrected: _____

_____

5. Unless you can lend me a few dollars.

corrected: _____

_____

6. Because Danielle forgot to buy bread. We have to toast hamburger rolls for breakfast.

corrected: _____

_____

7. My golden retriever loved everyone in the neighborhood. Except the bad-tempered man across the street.

corrected: _____

_____

8. Surveying my new apartment after signing the lease, I dreamed of transforming it into my personal sanctuary.

corrected: _____

_____

9. If I can get out of work early, I can meet you at the library and study for our algebra test.

corrected: If I can get out of work early, I can meet you at the library + study for our algebra test

10. My father doesn't need any more gifts of clothing. Such as sweaters or ties.

corrected: _____

_____

Collaborate

Exercise 8 **Correcting Fragments Two Ways**

The following groups of words all contain fragments. With a partner or group, construct two ways to eliminate the fragment. You can add words, phrases, or clauses; take out words; combine independent and dependent clauses; or attach a fragment to the sentence before or after it. When you have completed the exercise, be ready to share your answers with another group or with the class. The first one is done for you.

1. When she calls me and starts complaining.

   corrected: *When she calls me and starts complaining, I try to be sympathetic.*
   _____

   corrected: *She calls me and starts complaining.*
   _____

2. Although Ms. Norton's class is not one of my favorites.

   corrected: _____
   _____

   corrected: _____
   _____

3. Unless you advertise the garage sale. We won't be able to make any money for charity.

   corrected: _____
   _____

   corrected: _____
   _____

4. In the middle of the night, when I hear a strange noise.

   corrected: _____
   _____

   corrected: _____
   _____

5. Jaime grabbed more towels. As the leak in the bathtub spread across the floor.

   corrected: _____
   _____

   corrected: _____
   _____

6. Whenever I feel the first chill of October. I buy a pumpkin, carve it, and put it in my front window.

   corrected: _____
   _____

   corrected: _____
   _____

7. Helen ignoring the possibility of a divorce in her family.

   corrected: _____
   _____

corrected: _____

_____

8. If you need any help with the house painting.

corrected: _____

_____

corrected: _____

_____

9. After I met Julianne at the bowling alley. I couldn't stop thinking about her.

corrected: _____

_____

_____

corrected: _____

_____

_____

10. While the two boys poured chocolate syrup all over the kitchen floor.

corrected: _____

_____

corrected: _____

_____

Connect

Exercise 9 **Editing a Paragraph for Fragments**

Edit the paragraph below, correcting the sentence fragments by writing in the space above each fragment. There are six fragments.

    All my closest friends are optimists, Such as my cousin Jared. Jared is always willing to

expect the best outcome in a school, family, or work crisis. As a child, Jared had cancer,

yet he seemed to be the strongest member of the family. Even though he suffered terrible

pain and endured surgery, chemotherapy and radiation treatments, Jared stayed calm and

tough, He was an inspiration to me. Recently, Jared giving me strength and a positive atti-

tude, I lost my job at the movie theater and was depressed about finding work. However,

Jared encouraged me to transform my loss, Into an opportunity to find a job better suited

to my personality. His support led me to make an active and thorough job search. After a

few months, I got a position at a computer store, Where I enjoy helping the customers

choose the best technology. I like the work; in addition, I appreciate the rise in salary. My

loss turned into a gain, Because I took the advice of a close friend and acted on it.

Exercise 10 **Editing a Paragraph for Fragments**

Edit the paragraph below, correcting the sentence fragments by writing in the space above each fragment. There are six fragments.

I have the worst luck of everyone in my family. Except my Aunt Kristy. I have lost my passport, seen my engagement ring float down the drain, and broken my ankle minutes before cheerleading tryouts. Even though I can brag of suffering and surviving these misfortunes. They are not big compared to Aunt Kristy's disasters. She lost a winning lottery ticket, got a stomach flu on her wedding day, and was mistakenly identified as a bank robber. All in the same year. Our hard-luck stories seem funny to some people. But not to us. We are serious about the dark cloud hanging over us. In fact, avoiding each other just in case our dark cloud is contagious. We don't like to think about the potential for bad luck. If Aunt Kristy and I teamed up.

Chapter Test: Avoiding Sentence Fragments

Some of the following are complete sentences; some are sentence fragments. Put an *S* by each sentence and an *F* by each fragment.

1. __F__ A state senator to discuss the state's student loan policy with interested students at 2:00 p.m. in the Miller Conference Room.

2. __S__ Until Lynn can move out of her parents' house, she has to live by the family's rules.

3. __F__ If the plane fares to the Dominican Republic remain reasonable during the winter months and Victor can take some vacation time.

4. __S__ Except for a scratch on one leg, the chair was in perfect condition.

5. __F__ The hike in student activities fees causing many complaints from students without any interest in college-sponsored sports or social events.

6. __S__ Then a scowling woman shouted at the man holding back the rope line.

7. __F__ When three or four small children hear music and suddenly start to dance without any self-consciousness or inhibitions.

8. __F__ In order that the campus bookstore does not run out of the textbooks required in any college class.

9. __S__ A few houses down from my uncle's place was a family with a pet monkey.

10. __F__ Next to me in line at the supermarket a man with four apple pies and three pans of brownies in his shopping cart.

Using Parallelism in Sentences

Parallelism means balance in sentences. To create sentences with parallelism, remember this rule:

> **Similar points should get similar structures.**

Often, you will include two or more points—related ideas, examples, or details—in one sentence. If you express these ideas in a parallel structure, they will be clearer, smoother, and more convincing.

Here are some pairs of sentences with and without parallelism:

not parallel: Of all the household chores, the ones I hate the most are cooking, to iron, and dusting.

parallel: Of all the household chores, the ones I hate the most are *cooking, ironing,* and *dusting.* (Three words are parallel.)

not parallel: When I need a pencil, I look in my purse, the table, and beside the telephone.

parallel: When I need a pencil, I look *in my purse, on the table,* and *beside the telephone.* (Three prepositional phrases are parallel.)

not parallel: Inez should get the promotion because she gets along with her coworkers, she works hard, and a knowledge of the business.

parallel: Inez should get the promotion because *she gets along with her coworkers, she works hard,* and *she knows the business.* (Three clauses are parallel.)

From these examples you can see that parallelism involves matching the structures of parts of your sentence. There are two steps that can help you check your writing for parallelism.

INFO BOX: **Two Steps in Checking a Sentence for Parallel Structure**

Step 1: Look for the list in the sentence.

Step 2: Put the parts of the list into a similar structure.

You may have to change or add something to get a parallel structure.

ACHIEVING PARALLELISM

Let's correct the parallelism of the following sentence:

not parallel: If you want to pass the course, you have to study hard, taking good notes, and attendance at every class.

To correct this sentence, we'll follow the steps.

Step 1: Look for the list. If you want to pass the course, you have to do three things. Here's the list:
1. study hard
2. taking good notes
3. attendance at every class

Step 2: Put the parts of the list into a similar structure.
1. *to study* hard
2. *to take* good notes
3. *to attend* every class

Now revise to get a parallel sentence.

parallel: If you want to pass the course, you have *to study* hard, *to take* good notes, and *to attend* every class.

If you follow Steps 1 and 2, you can also write the sentence like this:

parallel: If you want to pass the course, you have to *study* hard, *take* good notes, and *attend* every class.

But you can't write the sentence like this:

not parallel: If you want to pass the course, you have to study hard, take good notes, and to attend every class.

Think of the list again. You can have
If you want to pass the course, you have

1. to study
2. to take   } parallel
3. to attend

Or you can have

If you want to pass the course, you have to

> 1. study
> 2. take   } parallel
> 3. attend

But your list can't be

If you want to pass the course, you have to

> 1. study
> 2. take   } not parallel
> 3. to attend

In other words, use *to* once (if it fits every part of the list) or use it with *every* part of the list.

Note: Sometimes making ideas parallel means adding something to the sentence because all the parts of the list cannot match exactly.

> **not parallel:** After the toddler threw his bowl of cereal, oatmeal splattered down the walls, the floor, and the table.

> **Step 1:** Look for the list. After the toddler threw his bowl of cereal, oatmeal splattered
> 1. down the walls
> 2. the floor
> 3. the table

As this sentence is written, *down* goes with *walls*, but it doesn't go with *floor* or *table*. Check the sense of this sentence by looking at each part of the list and how it is working in the sentence: "After the toddler threw his bowl of cereal, oatmeal splattered *down the walls*" is clear. But "oatmeal splattered *down the floor*"? Or "oatmeal splattered *down the table*"? These parts of the list are not right.

> **Step 2:** The sentence needs some words added to make the structure parallel.

> **parallel:** After the toddler threw his bowl of cereal, oatmeal splattered *down* the walls, *on* the floor, and *under* the table.

When you follow the two steps to check for parallelism, you can write clear sentences and improve your style.

Exercise 1   **Revising Sentences for Parallelism**

Some of the following sentences need to be revised so they have parallel structures. Revise the ones that need parallelism. Write *OK* for sentences that already have parallel structures.

> 1. Getting up early in the morning is not as bad as when you get up in the middle of the night.
>
> revised: ✗ _____
>
> _____

> 2. Colin can be immature and irritating at times, yet he can also be sympathetic and generous.
>
> revised: OK _____
>
> _____

3. My older brother warned me about flirting with his friends and to letting myself fall in love with one, but I didn't listen.

   revised: _X_____

   _____

4. Shane's outgoing personality, being naturally confident, and athletic ability made him popular in high school.

   revised: _X_____

   _____

5. In my family, children were taught to say "please" and "thank you," be kind to animals, and always telling the truth.

   revised: ~~OK~~ _____

   _____

6. André could grow up to be a man with strong principles and a heart that is filled with generosity.

   revised: _OK_____

   _____

7. I keep running into Mrs. Kelly on the bus, the movies, and in the hall.

   revised: _X_____

   _____

8. If my favorite entertainer ever goes on tour in the Southwest, I will travel to one of his concerts by car or plane.

   revised: _OK_____

   _____

9. When I am bored, I waste my time calling all my friends, eating large quantities of junk food, and watching endless hours of bad television.

   revised: _X_____

   _____

10. My final exams start on December 12; December 19 is when they end.

    revised: _My final exams start on December 12,_
    and end on December 19.

Collaborate

Exercise 2   Writing Sentences with Parallelism

With a partner or a group, complete each sentence. Begin by brainstorming a draft list; then revise the list for parallelism. Finally, complete the sentence in a parallel structure. You may want to assign one task (brainstorming a draft list, revising it, etc.) to each group member, then switch tasks on the next sentence. Following is a sample of how to work through each question, from list to sentence.

sample incomplete sentence: The three parts of college I like best are

Draft list
1. *new friends*
2. *doing well in English*
3. *Fridays off*

Revised list
1. *making new friends*
2. *doing well in English*
3. *having Fridays off*

sentence: *The three parts of college I like best are making new friends, doing well in English, and having Fridays off.*

1. Three reasons for getting regular exercise are

   Draft list
   1. _____
   2. _____
   3. _____

   Revised list
   1. _____
   2. _____
   3. _____

   sentence: _____

   _____

2. Two suggestions for fighting a cold are

   Draft list
   1. _____
   2. _____

   Revised list
   1. _____
   2. _____

   sentence: _____

   _____

3. Three signs that a person is lying are

   Draft list
   1. _____
   2. _____
   3. _____

   Revised list
   1. _____
   2. _____
   3. _____

   sentence: _____

   _____

4. Challenging adult rules gives teens a chance to

   Draft list
   1. _____
   2. _____
   3. _____

   Revised list
   1. _____
   2. _____
   3. _____

   sentence: _____

   _____

5. Four ways you can save money on clothes

Draft list	**Revised list**
1. _____	1. _____
2. _____	2. _____
3. _____	3. _____
4. _____	4. _____

sentence: _____

_____

Exercise 3   **Recognizing Parallelism in Famous Speeches**

Collaborate

Some of the most famous speeches in history contain parallel structures. This parallelism adds emphasis and dignity to the points expressed. Working in a group, have one member read each segment of a speech aloud while the others listen carefully. Then underline all the words, phrases, clauses, or sentences that are in parallel form. When you have completed the exercise, share your answers with another group.

1. Inaugural Address

John F. Kennedy

President John F. Kennedy delivered this speech when he was inaugurated on January 20, 1961. His theme was the renewal of American values and the changes and challenges we must face.

Let the word go forth from this time and place, to friend and foe alike, that the torch has been passed to a new generation of Americans—born in this century, tempered* by war, disciplined by a hard and bitter peace, proud of our ancient heritage—and unwilling to witness or permit the slow undoing of those human rights to which this nation has always been committed, and to which we are committed today at home and around the world.

*__tempered__ means hardened, toughened

2. I Have a Dream

Martin Luther King, Jr.

Martin Luther King, Jr., a Southern minister, was a leading advocate of civil rights in the 1960s. He delivered this speech to 200,000 people in Washington, D.C., where they had gathered to demonstrate peacefully for the cause of equality.

I have a dream that one day every valley shall be exalted, every hill and mountain shall be made low, the rough places shall be made plain, and the crooked places shall be made straight, and the glory of the Lord will be revealed, and all flesh shall see it together.

This is our hope. This is the faith that I go back to the South with.

> With this faith we will be able to hew* out of the mountain of despair a stone of hope. With this faith, we will be able to transform the jangling discords of our nation into a beautiful symphony of brotherhood.
>
> With this faith we will be able to work together, to pray together, to go to jail together, to stand up for freedom together, knowing that we will be free one day.

*hew means to make or shape with cutting blows

Connect

| Exercise 4 | **Combining Sentences and Creating a Parallel Structure** |

In the paragraph below, some sentences should be combined in a parallel structure. Combine each cluster of underlined sentences into one sentence with a parallel structure. Write your sentences in the lines above the old ones.

Everyone in my family did something risky and stupid when he or she was young. For example, at fifteen my father dived into a dangerous pond in the middle of winter. The pond had some treacherous shallow spots, and my father dived in from the high limb of a tree. <u>My father could have fallen from a snapped limb. My father also risked breaking his neck in a shallow spot. In addition, the icy water could have resulted in my father's death.</u> My mother's foolish behavior involved breaking the law. At thirteen, she was caught shoplifting in a store designed to attract young girls. <u>When the store manager caught her, my mother had a large purse full of cheap necklaces. Also inside it were glittering hair ornaments. The purse held fake silver rings as well.</u> My mother was lucky; the manager called my mother's parents and agreed not to prosecute the thirteen-year-old. My mother told us this humiliating story because she wanted to warn her children about reckless, impulsive behavior. <u>Unfortunately, her children have tested her patience. Ignoring her advice was frequent. Her children have made their own mistakes.</u> Risk-taking seems to be a family trait. <u>My older brother wrecked his first car by speeding. In a fight, he broke his nose. At a wild party, he got arrested.</u> My sister defied my parents and dated a man with a criminal record. <u>Worse, my younger brother risked an athletic scholarship by experimenting with drugs in his freshman year. In the same year, he skipped many of his classes. He failed two courses.</u> Finally, I put myself at risk by making the wrong friends. The people I associated with were older than I was and driven by anger. <u>Fortunately, my brothers, sister, and I have grown up. We have made better choices. We have all realized how close we came to disaster.</u>

Exercise 5 **Revising a Paragraph for Parallelism**

The following paragraph contains sentences with errors in parallelism. In the space above the lines, correct the sentences that contain errors in parallelism. There are five sentences with errors.

   Stillwater Park is the perfect place for a family picnic. Children love the range of activities. As soon as they enter, they see small children playing on the swings, are climbing the jungle gym, and racing through the colorful maze of cubes, tubes, and pyramids. Older children can enjoy the volleyball courts, basketball courts, and the softball fields. For people of all ages, there are bike paths, trails for jogging, and nature walks. The facilities for picnicking are as good as the ones for sports, for children's activities, and with enjoying nature. Beneath a cluster of trees are picnic tables and benches arranged in groups for family privacy. Barbecue pits are available; moreover, the picnic area is equipped with many trash containers so that visitors can keep the environment clean. There are also two water fountains (one for adults and one for children) and well-equipped restrooms. Stillwater Park offers the natural beauty, facilities that are clean, and varied activities that can please any picnicker.

Exercise 6 **Revising a Paragraph for Parallelism**

The following paragraph contains sentences with errors in parallelism. In the space above the lines, correct the sentences that contain errors in parallelism. There are four sentences with errors.

   Staying out of debt was never a problem for me until recently. Today money worries appear and reappear like wicked gremlins. The price of gas has risen, there's a higher rent on my apartment, and my heating bill has nearly doubled. At the same time, my salary remains low. Each day I struggle with money decisions. For instance, if I fill up my gas tank, I may not have enough cash to get a haircut. Sometimes, I have to think hard before I spend money at a pizza restaurant when I can save money by eating at home. The greatest temptation is to rely on credit cards, but I have seen the worst aspects of debt. My father used to juggle two or three credit cards, to pay a little each month, get deeper into debt, and then, out of desperation, sign up for another card. I have one credit card and use it only for emergencies. So far, I have managed to live within my means, but I miss the days when I could buy a movie ticket, a CD, or tee shirt without considering the effects on my budget. By the end of each pay period, my head is filled with money worries. Worse, each new paycheck seems to disappear as soon as I deposit it. By the time I pay my rent, put gas in my car, stocking the refrigerator with food, and settle my utility bills, I am broke again.

Chapter Test: Using Parallelism in Sentences

Some of the following sentences have errors in parallelism; some are correct. Put *OK* next to the correct sentences and *X* by the sentences with errors in parallelism.

1. __X__ After a long day at work, I relax by checking my e-mail, listening to music, and playing with my cat.

2. __ok__ Someone with common sense can be practical, reasonable, consider options, and flexible in a crisis.

3. __X__ I stopped buying fruit and vegetables at Gino's Market because the prices are too high, the lettuce can be rotten inside, the tomatoes taste like cardboard, and the frequent sale of mushy, bruised bananas.

4. __X__ The neighbors were surprised to learn that the man in the tiny frame house survived by selling aluminum cans, had no heat or electricity, and took in stray dogs.

5. __ok__ Whenever I get to my health and nutrition class early, I see students sleeping at their desks, gossiping about the teacher, and I notice them trying to finish the reading assignment.

6. __OK__ A dozen pairs of white socks, a stained sweatshirt, an evil-smelling tube of hair cream, trucker's hat, and a box of cough drops were crammed into my brother's top drawer.

7. __X__ Beth used to be afraid of yet curious about mountain climbing.

8. __ok__ On a typical weekday I wake up my two boys, get them dressed, prepare breakfast, searching for their jackets and backpacks, and drive them to preschool before 8:00 a.m.

9. __ok__ Coffee makes me jumpy, soft drinks are full of empty calories, and to drink bottled yogurt drinks doesn't appeal to me, so I stick to water most of the time.

10. __✓__ Whether it was a childhood of deprivation, a need for recognition, or a love of deal-making, something drove Sergio to make more and more money.

CHAPTER 8

Quick Question

Which sentence(s) is/are correct?

A. After I take my medicine, I feel well.

B. Something in the kitchen smells good.

(After you study this chapter, you will be confident of your answer.)

Using Adjectives and Adverbs

WHAT ARE ADJECTIVES?

Adjectives describe nouns (words that name persons, places, or things) or pronouns (words that substitute for a noun.)

adjectives:

She stood in a *dark* corner. (*Dark* describes the noun *corner.*)
I need a *little* help. (*Little* describes the noun *help.*)
She looked *happy.* (*Happy* describes the pronoun *she.*)

An adjective usually comes before the word it describes.

He gave me a *beautiful* ring. (*Beautiful* describes *ring.*)

Sometimes an adjective comes after a *being* verb, a verb that tells what something is. Being verbs are words like *is, are, was, am, has been.* Words like *feels, looks, seems, smells, sounds,* and *tastes* are part of the group called being verbs.

He seems *unhappy.* (*Unhappy* describes *he* and follows the being verb *seems.*)
Alan was *confident.* (*Confident* describes *Alan* and follows the being verb *was.*)
Your tires are *bald.* (*Bald* describes *tires* and follows the being verb *are.*)

Exercise 1   **Recognizing Adjectives**

Circle the adjective in each of the following sentences.

1. Beth and Kim are angry at their parents.
2. The fishermen saw a dark cloud fill the sky.
3. Your spice cake tastes delicious.
4. A tiny frog jumped on the bench.
5. The nasty remark hurt Rebecca.
6. Paul feels uncomfortable around strangers.
7. I am selling an old computer.
8. Abraham has been a loyal friend to me.
9. Alan slipped on the icy pavement.
10. Something in the attic smells rotten.

Exercise 2   **More on Recognizing Adjectives**

Circle the adjective in each of the following sentences.

1. Aggressive salespeople can frighten shoppers.
2. The children look excited about the trip to the zoo.
3. Dirty windows blocked the sun.
4. My boss gave me a small raise.
5. That man is wearing an expensive watch.
6. Curly hair runs in my family.
7. The top of the table feels sticky.
8. Your offer for the car sounds fair.
9. Our journey took us to an ancient site.
10. The foolish remark hurt Eva.

ADJECTIVES: COMPARATIVE AND SUPERLATIVE FORMS

The **comparative** form of an adjective compares two persons or things. The **superlative** form compares three or more persons or things.

> **comparative:** Your car is *cleaner* than mine.
> **superlative:** Your car is the *cleanest* one in the parking lot.

> **comparative:** Hamburger is *cheaper* than steak.
> **superlative:** Hamburger is the *cheapest* meat on the menu.

> **comparative:** Lisa is *friendlier* than her sister.
> **superlative:** Lisa is the *friendliest* of the three sisters.

For most adjectives of one syllable, add *-er* to form the comparative and add *-est* to form the superlative.

> The weather is *colder* today than it was yesterday, but Friday was the *coldest* day of the year.

Orange juice is *sweeter* than grapefruit juice, but the *sweetest* juice is grape juice.

For longer adjectives, use *more* to form the comparative and *most* to form the superlative.

I thought College Algebra was *more difficult* than English; however, Beginning Physics was the *most difficult* course I ever took.

My brother is *more outgoing* than my sister, but my father is the *most outgoing* member of the family.

The three forms of adjectives usually look like this:

adjective	comparative (two)	superlative (three or more)
sweet	sweeter	sweetest
fast	faster	fastest
short	shorter	shortest
quick	quicker	quickest
old	older	oldest

Or they may look like this:

adjective	comparative (two)	superlative (three or more)
confused	more confused	most confused
specific	more specific	most specific
dangerous	more dangerous	most dangerous
confident	more confident	most confident
beautiful	more beautiful	most beautiful

However, there are some *irregular forms* of adjectives:

adjective	comparative (two)	superlative (three or more)
good	better	best
bad	worse	worst
little	less	least
many, much	more	most *notecard*

Exercise 3 Selecting the Correct Adjective Forms

Write the correct form of the adjective in each of the following sentences.

1. You have __little__ (little) reason to worry about the results of your blood test.

2. Yesterday, Montrell looked at four apartments; the first one was the __most attractive__ (attractive).

3. On the menu at Colette's Café, steak is __more__ (expensive) than chicken; however, lobster is the __most__ (expensive) item of them all.

4. Professor Kaltenberg's final examination was the __toughest__ (tough) test I've ever taken.

5. Going to summer camp was a good experience for my son, but staying with his cousin in Mississippi was even __better__ (good).

6. The Rocky Mountains were __more beautiful__ (beautiful) than I had imagined.

7. Spending Saturday night with the wrong person can be
   worse (bad) than spending it alone.

8. Andy is _more_ (ambitious) than his brother Eddie.

9. Which of the four shirts is the _least_ (little) wrinkled?

10. My fourteen-year-old nephew is already _taller_ (tall) than
    his father.

Collaborate

Exercise 4 **Writing Sentences with Adjectives**

Working with a partner or group, write a sentence that correctly uses each of
the following adjectives. Be prepared to share your answers with another
group or with the class.

1. more dangerous _____

_____

2. best _____

_____

3. sillier _____

_____

4. most talented _____

_____

5. brightest _____

_____

6. more stubborn _____

_____

7. cleaner _My dog is cleaner than my next_
   door neighbors dog.

8. worst _The movie was the worst_
   out of all of them.

9. wiser _____

_____

10. most capable _____

_____

WHAT ARE ADVERBS?

Adverbs describe verbs, adjectives, or other adverbs.

adverbs:

As she spoke, Steve listened *thoughtfully*. (*Thoughtfully* describes the
   verb *listened*.)
I said I was *really* sorry for my error. (*Really* describes the adjective *sorry*.)
The cook worked *very* quickly. (*Very* describes the adverb *quickly*.)

Adverbs answer questions like "How?" "How much?" "How often?" "When?" "Why?" and "Where?"

| Exercise 5 | **Recognizing Adverbs**

Circle the adverbs in the following sentences.

1. At a children's concert, I heard a (naturally) talented, seven-year-old pianist.

2. Offered a free ticket to a hockey game, Mitchell was (not) (very) enthusiastic.

3. We'll rent a movie (tomorrow.)

4. The women looked (suspiciously) at the man with a briefcase full of cheap designer watches.

5. Pamela smiled (shyly) as the new boy looked at her.

6. If the traffic is heavy, the drive home can be (really) frustrating.

7. My boss is (usually) tolerant about sick days and other emergencies.

8. When the family needed help, the community responded (generously.)

9. Cory behaved (very foolishly) after his girlfriend left him.

10. The senior class heard (truly) inspiring advice from a former graduate.

| Exercise 6 | **More on Recognizing Adverbs**

Circle the adverbs in the following sentences.

1. Vincent was (intentionally) cruel to his opponent.

2. When the child kept fidgeting in his seat, his father responded (impatiently.)

3. The wedding reception was held at an (elegantly) decorated club.

4. Mr. Riccardi was (extremely) upset about his water bill.

5. That singer is (wildly) popular with pre-teen girls.

6. When my dog heard a noise at the door, he reacted (immediately.)

7. I (often) have cold pizza for breakfast.

8. At the sound of the bell, the students ran (happily) to the playground.

9. Lunch at the student center was (surprisingly) good.

10. The old movie seemed (unintentionally) funny to a modern audience.

| Exercise 7 | **Writing Sentences with Adverbs**

Collaborate

Working with a partner or group, write a sentence that correctly uses each of the following adverbs. Be prepared to share your answers with another group or with the class.

1. nearly _____

_____

2. sadly _____

_____

3. ever _____

_____

4. completely _____

_____

5. slowly _____

_____

6. partly _____

_____

7. clearly *She made her speech very*
clearly to understand.

8. rarely *Barely did the father*
got to see his son.

9. purely _____

_____

10. occasionally _____

_____

Hints about Adjectives and Adverbs

Do not use an adjective when you need an adverb. Some writers make the mistake of using an adjective when they need an adverb.

> **not this:** Talk to me ~~honest~~.
> **but this:** Talk to me honestly.
>
> **not this:** You can say it ~~simple~~.
> **but this:** You can say it simply.
>
> **not this:** He was breathing ~~deep~~.
> **but this:** He was breathing deeply.

Exercise 8   **Changing Adjectives to Adverbs**

In each pair of sentences, change the underlined adjective in the first sentence to an adverb in the second sentence. The first one is done for you.

1. a. That light is <u>bright</u>.

   b. That light gleams ____*brightly*____.

2. a. The traffic officer made a <u>tactful</u> reply.

   b. The traffic officer replied *tactfully*.

3. a. Two mechanics did a <u>thorough</u> check of the race car.

   b. Two mechanics checked the race car *thoroughly*.

4. a. The senator has a <u>decisive</u> way of speaking.

    b. The senator speaks _decisively_ .

5. a. Miguel has a <u>beautiful</u> voice.

    b. Miguel sings _beautifully_ .

6. a. Taylor makes <u>constant</u> references to his luck with women.

    b. Taylor _constantally_ refers to his luck with women.

7. a. Amy has a <u>simple</u> style of dressing.

    b. Amy dresses _simplely_ .

8. a. My son can be <u>impatient</u> in his actions.

    b. My son can act _impatentally_ .

9. a. Parker's complaints about his job are <u>rare</u>.

    b. Parker _rarely_ complains about his job.

10. a. The differences between coffee and tea are <u>significant</u>.

    b. Coffee and tea are _significantly_ different.

Do Not Confuse *Good* and *Well, Bad* and *Badly*

Remember that *good* is an adjective; it describes nouns. It also follows being verbs like *is, are, was, am,* and *has been.* Words like *looks, seems, smells, sounds,* and *tastes* are part of the group called being verbs. *Well* is an adverb; it describes verbs. (The only time *well* can be used as an adjective is when it means *healthy,* as in *I feel well today.*)

not this: You ran that race ~~good~~.
but this: You ran that race well.

not this: I cook eggs ~~good~~.
but this: I cook eggs well.

not this: How ~~good~~ do you understand grammar?
but this: How well do you understand grammar?

Bad is an adjective; it describes nouns. It also follows being verbs like *is, are, was, am, has been.* Words like *feels, looks, seems, smells, sounds,* and *tastes* are part of the group called being verbs. *Badly* is an adverb; it describes verbs.

not this: He feels ~~badly~~ about his mistake.
but this: He feels bad about his mistake. (*Feels* is a being verb; it is followed by the adjective *bad.*)

not this: That soup smells ~~badly~~.
but this: That soup smells bad. (*Smells* is a being verb; it is followed by the adjective *bad.*)

not this: He dances ~~bad~~.
but this: He dances badly.

Exercise 9 **Using *Good* and *Well*, *Bad* and *Badly***

Write the appropriate word in the following sentences.

1. Jonelle has been sick with the flu; she seemed really _____ (bad, badly) yesterday.

2. That room _____ (bad, badly) needs a new coat of paint.

3. Let me know if you feel _____ (good, well) enough to drive to Omaha next week.

4. André is behaving _____ (good, well) in his kindergarten class.

5. My chances of getting more financial aid look _____ (bad, badly).

6. Something in the kitchen smells _____ (good, well).

7. When Terrance asked you an embarrassing question, you answered it _____ (good, well).

8. After the team performed _____ (bad, badly) in the first half, the fans began to lose hope.

9. That new jacket looks _____ (good, well) on you.

10. The music of the new Jamaican group sounds _____ (bad, badly).

Do Not Use *More* + *-er,* or *Most* + *-est*

Be careful. Never write both an *-er* ending and *more,* or an *-est* ending and *most.*

> **not this:** I want to work with someone ~~more smarter~~.
> **but this:** I want to work with someone smarter.

> **not this:** Alan is the ~~most richest~~ man in town.
> **but this:** Alan is the richest man in town.

Use *Than,* Not *Then,* in Comparisons

When you compare things, use *than. Then* means *at a later time.*

> **not this:** You are taller ~~then~~ I am.
> **but this:** You are taller than I am.

> **not this:** I'd like a car that is faster ~~then~~ my old one.
> **but this:** I'd like a car that is faster than my old one.

When Do I Need a Comma Between Adjectives?

Sometimes you use more than one adjective to describe a noun:

> I visited a cold, dark cave.
> The cat had pale blue eyes.

If you look at the examples above, one uses a comma between the adjectives *cold* and *dark,* but the other doesn't have a comma between the adjectives *pale* and *blue.* Both sentences are correctly punctuated. To decide whether you need a comma, try one of these tests:

> **Test 1:** Try to put *and* between the adjectives. If the sentence still makes sense, put a comma between the adjectives.

Check for comma: I visited a cold, dark cave. (Do you need the comma? Add *and* between the adjectives.)
Add *and*: I visited a cold and dark cave. (Does the sentence still make sense? Yes. You need the comma.)
Correct sentence: I visited a cold, dark cave.

Check for comma: The cat had pale blue eyes. (Do you need the comma? Add *and* between the adjectives.)
Add *and*: The cat had pale and blue eyes. (Does the sentence still make sense? No. You do not need the comma.)
Correct sentence: The cat had pale blue eyes.

Test 2: Try to reverse the order of the adjectives. If the sentence still makes sense, put a comma between the adjectives.

Check for comma: I visited a cold, dark cave. (Do you need the comma? Reverse the order of the adjectives.)
Reverse the order of the adjectives: I visited a dark, cold cave. (Does the sentence still make sense? Yes. You need the comma.)
Correct sentence: I visited a cold, dark cave.

Check for comma: The cat had pale blue eyes. (Do you need a comma? Reverse the order of the adjectives.)
Reverse the order of the adjectives: The cat had blue pale eyes. (Does the sentence still make sense? No. You don't need a comma.)
Correct sentence: The cat had pale blue eyes.

You can use Test 1 or Test 2 to determine whether you need a comma between adjectives.

Exercise 10   **A Comprehensive Exercise on Using Adjectives and Adverbs**

Correct any errors in the use of adjectives and adverbs (including punctuation errors) in the following sentences. Some sentences do not need correcting.

1. Mrs. Hamilton seemed like a real helpful neighbor.
2. The little boy with the cut on his knee cried pitifully.
3. I've tried Book House and Loretto's Books, and Book House has better prices then Loretto's Books.
4. Reza found a slightly used suitcase at the hospital thrift shop.
5. Connor is the most daring of the three boys.
6. Alicia adopted a loving, loyal mutt with shiny white fur.
7. Hot soup smells well on a winter night.
8. I can't think of anyone more sweeter than my grandmother.
9. Ted feels badly about his argument with Terry.
10. Both Lester and Michelle are terrible drivers, but Lester is the worst.

Exercise 11   Another Comprehensive Exercise on Using Adjectives and Adverbs

Correct any errors in the use of adjectives and adverbs (including punctuation errors) in the following sentences. Some sentences do not need correcting.

1. I like your new cologne; it smells good.

2. Peter is ~~more~~ happier than he was in his previous job.

3. Luisa and John have three dogs; the little brown dachshund is the smartest.

4. We have been having a terrible winter; last Monday was the ~~most~~ coldest day since 1989.

5. Evan grew up in a poorly constructed apartment building in a bad neighborhood.

6. The little boy asked me ~~nice~~ *nicely* if he could have a cookie.

7. The real story behind the crime is a deep, dark secret.

8. My girlfriend is the ~~less~~ *least* athletic person I have ever known.

9. Noah dreams of something better ~~then~~ *than* the life his parents led.

10. I got up late, so I barely had time for a quick cup of coffee.

Connect

Exercise 12   Editing a Paragraph for Errors in Adjectives and Adverbs

Edit the following paragraph, correcting all the errors in the use of adjectives and adverbs. Write your corrections in the space above the errors. There are ten errors.

    Procrastination is a problem for me, especially at school. Every semester in the first few days of class, I promise myself to get organized, keep up with assignments, and start long-range projects immediately. Unfortunately, the early days of the semester are the ~~most~~ easiest time to put off assignments. Teachers ~~usual~~ *usually* spend a day explaining the class and another day introducing the subject. Many students complain about a shortage of textbooks, so I use their complaints as a ~~well~~ *good* excuse to put off buying my books. By the third week of class, I have already fallen behind. When I finally get my books, I feel bad about all the reading I have missed. As a result, I avoid getting down to the extreme*ly* difficult work of catching up. By mid-semester, I am more discouraged ~~then~~ *than* ever. At that point, I could drastically change my habits, or make some small attempts to establish a regular homework schedule, or avoid the problem entire*ly*. Since I am a procrastinator, I make the worse*t* choice. By the end of the term, I am hopelessly trapped by my own bad habits. Although I make foolish¸ desperate attempts to save my grades, I am disappointed with myself. This cycle of procrastination seems

pathetically, and it is. To break it, I will have to work ~~real~~ hard and change this

destructive pattern.

Exercise 13   **Editing a Paragraph for Errors in Adjectives and Adverbs**

Connect

Edit the following paragraph, correcting all the errors in the use of adjectives and adverbs. Write your corrections in the space above the lines. There are seven errors.

An old photograph in the right frame can combine to create a beautiful thoughtful gift. Everyone has at least one packet or box of photographs stashed in a closet or attic. When people take the time to look through older photos, they usual react with pleasure. Reactions such as, "Oh, that was your brother at four. Wasn't he a handsome little boy?" or "Don't we look ridiculously in our costumes?" are typical. Unfortunately, the photos generally end up back in a dusty box or packet. When a friend or family member takes the time to choose a special photo, the difficult part of the gift-giving process is complete. Finding a suitable frame is simple and even inexpensive. Photo frames are sold nearly everywhere, from drug stores to discount superstores to craft shops. Any frame is better then an unframed photo stuck in a box, but the most best frame is a careful chosen one. The gift of a framed photograph brings the past into the present, and that photograph will sit proud on someone's mantel, bureau, or desk.

Chapter Test: Using Adjectives and Adverbs

Some of the following sentences have errors in the use of adjectives and adverbs. Some are correct. Put *OK* by the correct sentences and *X* by the sentences with an error.

1. _OK_   Miguel and Estella are both grieving the loss of their father, but Miguel is the more devastated of the two.

2. _X_   No one saw the man enter the room because he came in very quiet.

3. _X_   I'm surprised that Jimmy looks ~~well~~ *good* even though he came directly from work and didn't have a chance to change his clothes.

4. _X_   My dog has a filthy, little blanket he insists on sleeping with every night.

5. _OK_   The Scion xB and the Honda Element both appeal to me; I'm not sure which one is the better buy.

6. _X_   At Thanksgiving, my aunts bake four kinds of pies; in my opinion, the coconut custard pie is the more delicious.

7. _X_   Erica's personality has changed; now I wonder how ~~good~~ *well* I know her.

8. _OK_   Sean has a really sincere way of convincing you to do what he wants.

9. _X_   The people who stopped to change my tire were unusually kindly to me.

10. _OK_   I've seen dozens of scary movies, but the most frightening one of all is an old one called <u>Night of the Living Dead</u>.

Correcting Problems with Modifiers

Modifiers are words, phrases, or clauses that describe (modify) something in a sentence. All of the following italicized words, phrases, and clauses are modifiers.

> **modifiers:**
> the *black* cat (word)
> the cat *in the corner* (phrase)
> the cat *that he adopted* (clause)

Sometimes modifiers limit another word. They make another word (or words) more specific.

> the basket *in the boy's bedroom* (tells which basket)
> *twenty* cookies (tells how many cookies)
> the card *that she gave me* (tells which card)
> They *seldom* visit. (tells how often)

97

Exercise 1 **Recognizing Modifiers**

In each of the following sentences, underline the modifiers (words, phrases, or clauses) that describe the italicized word.

1. An old *photograph* fell from the pages of the book.

2. In the back of the room sat a *boy* with piercing gray eyes.

3. The *soldiers* sent out of the country missed their families.

4. I was looking for a *chair* painted blue and white.

5. Katie loves the spring, but the season brings her terrible *allergies*.

6. Caught in the storm, the *travelers* found shelter in a turnpike plaza.

7. A demanding *customer* wasted an hour of my time yesterday.

8. The plump *baby* in the stroller began to gurgle and smile.

9. Sitting in the back row, *Dina* could barely see the movie screen.

10. My ancient stuffed *bear*, with its missing eye and scruffy fur, accompanied me to my first sleepover at a friend's house.

Exercise 2 **Finding Modifiers in Professional Writing**

Following is an excerpt from an essay by Pat Mora, a Chicana educator and writer. It is a remembrance of her favorite aunt, Lobo. The writing makes effective use of specific details, particularly through the use of modifiers. After you read the selection, underline the modifiers that describe each italicized word or phrase.

> We called her "Lobo." The word means "wolf" in Spanish, an odd name for a generous and loving *aunt*. Like all names it became synonymous* with her, and to this day returns me to my child self. Although the name seemed perfectly *natural* to us and to our friends, it did cause *frowns* from strangers throughout the years. I particularly remember one hot *afternoon* when on a crowded *streetcar* between the border cities of El Paso and Juarez, I momentarily *lost* sight of her. "Lobo! Lobo!" I cried in panic. Annoyed faces peered at me, disappointed at such disrespect to a white-haired woman.
>
> Actually the fault was hers. She lived with us for years, and when she arrived home from work in the evening, she'd knock on the front *door* and ask, "Donde estan mis lobitos?" "Where are my little *wolves*?" Gradually she became our lobo, a spinster* aunt who gathered the four of us around her, tying us to her life by giving us all she had.

*synonymous** means having the same or a similar meaning
*spinster** means an unmarried woman

CORRECTING MODIFIER PROBLEMS

Modifiers can make your writing more specific and more vivid. Used effectively and correctly, modifiers give the reader a clear picture of what you want to say, and they help you to say it precisely. But modifiers have to be used correctly. You can check for errors with modifiers as you revise your sentences.

> **INFO BOX:** **Three Steps in Checking for Sentence Errors with Modifiers**
>
> **Step 1:** Find the modifier.
>
> **Step 2:** Ask, "Does the modifier have something to modify?"
>
> **Step 3:** Ask, "Is the modifier in the right place, as close as possible to the word, phrase, or clause it modifies?"

If you answer no to either Step 2 or Step 3, you need to revise your sentence.

Review the three steps in the following example:

sample sentence: They were looking for a man walking a dog smoking a cigar.

Step 1: Find the modifier. The modifiers are *walking a dog* and *smoking a cigar.*

Step 2: Ask, "Does the modifier have something to modify?" The answer is yes. The man is walking a dog. The man is smoking a cigar. Both modifiers go with a *man.*

Step 3: Ask, "Is the modifier in the right place?" The answer is yes and no. One modifier is in the right place:

> a man *walking a dog*

The other modifier is not in the right place:

> a dog *smoking a cigar*

The dog is not smoking a cigar. The sentence needs to be revised.

revised sentence: They were looking for a man *smoking a cigar and walking a dog.*

Here is another example of how to apply the three steps:

sample sentence: Slathered in whipped cream and nuts, she ate the hot fudge sundae.

Step 1: Find the modifiers. The modifiers are *Slathered in whipped cream and nuts* and *hot fudge.*

Step 2: Ask, "Does the modifier have something to modify?" The answer is yes. The sundae is *slathered in whipped cream and nuts,* and the sundae is *hot fudge.*

Step 3: Ask, "Is the modifier in the right place?" The answer is yes and no. The phrase *hot fudge* is in the right place:

> *hot fudge* sundae

But *Slathered in whipped cream and nuts* is in the wrong place:

> *Slathered in whipped cream and nuts,* she

She is not slathered in whipped cream and nuts. The sundae is. The sentence needs to be revised.

revised sentence: She ate the *hot fudge* sundae *slathered in whipped cream and nuts.*

> **Caution:** Be sure to put words like *almost, even, exactly, hardly, just, merely, nearly, only, scarcely,* and *simply* as close as possible to what they modify. If you put them in the wrong place, you may write a confusing sentence.

confusing sentence: Brian only wants to buy toothpaste and shampoo. (The modifier that creates confusion here is *only*. Does Brian have only one goal in life—to be a toothpaste and shampoo buyer? Or are these the only items he wants to buy? To create a clearer sentence, move the modifier.)

revised sentence: Brian wants to buy *only* toothpaste and shampoo.

The preceding examples show one common error in using modifiers. This error involves **misplaced modifiers**—words that describe something but are not where they should be in the sentence. Here is the rule to remember:

Put the modifier as close as possible to the word, phrase, or clause it modifies.

Exercise 3 **Correcting Sentences with Misplaced Modifiers**

Some of the following sentences contain misplaced modifiers. Revise any sentences that have a misplaced modifier by putting the modifier as close as possible to whatever it modifies.

1. After falling from the tree, the doctor asked me if I could move my arms and legs.

   revised: The doctor asked me if I could move my arms and legs after falling from the tree.

2. Caitlin needed a ride to school, but in the past few weeks she had nearly asked all her friends and didn't want to ask again.

   revised: _____

   _____

3. I saw that the plane had crashed on television.

   revised: I saw on television that the plane had crashed.

4. You'll be sorry you missed this opportunity when you're old.

   revised: When you're old, you'll be sorry you missed this opportunity.

5. With a camera phone, all of these dramatic photos were taken by a boy.

   revised: _____

   _____

6. My parents saw beautiful animals on their African safari.

   revised: My parents saw beautiful animals when they went (on their African safari.)

7. Standing in line in the heat, Mrs. Klein began to feel dizzy.

   revised: Mrs. Klein began to feel dizzy while she was standing in line in the heat.

8. On the bus, I had a fascinating conversation with a woman who grooms famous people's pets named Mrs. Brinsley.

   revised: _____

   _____

9. When it was bedtime, my two-year-old son nearly screamed for twenty minutes.

   revised: _____

   _____

10. Covered in cheese and pepperoni, the hungry crowd reached for the pizzas.

    revised: The hungry crowd reached for the pizzas covered in cheese and pepperoni.

Correcting Dangling Modifiers

The three steps for correcting modifier problems can help you recognize another kind of error. For example, let's use the steps to check the following sentence.

Sample sentence: Cruising slowly through the Everglades, two alligators could be seen.

Step 1: Find the modifier. The modifiers are *Cruising slowly through the Everglades* and *two*.

Step 2: Ask, "Does the modifier have something to modify?" The answer is yes and no. The word *two* modifies *alligators*. But who or what is *cruising slowly through the Everglades*? There is no person mentioned in the sentence. The alligators are not cruising.

This kind of error is called a **dangling modifier**. It means that the modifier does not have anything to modify; it just dangles in the sentence. If you want to correct this kind of error, just moving the modifier will not work.

still incorrect: Two alligators could be seen cruising slowly through the Everglades. (There is still no person cruising, and the alligators are not cruising.)

The way to correct this kind of error is to add something to the sentence. If you gave the modifier something to modify, you might come up with several correct sentences.

revised sentences: *As we cruised slowly through the Everglades*, two alligators could be seen.
Two alligators could be seen *when the visitors were cruising slowly through the Everglades.*
Cruising slowly through the Everglades, the people on the boat saw two alligators.

Try the process for correcting dangling modifiers once more:

sample sentence: Having struggled in the snow all day, hot coffee was welcome.

Step 1: Find the modifier. The modifiers are *Having struggled in the snow all day,* and *hot.*

Step 2: Ask, "Does the modifier have anything to modify?" The answer is yes and no. The word *hot* modifies *coffee*, but *Having struggled in the snow all day* doesn't modify anything. Who struggled? There is nobody mentioned in the sentence. To revise, put somebody in the sentence.

revised sentences: Having struggled in the snow all day, Dan welcomed hot coffee.

After we struggled in the snow all day, hot coffee was welcome.

Remember that you cannot correct a dangling modifier just by moving the modifiers. You have to give the modifier something to modify, so you must add something to the sentence.

Exercise 4 **Correcting Sentences with Dangling Modifiers**

Some of the following sentences use modifiers correctly, but some have dangling modifiers. Revise the sentences that have dangling modifiers. To revise, you will have to add words and change words.

1. When driving a large car, small parking spaces can be a problem.

   revised: ~~Small parking spaces can be a problem when driving a large car.~~

2. Cooled by the ocean breeze, the porch was always a pleasant place to sit.

   revised: OK porch

3. ~~Without~~ a background in photography, the advanced photography course can be extremely challenging.

   revised: If one doesn't have —

4. At the age of three, my brother Isaac was born.

   revised: When I was three years old, my brother Isaac was born.

5. Covered in mud and slime, my old sneakers were ready for the trash bin.

   revised: Since my old sneakers was covered in mud and slime, they were ready for the trash bin.

6. While discussing the marketing plan for the new CD, a decision about the video was reached.

   revised: While we were

7. Spoiled by his grandparents and ignored by his parents, ~~childhood~~ Tony became confusing and uncertain. was

   revised: _____

8. Torn between my responsibilities to my family and my own desire for freedom, there was no way to avoid causing pain.

   revised: _____

   _____

9. To be a good parent, endless patience is needed. *a person*

   You need revised: Endless patience is needed to be a

   good parent.

10. When entering the restaurant, a shoving match between two impatient customers started.

    revised: When I was

    _____

REVIEWING THE STEPS AND THE SOLUTIONS

It is important to recognize problems with modifiers and to correct these problems. Modifier problems can result in confusing or even silly sentences, and when you confuse or unintentionally amuse your reader, the reader misses your point.

Remember to check for modifier problems by using the three steps and to correct each kind of problem appropriately.

INFO BOX: A Summary of Modifier Problems

Checking for Modifier Problems

Step 1: Find the modifier.

Step 2: Ask, "Does the modifier have something to modify?

Step 3: Ask, "Is the modifier in the right place?"

Correcting Modifier Problems

- If a modifier is in the wrong place (a misplaced modifier), put it as close as possible to the word, phrase, or clause it modifies.

- If a modifier has nothing to modify (a dangling modifier), add or change words so that it has something to modify.

Exercise 5 Revising Sentences with Misplaced or Dangling Modifiers

All of the sentences below have some kind of modifier problem. Write a new, correct sentence for each one. You can move, remove, add, or change words. The first one is done for you.

1. Shot in the chest, the ambulance took the robber to the emergency room.

   revised: *The ambulance took the robber, shot in the chest, to the emergency room.*

2. Floating on the polluted river, Melissa saw empty cans, food wrappers, and cigarette butts.

   revised: _Melissa saw empty cans, food wrappers,_ _+ cigarette butts floating on the polluted river_

3. To be happy, great wealth and fame are not necessary.

   revised: _Great wealth and fame are not_ _necessary_ (for someone) _to be happy._

4. Baked in butter and garlic, Larry served the giant shrimp.

   revised: _Larry served the giant shrimp that_ _was baked in butter and garlic._

5. The governor's speech to the graduates almost lasted an hour.

   revised: _____

   _____

6. A dozen antique toys were discovered at a local garage sale that could be 150 years old.

   revised: _A dozen antique toys that could be 150_ _years old were discovered at a local garage_ _sale._

7. Bouncing wildly on the king-sized bed, the father discovered his happy children.

   revised: _The father discovered his happy children_ _bouncing wildly on the king-sized bed._

8. Concerned about the many homeless pets in the area, money for an animal shelter was raised by the small town.

   revised: _____

   _____

9. Sailing in rough waters, seasickness hit the passengers and crew.

   revised: _____

   _____

10. Ripping a tennis ball to shreds, Wanda finally found her rambunctious golden retriever.

   revised: _____

   _____

Collaborate

Exercise 6 **Completing Sentences with Modifiers**

Do this exercise with a partner or group. Below are the beginnings of sentences. Complete each sentence by adding your own words. Be sure that each new sentence is free of modifier problems. When you have completed the exercise, share your sentences with another group or with the class. The first one is done for you.

1. Scorched and dry, *the toasted English muffin tasted like a chunk of* _____ *charcoal.* _____

2. Furious about his friend's betrayal, _____

   _____

3. Sitting around the campfire on a starless night, _____

   _____

4. When making an excuse, he was lieing to his _____

   friends, _____

5. Stuck at work until 9:00 p.m., _____

   _____

6. To make friends in a new town, _____

   _____

7. Suddenly encountering a huge bear, _____

   _____

8. Loved by millions, _____

   _____

9. While trying to install a ceiling fan, _____

   _____

10. Filled with money, _____

    _____

| Exercise 7 | **Revising for Modifier Problems** |

Connect

The following paragraph has some modifier problems. Correct the errors by writing above the lines. There are six errors.

    I worry about my brother Jack because he only trusts one person, his best friend, Lou. Having grown up together, their close friendship developed over many years. The problem lies with Jack, who can't seem to open up to anyone besides Lou. Lou has several people he confides in; he turns to his father, his girlfriend, an old teammate, and Jack for support and advice. However, my brother's small support system makes him dependent and secretive. Without Lou, it would be hard for Jack to function. In addition, I often feel left out of my brother's life. Even though I am Jack's brother, I seem to just be a stranger. After years of shutting me out, some brotherly connection should be established. While learning to trust more than one person, more security can be found for Jack. Of course, I would be happy to have a genuine brotherly relationship.

Connect

Exercise 8　Revising for Modifier Problems

The following paragraph has some modifier problems. Correct the errors by writing above the lines. There are five errors.

Going online, the time speeds by. I am capable of sitting at my computer for five hours and losing all sense of the passing of time. After checking my messages, replies must be sent to all my friends. Involved in the resulting conversations, a new world is entered, one without clocks. I can spend hours on my favorite sites and blogs. I can play games, chat, watch videos, listen to music, and shop. My computer offers a new world for me. In this world, I can choose what I want to see and hear. First becoming popular years ago, some people worried about the power of television. They worried about television's ability to fascinate huge audiences. However, spending hours in front of a television does not erase a person's sense of time. An online experience can only do that.

Chapter Test: Correcting Problems with Modifiers

Some of the sentences below have problems with modifiers; some are correct. Put *OK* by each correct sentence and *X* by each sentence with a modifier problem.

1. __X__　Dancing on his hind legs, the trainer gave a treat to the performing dog.

2. __OK__　Stranded at the airport, the travelers stared at the blizzard swirling outside.

3. __X__　At barely five years old, my family left the Philippines to start a new life in the United States.

4. __OK__　Immediately pleased by the offer of a new toy, the spoiled child stopped crying.

5. __X__　Falling off the table, I reached for the jar of jam.

6. __X__　Holding her tight, the evening seemed like a dream.

7. __X__　Torn into pieces, Ally threw the photograph into the trash bin.

8. __OK__　While shopping in the new music store, Celia and I found a great CD for our parents.

9. __X__　With my heart beating wildly, speaking in front of fifty people seemed impossible.

10. __OK__　My brother taught me nearly everything I needed to know about taking care of a car.

CHAPTER 10

Quick Question

Which sentence(s) is/are correct?

A. The light from the streetlight shone into my bedroom all night.

B. The light from the streetlight shined into my bedroom all night.

(After you study this chapter, you will be confident of your answer.)

Verbs: The Four Main Forms

Verbs are words that show some kind of action or being:

> verb
> My brother *washes* my car.
> verb
> The teddy bear *is* his oldest toy.
> verb
> Your cinnamon cake *smells* wonderful.

Verbs also tell about time:

> verb
> My brother *will wash* my car. (The time is future.)
> verb
> The teddy bear *was* his oldest toy. (The time is past.)
> verb
> Your cinnamon cake *smells* wonderful. (The time is present.)

The time of a verb is called its **tense.** You can say a verb is in the **present tense,** the **future tense,** the **past tense,** or many other tenses.

Using verbs correctly involves knowing which form of the verb to use and choosing the right verb tense.

USING STANDARD VERB FORMS

Many people use nonstandard verb forms in everyday conversation. But everyone who wants to write and speak effectively should know different levels of language, from the slang and dialect of everyday conversation to the **standard English** of college, business, and professional environments.

In everyday conversation, you might use nonstandard forms like the ones that follow:

Nonstandard Verb Forms

it seem	I faces	we was	you was
we goes	they doesn't	they talks	she work
you be	I be	he sell	it don't

But these are not correct forms in standard English. To become more familiar with standard verb forms, start with a review of the present tense.

THE PRESENT TENSE

Following are the standard verb forms of the verb *walk*.

INFO BOX: Standard Verb Forms in the Present Tense

I walk	we walk
you walk	you walk
he, she, it walks	they walk

Take a closer look at the standard verb forms. Only one form is different:

> he, she, it *walks*

This is the only form that ends in -*s* in the present tense.

In the present tense, use an -*s* or -*es* ending on the verb only when the subject is *he*, *she*, or *it*, or the equivalent of *he*, *she*, or *it*.

> **examples:**
> He *drives* to the store on Saturdays.
> Larry *walks* his dog on Saturdays. (*Larry* is the equivalent of *he.*)
> The cat *chases* the birds in my garden. (The *cat* is the equivalent of *it.*)
> She *reminds* me of my sister.
> It *looks* like a new car.
> Your engine *sounds* funny. (The word *engine* is the equivalent of *it.*)
> My daughter *watches* the news on television. (The word *daughter* is the equivalent of *she.*)

Take another look at the present tense. If the verb is a standard verb, like *work*, it will follow this form in the present tense:

I *work* on the weekends.	We *work* well together.
You *work* too hard.	You two boys *work* with Joe.
He *works* for his father.	They *work* near the mall.
She *works* in a bakery.	
It *works* on solar power.	

Exercise 1 **Picking the Right Verb in the Present Tense**

To familiarize yourself with standard verb forms in the present tense, underline the subject and circle the correct verb form in each of the following sentences.

1. She (collect / collects) antique spoons.
2. The building (contain / contains) offices and a small coffee shop.
3. At night, the cat (like / likes) to explore the back yard.
4. Joe and his uncle (make / makes) a good living in the family business.
5. Traveling to exotic places (fascinate / fascinates) Sergio.
6. My watch (need / needs) a new battery.
7. A smile from my little daughter (brighten / brightens) my day.
8. After a big dinner, we (go / goes) for a long walk.
9. Dreaming of a medical career, Wanda (work / works) part time at a children's clinic.
10. The price of his cashmere coat (equal / equals) two month's rent for me.

Exercise 2 **More on Picking the Right Verb in the Present Tense**

To familiarize yourself with standard verb forms in the present tense, underline the subject and circle the correct verb form in each of the following sentences.

1. On Thanksgiving, the restaurant (serve / serves) free dinners to the poor.
2. A week without studying (seem / seems) impossible.
3. Her quick temper (cause / causes) problems in the family.
4. Next week, you (drive / drives) Keisha to Orlando.
5. Anthony (look / looks) worried about the sociology exam.
6. In the attic of the old house (live / lives) a raccoon.
7. Your bathroom (smell / smells) like a beauty salon.
8. They rarely (offer / offers) me any advice.
9. At a party, I usually (spend / spends) most of my time with friends.
10. Constant jealousy (damage / damages) any relationship.

Exercise 3 **Writing Sentences with Verbs in the Present Tense**

Collaborate

Below are pairs of verbs. Working with a partner or group, write a sentence using each verb. Be sure your verbs are in the present tense, and make your sentences at least five words long. When you have completed the exercise, share your sentences with another group. The first one is done for you.

1. **verbs:** listen, listens

   sentence 1. *Every morning on their way to work, my parents listen to a boring radio station.*

sentence 2. *Sam always listens to my sad stories and silly complaints.*

_____

2. **verbs:** cook, cooks

sentence 1. _____

_____

sentence 2. _____

_____

3. **verbs:** choose, chooses

sentence 1. _____

_____

sentence 2. _____

_____

4. **verbs:** complain, complains

sentence 1. _____

_____

sentence 2. _____

_____

5. **verbs:** ignore, ignores

sentence 1. _____

_____

sentence 2. _____

_____

6. **verbs:** speak, speaks

sentence 1. _____

_____

sentence 2. _____

_____

7. **verbs:** enjoy, enjoys

sentence 1. _____

_____

sentence 2. _____

_____

8. **verbs:** encourage, encourages

sentence 1. _____

_____

sentence 2. _____

_____

9. **verbs:** remember, remembers

sentence 1. _____

_____

sentence 2. _____

_____

10. **verbs:** avoid, avoids

sentence 1. _____

_____

sentence 2. _____

_____

Connect

| Exercise 4 | **Revising a Paragraph for Errors in the Present Tense** |

The following paragraph contains ten errors in the present tense verb forms. Correct the errors in the spaces above the lines.

Sometimes my psychology professor go too fast when she lectures, and in order to understand the information in the lecture and take good notes, I rely on two strategies. Whenever I finds myself listening to several sentences full of strange new terms, I raise my hand and asks the teacher to explain the meaning of the terms. At other times, when the teacher stress the importance of a concept like low self-esteem or irrational fear, I requests an example. Asking so many questions can make me feel foolish, especially when the other students sits back and stares at me in silence. However, I know that I need to be involved in my education and not just sit back and let the words flows over me. Once the ideas in the lecture floats by me, they disappears.

THE PAST TENSE

The past tense of most verbs is formed by adding -d or -ed to the verb.

> **INFO BOX:** **Standard Verb Forms in the Past Tense**
>
> | I walked | we walked |
> | you walked | you walked |
> | he, she, it walked | they walked |

Add -ed to *walk* to form the past tense. For some other verbs, you may add -d.

The zookeeper *chased* the chimpanzee.
I *trembled* with excitement.
Paul *baked* a birthday cake for his daughter.

Exercise 5 **Writing the Correct Form of the Past Tense**

To familiarize yourself with the past tense, write the correct past tense form of each verb in the blank space.

1. Fifty years ago, my great aunt _introduced_ (introduce) my grandfather to his future wife.

2. Last weekend, I _played_ (play) soccer with some friends from Pakistan.

3. At my first job, I always _arrived_ (arrive) early.

4. After washing my mother's car, my brother _waxed_ (wax) it.

5. The room deodorizer in Maria's kitchen _smelled_ (smell) like strong chemicals.

6. During my semester break, I _volunteered_ (volunteer) to help clean up the yard and house of an elderly man in my neighborhood.

7. Last night, the six o'clock news _reported_ (report) a robbery at my favorite restaurant.

8. When he was sixteen, my uncle _lied_ (lie) about his age to get into the Navy.

9. Before the show, the comedian _asked_ (ask) for a bottle of water.

10. Caught borrowing my jacket without permission, my sister _mumbled_ (mumble) some excuse.

Exercise 6 **More on Writing the Correct Form of the Past Tense**

To familiarize yourself with the past tense, write the correct past tense form of each verb in the blank space.

1. During the early morning hours, someone _knocked_ (knock) on my door.

2. At the beginning of class, one brave student _asked_ (ask) to postpone the test.

3. Two weeks ago, Jessica _promised_ (promise) me a ride in her new car.

4. All afternoon, my cat _stared_ (stare) at the birds perched on the outdoor bird feeder.

5. Last night at a family dinner, I _spilled_ (spill) tomato sauce on my mother's best tablecloth.

6. After hours of hard, physical labor, Calvin _longed_ (long) for a hot shower and a good night's sleep.

7. An old girlfriend from my high school days _reappeared_ (reappear) in my life last fall.

8. In 1999, Beth Cho _created_ (create) a popular cartoon character and a nationally known comic strip.

9. Upset by all the rumors and criticism, Taylor __resigned__ (resign) from the team yesterday.

10. At the end of the meeting, no one __stayed__ (stay) to chat.

Exercise 7   **Writing Sentences with Verbs in the Present and Past Tense**

Collaborate

Below are pairs of verbs. Working with a partner or group, write a sentence using each verb. Each sentence should be five or more words long. When you have completed the exercise, share your sentences with another group. The first one is done for you.

1. **verbs:** recognizes, recognized

    sentence 1. *Whenever I go to that coffee shop, the owner recognizes me.*

    _____

    sentence 2. *Yesterday my sister recognized a famous actor walking down our street.*

2. **verbs:** delay, delayed

    sentence 1. _____

    _____

    sentence 2. _____

    _____

3. **verbs:** argues, argued

    sentence 1. _____

    _____

    sentence 2. _____

    _____

4. **verbs:** explain, explained

    sentence 1. _____

    _____

    sentence 2. _____

    _____

5. **verbs:** believes, believed

    sentence 1. _____

    _____

    sentence 2. _____

    _____

6. **verbs:** look, looked

    sentence 1. _____

    _____

    sentence 2. _____

    _____

7. **verbs:** hopes, hoped

    sentence 1. _____

    _____

    sentence 2. _____

    _____

8. **verbs:** remind, reminded

    sentence 1. _____

    _____

    sentence 2. _____

    _____

9. **verbs:** causes, caused

    sentence 1. _____

    _____

    sentence 2. _____

    _____

10. **verbs:** react, reacted

    sentence 1. _____

    _____

    sentence 2. _____

    _____

Connect

Exercise 8   Rewriting a Paragraph, Changing the Verb Tense

Rewrite the following paragraph, changing all the present tense verbs to the past tense. Write the changes in the lines above the original words.

Whenever my boss praises me, I experience a rush of pride. My new job involves selling shoes, and the mysteries of ringing up a sale with the proper codes present a challenge. My boss, Mrs. Kelly, shows great patience. However, sometimes I notice an irritable tone in her voice as she explains a process to me for the third time. I want to do well, not only to please Mrs. Kelly and to hold on to my job, but to demonstrate my ability. Therefore, a kind word or two from my boss encourages me. It represents a step in my progress.

THE FOUR MAIN FORMS OF A VERB

When you are deciding what form of a verb to use, you will probably rely on one of four verb forms: the present tense, the past tense, the present participle, or the past participle. You will use one of these forms or add a helping verb to it. As an example, look at the four main forms of the verb *walk*.

> INFO BOX: The Four Main Forms of a Verb
>
> | Present | Past | Present Participle | Past Participle |
> |---------|------|--------------------|-----------------|
> | walk | walked | walking | walked |

You use the four verb forms—present, past, present participle, past participle—alone or with helping verbs to express time (tense). Forms of regular verbs like *walk* are easy to remember.

> Use the **present** form for the present tense:
> They *walk* three miles every day.

The **past** form expresses past tense:

> Steve *walked* to work yesterday.

The **present participle,** or *-ing* form, is used with helping verbs:

> He *was walking* in a charity fund-raiser.
> I *am walking* with a neighbor.
> You *should have been walking* faster.

The **past participle** is the form used with the helping verbs *have, has,* or *had:*

> I *have walked* down this road before.
> She *has walked* to church for years.
> The children *had walked* the dog before they went to school.

Of course, you can add many helping verbs to the present tense:

> **present tense:**
> We *walk* in a beautiful forest.

> **add helping verbs:**
> We *will* walk in a beautiful forest.
> We *must* walk in a beautiful forest.
> We *can* walk in a beautiful forest.

In **regular verbs,** the four verb forms are simple: the past form is created by adding *-d* or *-ed* to the present form. The present participle is formed by adding *-ing* to the present form, and the past participle is the same as the past form.

Exercise 9 **Writing Sentences Using the Four Main Forms of a Verb**

Collaborate

Do this exercise with a partner or group. Below are pairs of verbs. Write a sentence for each verb. Your sentences should be at least five words long. When you have completed this exercise, share your answers with another group or with the class. The first one is done for you.

    1. **verbs:** hesitate, hesitating

        sentence 1. *Since I had a car accident, I hesitate before getting into a car.*

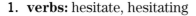

        sentence 2. *The lawyers might have been hesitating about the deal.*

2. **verbs:** conceal, concealed (Put *have* in front of *concealed.*)

sentence 1. _____

_____

sentence 2. _____

_____

3. **verbs:** smiled, smiling

sentence 1. _____

_____

sentence 2. _____

_____

4. **verbs:** support, supported

sentence 1. _____

_____

sentence 2. _____

_____

5. **verbs:** wandering, wandered (Put *has* in front of *wandered.*)

sentence 1. _____

_____

sentence 2. _____

_____

6. **verbs:** close, closed (Put *had* in front of *closed.*)

sentence 1. _____

_____

sentence 2. _____

_____

7. **verbs:** ignore, ignoring

sentence 1. _____

_____

sentence 2. _____

_____

8. **verbs:** create, created (Put *has* in front of *created.*)

sentence 1. _____

_____

sentence 2. _____

_____

9. **verbs:** exaggerating, exaggerated (Put *have* in front of *exaggerated.*)

sentence 1. _____

_____

sentence 2. _____

_____

10. **verbs:** remained, remaining

sentence 1. _____

_____

sentence 2. _____

_____

IRREGULAR VERBS

The Present Tense of *Be, Have, Do*

Irregular verbs do not follow the same rules for creating verb forms that regular verbs do. Three verbs that we use all the time—*be, have, do*—are irregular verbs. You need to study them closely. Look at the present tense forms for all three, and compare the standard present tense forms with the nonstandard ones. *Remember to use the standard forms for college or professional writing.*

present tense of *be:*

Nonstandard	Standard
~~I be or I is~~	I am
~~you be~~	you are
~~he, she, it be~~	he, she, it is
~~we be~~	we are
~~you be~~	you are
~~they be~~	they are

present tense of *have:*

Nonstandard	Standard
~~I has~~	I have
~~you has~~	you have
~~he, she, it have~~	he, she, it has
~~we has~~	we have
~~you has~~	you have
~~they has~~	they have

present tense of *do:*

Nonstandard	Standard
~~I does~~	I do
~~you does~~	you do
~~he, she, it do~~	he, she, it does
~~we does~~	we do
~~you does~~	you do
~~they does~~	they do

Caution: Be careful when you add *not* to *does*. If you're using the contraction of *does not*, be sure you write *doesn't* instead of *don't*. Contractions should be avoided in most formal reports and business writing courses. Always check with your instructor about the use of contractions in your personal writing.

> **not this:** ~~He don't call me very often.~~
> **but this:** He doesn't call me very often.

Exercise 10   Choosing the Correct Form of *Be, Have,* and *Do* in the Present Tense

Circle the correct form of the verb in each sentence.

1. I hope that my brother (**doesn't** / don't) forget to bring the tickets.

2. Keep the music low when Selena (be / **is**) studying for her child development test.

3. On Fridays, my mother (**has** / have) a busy schedule at her office.

4. In my large family, somebody (do / **does**) a load of laundry nearly every day.

5. When I look at my friends and family, I (**am** / be) grateful for my good luck.

6. Living outside the city, we (has / **have**) a long drive to work.

7. My dog and my cat (**are** / be) surprisingly good friends.

8. A car with bald tires (**does** / do) some dangerous skidding on slick roads.

9. Tyrone, my neighbor, (**has** / have) a bad attitude about keeping his place clean.

10. When Carl and I get together on the weekends, we (**are** / be) ready to relax.

Exercise 11   More on Choosing the Correct Form of *Be, Have,* and *Do* in the Present Tense

Circle the correct form of the verb in each sentence.

1. Mark likes to talk too much, but he (do / **does**) tell a good story.

2. I (**have** / has) not had a raise in two years.

3. I love my speech class, so I (**am** / be) thinking about taking another class in public speaking.

4. Both colleges offer the classes you want; you (has / **have**) a choice to make.

5. The coffeemaker in the lunchroom (**is** / be) making a strange sound.

6. Sondra (do / **does**) everything to make her children happy.

7. Every time I see Marlon, he (**has** / have) another story about his new baby.

8. Whenever I see a terrible movie, I (is / **am**) determined never to waste my money on trash again.

9. If I stay out too late, my brain (doesn't / don't) work well in the morning.

10. The band members at Sequoia High School (have / has) a practice tomorrow morning.

Exercise 12   Revising a Paragraph with Errors in the Present Tense of *Be, Have,* and *Do*

Connect

The following paragraph contains eight errors in the use of the present tense forms of *be, have,* and *do.* Correct the errors above the lines.

Darnell and I share a small apartment, and Darnell's habits be making it difficult for me to live with him. For example, Darnell's dirty jeans, shoes, and even underwear fill the living room; Darnell be too lazy to carry them as far as the bedroom. The refrigerator have no space for food because Darnell never throws out the sour milk, rotten fruit, and moldy pizza that fill the shelves. Darnell don't seem to care about the mess in the bathroom, either. I clean the bathroom once a week, but one day after I clean it, it is filthy again. Darnell do nothing about the hair in the sink, the toothpaste caked on the faucets, and the shaving cream crusted on the mirror. I am the only one who have concerns about scrubbing the shower after I use it. Clearly, I has to take a stand with Darnell because we be living in an endless mess.

The Past Tense of *Be, Have, Do*

The past tense forms of these irregular verbs can be confusing. Again, compare the nonstandard forms with the standard forms. *Remember to use the standard forms for college or professional writing.*

past tense of *be*

Nonstandard	Standard
I were	I was
you was	you were
he, she, it were	he, she, it was
we was	we were
you was	you were
they was	they were

past tense of *have*

Nonstandard	Standard
I has	I had
you has	you had
he, she, it have	he, she, it had
we has	we had
you has	you had
they has	they had

past tense of *do*

Nonstandard	Standard
~~I done~~	I did
~~you done~~	you did
~~he, she, it done~~	he, she, it, did
~~we done~~	we did
~~you done~~	you did
~~they done~~	they did

Exercise 13 **Choosing the Correct Form of *Be, Have,* and *Do* in the Past Tense**

Circle the correct verb form in each sentence.

1. After Mitchell and I argued, I (**did** / done) the right thing and apologized.

2. At yesterday's open-air market, one stall (have / **had**) fresh mangoes.

3. When the car broke down, you (**had** / has) no idea how to fix it.

4. In high school, you (was / **were**) always a rebel; now you are a leader.

5. A week ago, an old friend called, and I (**had** / has) a long conversation with him about old times.

6. In my first weeks in a new town, my neighbors (done / **did**) their best to make me feel welcome.

7. I enjoyed the singers last night; they (was / **were**) talented and lively.

8. When Roberto came back from New Jersey, he (**was** / were) a different person from the one I used to know.

9. No matter how hard Kyra tried to learn the new dance, she (**did** / done) it wrong.

10. After Peter made his sarcastic remark, he (have / **had**) no idea how many people he offended.

Exercise 14 **More on Choosing the Correct Form of *Be, Have,* and *Do* in the Past Tense**

Circle the correct verb form in each sentence.

1. Lisa and Danny (done / **did**) most of the work in the office; the other members of the staff were on the road most of the time.

2. After my grandmother retired, she finally (have / **had**) the time to enjoy her favorite hobbies: photography and ballroom dancing.

3. For two years, I (**was** / were) the proud owner of a large snake.

4. When I first saw my sister's cats, they (was / **were**) tiny kittens curled up in an old baseball cap.

5. My brothers never helped with chores around the house; they always (**have** / had) a million excuses for getting out of housework.

6. The cake at Kelly's birthday party (was̲/ were) so large that we all took the leftover pieces home.

7. For months, Saul and his friends (done /did̲) nothing but complain about their bad luck.

8. Because our parents died young, my sister and I (has / had̲) very little guidance in our teen years.

9. A month after we moved into our new house, we (was / were̲) still unpacking boxes of clothes, dishes, and other household items.

10. Getting a cell phone (did̲/ done) nothing to make my day easier.

Exercise 15 Revising a Paragraph with Errors in the Past Tense of *Be, Have,* and *Do*

Connect

The following paragraph contains twelve errors in the use of the past tense of *be, have,* and *do.* Correct the errors above the lines.

Last week, my cousin done me a big favor, but his kindness were not enough to change my opinion of him. My cousin Lennie and I grew up together because our mothers was sisters. Even though Lennie and I used to spend days and nights in each other's house, Lennie and I was more like rivals than friends. Lennie were a bully around smaller and weaker boys, so I have to fight him often to protect other children. In our teens, Lennie and I saw less of each other, but I heard stories of the cruel and selfish things that Lennie done to get ahead and to dominate others. Once we was both in our twenties, we rarely met. Then, last month, I faced an emergency. My mother needed expensive medical care, and I could not pay for it. She and I has no one to turn to except Lennie, the wealthiest person in the family. Lennie lent me the money, and I were grateful. However, I believe Lennie have a hidden motive for what he done. He bragged about his generosity so that everyone knew about his money. Once again, his actions made him look powerful and another person look small.

More Irregular Verb Forms

Be, have, and *do* are not the only verbs with irregular forms. There are many such verbs, and everybody who writes uses some form of an irregular verb. When you write and you are not certain you are using the correct form of a verb, check the following list of irregular verbs.

For each verb listed, the *present,* the *past,* and the *past participle* forms are given. The present participle isn't included because it is always formed by adding *-ing* to the present form.

Irregular Verb Forms

Present	Past	Past Participle
(Today I *arise*.)	(Yesterday I *arose*.)	(I have/had *arisen*.)
arise	arose	arisen
awake	awoke, awaked	awoken, awaked
bear	bore	born, borne
beat	beat	beaten
become	became	become
begin	began	begun
bend	bent	bent
bite	bit	bitten
bleed	bled	bled
blow	blew	blown
break	broke	broken
bring	brought	brought
build	built	built
burst	burst	burst
buy	bought	bought
catch	caught	caught
choose	chose	chosen
cling	clung	clung
come	came	come
cost	cost	cost
creep	crept	crept
cut	cut	cut
deal	dealt	dealt
draw	drew	drawn
dream	dreamed, dreamt	dreamed, dreamt
drink	drank	drunk
drive	drove	driven
eat	ate	eaten
fall	fell	fallen
feed	fed	fed
feel	felt	felt
fight	fought	fought
find	found	found
fling	flung	flung
fly	flew	flown
freeze	froze	frozen
get	got	got, gotten
give	gave	given
go	went	gone
grow	grew	grown
hear	heard	heard
hide	hid	hidden
hit	hit	hit
hold	held	held
hurt	hurt	hurt
keep	kept	kept
know	knew	known

Present	Past	Past Participle
☆ lay (to put)	laid	laid
lead	led	led
leave	left	left
lend	lent	lent
let	let	let
☆ lie (to recline)	lay	lain
light	lit, lighted	lit, lighted
lost	lost	lost
make	made	made
mean	meant	meant
meet	met	met
pay	paid	paid
ride	rode	ridden
ring	rang	rung
rise	rose	risen
run	ran	run
say	said	said
see	saw	seen
sell	sold	sold
send	sent	sent
sew	sewed	sewn, sewed
shake	shook	shaken
shine	shone, shined	shone, shined
shrink	shrank	shrunk
shut	shut	shut
sing	sang	sung
sit	sat	sat
sleep	slept	slept
slide	slid	slid
sling	slung	slung
speak	spoke	spoken
spend	spent	spent
stand	stood	stood
steal	stole	stolen
stick	stuck	stuck
sting	stung	stung
stink	stank, stunk	stunk
string	strung	strung
swear	swore	sworn
swim	swam	swum
teach	taught	taught
tear	tore	torn
tell	told	told
think	thought	thought
throw	threw	thrown
wake	woke, waked	woken, waked
wear	wore	wore
win	won	won
write	wrote	written

Exercise 16   Choosing the Correct Form of Irregular Verbs

Write the correct form of the verb in parentheses in the following sentences. Be sure to check the list of irregular verbs.

1. Yesterday Silvio _wore_ (wear) his new jacket to work.

2. Julia has _written_ (write) a beautiful poem for her parents' wedding anniversary.

3. I think the puppy's scratching has _torn_ (tear) a hole in the upholstery.

4. My father _taught_ (teach) me how to drive, and I would not recommend this father–son activity.

5. Keith told a silly joke, but he never _meant_ (mean) to hurt anyone's feelings.

6. A huge SUV _slid_ (slide) into the parking space before I could grab the spot.

7. Last night, in the last minutes of the game, my favorite team _beaten_ (beat) its most powerful rival.

8. Everything on the menu was expensive, so I _chose_ (choose) one of the cheaper items.

9. My brother _bore_ (bear) his supervisor's criticism for five long years.

10. After years of avoiding physical exercise, Raymond has _began_ (begin) to enjoy a morning walk.

Exercise 17   More on Choosing the Correct Form of Irregular Verbs

Write the correct form of the verb in parentheses in the following sentences. Be sure to check the list of irregular verbs.

1. When the spotlight turned to me, I _shook_ (shake) with nervousness.

2. Be careful; that little puppy has _bitten_ (bite) me with his sharp little teeth.

3. Our basement was full of water because the pipes had _burst_ (burst) while we were out of town.

4. When the storm hit, the wind _blew_ (blow) through the smallest cracks in the log cabin's walls.

5. After class, Alicia _went_ (go) to the computer lab to work on her political science assignment.

6. My mother saved old buttons and _strung_ (string) them together to make a necklace for her little granddaughter.

7. I have never _slept_ (sleep) on the top bunk of a bunk bed.

8. For years, my father has _risen_ (rise) at 5:30 a.m. and cooked himself a large breakfast.

9. By the time dinner was served, the children had ___ate___ (eat) so many snacks that they were no longer hungry.

10. Yesterday my husband ___bought___ (buy) our toddler a tiny basketball.

Collaborate

Exercise 18   **Writing Sentences with Correct Verb Forms**

With a partner or with a group, write two sentences that correctly use each of the following verb forms. Each sentence should be five or more words long. In writing these sentences, you may add helping verbs to the verb forms, but you may *not* change the verb form itself. When your group has completed the exercise, share your answers with another group or with the class. The first one has been done for you.

1. **verb:** seen

   sentence 1. *Until Suzanne moved to Vermont, she had never seen snow.*

   sentence 2. *The refugees from Africa have seen too much misery for anyone to bear.*

2. **verb:** lain

   sentence 1. _____

   _____

   sentence 2. _____

   _____

3. **verb:** crept

   sentence 1. _____

   _____

   sentence 2. _____

   _____

4. **verb:** stuck

   sentence 1. _____

   _____

   sentence 2. _____

   _____

5. **verb:** dealt

   sentence 1. _____

   _____

   sentence 2. _____

   _____

6. **verb:** swam

   sentence 1. _____

   _____

sentence 2. _____

_____

7. verb: grown

sentence 1. _____

_____

sentence 2. _____

_____

8. verb: taught

sentence 1. _____

_____

sentence 2. _____

_____

9. verb: stunk

sentence 1. _____

_____

sentence 2. _____

_____

10. verb: gotten

sentence 1. _____

_____

sentence 2. _____

_____

Connect

Exercise 19   **Revising a Paragraph That Contains Errors in Irregular Verb Forms**

Nine of the irregular verb forms in the following paragraph are incorrect. Write the correct verb forms in the space above the lines.

Last Friday, I became a kind of Sleeping Beauty, but the results were not so

beautiful. It all began when I come home from work at 6:00 p.m. and my roommate

said I looked tired. I feeled a little worn out, so I decided to take a short nap before

dinner. My roommate leaved for her job, and the house was quiet. I laid down on the

living room couch, and within minutes I fell into a deep sleep. I remember turning

over once and pulling an old quilt over my knees. I thinked I heared a phone ring in

the distance, but the sound seemed far away. The next thing I knowed my roommate

was shaking me. It was 9:00 a.m.! She had finished her shift at work, had went out to

breakfast, and had even done some shopping. Meanwhile, I had laid asleep on the couch for more than twelve hours. Worse, my boyfriend had called three times during

the night, and I hadn't answered the phone. I had some explaining to do. In his eyes,

my long sleep was not pretty.

Connect

Exercise 20 Revising Another Paragraph That Contains Errors in Irregular Verb Forms

Nine of the irregular verb forms in the following paragraph are incorrect. Write the correct verb forms in the space above the lines.

Waiting for a loved one to come out of surgery can mean spending hours filled with emotions. When I waited for my sister as she was undergoing surgery for breast cancer, the time seemed endless. Impatience builded in me until I wanted to hit something. I tried to distract myself by observing the other people waiting for loved ones, but they all appeared calm and even unconcerned. Two people, for example, talked and drinked cans of soda as if they had no worries. Another woman slept in her chair for an hour. Meanwhile, I growed more tense and impatient. I knowed the surgeon was supposed to come out and talk to me and my aunt when he had finished the operation. I began to think he had gave up on my sister and didn't want to talk to us. Fear replaced my anger. I feeded my imagination with all kinds of horrible situations such as funerals and burials. Hours later, my sister's surgeon bursted through the swinging doors. He had good news. Now I felt intense joy and, underneath it, relief. I could not have beared the loss of my sister.

Chapter Test: Verbs: The Four Main Forms

Some of the sentences use verbs correctly; others do not. Put *OK* by each correct sentence and *X* by each sentence with an error in using verbs.

1. _X_   After I got disappointing grades on my first two accounting quizzes, I speaked to my instructor.

2. _OK_   Lamar rose to his feet and flung a stack of dollar bills on the counter.

3. _X_   My mother lay in bed all day yesterday; her head and neck hurt.

4. _X_   Lawrence should not feel guilty about losing his job because he done all that he could to be a good employee.

5. _OK_   My car has cost me more in repairs than I originally paid for it.

6. _OK_   At work, a funny joke travels fast, but nasty rumors flies like lightning.

7. _OK_   My son slid down the water slide so many times that he was worn out by late afternoon.

8. _X_   You chose to go to a party when you was supposed to spend time with me.

9. _OK_   Pamela spoke to me about some personal problem, but I didn't know what she meant.

10. _OK_   When my brother was ten, he had more friends than anyone else on the block.

More on Verb Tenses

HELPING VERBS AND VERB TENSES

The main verb forms—present, past, present participle, and past participle—can be combined with **helping verbs** to create more verb tenses. Following is a list of some common helping verbs.

INFO BOX: Some Common Helping Verbs			
is	was	does	have
am	were	did	had
are	do	has	

These verbs change their form, depending on the subject:

She *is* calling the ticket booth.
I *am* calling the ticket booth.

Fixed-Form Helping Verbs

Some other helping verbs always keep the same form, no matter what the subject. These are the **fixed-form helping verbs.** Following are the fixed-form helping verbs.

INFO BOX: Fixed-Form Helping Verbs				
can	will	may	shall	must
could	would	might	should	

Notice how the helping verb *can* is in the same form even when the subject changes:

> She *can* call the ticket booth.
> I *can* call the ticket booth.

Helping Verbs *Can* and *Could, Will* and *Would*

Can is used to show the present tense:
> Today, David *can* fix the washer.

Could is used to show the past tense:
> Yesterday, David *could* fix the washer.

Could is also used to show a possibility or a wish:
> David *could* fix the washer if he had the right tools.
> Harry wishes he *could* fix the washer.

Will points to the future from the present:
> Cecilia is sure she *will* win the case. (Today, in the present, Cecilia is sure she will win, in the future.)

Would points to the future from the past:
> Cecilia was sure she *would* win the case. (In the past, Cecilia was sure she would win, in the future.)

Would is also used to show a possibility or a wish:
> Cecilia *would* win the case if she prepared for it.
> Cecilia wishes she *would* win the case.

Exercise 1 Recognizing Helping Verbs

Underline the helping verbs in the following sentences.

1. My father <u>does</u> appreciate his children's visits.

2. When I become King of England, I <u>shall</u> give half of my wealth to charity.

3. If you're looking for a good college, you <u>might</u> want to look at the ones near your home.

4. You have beautiful dark hair; however, you <u>do</u> need a haircut.

5. When my son was ten months old, he <u>could</u> walk across a room by himself.

6. If the weather is bad, I <u>may</u> skip my weekly visit to the Farmers' Market.

7. Last week, Billy wasn't certain he <u>would</u> get the promotion at work.

8. When you visit New York City, you <u>must</u> stop at Rockefeller Center.

9. Elena <u>was</u> chosen for the lead role in the school play.

10. I <u>should</u> spend more time with my best friend.

Exercise 2 Selecting *Can* or *Could, Will* or *Would*

In each of the following sentences, circle the correct helping verb.

1. If Mike spent less money on his social life, he (will / (would)) be able to save for a car.

2. When I lived at home, I ((can) / could) wash my clothes in my parents' washer.

3. All your friends wish you (will / (would)) take better care of your health.

4. When the sun shines, my cat ((can) / could) spend hours dozing on a sunny windowsill.

5. The teacher knew the children (will / (would)) enjoy the puppet show.

6. Maya is confident that she ((will) / would) find work in her field.

7. Last month, my brother and I thought we (can / (could)) drive to South Carolina for a long weekend.

8. I'm sure that my old parka ((will) / would) last through another winter.

9. Once the door was locked, no one (can / (could)) get into the bank vault.

10. This morning, I ((can) / could) sleep an hour later than I usually do.

PRESENT PROGRESSIVE TENSE

The **present progressive tense** uses the present participle (the *-ing* form of the verb) plus some form of *to be*. Following are examples of the present progressive tense:

INFO BOX: Present Progressive Tense

I am walking		we are walking	
you are walking	Singular	you are walking	Plural
he, she, it is walking		they are walking	

All these forms of the present progressive tense use an *-ing* form of the verb (*walking*) plus a present form of *to be* (*am, is, are*).

Be careful not to confuse the present progressive tense with the present tense:

present tense: Terry *listens* to music. (This sentence means that Terry *does* listen to music, but it does not say she is doing so at this moment.)

present progressive: Terry *is listening* to music. (This sentence means that Terry is listening to music at this moment.)

The present progressive tense shows us that the action is happening right now. The present progressive tense can also show future time.

Terry *is listening* to music later. (This sentence means that Terry will be listening to music in the future.)

Exercise 3 **Distinguishing between the Present Tense and the Present Progressive Tense**

Circle the correct verb tense in each of the following sentences. Be sure to look carefully at the meaning of each sentence.

1. You can't talk to Kelly right now; she (is taking / takes) a nap.

2. Every Friday, we (are going / go) out for dinner.

3. The new neighbors look lonely, so I (am inviting / invite) them over for coffee tomorrow.

4. Sometimes you (are complaining / complain) about trivial problems.

5. When it is sunny, Shondra (takes / is taking) her baby to the playground.

6. Jerome and Holly seem preoccupied; maybe they (are thinking / think) about their financial problems.

7. At this moment, my girlfriend (is boarding / boards) a plane for Barbados.

8. Early in the morning, my neighbor's cat (is crying / cries) outside my window.

9. You may see your father now; he (is resting / rests) comfortably in his hospital room.

10. Occasionally, my brothers (are visiting / visit) the old neighborhood.

PAST PROGRESSIVE TENSE

The **past progressive tense** uses the present participle (the *-ing* form of the verb) plus a past form of *to be* (*was, were*). Following are examples of the past progressive tense.

INFO BOX: Past Progressive Tense

I was walking		we were walking	
you were walking	Singular	you were walking	Plural
he, she, it was walking		they were walking	

Be careful not to confuse the past progressive tense with the past tense:

past tense: George *walked* carefully. (This sentence implies that George has stopped walking.)

past progressive tense: George *was walking* carefully when he slipped on the ice. (This sentence says that George was in the process of walking when something else happened: he slipped.)

Use the progressive tenses, both present and past, when you want to show that something was or is in progress.

| Exercise 4 | **Distinguishing between the Past Tense and the Past Progressive Tense** |

Circle the correct verb tense in each of the following sentences. Be sure to look carefully at the meaning of each sentence.

1. One summer, my little sister Felicia (was following / followed) me everywhere.

2. Before the light changed from yellow to red, Norman (was stepping / stepped) hard on the gas pedal.

3. I (was sleeping / slept) soundly when the phone rang.

4. More than a year ago, you and I (were meeting / met) at your sister's house.

5. Chelsea and Lurleen (were sitting / sat) at the breakfast table when the toaster caught fire.

6. When you were a baby, you (were loving / loved) baby food such as applesauce and tapioca pudding.

7. The hailstorm (was hitting / hit) the suburbs before it moved to the city.

8. After my nephews' visit to the aquarium, the boys (were pleading / pleaded) for pizza and soft drinks.

9. Derrick (was finishing / finished) his psychology project last night.

10. The old Honda (was making / made) a sound like metal scraping on metal.

PRESENT PERFECT TENSE

The **present perfect tense** is made up of the past participle form of the verb plus *have* or *has* as a helping verb. Following are examples of the present perfect tense.

INFO BOX: **Present Perfect Tense**

I have walked		we have walked	
you have walked	Singular	you have walked	Plural
he, she, it has walked		they have walked	

Be careful not to confuse the present perfect tense with the past tense:

past tense: Jacqueline *studied* yoga for two years. (This sentence means that Jacqueline doesn't study yoga anymore, but she did study it in the past.)

present perfect tense: Jacqueline *has studied* yoga for two years. (This sentence means that Jacqueline started studying yoga two years ago; she is still studying it.)

The present perfect tense is used to show an action that started in the past but is still going on in the present.

Exercise 5 **Distinguishing between the Past Tense and the Present Perfect Tense**

Circle the correct verb tense in each of the following sentences. Be sure to look carefully at the meaning of each sentence.

1. Mrs. Bernsen (taught / has taught) at Roosevelt Elementary School since 1998.

2. I (stood / have stood) in the ticket line for thirty minutes and still couldn't see the ticket booth.

3. Lewis (applied / has applied) to ten fire departments and received an encouraging reply from one of them.

4. Linda and Francine (studied / have studied) together at the Art Institute for two years and they are now starting internships at a design company in New York.

5. For years now, Formal Fashions (was / has been) the place to go for prom clothes.

6. A frightened resident of Tower Apartments called the police and (reported / has reported) the strange sounds coming from the parking lot.

7. My mother (was / has been) nagging me about my smoking habit, but I don't pay much attention to her.

8. My grandparents (held / have held) a big party on New Year's Day for many years now.

9. Dr. Torelli (worked / has worked) for the Department of Health but left to practice medicine at a clinic in Sierra Leone.

10. Yesterday, the governor (signed / has signed) a bill that will raise tuition at the state's colleges and universities.

PAST PERFECT TENSE

The **past perfect tense** is made up of the past participle form of the verb with *had* as a helping verb. You can use the past perfect tense to show more than one event in the past; that is, you can use it to show when two or more events happened in the past but at different times.

past tense: Alan *cut* the grass.

past perfect tense: Alan *had cut* the grass by the time David arrived. (Alan cut the grass *before* David arrived. Both events happened in the past, but one happened earlier than the other.)

past tense: The professor *lectured* for an hour.

past perfect tense: The professor *had lectured* for an hour when he pulled out a surprise quiz. (Lecturing came first; pulling out a surprise quiz came second. Both actions are in the past.)

The past perfect is especially useful because you write most of your essays in the past tense, and you often need to get further back into the past. Just remember to use *had* with the past participle of the verb, and you'll have the past perfect tense.

Exercise 6   **Distinguishing between the Past Tense and the Past Perfect Tense**

Circle the correct verb tense in the following sentences. Be sure to look carefully at the meaning of each sentence.

1. When Julio honked the car horn, Eric (**dashed** / had dashed) outside.

2. Molly worried that her husband (forgot / **had forgotten**) to lock the front door earlier that morning.

3. By the time I arrived at the sale, all the best bargains (**were** / had been) taken by smart shoppers.

4. As Mark (**shouted** / had shouted) into his cell phone, he turned red with rage.

5. Colin asked if we (saw / **had seen**) the martial arts movie at the multiplex.

6. Every Saturday, my mother (called / **had called**) to invite me to Sunday dinner.

7. At the summer festival, my little boy (held / **had held**) my hand while his cousin raced ahead of us.

8. By the time I dragged myself out of bed, my roommate (**spent** / had spent) two hours studying for his science test.

9. Lauren was sure that her brother (used / **had used**) her computer before she arrived home from work.

10. Tom went to traffic court yesterday to fight a ticket he (received / **had received**) three weeks ago.

A Few Tips about Verbs

There are a few errors that people tend to make with verbs. If you are aware of these errors, you will be on the lookout for them as you edit your writing.

Used to: Be careful when you write that someone *used to* do, say, or feel something. It is incorrect to write *use to*.
   not this: Wendy ~~use to~~ make pancakes for breakfast.
   but this: Wendy *used to* make pancakes for breakfast.

   not this: They ~~use to~~ live on my street.
   but this: They *used to* live on my street.

Supposed to: Be careful when you write that someone is *supposed to* do, say, or feel something. It is incorrect to write *suppose to*.
   not this: He was ~~suppose to~~ repair my watch yesterday.
   but this: He was *supposed to* repair my watch yesterday.

not this: I am ~~suppose to~~ make dinner tomorrow.
but this: I am *supposed to* make dinner tomorrow.

Could have, should have, would have: Using *of* instead of *have* is another error with verbs.
not this: He ~~could of~~ sent me a card.
but this: He *could have* sent me a card.

not this: You ~~should of~~ been more careful.
but this: You *should have* been more careful.

not this: Norman ~~would of~~ enjoyed the music.
but this: Norman *would have* enjoyed the music.

Would have/had: If you are writing about something that might have been possible but that did not happen, use *had* as the helping verb.
not this: If he ~~would have~~ been friendlier, he would not be alone now.
but this: If he *had* been friendlier, he would not be alone now.

not this: I wish the plane fare ~~would have~~ cost less.
but this: I wish the plane fare *had* cost less.

not this: If David ~~would have~~ controlled his temper, he would be a free man today.
but this: If David *had* controlled his temper, he would be a free man today.

Connect

Exercise 7   **Editing a Paragraph for Common Errors in Verbs**

Correct the seven errors in *used to, supposed to, could have, should have, would have,* and *would have/had* in the following paragraph. Write your corrections above the lines.

When I got my first job, I was so excited about having my own money to spend that I spent it foolishly. My first job was working as a package helper in a supermarket. I use to pack the customers' groceries and sometimes carry the bags to the customers' cars. I was suppose to be efficient, polite, and helpful. The pay was not great but at fifteen, I was pleased to get any pay at all. As soon as I got each paycheck, I spent it all at once on silly items: junk food, games, CDs, and DVDs. I soon tired of the games, movies, and music I had bought. But every time payday came around, I spent more money recklessly. I could of saved half of what I made and had enough for a small savings account. If I would have saved even a third of each check, I would of accumulated enough to start saving for college or a car. My parents let me take my first job and spend my own money because the experience was suppose to teach me how to handle money responsibly. Instead, I behaved like a child, and what should of been a lesson in managing my cash became an exercise in wasting it.

Exercise 8   **Writing Sentences with the Correct Verb Forms**

Collaborate

Do this exercise with a partner or with a group. Write or complete each of the following sentences. When you have finished the exercise, be ready to share your answers with another group or with the class.

1. Complete this sentence and add a verb in the correct tense: Ethan had never seen the ocean until he

_____

_____

2. Write a sentence that uses the words *given me the same birthday gift* in the middle of the sentence.

_____

_____

3. Complete this sentence and add a verb in the correct tense: I was falling asleep at my desk when

_____

_____

4. Write a sentence that includes the phrases *has guided* and *for many years.*

_____

_____

5. Complete this sentence: If only you had asked me,

_____

_____

6. Write a sentence that contains the words *should have.*

_____

_____

7. Write a sentence that includes both these helping verbs: *will* and *would.*

_____

_____

8. Complete this sentence: By the time the battle ended, six soldiers

_____

_____

9. Write a sentence that includes the words *for weeks* and *have been nagging.*

_____

_____

10. Write a sentence that includes the words *movies used to.*

_____

_____

Connect

Exercise 9   **A Comprehensive Exercise in Editing a Paragraph for Errors in Verb Tense**

Correct the nine errors in verb tense in the following paragraph. Write your corrections in the space above the lines.

Andrew is an attractive, generous, and good-natured person, but his lack of confidence often keeps him from making friends. I remember one time when he and I was sitting on a patio at our college, eating pizza and drinking Pepsi. Three women at a nearby table were giggling and glancing our way. I took this behavior as a sign that the women can be interested in a little conversation, but even when Andrew and I joined the women's table, Andrew will not talk. He remained silent and uneasy until we had to leave for class. Andrew behaved this way for years. Once, when he and I were in middle school, I was dragging him to a school talent show. I figured that Andrew will not be nervous because he did not have to make conversation with strangers; he could just sit in the audience and watch the show. After I found us two seats near the front of the crowded auditorium, I left my seat to talk to a friend. By the time I came back, Andrew moved to a seat in the last row, all alone. Andrew's shyness causes some problems; however, his good qualities sometimes shine through his bashful exterior. Right now, for example, he sits at the movies with a woman he had met last month. She says she likes Andrew's quiet, calm personality.

Exercise 10   **A Comprehensive Exercise in Editing a Paragraph for Errors in Verb Tense**

Correct the six errors in verb tense in the following paragraph. Write your corrections above the lines.

Too much quiet can be hard on a person's nerves. If a person has walked into a totally quiet department store, for example, he or she would suspect a robbery was in progress. Similarly, a person who entered a classroom full of silent students will feel uneasy. The person can fear that a boring lecture or a tough exam was in progress. Sitting in an airport lounge at night after most of the passengers and staff departed is a strange experience, too. In addition, many parents are having a hard time dealing with the silence in the house after the last child has left home. Places that are usually full of sound had become strange and even sinister when they are quiet.

Chapter Test: More on Verb Tenses

Some of the sentences below are correct; some have errors in verb tenses or other common errors. Put *OK* next to the correct sentences and *X* next to the sentences with errors.

1. _OK_ When Danny was a senior in high school, he was thinking about becoming a pilot.

2. _OK_ My grandfather has been my fishing buddy and advisor for as long as I can remember.

3. _X_ Lenny and David were laughing when I entered the room.

4. _X_ She has spent an hour on the phone, trying to get through to Keith, and then she left the club.

5. _X_ College costs more than I thought; I should of saved more of my salary when I was still living at home.

6. _X_ Henry was convinced he will persuade Linda to go to Idaho with him.

7. _OK_ Mrs. Jensen asked me if I had seen her cat wandering around the neighborhood.

8. _OK_ Gina is lending me her suitcase tomorrow so that I can use it on my trip to Brazil.

9. _X_ Once a week, my brother is playing cards at his friend Carl's house.

10. _OK_ After a bad experience with online dating, Mark wishes he would have been more careful and less trusting.

Verbs: Consistency and Voice

Remember that your choice of verb form indicates the time (tense) of your statements. Be careful not to shift from one tense to another unless you have a reason to change the time.

CONSISTENT VERB TENSES

Staying in one tense (unless you have a reason to change tenses) is called **consistency of verb tense.**

> **incorrect shifts in tense:**
> He *raced* through the yellow light, *stepped* on the gas, and *cuts* off a driver in the left lane.
> A woman in a black dress *holds* a handkerchief to her face and *moaned* softly.

You can correct these errors by putting all the verbs in the same tense.

> **consistent present tense:**
> He *races* through the yellow light, *steps* on the gas, and *cuts* off a driver in the left lane.
> A woman in a black dress *holds* a handkerchief to her face and *moans* softly.

consistent past tense:

He *raced* through the yellow light, *stepped* on the gas, and *cut* off a driver
   in the left lane.
A woman in a black dress *held* a handkerchief to her face and *moaned* softly.

Whether you correct the errors by changing all the verbs to the present
tense or by changing them all to the past tense, you are making the tense
consistent. Consistency of verb tenses is important when you describe events
because it helps the reader understand what happened and when it happened.

Exercise 1   Correcting Sentences That Are Inconsistent in Tense

In each sentence that follows, one verb is inconsistent in tense. Cross it out and
write the correct tense above. The first one is done for you.

1. Even though food ~~tasted~~ *tastes* better when I am hungry, food still tastes

    good whenever I eat it.

2. On my day off, I studied for my science test, paid all my bills, and

    shopped for food, but I ~~avoid~~ *avoided* the hard task of starting my sociology

    book report.

3. Because the mayor and city council cut the budget, the community

    center closed earlier each day, the cost of trash collection ~~goes~~ *went* up,

    and the library lost funds for expansion.

4. Kyra treats me like a child and laughs at me if I ~~asked~~ *ask* her a serious

    question.

5. For a week I remained silent when my coworker complained about

    our supervisor and gossiped about the other staff, but I ~~lose~~ *lost* my

    temper when the complaints and gossip turned into lies.

6. I get my hair cut at Vincenzo's because the prices are reasonable, the

    location ~~was~~ *is* convenient, and the staff knows the latest styles.

7. Melissa and I take the same algebra class at the college, so she ~~let~~ *lets* me

    see her notes when I miss class.

8. All last summer, swarms of mosquitoes attacked us outdoors, found

    their way into the house, and torment us when we were sleeping.

9. When the first flowers bloom in the spring, I packed up my winter

    clothes and look forward to months without wet boots, heavy jackets,

    and layers of shirts and sweaters.

10. My college counselor was extremely helpful: he reviewed all the courses I have taken, matches them against a list of required courses, and suggested a schedule for next term.

Connect

Exercise 2 Editing a Paragraph for Consistency of Tense

Read the following paragraph. Then cross out any verbs that are inconsistent in tense and write the corrections above them. The paragraph has four errors.

Every Saturday, I meet my friend Daniel at The Ranch restaurant, and we catch up on each other's news. Most of the time, we talked about the same topics: our jobs, our families, and the sports teams we love. We always ordered the same breakfast, too; we choose scrambled eggs, ham, bacon, sausage, and pancakes. We eat fast and then linger over endless refills of coffee. The wait staff is kind and never tried to kick us out of our booth. Not much changes in our Saturday routine, but it was the sameness of it that Daniel and I enjoy. Our breakfasts are a calm moment in our hectic lives.

Connect

Exercise 3 Editing a Paragraph for Consistency of Tense

Read the following paragraph. Then cross out any verbs that are inconsistent in tense and write the corrections above them. The paragraph has six errors.

Last night, someone did me a great favor, and I never got to thank that person. At 10:00 p.m., when I came home from work, I park my car in the parking lot next to my apartment and settled in for the night. After eating a microwave pizza and some cookies, I checked my e-mail, listen to some music, and fell into a deep sleep by midnight. When my alarm rings at 7:00 a.m., I was still sleepy. Half awake, I stumbled into the shower, brush my teeth, and threw on some clothes. Grabbing a cold can of Coke, I walked to my car in a daze. I was about to turn the key in the ignition when I see a note placed under one of the windshield wipers. Irritated, I thought it was another advertising flyer and planned to crumple it up and toss it in the back of my car. However, it was a handwritten note that warned me about my left front tire, which was nearly flat. That note kept me from driving off, still half asleep and unaware of any danger, with a bad tire. Thanks to a stranger, I was able to take care of my tire before I wind up stuck on the highway—or worse.

Exercise 4 **Rewriting a Paragraph for Consistent Verb Tenses**

Collaborate

The following paragraph has some inconsistencies in verb tenses: it shifts between past and present tenses. Working with a group, correct the errors in consistency by writing all the verbs in the past tense. You can write your corrections in the space above the errors. When you have completed the corrections, have one member of the group read the paragraph aloud as a final check.

My little nephew Joshua was an adventurous child. At two years old, he knew how to turn the front door knob and begins to venture out into the world. Fortunately, my sister-in-law, his mother, and my brother, his father, watched him carefully. Nevertheless, Joshua manages to travel into the next-door neighbor's yard, where he was found digging a hole with the help of the neighbor's large golden retriever. By the time he is four years old, Joshua was known throughout the neighborhood as the child who could climb a tree, dig under a fence, fall off a bike, crawl into a cellar, or hide in a closet before anyone notices. Of course, his parents, grandparents, aunts, and uncles are terrified of what this boy would do next. Elementary school promised to be a challenge, not so much for my nephew as for his family and even for his teachers. Fortunately, Joshua's first teacher knows how to channel all my nephew's drive to explore into acceptable and safe activities. In kindergarten, Joshua always jumps into new experiences and tasks. He loved being a team leader and a teacher's helper. Joshua is not afraid to touch a snake on a field trip to a petting zoo or to sing a song in front of the class. Once he started school, this reckless little boy finds a place where learning was his new adventure.

PASSIVE AND ACTIVE VOICE

Verbs not only have tenses; they have voices. When the subject in the sentence is doing something, the verb is in the **active voice.** When something is done to the subject, the verb is in the **passive voice.**

> **active voice:**
> I designed the album cover. (*I*, the subject, did it.)
> My friends from college raised money for the homeless shelter. (*Friends*, the subject, did it.)
>
> **passive voice:**
> The album cover was designed by me. (The *cover*, the subject, didn't do anything. It received the action—it was designed.)

Money for the homeless shelter was raised by my friends from college. (*Money*, the subject, didn't do anything. It received the action—it was raised.)

Notice what happens when you use the passive voice instead of the active voice:

active voice: I designed the album cover.
passive voice: The album cover was designed by me.

The sentence in the passive voice is two words longer than the one in the active voice. Yet the sentence that used the passive voice doesn't say anything different, and it doesn't say it more clearly than the one in the active voice.

Using the passive voice can make your sentences wordy, it can slow them down, and it can make them boring. The passive voice can also confuse readers. When the subject isn't doing anything, readers may have to look carefully to see who or what *is doing* something. Look at this sentence, for example:

A famous city landmark is being torn down.

Who is tearing down the landmark? In this sentence, it's impossible to find the answer to that question.

Of course, there will be times when you have to use the passive voice. For example, you may have to use it when you don't know who did something, as in these sentences:

Lana's car was stolen last week.
A bag of garbage was scattered all over my neighbor's lawn.

But in general, you should avoid using the passive voice; instead, rewrite sentences so they are in the active voice.

Collaborate

| Exercise 5 | **Rewriting Sentences, Changing the Passive Voice to the Active Voice** |

In the following sentences, change the passive voice to the active voice. If the original sentence doesn't tell you who or what performed the action, add words that tell you who or what did it. The first one is done for you.

1. One of Shakespeare's plays was performed at Peace River High School last night.

   rewritten: *Students at Peace River High School performed one of*

   Shakespeare's plays last night.

2. A series of safety measures was recommended by the superintendent of the Water Management District.

   rewritten: _____

   _____

3. Tremendous effort went into restoring the historic house.

   rewritten: _____

   _____

4. A new contract for workers at the plant has been proposed.

   rewritten: _____

   _____

5. A decision was made not to hire more security guards for the shopping center.

rewritten: _____

_____

6. A famous musician has been invited to speak at the college graduation ceremony.

rewritten: _____

_____

7. On most days, my mail is delivered after 5:00 p.m.

rewritten: _____

_____

8. Advice for dealing with stress was offered by a local psychologist.

rewritten: _____

_____

9. Cigarette butts, plastic bottles, and soda cans had been tossed on the sand.

rewritten: _____

_____

10. Several options for reducing traffic in the downtown area were proposed by the city manager.

rewritten: _____

_____

Exercise 6   **Rewriting a Paragraph, Changing It to the Active Voice**

Collaborate

Do this exercise with a partner or group. Rewrite the paragraph below, changing all the verbs that are in the passive voice to the active voice. To make these changes, you may have to add words, omit words, and change the structure of sentences. Write your changes in the space above the lines. Be ready to read your new version of the paragraph to another group or to the class.

A new system for filing insurance claims has been created by the Safety First

Automobile Insurance Company. Starting next month, all damage claims must be filed

by policyholders within thirty days of the accident. It is hoped that this early filing

deadline will help our customers. Earlier reimbursements for repairs can be enjoyed

by our policyholders if the claims process is streamlined and accelerated by the

company. As always, decisions at the company are reached with the welfare of our

customers in mind. Any questions about the new system can be answered by your local Safety First representative. Remember, Safety First can be trusted to think of

our customers' safety first.

Avoiding Unnecessary Shifts in Voice

Just as you should be consistent in the tense of verbs, you should be consistent in the voice of verbs. Do not shift from active to passive, or vice versa, without a good reason to do so.

　　　　　　　　active　　　　　　　　　　passive
shift: *Carl wrote* the song, but the *credit was taken* by Tom.

　　　　　　　　active　　　　　　active
rewritten: *Carl wrote* the song, but *Tom took* the credit.

　　　　　　　　　　　　　　passive
shift: Several *suggestions were made* by the vice president, yet the

　　　　active
president rejected all of them.

　　　　　　　　　　　　　active
rewritten: The *vice president made* several suggestions, yet the

　　　　active
president rejected all of them.

Being consistent can help you to write clearly and smoothly.

Exercise 7 **Rewriting Sentences to Correct Shifts in Voice**

Rewrite the following sentences so that all the verbs are in the active voice. You may change the wording to make the sentences clear, smooth, and consistent in voice.

1. Andre Hall was awarded a scholarship by the New Vistas organization; Andre is a remarkable young man.

   rewritten: _____

   _____

2. My mother and her friends are obsessed with a soap opera; its stars and plots are constantly analyzed by the women.

   rewritten: _____

   _____

3. The drill sergeant bullied the new recruits, and the last drop of energy was squeezed from them.

   rewritten: _____

   _____

4. If plans for a holiday party were made by my parents, they didn't include me in their arrangements.

   rewritten: _____

   _____

5. Palmer Heights was a desirable place to live until the area was struck by a series of violent robberies.

   rewritten: _____

   _____

6. The spectators roared with approval as sports history was made by the pitcher.

   rewritten: _____

   _____

7. It has been arranged by volunteer firefighters to sponsor a food drive next week; they will collect canned goods.

   rewritten: _____

   _____

8. Because Kelly is so eager to please her boyfriend, her ambitions can easily be stifled by him.

   rewritten: _____

   _____

9. A wallet was found in the vacant hotel room; the housekeeping staff also discovered a diamond ring.

   rewritten: _____

   _____

10. When the art school rejected my application for admission, my dreams of a career in fashion were shattered.

    rewritten: _____

    _____

| Exercise 8 | **Editing a Paragraph for Consistency in Voice**

Connect

The following paragraph contains seven unnecessary shifts to the passive voice. Write your corrections in the space above the errors. You can add words, omit words, or change words.

Christopher and I did not want to ask our roommate Eugene to move out, but it was believed that we had no choice. Eugene was a careless person. A lighted cigarette would sometimes be left burning when he left the apartment, and Christopher and I were afraid that one day he would start a fire. He was also an angry person. He could be provoked to violence by an offhand remark. Casual destruction was also caused by Eugene. Eugene borrowed my car, and it was dented. He never even bothered to tell me about the incident, and when the damage was discovered by me, he laughed about the dent. Eugene used to take Christopher's best shirts and wear them

to play sweaty games of football. Then the filthy shirts would be tossed on the floor.

Christopher and I kicked Eugene out because we feared what Eugene would do next.

Connect

| Exercise 9 | A Comprehensive Exercise: Editing a Paragraph for Errors in Consistent Verb Tense and Voice |

The following paragraph has six errors related to verb tense and voice. Correct
the errors in the space above the lines.

Yesterday I went shopping with Nadia, and the experience ~~teaches~~ *taught* me never to enter

a store with her again. At the first shop, Nadia didn't simply try on a dress. ~~The dressed~~ *She tried*

the dress on, ~~was tried on,~~ she viewed it from every angle of the three-way dressing room mirror, and

she analyzed the dress for hours. Then Nadia vowed never to wear such an ugly style

promised

and ~~promises~~ never to shop at the store again. After she repeated this process of trying

Nadia returned

on, considering, analyzing, and rejecting clothes at four more stores, ~~the original store~~

to the original store,

~~was returned to by Nadia.~~ Here she reconsidered and reevaluated the first dress of her

an enraged salesperson would

shopping trip. By this time, I hoped that Nadia would be thrown out of the store by an

throw Nadia out.

enraged salesperson. Unfortunately, it wasn't until the store was closed by the manager

that I was able to drag Nadia out of the mall.

Connect

| Exercise 10 | A Comprehensive Exercise: Editing a Paragraph for Errors in Consistent Verb Tense and Voice |

The following paragraph has six errors related to verb tense and voice. Correct
the errors in the space above the lines.

One of the greatest pleasures in life is watching little children dance. From age

three to five, children are utterly spontaneous. When lively music is heard, the children

jump up and danced. They are not self-conscious about their bodies or dancing abilities

and were too involved in their movements to look around. They dance in their own

style, totally enchanted by the music. One child jumps, another twirled, and another

shakes. Every kind of dance is acceptable, for judgment and cruelty have not been

learned by these young dancers. Everyone who is lucky enough to observe young

children dancing had a chance to see the beauty of one childhood moment.

Chapter Test: Verbs: Consistency and Voice

Some of the sentences below are correct; others have errors related to consistency in verb tense or voice. Put *OK* next to the correct sentences and *X* next to the sentences with errors.

1. _OK_   Pamela sent me a beautiful poem about love and loss; Emily Dickinson, a famous poet, wrote it many years ago.

2. _OK_   Gloria buys many of her clothes at thrift shops because she likes to create her own style from bits and pieces of vintage clothing.

3. _X_   At breakfast this morning, I told my father about the free concert in town and asked him if he wanted to go, but he ~~leaves~~ left without making up his mind.

4. _OK_   Marcia lent me her coat, Kelly stuffed some spending money into my pocket, and Tom drove me to the bus station for my trip to Vermont.

5. _X_   The unhappiest children in my neighborhood have the most expensive toys and clothes; however, more time with their parents is craved by these sad boys and girls.

6. _X_   Miami is viewed by those who have never visited the city as an exciting, exotic destination for nonstop fun; people who live in the city view it differently.

7. _X_   On most weekends, I go grocery shopping, Gina does the laundry, Casey cleaned the kitchen, and Mike scrubs the bathroom.

8. _X_   Although my dog ~~loved~~ loves peanuts, I can't give them to him because he is allergic to peanuts.

9. _OK_   Nathan shakes my hand firmly and looks me straight in the eye every time I meet him at the bank.

10. _OK_   When I saw Lindsay, she looked tired and said very little about her divorce.

Making Subjects and Verbs Agree

Subjects and verbs have to agree in number. That means a singular subject must be matched with a singular verb form; a plural subject must be matched with a plural verb form.

singular subject, singular verb
Nicole races out of the house in the morning.

plural subject, plural verb
Christine, Michael, and Marie take the train to work.

singular subject, singular verb
The old *song reminds* me of Mexico.

plural subject, plural verb
Greasy *hamburgers upset* my stomach.

Caution: Remember that a regular verb has an -*s* ending in one singular form in the present tense—the form that goes with *he*, *she*, *it*, or their equivalents.

s **endings in the present tense:**

He *takes* good care of his dog.

She *concentrates* on her assignments.

It *looks* like a nice day.

Eddie *buys* high-octane gasoline.

Nancy *seems* pleased.

The apartment *comes* with cable television.

PRONOUNS USED AS SUBJECTS

Pronouns can be used as subjects. **Pronouns** are words that take the place of nouns. When pronouns are used as subjects, they must agree in number with verbs.

Following is a list of the subject pronouns and the regular verb forms that agree with them in the present tense.

INFO BOX: **Subject Pronouns and Present Tense Verb Forms**

pronoun	verb	
I	walk	
you	walk	all singular forms
he, she, it	walks	
we	walk	
you	walk	all plural forms
they	walk	

In all the following sentences, the pronoun used as the subject of the sentence agrees in number with the verb:

singular pronoun, singular verb
>*I take* good care of my daughter.

singular pronoun, singular verb
>*You sing* like a professional entertainer.

singular pronoun, singular verb
>*She argues* with conviction and courage.

plural pronoun, plural verb
>*We want* a better deal on the apartment.

plural pronoun, plural verb
>*They accept* my decision about moving.

Exercise 1   Editing a Paragraph for Simple Errors in Subject–Verb Agreement

Connect

There are eight errors in subject–verb agreement in the following paragraph. If the verb does not agree with the subject, cross out the incorrect verb form and write the correct one above it.

Some people believes that dogs make more exciting pets than cats, but my cat prove these people wrong. Astro is an adventurous cat, and in most of her adventures, I plays an important role. Sometimes she stalks me, hiding under the edge of the bed until I walk by. At that moment, my fearless cat race out and puts her teeth into my ankle. She has caught her prey and feel victorious. While some might note that I am the victim in this game, I feel that a few small bites on the ankle are a small price to pay for such a suspenseful game. Another game that Astro loves involve surprise. Astro loves to startle me at night. I can be fast asleep when suddenly a large furry object leap onto my chest or lands on my head. It is, of course, Astro, playing her version of Supercat in the dark. People who don't know Astro may think that cats are just cozy little pets looking for a lap to sleep in, but my friends knows better. Astro likes to hunt them, too.

SPECIAL PROBLEMS WITH AGREEMENT

Agreement seems fairly simple, doesn't it? If a subject is singular, use a singular verb form; if a subject is plural, use a plural verb form. However, certain problems with agreement will come up in your writing. Sometimes it is difficult to find the subject of a sentence; at other times, it can be difficult to determine if a subject is singular or plural.

Finding the Subject

When you are checking for subject–verb agreement, you can find the real subject of the sentence by first eliminating the prepositional phrases. To find the real subject, put parentheses around the prepositional phrases. Then it will be easy to find the subject because nothing in a prepositional phrase can be the subject of a sentence.

prepositional phrases in parentheses:

A *person* (with good math skills) *is* a good candidate (for the job).

One (of the children) (from the village) (in the hills) *is* my cousin.

The *restaurant* (down the road) (from Cindy's house) *is* open all night.

Roy, (with his charm and style), *is* popular (with the ladies).

Exercise 2 Finding the Subject and Verb by Recognizing Prepositional Phrases

Put parentheses around all the prepositional phrases in the following sentences, and identify the subject and verb by writing an *S* or a *V* above them.

1. (On Simon's busiest days,) a giant container of coffee (from a drive-through restaurant window) substitutes (for a real breakfast.)

2. (In a moment (of weakness,) my boyfriend promised his five-year-old nephew a trip (to the water park) (over the Memorial Day weekend.)

3. (From my first day (of work) (at the warehouse) to my last moments, I enjoyed the friendly atmosphere (among the workers.)

4. A woman (with a background in bookkeeping) examined the pile (of bills and receipts) (at the office) (of the local charity.)

5. The old house (by the lake) stands (between a small pine grove) and (an old farmers' market.)

6. A set (of tools for changing a tire) belongs (in the trunk) (of every car.)

7. The best special effects (in the movie) came (at the end) (of the chase) (through the dark cave.)

8. (After the last exam) (of the semester,) a few (of us) went (to a coffee shop) (near the school.)

9. I searched (inside my wallet) for the receipt (from the repair shop.)

10. Carly dozed (during the three-hour ceremony) (in the hot, crowded gymnasium.)

Exercise 3   **Selecting the Correct Verb Form by Identifying Prepositional Phrases**

In the following sentences, put parentheses around all the prepositional phrases; then circle the verb that agrees with the subject.

1. A friend (of mine) (from the Philippines) (is / are) visiting me (after his graduation) (in June.)

2. A delicious breakfast (in the summer months) (is / are) a bowl of cereal (with cold milk and fresh strawberries.)

3. The musty smell (inside my apartment) (has / have) got me concerned (about mold) (in the building.)

4. (Between midnight and the early hours) (of the morning,) several trucks (was / were) unloading supplies (at the warehouse) (across the street.)

5. The sight (of small birds) (on the lawn) (turn / turns) my sweet cat (from a pet) (into a hunter.)

6. The plastic chairs (inside the garage) (was / were) used (for outdoor barbeques or other warm-weather activities.)

7. (During the worst hours) (of the storm,) my sister's behavior (around her children) (was / were) calm and reassuring.

8. A young man (with blue eyes) (is / are) staring at me (from across the dance floor.)

9. Kevin's victory (over years of addiction) (was / were) a story (of his determination and his family's support.)

10. A spokesperson (from the television network) (has / have) announced a press conference (for this afternoon) (at 3:00 p.m.)

Changed Word Order

You are probably used to looking for the subject of a sentence in front of the verb, but not all sentences follow this pattern. Questions, sentences beginning with words like *here* or *there*, and other sentences can change the word order. Therefore, you have to look carefully to check for subject–verb agreement.

sentences with changed word order:

       V   S

Where *are* the *packages?*

       V   S   V

When *is Mr. Hernandez giving* the exam?

              V   S

Behind the trees *is* a picnic *table.*

     V   S

There *are crumbs* on the floor.

     V   S

There *is* an *answer* to your question.

Exercise 4   **Making Subjects and Verbs Agree in Sentences with Changed Word Order**

In each of the following sentences, underline the subject; then circle the correct verb form.

1. Where (is / are) the ketchup and mustard for the hot dogs?
2. Below the bridge (is / are) a paved walking path with benches.
3. At the back of the theater (stands / stand) two ushers.
4. There (was / were) hope and peace in the old man's eyes.
5. Near the top of the hill (was / were) a restaurant with a view of the surrounding countryside.
6. Here (was / were) the lost photo album and my grandfather's old war mementos.
7. Among my oldest dreams (was / were) a wish for a large and loving family of my own.
8. When (is / are) Lisa and the boys coming for dinner?
9. At the end of a good day at my job (come / comes) a sense of achievement.
10. Here (is / are) the man with all the answers.

Collaborate

Exercise 5   **Writing Sentences with Subject–Verb Agreement in Changed Word Order**

Do this exercise with a partner or group. Complete the following, making each into a sentence. Be sure the subject and verb agree. The first one is done for you.

1. From the back of the room came *three loud cheers.*
2. Behind the castle wall lurks a dangerous wolf.
3. Here are _____
4. Under the pile of old newspapers was _____
5. With the famous basketball star come _____
6. After the scream, there was _____
7. Into the glass skylight crashes _____
8. At the top of the mountain are _____

9. Toward me run _____

10. Where is my _____

Compound Subjects

A **compound subject** is two or more subjects joined by *and*, *or*, or *nor*.

When subjects are joined by *and*, they are usually plural.

compound subjects joined by *and*:

S   S   V
Bill and *Chris are* good tennis players.

S   V
The *garage* and the *basement are* full of water.

S   S V
A *restaurant* and a *motel are* across the road.

Caution: Be sure to check for a compound subject when the word order changes.

compound subjects in changed word order:

V   S   S
There *are* a *restaurant* and a *motel* across the road. (Two things, a restaurant and a motel, are across the road.)

V   S   S
Here *are* your *notebook* and *pencil*. (Your notebook and pencil, two things, are here.)

When subjects are joined by *or*, *either . . . or*, *neither . . . nor*, *not only . . . but also*, the verb form agrees with the subject closest to the verb.

compound subjects with *or*, *either . . . or*, *neither . . . nor*, *not only . . . but also*:

singular S   plural S,   plural V
Christine or the *neighbors are* making dinner.

plural S   singular S, singular V
The *neighbors* or *Christine is* making dinner.

singular S   plural S, plural V
Not only my *mother* but also my *brothers were* delighted with the gift.

plural S   singular S, singular V
Not only my *brothers* but also my *mother was* delighted with the gift.

plural S   singular S, singular V
Either the *tenants* or the *landlord has* to back down.

singular S   plural S, plural V
Either the *landlord* or the *tenants have* to back down.

plural S   singular S, singular V
Neither the rose *bushes* nor the lemon *tree fits* in that corner of the yard.

singular S   plural S, plural V
Neither the lemon *tree* nor the rose *bushes fit* in that corner of the yard.

Exercise 6 **Making Subjects and Verbs Agree: Compound Subjects**

Circle the correct form of the verb in each of the following sentences.

1. Constant restlessness and a quick temper (was)/ were) Arthur's worst traits.

2. Dr. Litwack or Dr. Karrim (is / are) keeping the clinic open on Wednesday evenings.

3. Not only my nephews but also their mother (is / are) taking lessons in the martial arts.

4. Here (is / are) a bag of popcorn and a large Diet Pepsi for you to enjoy during the movie.

5. My parents or my sister (takes / take) the dog for a walk in the morning.

6. In the medicine cabinet (is / are) a new tube of toothpaste and a toothbrush.

7. Neither my sweaters nor my jacket (is / are) heavy enough to protect me in a snowstorm.

8. There (is / are) a right way and a wrong way to apologize to your friend.

9. Either stress or nightmares (has / have) kept me from sleeping soundly all week.

10. Before the ceremony began, the bride and her father (was / were) waiting in the hall.

Exercise 7   **Recognizing Subjects and Verbs: A Review**

Being sure that subjects and verbs agree often depends on recognizing subjects and verbs in sentences with changed word order, prepositional phrases, and compound subjects. To review the subject–verb patterns of sentences, underline all the subjects and verbs in the following selection. Put an *S* above the subjects and a *V* above the verbs.

The following excerpt is from an essay by Edna Buchanan, a former prize-winning journalist for the *Miami Herald* and now a famous crime novelist.

Miami's Most Dangerous Profession

Miami's most dangerous profession is not police work or fire fighting; it is driving a cab. For taxi drivers, many of them poor immigrants, murder is an occupational hazard. All-night gas station attendants and convenience store clerks used to be at high risk, but steps were taken to protect them. All gas pumps now switch to self-serve after dark, with exact change only, and the attendants are locked in bullet-proof booths. Convenience stores were redesigned, and drop safes were installed, leaving little cash available.

But the life of a taxi driver is just as risky as it was twenty years ago when I covered my first killing of a cabbie.

Bullet-proof glass could be placed between the driver and passengers, but most owners say it is too expensive, and besides, there is no foolproof way to protect oneself totally from somebody riding in the same car.

Indefinite Pronouns

Certain pronouns, called **indefinite pronouns,** always take a singular verb.

INFO BOX: Indefinite Pronouns			
one	nobody	nothing	each
anyone	anybody	anything	either
someone	somebody	something	neither
everyone	everybody	everything	

If you want to write clearly and correctly, you must memorize these words and remember that they always use singular verbs. Using common sense isn't enough because some of these words seem plural: for example, *everybody* seems to mean more than one person, but in grammatically correct English, it takes a singular verb. Here are some examples of the pronouns used with singular verbs:

indefinite pronouns and singular verbs:

singular S   singular V
Each of my friends *is* athletic.

singular S   singular V
Everyone in the supermarket *is looking* for a bargain.

singular S   singular V
Anybody from our Spanish class *is* capable of translating the letter.

singular S   singular V
Someone from the maintenance department *is working* on the heater.

singular S   singular V
One of Roberta's nieces *is* in my sister's ballet class.

singular S   singular V
Neither of the cakes *is* expensive.

You can memorize the indefinite pronouns as the *-one, -thing,* and *-body* words—*everyone, everything, everybody,* and so on—plus *each, either,* and *neither.*

Exercise 8   Making Subjects and Verbs Agree: Using Indefinite Pronouns

Circle the correct verb in the following sentences.

1. One of my happiest childhood memories (is / are) of a visit to my grandmother's house.

2. Anything with cinnamon and cloves in it (fills / fill) the whole house with a welcoming smell.

3. When Thanksgiving rolls around, nobody in our family (wants / want) to experiment with the traditional menu.

4. Everything in my studio apartment (comes / come) from a thrift shop or yard sale.

5. Yesterday, someone at the movies (was / were) snoring during the most exciting part of the film.

6. Neither of your friends (spends / spend) much money on rent.

7. Nothing in my closet (fits / fit) me anymore.

8. (Was / Were) something unusual about Cassie's behavior?

9. Each of the cars (comes / come) with a warranty.

10. Anybody with experience around boats (knows / know) about the dangers of rough seas.

Exercise 9 **Another Exercise on Making Subjects and Verbs Agree: Using Indefinite Pronouns**

Circle the correct verb in the following sentences.

1. Sal and Todd are both trustworthy and discreet; either (makes / make) a good listener when you are in trouble.

2. Anyone from our old graduating class still (remembers / remember) Mrs. Marciano, the sweetest lady in the cafeteria.

3. Each of the sequined tee shirts (costs / cost) more than my weekly paycheck.

4. Fortunately, neither of my sisters (has / have) inherited my mother's restless spirit.

5. Be sure to read the entire contract; nothing in all those pages (covers / cover) electrical problems.

6. Somebody from the airlines (was / were) explaining the flight delays.

7. (Has / Have) anyone in the office made coffee yet?

8. Everybody in my math class (complains / complain) about all the homework.

9. Nobody with money problems (needs / need) to be bombarded with offers for more credit cards.

10. There (is / are) everyone from your old softball team.

Connect

Exercise 10 **Editing for Subject–Verb Agreement in a Paragraph with Indefinite Pronouns**

The following paragraph has five errors in the agreement of indefinite pronouns and verbs. Correct the errors in the spaces above the lines.

Whenever I go to the local mall, I wonder what everybody are doing there. First, I

become irritated by the crowds. At the food court, for instance, I am frustrated that

everyone have taken the best tables. As I hunch over a tiny table near the garbage

bins, I convince myself that something have to be very wrong in our society. Hundreds

of people, aimlessly wandering around the same stores every weekend, eating junk

food and wasting their money, should have something better to do. Anyone with a

little imagination know better ways to spend free time. Nothing about shopping make a person healthier or even more content. In contrast, a walk outdoors can stimulate

the mind and body; playing a sport is healthy and allows people to interact. Either

books or art offers a way into new worlds. But what draws people into the mall? Of

course, to answer this question, I should look inside. I should consider why *I* am

making regular visits to shop, stroll, and eat at the mall.

Collective Nouns

Collective nouns refer to more than one person or thing.

INFO BOX: **Some Common Collective Nouns**

team	company	council
class	corporation	government
committee	family	group
audience	jury	crowd

Collective nouns usually take a singular verb.

collective nouns and singular verbs:

singular S, singular V
The *class is meeting* in the library today.

singular S,   singular V
The *audience was* bored.

singular S, singular V
The *jury is examining* the evidence.

A singular verb is used because the group is meeting, or feeling bored, or examining, *as one unit.*

Collective nouns take a plural verb *only* when the members of the group are acting individually, not as a unit.

collective noun with a plural verb:

plural S,   plural V
The football *team are arguing* among themselves. (The phrase *among themselves* shows that the team is not acting as one unit.)

Exercise 11   **Making Subjects and Verbs Agree: Using Collective Nouns**

Circle the correct verb in each of the following sentences.

1. The Advertising Council of Springfield (is / are) sponsoring a student poster contest with cash prizes.

2. Whenever the stadium is packed with enthusiastic fans, the team (plays / play) with more spirit.

3. Once the featured performer began to sing, the audience (was / were) overcome with happiness.

4. A family of famous ocean explorers (is / are) planning a campaign to save endangered reefs.

5. The group of schoolchildren on a field trip (was / were) fighting among themselves over the best seats on the bus.

6. Behind closed doors, the jury (analyzes / analyze) the evidence in the case.

7. Once the project begins, the team of volunteers from the Fire Department always (works / work) with enthusiasm and purpose.

8. Morrison Shoe Company (sells / sell) some long-lasting athletic shoes.

9. The advisory board (has / have) recommended a few minor improvements to the public parking garage.

10. The Camaro Club (invite / invites) all owners of classic Camaro automobiles to an auto show at the fairgrounds.

MAKING SUBJECTS AND VERBS AGREE: A REVIEW

As you have probably realized, making subjects and verbs agree is not as simple as it first appears. But if you can remember the basic ideas in this section, you will be able to apply them automatically as you edit your own writing. Following is a quick summary of subject–verb agreement.

INFO BOX: Making Subjects and Verbs Agree: A Summary

1. Subjects and verbs should agree in number: singular subjects get singular verbs; plural subjects get plural verbs.

2. When pronouns are used as subjects, they must agree in number with verbs.

3. Nothing in a prepositional phrase can be the subject of a sentence.

4. Questions, sentences beginning with *here* or *there,* and other sentences can change word order.

5. Compound subjects joined by *and* are usually plural.

6. When subjects are joined by *or, either . . . or, neither . . . nor, not only . . . but also,* the verb form agrees with the subject closest to the verb.

7. Indefinite pronouns always take singular verbs.

8. Collective nouns usually take singular verbs.

Exercise 12   **A Comprehensive Exercise on Subject–Verb Agreement**

This exercise covers all the rules on subject–verb agreement. Circle the correct verb form in the following sentences.

1. Unless the city installs speed bumps on this street, someone in the neighborhood (is / are) going to be killed in an accident.

2. A teenager with endless reserves of energy and hours of free time (needs / need) a safe place to burn that energy.

3. Neither my mother nor her brothers (wants / want) to give up the family business.

4. Each of the apartments in the old building (has / have) the potential to be an attractive home.

5. Behind all Tito's bossiness and bluster (is / are) a kind person with a generous heart.

6. Anybody from Florida (knows / know) the meaning of the word "humidity."

7. Sometimes, when feuding family members meet over a meal, food and personal contact (leads / lead) to forgiveness.

8. How (was / were) the coffee and cake at the housewarming party?

9. The insurance corporation from Glenn Falls (is / are) planning to build a branch office nearby.

10. If the unruly crowd (is / are) fighting among themselves, then stadium security will have to intervene.

Exercise 13 **Another Comprehensive Exercise on Subject–Verb Agreement**

This exercise covers all the rules on subject–verb agreement. Circle the correct verb form in the following sentences.

1. Occasionally, famous celebrities (wants / want) nothing more than privacy.

2. After spring break, everyone in school (was / were) longing for the semester to end.

3. If you want to send your girlfriend a picture of you, either of the photographs from the picnic (is / are) an excellent choice.

4. Where on earth (is / are) my license and registration?

5. Every week, there (is / are) a classic film and a discussion group at the National Cinema.

6. For years, the United States (has / have) offered free public education to all students.

7. At the end of the term, the early childhood education class (gives / give) a party for children at a local daycare center.

8. To me, nothing in Mario's apology (seems / seem) sincere.

9. There (is / are) an empty box of tissues and a yellowed newspaper on the floor of your car.

10. Either the hot water heater or the pipes is / are making a strange noise.

Exercise 14 **Writing Sentences with Subject–Verb Agreement:**
             A Comprehensive Exercise

Collaborate

With a partner or group, write two sentences for each of the following phrases. Use a verb that fits and put it in the present tense. Be sure that the verb agrees with your subject. The first one is done for you.

1. A group of Ecuadoran students *visits my high school once a year in the fall.*

   A group of Ecuadoran students *corresponds with a group of high school seniors from Milwaukee.*

2. Nothing at the movies seems interesting to go see.

   Nothing at the movies _____

3. My cell phone provider is trying to sell me a better phone.

   My cell phone provider _____

4. Anyone with common sense would know how to work a telephone.

   Anyone with common sense _____

5. Each of my children wants to go outside.

   Each of my children _____

6. Not only my mother but also the neighbors wants to have me over for dinner.

   Not only my mother but also the neighbors _____

7. Everyone on the stairs _____

   Everyone on the stairs _____

8. The group by the copy machine is waiting for someone their turn.

   The group by the copy machine _____

9. Neither the eggs nor the bacon is ready right now.

   Neither the eggs nor the bacon _____

10. Books about sports or a sports DVD _____

   _____

   Books about sports or a sports DVD _____

   _____

Exercise 15 **Create Your Own Text on Subject–Verb Agreement**

Work with a partner or group to create your own grammar handbook. Following is a list of rules on Subject–Verb agreement. Write two sentences that are examples of each rule. Write an *S* above the subject of each sentence and a *V* above the verb. After you've completed this exercise, trade it for another group's exercise. Check that group's examples while it checks yours. The first one is done for you.

Rule 1: Subjects and verbs should agree in number: singular subjects get singular verb forms; plural subjects get plural verb forms.

   S   V
example 1: *An apple is a healthy snack.* _____

   _____

   S   V
example 2: *Runners need large quantities of water.* _____

   _____

Rule 2: When pronouns are used as subjects, they must agree in number with verbs.

example 1: _____

   _____

example 2: _____

   _____

Rule 3: Nothing in a prepositional phrase can be the subject of a sentence.

example 1: _____

   _____

example 2: _____

   _____

Rule 4: Questions, sentences beginning with *here* or *there*, and other sentences can change word order.

example 1: _____

   _____

example 2: _____

   _____

Rule 5: Compound subjects joined by *and* are usually plural.

example 1: _____

_____

example 2: _____

_____

Rule 6: When subjects are joined by *or, either . . . or, neither . . . nor,* or *not only . . . but also,* the verb form agrees with the subject closest to the verb.

example 1: _____

_____

example 2: _____

_____

Rule 7: Indefinite pronouns always take singular verbs.

example 1: _____

_____

example 2: _____

_____

Rule 8: Collective nouns usually take singular verbs.

example 1: _____

_____

example 2: _____

_____

Connect

Exercise 16 **A Comprehensive Exercise: Editing a Paragraph for Subject–Verb Agreement**

The following paragraph has seven errors in subject–verb agreement. Correct the errors in the spaces above the lines.

The Arts Council of Springfield ~~are~~ is offering a wonderful opportunity for students studying design, graphics, illustration, painting, or many other aspects of art. As part of a planned downtown renovation, the council ~~have~~ has received a grant to paint two large murals depicting Springfield today and yesterday. Anyone interested in becoming a part of this project ~~are~~ is invited to apply. The most experienced artists or the college freshman in a beginning art course ~~are~~ is eligible for a small grant. A team from the council is accepting applications and conducting interviews next month. My friend

Marty and I are excited about the possibility of working with other artists and con-

tributing to a major project. In fact, everyone in my painting class *are* [is] talking about

the chance to gain real experience in the field. Not only the learning experience but

also the opportunities for making contacts in the art world *is* [are] valuable. In the crowded

field of art, there *is* [are] few opportunities for students like me to learn, make a little

money, and make contacts on the job.

Exercise 17 **Another Comprehensive Exercise: Editing a Paragraph for Subject–Verb Agreement**

Connect

The following paragraph has six errors in subject–verb agreement. Correct the errors in the spaces above the lines.

One of the cashiers at the local market *are* [is] known for her great disposition. Kath-

leen Monaghan greets all her customers with a big smile and a cheery, "Hey! How are

you doing?" If she knows the customer, she will add a compliment such as, "You're

looking good today!" Strangers will hear Kathleen shout, "Hi! Come on in!" Something

about her tone *make* [makes] people feel special. Once a shopper arrives at Kathleen's check-

out counter, he or she *see* [sees] more of Kathleen's sunny personality. She will chat about

the weather, sports, or local news. Her conversation *is* [are] always upbeat. There is too

many high points in every day for a person to focus on low moments, she believes. By

the time Kathleen hands a customer a receipt and change, he or she *are* [is] in a good

mood. "Good-bye, Honey," she calls to each customer who walks out the door. She

adds, "Have a great day." Neither the old-timers nor the first-time customer *are* [is] able to

leave without smiling.

Chapter Test: Making Subjects and Verbs Agree

Some of the sentences below are correct; others have errors in making subjects and verbs agree. Put *OK* next to the correct sentences and *X* next to the sentences with errors.

1. _OK_ Here are Maggie and her friend from Costa Rica.

2. _X_ Either two small gifts or one big one are enough for Abraham's birthday.

3. _OK_ Something about the new neighbor and his friends is slightly suspicious.

4. _OK_ My favorite basketball team is having a difficult season, and many fans are losing interest in the games.

5. _X_ Every time it rains, not only the roof but also the windows leaks.

6. _OK_ Alonzo, with all his so-called friends and admirers, remains a lonely man at heart.

7. _OK_ There are a man in a gray suit and a small child waiting to see you.

8. _OK_ The boys across the street or the little girl at the corner plays at the empty lot nearly every day.

9. _X_ Each of my math assignments take me about an hour to complete.

10. _X_ Where is the special cake and the balloons for Aunt Cecilia's party?

Using Pronouns Correctly: Agreement and Reference

Pronouns are words that substitute for nouns. A pronoun's **antecedent** is the word or words it replaces.

pronouns and antecedents:

antecedent   pronoun
George is a wonderful father; *he* is loving and kind.

               antecedent   pronoun
Suzanne wound *the clock* because *it* had stopped ticking.

       antecedent   pronoun
Talking on the phone is fun, but *it* takes up too much of my time.

      antecedent   pronoun
Joanne and David know what *they* want.

antecedent   pronoun
Christopher lost *his* favorite baseball cap.

      antecedent   pronoun
The *horse* stamped *its* feet and neighed loudly.

| Exercise 1 | Identifying the Antecedents of Pronouns |

In each of the following sentences, a pronoun is underlined. Circle the word or words that are the antecedent of the underlined pronoun.

1. Several people at the park were eating their lunches in the fresh air.

2. The twins begged their mother for more time in front of the television, but she paid no attention.

3. Aggressive drivers feel that they can dominate the road.

4. After all the heavy rain, my lemon tree lost most of its leaves.

5. Yesterday my boyfriend and I felt great; we found jobs at a new restaurant near school.

6. Madison, can you lend me a few dollars?

7. Unfortunately, Curtis was unwilling to face his problem with alcohol.

8. Waiting in a long line can be frustrating; it allows you to think about better things to do with the wasted time.

9. My father loves to snack on pistachio nuts, but I don't care for them.

10. Angela and her fiancé wanted to buy an old house they could remodel.

AGREEMENT OF A PRONOUN AND ITS ANTECEDENT

A pronoun must agree in number with its antecedent. If the antecedent is singular, the pronoun must be singular. If the antecedent is plural, the pronoun must be plural.

singular antecedents, singular pronouns:
singular antecedent   singular pronoun
The *dog* began to bark wildly; *it* hated being locked up in the cellar.
singular antecedent   singular pronoun
Maria spends most of *her* salary on rent.

plural antecedents, plural pronouns:
plural antecedent   plural pronoun
Carlos and Ronnie went to Atlanta for a long weekend; *they* had a good
    time.
plural antecedent   plural pronoun
Cigarettes are expensive, and *they* can kill you.

SPECIAL PROBLEMS WITH AGREEMENT

Agreement of pronoun and antecedent seems fairly simple: if an antecedent is singular, use a singular pronoun; if an antecedent is plural, use a plural pronoun. There are, however, some special problems with agreement of pronouns, and these problems will come up in your writing. If you become familiar with the explanations, examples, and exercises that follow, you'll be ready to handle special problems.

Indefinite Pronouns

Certain words, called **indefinite pronouns,** are always singular. Therefore, if an indefinite pronoun is the antecedent, the pronoun that replaces it must be singular. Here are the indefinite pronouns:

> ### INFO BOX: Indefinite Pronouns
>
> | | | | |
> |---|---|---|---|
> | one | nobody | nothing | each |
> | anyone | anybody | anything | either |
> | someone | somebody | something | neither |
> | everyone | everybody | everything | |

You may think that *everybody* is plural, but in grammatically correct English, it is a singular word. Therefore, if you want to write clearly and correctly, memorize these words as the *-one*, *-thing*, and *-body* words: *everyone, everything, everybody, anyone, anything,* and so on, plus *each, either,* and *neither.* If any of these words is an antecedent, the pronoun that refers to it is singular.

indefinite pronouns as antecedents:

indefinite pronoun antecedent, singular pronoun
Each of the women skaters did *her* best in the Olympic competition.

indefinite pronoun antecedent   singular pronoun
Everyone nominated for Father of the Year earned *his* nomination.

Avoiding Gender Bias

Consider this sentence:

Everybody in the cooking contest prepared _____ best dish.

How do you choose the correct pronoun to fill this blank? You can write

Everybody in the cooking contest prepared *his* best dish.

if everybody in the contest is male. Or you can write

Everybody in the cooking contest prepared *her* best dish.

if everybody in the contest is female. Or you can write

Everybody in the cooking contest prepared *his or her* best dish.

if the contest has male and female entrants.

In the past, most writers used *his* to refer to both men and women when the antecedent was an indefinite pronoun. Today, many writers try to use *his or her* to avoid gender bias. If you find using *his or her* is getting awkward and repetitive, you can rewrite the sentence and make the antecedent plural.

Correct: *The entrants* in the cooking contest prepared *their* best dishes.

But you cannot shift from singular to plural:

Incorrect: ~~Everybody in the cooking contest prepared their best dish.~~

> **Exercise 2** Making Pronouns and Their Antecedents Agree:
> Simple Agreement and Indefinite Pronouns

In each of the following sentences, write the appropriate pronoun in the blank space. Look carefully for the antecedent before you choose the pronoun.

1. Each of the brothers wants a chance to open ____his____ own business.

2. Writing a thank-you note can be a chore; however, _____it_____ is the best way to show your appreciation.

3. A busy mother with responsibilities at home and at work would love a few hours away from _____her_____ daily routine.

4. One of the women in my night class lent me _____her_____ umbrella after class.

5. Either of your uncles could have given you _____his_____ help with your landscaping project.

6. Take a look at the little girls on the swings; _____they_____ are having a wonderful time.

7. Does anyone on the men's softball team want _____his_____ picture taken?

8. An inmate at the women's prison turned _____her_____ experiences into a book.

9. Most of the servers at the restaurant rely on _____their_____ tips to survive.

10. Once Stephanie took the first step in applying to college, _____she_____ began to feel optimistic.

Connect

Exercise 3 **Editing a Paragraph for Errors in Agreement: Indefinite Pronouns**

The following paragraph contains five errors in agreement where the antecedents are indefinite pronouns. Correct the errors in the space above the lines.

When I was ten years old, I had my first experience of a summer camp. My parents enrolled me in a city-sponsored sleepaway camp for boys. The bus ride to the camp was chaotic; everybody on the bus was shouting at the top of their lungs and pushing and shoving. Still, it was exciting to leave the stifling heat of the city for green trees and lakes. Once the campers arrived, each of the boys was assigned to ~~their~~ his bunk in one of several large tents. Then a camp counselor herded all the boys belonging to one tent to their new home. Everybody got a narrow bunk with a thick, scratchy blanket, a box for their clothes, a towel, soap, and a washcloth. There were no chairs in the tent, just rough wooden benches. Anyone who had never been to camp before felt like they he? had joined the army. Fortunately, after a few days of rough living, all the boys settled into their new existence. Nobody who attended the camp will ever forget the swimming, the games, the contests, the campfires, and even the bad food—all part of their great adventure.

Collective Nouns

Collective nouns refer to more than one person or thing.

INFO BOX: Some Common Collective Nouns

team	company	council
class	corporation	government
committee	family	group
audience	jury	crowd

Most of the time, collective nouns take a singular pronoun.

collective nouns and singular pronouns:
collective noun   singular pronoun
The *jury* in the murder trial announced *its* verdict.
collective noun   singular pronoun
The *company* I work for has been in business a long time; *it* started in
   Atlanta, Georgia.

Collective nouns are usually singular because the group is announcing a verdict
or starting a business as one, as a unit. Collective nouns take a plural *only* when
the members of the group are acting individually, not as a unit.

collective noun and a plural pronoun:
collective noun, plural pronoun
The *team* signed *their* contracts yesterday. (The members of the team
   sign contracts individually.)

Exercise 4   **Making Pronouns and Antecedents Agree: Collective Nouns**

Circle the correct pronoun in each of the following sentences.

1. The Morton Company is having (its / their) holiday party early this year.

2. My favorite team began to suffer many losses when the players
    began to quarrel among (itself / themselves).

3. When the featured singer arrived an hour late, the audience lost
    (its / their) faith in the show.

4. Several of the pharmaceutical corporations agreed to donate part of
    (its / their) profits to medical research.

5. Over the years, bad feelings broke the family apart; (it / they) never
    resolved an old feud and lost touch with one another.

6. Aqua Sports created a cheaper version of (its / their) popular per-
    sonal watercraft.

7. The Helping Hands Club lost (its / their) president last week.

8. The committee that interviewed me for the job will let me know
    (its / their) decision next week.

9. The Air Force brings (its / their) best jets to the air show.

10. My son's kindergarten class had (its / their) graduation party yesterday.

Connect

Exercise 5 Editing a Paragraph for Errors in Agreement: Collective Nouns

The following paragraph contains eight errors in agreement where the antecedent is a collective noun. Correct the errors in the spaces above the lines.

My mother is involved in an endless argument with the electric company. Two months ago, our area suffered some major damage from a storm. Part of that damage was a loss of power, and our neighborhood was without electricity for ten days. Living without light, fans, air conditioning, hot water, and refrigeration was bad enough, but my mother lost her patience *after* the power was restored. At that time, she received an enormous monthly bill from the electric company, more than they had ever charged her before. My mother questioned why the company would charge her so much when she had been without power for almost one third of the month. However, the company explained that they had been unable to read their customers' meters after the storm, so the bill they sent was merely their estimate. The electric company added that they would research the real cost and refund any overcharges in the next month's bill. My mother, already stressed by the storm, said she could not believe that the company would treat their customers so badly. She refused to pay the bill. After four calls and three letters from my mother and several replies from the company, the battle continues. I can only hope that this issue is resolved before the company loses their patience and cuts off our electricity.

Collaborate

Exercise 6 Writing Sentences with Pronoun–Antecedent Agreement

With a partner or with a group, write a sentence for each of the following pairs of words, using each pair as a pronoun and its antecedent(s). The first pair is done for you.

1. men . . . their

   sentence: *The men at the dance were wearing their best clothes.*

   _____

2. The Eastville Sheriff's Department . . . its

   sentence: _____

   _____

3. parrot . . . its

   sentence: _____

   _____

4. anyone . . . his or her

   sentence: _____

   _____

5. Graciela and Brandon . . . their

   sentence: _____

   _____

6. nothing . . . its

   sentence: _____

   _____

7. neither . . . her

   sentence: _____

   _____

8. bragging . . . it

   sentence: _____

   _____

9. everyone . . . his or her

   sentence: _____

   _____

10. celebrities . . . they

   sentence: _____

   _____

PRONOUNS AND THEIR ANTECEDENTS: BEING CLEAR

Remember that pronouns are words that replace or refer to other words, and those other words are called *antecedents*.

Make sure that a pronoun has one clear antecedent. Your writing will be vague and confusing if a pronoun appears to refer to more than one antecedent or if a pronoun doesn't have any specific antecedent to refer to. Such confusing language is called a problem with *reference of pronouns*.

When a pronoun refers to more than one thing, the sentence can become confusing or silly.

pronouns below refer to more than one thing (unclear antecedent):

Carla told Elaine that her car had a flat tire. (Whose car had a flat tire? Carla's? Elaine's?)

Josh woke to the shrieking alarm clock, buried his head in his pillow, and threw it across the room. (What did Josh throw? The pillow? The clock? His head?)

If there is no one, clear antecedent, you must rewrite the sentence to make the reference clear. Sometimes the rewritten sentence may seem repetitive, but a little repetition is better than a lot of confusion.

unclear: Carla told Elaine that her car had a flat tire.
clear: Carla told Elaine that Carla's car had a flat tire.

clear: Carla told Elaine that Elaine's car had a flat tire.
clear: Carla told Elaine, "Your car has a flat tire."
clear: Carla told Elaine, "My car has a flat tire."

unclear: Josh woke to the shrieking alarm clock, buried his head in his pillow, and threw it across the room.
clear: Josh woke to the shrieking alarm clock, buried his head in his pillow, and threw the clock across the room.

Sometimes the problem is a little more confusing. Can you spot what's wrong with this sentence?

Linda was able to negotiate for a raise, which pleased her. (What pleased Linda? The raise? Or the fact that she was able to negotiate for it?)

Be very careful with the pronoun *which*. If there is any chance that using *which* will confuse the reader, rewrite the sentence and get rid of *which*.

clear: Linda was pleased that she was able to negotiate for a raise.
clear: Linda was pleased by the raise she negotiated.

Sometimes a pronoun has nothing to refer to; it has no antecedent.

pronouns with no antecedent:
When Mary took the television to the repair shop, they said the television couldn't be repaired. (Who are "they"? Who said the television couldn't be repaired? The television service personnel? The customers? The repairmen?)

I have always been interested in designing clothes and have decided that's what I want to be. (What does "that" refer to? The only word it could refer to is *clothes*. You certainly don't want to be clothes. You don't want to be a dress or a suit.)

If a pronoun lacks an antecedent, add an antecedent or eliminate the pronoun.

add an antecedent: When Mary took the television to the repair shop and asked *the service personnel* for an estimate, they said the television couldn't be repaired.
eliminate the pronoun: I have always been interested in designing clothes and have decided I want to be a fashion designer.

To check for clear reference of pronouns, underline any pronouns that may not be clear. Then try to draw a line from that pronoun to its antecedent. Are there two or more possible antecedents? Is there no antecedent? In either case, you need to rewrite.

Exercise 7 **Rewriting Sentences for Clear Reference of Pronouns**

Rewrite the following sentences so that the pronouns have clear references. You can add, take out, or change words.

1. Alice rarely has a free weekend, which depresses her.

   rewritten: *Rarely having a free weekend depresses Alice.*

2. Charlie warned his brother, "your/my" that his money is was running out."

   rewritten: *Charlie's brother was warned that he was running out of money*

3. They didn't tell me that late registration had ended.

   rewritten: _Nobody had told me that late_
   registration had ended.

4. Mark dropped a china candlestick on the glass coffee table, but it didn't break.

   rewritten: _The china candlestick didn't break_
   when Mark dropped it on the glass coffee table.

5. Natalie quizzed Deanna, trying to find out what Adam had said about her. _Natalie_

   rewritten: _____

   _____

6. My sister stopped speaking to Stephanie because _My sister_ she has a quick temper.

   rewritten: _____

   _____

7. My parents want me to consider the healthcare field, but I don't want to be ~~one.~~ _a nurse_

   rewritten: _____

   _____

8. Bill returned the expensive new truck, which infuriated his wife.

   rewritten: _Returning the expensive new truck,_
   infuriated Bill's wife.

9. Valerie always buys her groceries at Daria's Market because they _market_ have good deals on meat and produce.

   rewritten: _Because Daria's Market has good deals_
   on meat and produce, valerie always buys her groceries there.

10. Lauren complained to Chantelle ~~that her~~ _your_ room ~~was~~ _is_ a mess."

    rewritten: _____

    _____

| Exercise 8 | **Revising Sentences with Problems in Pronoun Reference: Two Ways** |

Collaborate

Do this exercise with a partner or group. Each of the following sentences contains a pronoun with an unclear antecedent. Because the antecedent is unclear, the sentence can have more than one meaning. Rewrite each sentence twice to show the different meanings. The first one is done for you.

1. Mrs. Klein told Mrs. Yamaguchi her dog was digging up the flower beds.

   sentence 1: _Mrs. Klein told Mrs. Yamaguchi, "Your dog is digging up the_
   flower beds."

sentence 2: *Mrs. Klein told Mrs. Yamaguchi that Mrs. Klein's dog was digging up the flower beds.*

2. Jimmy asked Lewis if he could bring a friend to the party.

sentence 1: Jimmy asked Lewis, " can I bring a friend to the party?"

sentence 2: _____

_____

3. Patty ran into her mother at ~~her~~ Patty's favorite restaurant.

sentence 1: _____

_____

sentence 2: _____

_____

4. Leonard took a five-dollar bill out of the envelope and gave it to me.

sentence 1: _____

_____

sentence 2: _____

_____

5. Once the guests had petted the dogs, ~~they~~ the guests left the room.

sentence 1: _____

_____

sentence 2: _____

_____

6. Pete soon got a new job, which brightened his mood.

sentence 1: ~~Pete~~ _____

_____

sentence 2: _____

_____

7. Yolanda told Melissa, she worried too much about little things."

sentence 1: _____

_____

sentence 2: _____

_____

8. When Jolene picked up her little daughter, she began to cry.

sentence 1: _____

_____

sentence 2: _____

_____

9. Emma's sister asked her to bring her big cooler to the picnic.

sentence 1: _____

_____

sentence 2: _____

_____

10. After my two beagles met my sister's bossy cats, they were never the same.

sentence 1: _____

_____

sentence 2: _____

_____

Exercise 9   **Editing a Paragraph for Errors in Pronoun Reference**   Connect

The following paragraph contains four errors in pronoun reference. Correct the errors in the spaces above the lines.

I'm never going to eat at the Sunny Side Restaurant again. I went there for the first

time about ten days ago because the place had just opened and is near my house. I

ordered a garden salad and a bowl of onion soup, but I didn't like it. In addition, they
[the soup]   [the waiter was]

were sloppy and spilled some of the soup on the table. Yesterday, my friends Rocco

and Paul asked me if I wanted to give the restaurant another try. I agreed, but the
                                                [I was upset that]

experience turned out to be horrible. First, the only chicken dish on the menu was

chicken wings, which disappointed me. Second, as we began to eat, Rocco suddenly
                [my]
told Paul that his chili had a dead insect in it. Sure enough, there was a small, dead

cockroach that could easily have been mistaken for a bean. Paul, Rocco, and I decided

that in the future, we would find somewhere else to eat.

Exercise 10   **Editing a Paragraph for Errors in Agreement and Reference**   Connect

The following paragraph contains five errors in pronoun agreement and reference. Correct the errors in the space above the lines.

A pet can be a terrible nagger. Although I love my animals, each of the critters can

be a torment at various times. If my dog Chance wants to go outside, for instance, he

knows how to tell me. Whenever he looks out the window and sees a squirrel playing

in the yard, he whines and paws the glass until I let him outside. Chance is sure that

whatever I am doing, even if it is studying for a test or standing on a ladder to change a light bulb, cannot be as important as chasing a squirrel. When Chance sees a squirrel, nothing ~~matter~~ *matters*. He has to go out and chase that pesky creature. My cat Ethel is equally impatient when she wants to be fed. Unfortunately, she has decided that she wants to be fed at 3:00 a.m. At that ghastly hour, she sits next to my head on the pillow and repeatedly licks my face with her sandpaper tongue which makes me crazy. When I finally crawl out of bed and stagger to the kitchen, Puffy, my parrot, wakes up. Puffy resents the early wake-up call and begins to scold me. He squawks until my cat and I have left the room and quiet has returned to the kitchen. Everyone who hears about my pets' little imperfections has ~~their~~ *his or her* own opinion about animal behavior and training. But I know that each of my pets has demonstrated ~~their~~ *his or her* capacity to learn and grow. Unfortunately, the group of animals in my house ~~have~~ *has* learned how to train *me*.

Chapter Test: Using Pronouns Correctly: Agreement and Reference

Some of the sentences below are correct; others have errors in pronoun agreement or reference. Put *OK* next to the correct sentences and *X* next to the sentences with errors.

1. *OK* Living in a big city can be exciting; it can also be expensive.

2. *X* Everyone in the finals of the women's tennis tournament tried their best to beat the reigning champion.

3. *OK* Everything about the Rocky Mountains lost its charm for me when my brother was hurt in a skiing accident.

4. *OK* My father refuses to go to the Oaks Movie Theater because he thinks they charge too much for popcorn.

5. *X* The Inspiration Music Company is opening their new headquarters in Los Angeles next week.

6. *X* Brad had a long talk with Rick about his reckless behavior.

7. *X* A flagpole in the back yard fell against the roof, but it wasn't badly damaged.

8. *OK* Cristina wanted to try out for a part in a movie, which upset her parents.

9. *X* Antonio's mother makes a good salary selling cars, but Antonio doesn't want to be one.

10. *OK* Someone in our apartment building left his or her bicycle on the third-floor landing.

CHAPTER 15

Quick Question

Which sentence(s) is/are correct?

A. The flea market is a good place for me to shop because you can get bargains on tee shirts and sandals.

B. Abigail wants to go to Santa Fe with Adam and me.

(After you study this chapter, you will be confident of your answer.)

Using Pronouns Correctly: Consistency and Case

When you write, you write from a point of view, and each point of view gets its own form. If you write from the first person point of view, your pronouns are in the *I* (singular) or *we* (plural) forms. If your pronouns are in the second person point of view, your pronouns are in the *you* form, whether they are singular or plural. If you write from the third person point of view, your pronouns are in the *he, she,* or *it* (singular) or *they* (plural) forms.

Different kinds of writing may require different points of view. When you are writing a set of directions, for example, you might use the second person (you) point of view. For an essay about your childhood, you might use the first person (I) point of view.

Whatever point of view you use, be consistent in using pronouns. That is, do not shift the form of your pronouns without some good reason.

not consistent: The last time *I* went to that movie theater, the only seat *you* could get was in the front row.

consistent: The last time *I* went to that movie theater, the only seat *I* could get was in the front row.

not consistent: By the time the shoppers got into the store, *they* were so jammed into the aisles that *you* couldn't get to the sales tables.

consistent: By the time the shoppers got into the store, *they* were so jammed into the aisles that *they* couldn't get to the sales tables.

Exercise 1   Consistency in Pronouns

Correct any inconsistency in point of view in the following sentences. Cross out the incorrect pronoun and write the correct one above it.

1. When I first saw Hamilton Hills, I thought the town was so perfect that ~~you~~ [I] would never want to leave it.

2. Whenever my brother calls me, ~~you~~ [I] know he is going to ask me for a favor.

3. During the weekend that Michael and I spent in Vermont, the snow-fall was so heavy that ~~you~~ [we] could barely leave the house.

4. People liked Matthew because ~~you~~ [they] could always count on him for a favor or a kind word.

5. Gina is extra careful when the light turns green at the Grove and Morton Street intersection; she waits a few extra seconds before she moves because ~~you~~ [she] can see many people running red lights at that crossroads.

6. In the new county library, residents can check out books, CDs, or DVDs, read magazines and newspapers, or research ~~your~~ [their] favorite subject on the new computers.

7. College students have to be careful when they receive dozens of offers for credit cards; promises of easy credit can lead ~~you~~ [them] to bankruptcy.

8. Once the plane has reached cruising altitude and the passengers have unfastened their seat belts, a flight attendant comes down the aisles and offers ~~you~~ [them] a beverage.

9. On even a short car trip, my parents always carried bottles of water because ~~your~~ [their] car could break down and leave them stranded and thirsty.

10. I hate shopping at that shopping center because ~~you~~ $\overset{I}{}$ always have to

    drive around for hours to get a parking space.

Collaborate

Exercise 2   Rewriting Sentences with Consistency Problems

Do this exercise with a partner or group. Rewrite the following sentences, correcting any errors in the consistency of pronouns. To make the corrections, you may have to change, add, or take out words.

1. I don't see why I should give Ella another chance; after she makes new promises, she always hurts you again.

   rewritten: _____

   _____

   _____

2. Once my father has sautéed the onions, you add them to the grilled steaks and buns, and he serves his famous steak sandwiches.

   rewritten: _____

   _____

   _____

3. The first time I worked in the kitchen at the pizza place, the pace of the workers was so fast that you could hardly keep up.

   rewritten: _____

   _____

   _____

4. The most rewarding part of my job at the day-care center is seeing the children run to you when they enter the door.

   rewritten: _____

   _____

   _____

5. Customers who want to take advantage of the store's weekly sales and special offers must remember to present your discount cards at the register.

   rewritten: _____

   _____

   _____

6. Samantha isn't going to invite her cousin Rick to her graduation party because he'll just make you want to scream if he keeps following her around with his camera.

   rewritten: _____

   _____

   _____

7. Parents who return to school need support, for you can get lost balancing school, home, and work responsibilities.

   rewritten: _____

   _____

   _____

8. Manny's favorite holiday is the Fourth of July when you can relax in shorts and a tee shirt, get some sun, and, if he has the energy, go to the park and see the fireworks.

   rewritten: _____

   _____

   _____

9. You knew this was a happy family as soon as we walked in and saw the children helping their parents set the table.

   rewritten: _____

   _____

   _____

10. Drivers on the Tillotson Expressway this weekend are advised to keep a close eye on your speedometers because the Highway Patrol will be ticketing speeders.

    rewritten: _____

    _____

    _____

Connect

Exercise 3 Editing a Paragraph for Pronoun Consistency

The following paragraph has four errors in consistency of pronouns. Correct the errors above the lines.

When Stephen and I went to visit the Colonial Museum, we were fascinated. We were surprised to discover that the museum is an old house, built in 1760. The house has been restored so that it looks like it would have when the original residents lived in it. The first thing that happened when ~~you~~ we entered the museum was that a tour guide greeted us and led us through the house. Stephen and I loved the sense of history but could not imagine anyone living in such primitive conditions. We couldn't believe that, in 1760, taking a bath meant that people had to get water from a well or pump and heat it over a fire or on the stove. Then ~~you~~ they poured the water into a large, heavy tub that they carried close to a warm fire. Going to bed meant sleeping in a cold or even freezing room because most people couldn't afford a fireplace in every room

or ~~you~~ *they* could not risk the danger of leaving a fire burning overnight. Once Stephen and

I realized that life in 1760 was so hard, ~~you~~ *we* had to admire families like the one that had

lived in the museum house.

CHOOSING THE CASE OF PRONOUNS

Pronouns have forms that show number and person, and they also have forms
that show **case.** Following is a list of three cases of pronouns:

INFO BOX: **Pronouns and Their Case**

Singular Pronouns

	Subjective case	Objective case	Possessive case
1st person	I	me	my
2nd person	you	you	your
3rd person	he, she, it	him, her, it	his, her, its

Plural Pronouns

	Subjective case	Objective case	Possessive case
1st person	we	us	our
2nd person	you	you	your
3rd person	they	them	their

(handwritten margin notes)
Reflexive
myself
yourself
himself, herself, itself

ourselves
yourself
themselves

Rules for Choosing the Case of Pronouns

The rules for choosing the case of pronouns are simple:

1. When a pronoun is used as a subject, use the subjective case.
2. When a pronoun is used as the object of a verb or the object of a
   preposition, use the objective case.
3. When a pronoun is used to show possession, use the possessive case.

   Here are some examples of the correct use of pronouns:

   pronouns used as subjects:
   She calls the office once a week.
   Sylvia wrote the letter, and *we* revised it.
   When Guy called, *I* was thrilled.

   pronouns used as objects:
   The loud noise frightened *me.*
   The card was addressed to *him.*
   Sadie's dog always traveled with *her.*

   pronouns used to show possession:
   The criticism hurt *her* feelings.
   Our car is nearly new.
   The restaurant changed *its* menu.

Exercise 4 Choosing the Correct Pronoun Case: Simple Situations

Circle the correct pronoun in each of the following sentences.

1. Peter spent all night studying for the science test, but (**I** / me / my) fell asleep at midnight.

2. (They / Them / **Their**) front porch is falling apart.

3. Last year, my boyfriend's parents were extremely kind to (we / **us** / our).

4. Coco and George bought (they / them / **their**) house two years ago.

5. Aunt Maria is thoughtful; I just received a lovely birthday card from (she / **her**).

6. When Larry and I were children, Uncle William used to take (we / **us** / our) to a miniature golf course.

7. Be sure to keep (you / **your**) eyes on the road.

8. The surfers spent every daylight hour in the water; then (**they** / them / their) spent the evening talking about the waves.

9. On Sunday, my wife gave (I / **me** / my) the best gift of (I / me / **my**) life, a baby.

10. Harry will do well in the army; (**he** / him / his) likes a structured environment.

PROBLEMS CHOOSING PRONOUN CASE

Choosing the Correct Pronoun Case in a Related Group of Words

You need to be careful in choosing pronoun case when the pronoun is part of a related group of words. If the pronoun is part of a related group of words, isolate the pronoun. Next, try out the pronoun choices. Then decide which pronoun is correct and write the correct sentence. For example, which of these sentences is correct?

Diane had a big surprise for Jack and *I*.
            or
Diane had a big surprise for Jack and *me*.

To choose the correct sentence, follow these steps:

Step 1: Isolate the pronoun. Eliminate the related words *Jack and*.

Step 2: Try each case.

Diane had a big surprise for *I*.
        or
Diane had a big surprise for *me*.

Step 3: Decide which pronoun is correct and write the correct sentence.

correct sentence: Diane had a big surprise for Jack and *me*.

The pronoun acts as an object, so it takes the objective case.
To be sure that you understand the principle, try working through the steps once more. Which of the following sentences is correct?

Next week, my sister and *me* will start classes at Bryant Community College.
            or
Next week, my sister and *I* will start classes at Bryant Community College.

Step 1: Isolate the pronoun. Eliminate the related words *my sister and.*

Step 2: Try each case.

> Next week, *me* will start classes at Bryant Community College.
> Next week, *I* will start classes at Bryant Community College.

Step 3: Decide which pronoun is correct and write the correct sentence.

correct sentence: Next week, my sister and *I* will start classes at Bryant Community College.

Common Errors with Pronoun Case

In choosing the case of pronouns, be careful to avoid these common errors:

1. *Between* is a preposition. The pronouns that follow it are objects of the preposition: between *us*, between *them*, between *you and me.* It is never correct to write between *you and I.*

   examples:
   not this: What I'm telling you must be kept strictly between you and ~~I~~.
   but this: What I'm telling you must be kept strictly between you and me.

2. Never use *myself* as a replacement for *I* or *me.*

   examples:
   not this: My family and ~~myself~~ are grateful for your expressions of sympathy.
   but this: My family and I are grateful for your expressions of sympathy.

   not this: The scholarship committee selected Nadine and ~~myself~~.
   but this: The scholarship committee selected Nadine and me.

3. The possessive pronoun *its* has no apostrophe.

   examples:
   not this: The stale coffee lost ~~it's~~ flavor.
   but this: The stale coffee lost its flavor.

Exercise 5 **Choosing the Correct Pronoun Case: Problems with Pronoun Case**

Circle the correct pronoun in each of the following sentences.

1. Alonzo and (I / me) sat around, listening to music all afternoon.

2. A trip to China has long been a dream for Anna and (I / me).

3. My cousins and (we / us) are planning a surprise party for our grandparents' anniversary.

4. One dog in the neighborhood barks at (I / me) and Sylvia whenever we walk by.

5. On behalf of (me / myself) and Mr. Inada, I want to say "thank you" for your confidence and support.

6. Trapped in the elevator, Mrs. Rosenblatt and (he / him) waited for help to arrive.

7. After I dressed the children, I took (they / them) and Anne to a movie.

8. Francine knew that she could spend the weekend with Sheila and (I / me).

9. I used to love watching baseball, but now the sport has lost (it's / its) appeal for me.

10. As a child, Nick endured constant teasing from Andrew and (me / myself).

Exercise 6 More on Choosing the Correct Pronoun Case: Problems with Pronoun Case

Circle the correct pronoun in each of the following sentences.

1. The bird on the lawn has not flown in an hour; I hope it has not hurt (it's / its) wing.

2. Last year was a challenging one for my family and (I / me).

3. Over the weekend, David and (he / him) couldn't find the right part for David's motorcycle.

4. Pari's appearance at the ceremony was a complete surprise to Craig and (I / me).

5. At dawn, Kathy and (she / her) packed the car for the long drive to Albuquerque.

6. Without the constant encouragement of Mike and (I / me), Blake would never have tried out for the team.

7. My sister did her best to end the constant bickering between Julio and (me / myself).

8. After ten years, I visited my birthplace, and the city still holds (its / it's) charm for me.

9. My coworkers and (I / myself) are concerned about safety conditions at the packing plant.

10. I thought you understood that our arrangement was to be a secret between you and (I / me).

Collaborate

Exercise 7 Write Your Own Text on Pronoun Case

With a partner or group, write two sentences that could be used as examples for each of the following rules. The first one is done for you.

Rule 1: When a pronoun is used as a subject, use the subjective case.

example 1: *They study for tests in the math lab.*

example 2: *Caught in the rain, she ran for cover.*

Rule 2: When a pronoun is used as the object of a verb or the object of a preposition, use the objective case. (For examples, write one sentence in which the pronoun is the object of a verb and one in which the pronoun is the object of a preposition.)

example 1: _____

example 2: _____

Rule 3: When a pronoun is used to show ownership, use the possessive case.

example 1: _____

example 2: _____

Rule 4: When a pronoun is part of a related group of words, isolate the pronoun to choose the case. (For examples, write two sentences in which the pronoun is part of a related group of words.)

example 1: _____

example 2: _____

| Exercise 8 | **Editing a Paragraph for Correct Pronoun Case** |

Connect

The following paragraph has five errors in pronoun case. Correct the errors above the lines.

Yesterday brought some unexpected excitement to Suzanne and I [me] when we got lost

on the back roads of Granville. On our way to visit a friend in North Madison, we saw

a traffic jam ahead of us on the highway. Suzanne said she knew a shortcut and

directed me to the next exit. From the exit I pulled onto a desolate stretch of road and

looked at Suzanne for more directions. "Keep going," she said, "I think there is a

turnoff to Granville soon." Twenty minutes later, the road was narrower and emptier.

Then we tried to find our way back to the highway, but the situation became more

complicated. Between Suzanne and I [me], we must have taken several wrong turns

because we wound up at a gas station and food mart in a strange town. Fortunately,

the man behind the counter gave us clear directions back to the highway. Although the

afternoon provided action and suspense for Suzanne and myself [me], I am not eager to try

a shortcut again. Driving on the back roads has lost it's [its] appeal for me. From now on,

Suzanne and me [I] will stick to the highway, even if it's crowded.

| Exercise 9 | **Editing a Paragraph for Pronoun Consistency and Correct Pronoun Case** |

Connect

The following paragraph has six errors in pronoun consistency and case. Correct the errors above the lines.

I love to go to the movies, but I am disgusted by the condition of the movie the-

aters. Even before you find a seat, the sticky floors make me wonder what I've just

stepped on or into. The mess could be gum, melted candy, or half-dried cola. The noise

of a crackle or an oozy texture under your shoe as I make my way down the aisle does not welcome me into the room. The fact that the room is dark makes the search for a seat even more unpleasant. In a theater with stadium seating, you face the possibility of sliding on a slick substance and falling down the stairs. After I find a seat, two more problems confront me. One is more trash. Last week, me and my girlfriend climbed into two seats in the middle of a row and had to fight our way around half-empty boxes of popcorn, huge paper cups, and crumpled paper plates. When we finally got to the center seats, they were covered in another sticky substance. My girlfriend and myself felt as if we were sitting on garbage in a trash heap. On another occasion, I found another problem: broken seats. I sat back, expecting to relax in a rocking-chair seat, but I relaxed a little too far. The seat had no spring attached, and I slid into an endless slope. Feeling like a fool and hoping no one had noticed me, I scrambled to another seat. It, too, was damaged. This time, the armrest fell off the chair. I know that movie theaters get a large, continuous stream of patrons. I also know that the ushers and cleaners work hard and fast between showings so that the theaters will be fresh. But between you and I, I must confess that, after my recent experiences, renting DVDs is looking better than moviegoing.

Chapter Test: Using Pronouns Correctly: Consistency and Case

Some of the sentences below are correct; others have errors in pronoun consistency or case. Put *OK* next to the correct sentences and *X* next to the sentences with errors.

1. __X__   Sarah has to get to work early because, in that part of town, you can't find a place to park after 8:00 a.m.

2. __OK__   I and my younger sister spent the night in a small tent in the woods.

3. __X__   When my brother gets restless, him and his best friend drive aimlessly around town, looking for excitement.

4. __X__   My coworkers and myself gratefully accept this donation to the emergency relief fund.

5. __X__   Once we had taken our seats in the plane, a flight attendant came around to check whether you had put your carry-on luggage in the overhead bins.

6. __OK__   The promise Eddie and I made as children remained a secret between me and him.

7. __X__   These days, when I take the expressway to school, I am extra careful since the endless construction detours can lead you onto rocky or narrow paths.

8. __OK__   Summer made its first appearance today when the temperature soared and people sunbathed in the park.

9. __X__   A series of family and financial problems caused my girlfriend and I to drop out of college last semester.

10. __X__   I had a long talk with Justina last night; me and her can't understand the reasons behind the sudden closing of the tire plant.

Punctuation

You probably know much about punctuation already. In fact, you probably know many of the rules so well that you punctuate your writing automatically. However, there are times when every writer wonders, "Do I need a comma here?" or "Should I capitalize this word?" The following review of the basic rules of punctuation can help you answer such questions.

THE PERIOD

Periods are used two ways:

1. Use a period to mark the end of a sentence that makes a statement.

   examples:
   My father gave me an exciting new book.
   After the dance, we went to a coffeehouse for a snack.

2. Use a period after abbreviations.

   examples:
   Mr. Vinh
   Carlos Montoya, Sr.

11:00 a.m.
Dr. J. T. Mitchell

THE QUESTION MARK

Use a question mark after a direct question.

examples:

Do you have any spare change?
Wasn't that song beautiful?

If a question is not a direct question, do not use a question mark.

examples:

I wonder if it will rain tonight.
Nadine asked whether I had cleaned the kitchen.

Exercise 1   Punctuating with Periods and Question Marks

Add the necessary periods and question marks to the following sentences.

1. Why isn't Cecilia at work today?

2. Dr. Michalski was appointed to the Water Management Board

3. The mail carrier wanted to know if the people next door had moved
   away

4. When does the plane from LaGuardia Airport arrive

5. My brother was out until 4:00 a m, so I don't think he wants to play
   basketball this morning

6. Carmine and Rosanna wondered whether the little dog on the street
   belonged to anyone

7. Mr Sutton has a B A in African History

8. If you have a minute, can you explain this math problem to me

9. I am not sure when I will be able to go back to work

10. Patrick questioned the truth of Leon's account of the accident

Exercise 2   Punctuating with Periods and Question Marks

Collaborate

Do this exercise with a partner. First, by yourself, write a paragraph that needs periods and question marks, but leave out those punctuation marks. Then exchange paragraphs with your partner, and add the necessary periods and question marks to your partner's paragraph. Finally, you and your partner should check each other's punctuation.

Write a paragraph of at least six sentences, using the topic sentence below.

New students have many questions about college, but their questions are soon

answered. _____

_____

_____

_____

_____

_____

_____

THE SEMICOLON

There are two ways to use semicolons:

1. Use a semicolon to join two independent clauses.

    examples:
    Aunt Celine can be very generous; she gave me fifty dollars for my birthday.
    The ice storm was horrible; our town endured five days without electricity.

If the independent clauses are joined by a conjunctive adverb, you still need a semicolon. You will also need a comma after the conjunctive adverb if the conjunctive adverb is more than one syllable long.

    examples:
    I called the towing service; then I waited impatiently for the tow truck to
        arrive.
    Stephen forgot about the exam; therefore, he was not prepared for it.

2. If a list contains commas and the items on it need to be clarified, use a semicolon to separate the items. Note how confusing the following lists would be without the semicolons.

    examples:
    The student government presidents at the conference represented Mill
        Valley High School, Springfield; Longfellow High School, Riverdale;
        Kennedy High School, Deer Creek; and Martin Luther King High
        School, Rocky Hills.
    The members of the musical group were Janet Reese, guitar; Richelle
        Dennison, drums; Sandy Simon, bass; and Lee Vickers, vocalist.

Exercise 3 Punctuating with Semicolons

Some of the following sentences need semicolons; some do not. Add the necessary semicolons. (You may need to change some commas to semicolons.)

1. Bananas are a great snack they are full of potassium and fiber.

2. If you go to the beach tomorrow, be sure to bring heavy sunscreen, a big towel or blanket, several bottles of water, and a hat.

3. Give me the jar I can open it for you.

4. Riding a bicycle to work or school can help you lose weight and can keep you fit.

5. In the summer, my mother took us to free concerts in the park thus we grew up loving all kinds of music.

6. Yesterday, the Neighborhood Crime Watch Association elected these officers: Pierre Nilon, president, Estelle Moreno, vice president, Stanley Rosen, treasurer, and Alan Chang, secretary.

7. Edward spent all afternoon looking for some paint for the kitchen but couldn't decide on the right shade of blue.

8. Dr. Wing has all the academic qualifications for the job of head of the pediatrics department furthermore, he is devoted to his patients.

9. The guests at Kimberly's wedding came from as far away as San Francisco, California, Portland, Oregon, Denver, Colorado, and Honolulu, Hawaii.

10. A handsome man answered the door he looked at me suspiciously.

Exercise 4 **Punctuating with Semicolons**

Connect

Add semicolons where they are needed in the following paragraph. You may need to change some commas to semicolons.

When Sean started work at the Rose Inn, he struggled to adapt to the personalities and demands of his bosses. At work, Sean had to answer to four people: Alice Lejeune, the head of reservations, Don Davis, the day manager, Catherine Chinn, the night manager, and John Carney, the chief accountant. As a new member of the reservations staff, Sean had to learn how to deal with the hotel guests in addition, he had to learn what each of his superiors required from him. John Carney, for example, cared about money problems he did not want Sean to make any promises of discounts or refunds to customers. If Sean worked the night shift, Catherine Chinn wanted him to be lively and energetic when guests checked in late at night. The day manager was a calm and tolerant man, consequently, Sean learned to relax around Mr. Davis. On the other hand, Alice Lejeune, the head of reservations, expected the best of her staff. Sean worked extra hard to please Ms. Lejeune as a result, he became a competent and confident staff member. For Sean, dealing with the hotel guests was a challenge dealing with four bosses was an education.

Connect

| Exercise 5 | **Punctuating with Semicolons** |

Add semicolons where they are needed in the following paragraph. You may need to change some commas to semicolons.

After many years of hard work, Jonathan Reilly was able to buy a home, next he wanted to create a good life for his children. He felt that he could provide opportunities that he had never had to Crystal, seven years old, Marcus, four years old, and Anthony, eighteen months old. Mr. Reilly never gave his children expensive clothes, fancy cars, or lavish vacations. Mr. Reilly didn't believe that a childhood full of luxuries would open doors for his sons and daughter instead, he focused on their education. Even if he had to work at two jobs, he found a way to save the money for three children's college educations. From their earliest years, Crystal, Marcus, and Anthony learned to focus on their academic strengths and improve their academic weaknesses. Mr. Reilly challenged his children to open their minds, in addition, he showed them the pleasures of learning. Books filled the Reilly home, and the children learned the pleasures of stargazing, exploring nature, camping, and caring for animals. By the time they were old enough for college, the Reilly children had focused on their career paths. Crystal chose veterinary science, Marcus decided to become a writer. The third child, Anthony, focused on marine biology. Jonathan Reilly lived to see his children find fulfillment and happiness. The Reillys are a remarkable family. I know them intimately. Jonathan is my grandfather Anthony is my father. One day, I hope to be as hardworking and committed as they are.

THE COMMA

There are four main ways to use a comma, and there are other, less important ways. Memorize the four main ways. If you can learn and understand these four rules, you will be more confident and correct in your punctuation. That is, you will use a comma only when you have a reason to do so; you will not be scattering commas in your sentences simply because you think a comma might fit, as many writers do. The four main ways to use a comma are as a *lister*, a *linker*, an *introducer*, or an *inserter* (two commas).

1. **Comma as a lister**
    Commas separate items in a series. These items can be words, phrases, or clauses.

    commas between words in a list:
    Charles was fascinated by Doreen because she was smart, sassy, and funny.

commas between phrases in a list:
I wanted a house on a quiet street, in a friendly neighborhood, and with a
school nearby.

commas between clauses in a list:
In a single year my uncle joined the army, he fought in the Gulf War, and
he was decorated for valor.

> **Note:** In a list, the comma before *and* is optional, but most writers use it.

Exercise 6   Using the Comma as a Lister

Add commas only where they are needed in the following sentences.

1. Living on my own turned out to be stressful scary and difficult, but it
   was also exciting liberating and fun.

2. After they heard the news, Melanie was upset Robert got angry and
   Henry felt guilty.

3. By the time I was ten, my family had lived in four cities: Miami
   Orlando Atlanta and Charlotte.

4. Babysitting a toddler working in a preschool and volunteering at a
   children's hospital are all good training for becoming a parent.

5. Brian always checked the tires changed the oil washed the windshield and changed the filters on his sister's old car.

6. With very little money, Aunt Eva serves large tasty and nutritious
   meals to her family of six.

7. When my grandmother was young, the only good jobs available to
   most women were secretary nurse and teacher.

8. Get me some shampoo toothpaste deodorant and cough drops when
   you go to the drugstore.

9. Billy could be at his father's house at the movies or at the gym.

10. Thinking planning and revising are all part of the writing process.

2. **Comma as a linker**
   A comma and a coordinating conjunction link two independent clauses.
   The coordinating conjunctions are *for, and, nor, but, or, yet, so.* The
   comma goes before the coordinating conjunction.

   comma before coordinating conjunctions:
   Norbert was thrilled by the A in Organic Chemistry, for he had studied
   really hard all semester.
   You can pick up the pizza, and I'll set the table.
   Our house had no basement, nor did it have much of an attic.
   The movie was long, but it was action-packed.
   Diane will fly home for summer vacation, or her parents will visit her.
   Mr. Weinstein has lived in the neighborhood for a year, yet no one knows
   him very well.
   The front door was open, so I went right in.

> **Note:** Before you use a comma, be careful that the coordinating conjunction is
> linking two independent clauses.

no comma: Veronica wrote poetry and painted beautiful portraits.
use a comma: Veronica wrote poetry, and she painted beautiful portraits.

Exercise 7 **Using the Comma as a Linker**

Add commas only where they are needed in the following sentences.

1. I really need a haircut but I can't afford one right now.

2. Thomas rarely says much yet he always seems quite intelligent.

3. The new neighbors painted the exterior of their house and they planted some bushes in the front yard.

4. Some of my friends from work get together on Fridays and have dinner at a Caribbean restaurant.

5. My dentist rarely hurts me nor does he give me any anesthetic.

6. Sam is shy so he sometimes appears arrogant or aloof.

7. Many people have dealt with addiction in their own families or have seen friends cope with substance abuse.

8. We have to call an electrician for we need to check the wiring in the basement.

9. Callie checked her e-mail several times last night but didn't find any messages from Mercedes.

10. The kitten loves people and it is already litter-trained.

3. **Comma as an introducer**
   Put a comma after introductory words, phrases, or clauses in a sentence.

   comma after an introductory word:
   No, I can't afford that car.

   comma after an introductory phrase:
   In my opinion, that car is a lemon.

   comma after an introductory clause:
   When the baby smiles, I am the happiest father on earth.

Exercise 8 **Using the Comma as an Introducer**

Add the necessary commas to the following sentences.

1. With no apology the stranger cut ahead of me in the ticket line.

2. Before you go to bed lock the doors.

3. Fortunately I have never had to borrow money from my family.

4. On the first day of spring Amanda married her childhood sweetheart.

5. Laughing with pleasure Mitchell recognized some old friends at the surprise party in his honor.

6. On a cold winter day I want to stay in my warm bed forever.

7. When my instructor asks me a question I hesitate before answering him.

8. If someone at the college is advertising for a roommate I might call the number on the advertisement.

9. As soon as I drank some water I stopped coughing and choking.

10. Sure you can borrow my notes from psychology class.

4. Comma as an inserter

When words or phrases that are not necessary are inserted into a sentence, put a comma on *both* sides of the inserted material.

commas around inserted material:
Her science project, a masterpiece of research, won first prize.
Selena's problem, I believe, is her fear of failure.
Julio, stuck by the side of the road, waited for the tow truck.
Artichokes, a delicious vegetable, are not always available at the local market.

Using commas as inserters requires that you decide what is *essential* to the meaning of the sentence and what is *nonessential*.

If you do not need material in a sentence, put commas around the material.
If you need material in a sentence, do not put commas around the material.

For example, consider this sentence:

The woman who was promoted to captain was Jack's wife.

Do you need the words *who was promoted to captain* to understand the meaning of the sentence? To answer this question, write the sentence without the words:

The woman was Jack's wife.

Reading the shorter sentence, you might ask, "What woman?" The words *who was promoted to captain* are essential to the sentence. Therefore, you do not put commas around them.

correct: The woman who was promoted to captain was Jack's wife.

Remember that the proper name of a person, place, or thing is always sufficient to identify it. Therefore, any information that follows a proper name is inserted material; it is not essential and gets commas on both sides.

proper names and inserted material:
Gloria Chen, who lives in my apartment building, won the raffle at Dominion High School.
Suarez Electronics, which just opened in the mall, has great deals on color televisions.

Inserted material often begins with one of these **relative pronouns:** *who, which, that.* If you have to choose between *which* and *that, which* usually begins inserted material that is not essential:

The movie, which was much too long, was a comedy.

That usually begins inserted material that is essential.

The puppy that I want is a miniature poodle.

Note: Sometimes the material needed in a sentence is called *essential* (or *restrictive*), and the material not needed is called *nonessential* (or *nonrestrictive*).

Exercise 9 **Using Commas as Inserters (Two Commas)**

Add commas only where they are needed in the following sentences.

1. The man who identified the suspect was a witness to the crime.

2. One piece of furniture that I would love to own is a huge entertainment unit.

3. Catherine gave me a DVD of <u>The Incredibles</u> one of my favorite movies to cheer me up.

4. Anyone who can speak a second language has an advantage in this job market.

5. Snickers bars which I first tasted as a child remain my favorite candy.

6. My brother's apology which came a year too late did not change my mind about his character.

7. Professor Gilman taking pity on the class postponed the test for a week.

8. The woman it appears is trying to make friends in a new town.

9. Jason McNeill from my old high school has just been elected to the city council.

10. The stuffed teddy bear that Alan gave me is sitting on my bed.

Exercise 10 **Punctuating with Commas: The Four Main Ways**

Add commas only where they are needed in the following sentences.

1. While Alex played video games Bobby made some popcorn.

2. After we eat dinner we'll have some time to look at the old photograph albums and talk about old times.

3. Karen had candles on her coffee table in the kitchen and near her bathtub.

4. I would love to have a piece of coconut cake but I have to watch my weight.

5. It's my brother's birthday tomorrow so I have to find a funny card for him.

6. Isabel found a denim jacket some leather gloves and a red cap at the thrift shop.

7. Sizzling Seafood which is near my apartment offers weekday specials on shrimp dinners.

8. The speeding car slid across the icy road but managed to stop on the hilltop.

9. Only Gregory with all his charm and sincerity could have talked the officer out of issuing a traffic ticket.

10. Whether you like it or not you have to apologize to your friend.

Exercise 11 **More on Punctuating with Commas: The Four Main Ways**

Add commas only where they are needed in the following sentences.

1. Until Neal took me out to dinner I had never tasted sushi.

2. Most of my friends don't like to gossip nor do they enjoy constant complaining.

3. Mom can you lend me ten dollars?

4. Sarah didn't know anyone at the party yet she quickly made friends with two engineering students.

5. Penelope Greenberg who started a chain of clothing stores is going to speak to our Introduction to Business class next week.

6. Nelson will of course want to spend the long weekend with his family.

7. The house that I wanted was a fishing cabin near a beautiful lake.

8. The girl who won the spelling bee will receive a $10,000 college scholarship.

9. My sister spends most of her time putting on her makeup touching up her makeup and removing her makeup.

10. In my mother's big kitchen we have long conversations about everything from family to French toast and we have leisurely meals.

Exercise 12 **The Four Main Ways to Use Commas: Create Your Own Examples**

Collaborate

Do this exercise with a partner or group. Below are the rules for the four main ways to use commas. For each rule, write two sentences that are examples. The first one is done for you.

Rule 1: Use a comma as a lister.

example 1: *I have old photos stashed in my attic, in my closet, and in the garage.*

example 2: *The movie was long, dull, and pointless.*

_____

Rule 2: Use a comma as a linker.

example 1: _____

_____

example 2: _____

_____

Rule 3: Use a comma as an introducer.

example 1: _____

_____

example 2: _____

_____

Rule 4: Use a comma as an inserter (two commas).

example 1: _____

_____

example 2: _____

_____

Connect

Exercise 13   **The Four Main Ways to Use Commas**

Add commas where they are needed in the following paragraph. Do not add or change any other punctuation; just add commas.

When I have achieved some goal I have a secret way of celebrating. Believe it or not I reward myself by making brownies. Last week for example I passed a really difficult chemistry test that had kept me awake for many nights. I had reviewed for the test joined a study group and even worked with a tutor but I was still uncertain about the test. As soon as I saw my passing score I rushed out and bought the ingredients for a pan of brownies. I spent some happy moments in my kitchen for I loved mixing the gooey batter licking the bowl watching the brownies bake and frosting the moist squares of chocolate heaven. Naturally I had to taste a large portion of the frosting and the warm brownies while I prepared them. The chemistry test which had caused me so much misery seemed a distant memory once I enjoyed my reward.

Connect

Exercise 14   **The Four Main Ways to Use a Comma**

Add commas where they are needed in the following paragraph. Do not add or change any other punctuation; just add commas.

Richie Scott my boyfriend was killed last week on a sunny street in our town, and his death was his own fault. Richie was street racing. He and another driver were weaving though rush-hour traffic on a busy avenue bordered by apartments and strip malls. According to eyewitness reports Richie driving at high speed bolted into oncoming traffic and the other racer followed. Richie's Mustang was torn in half; he died at the scene. Three other cars were involved in the crash. The other street racer was taken to the hospital but he is expected to survive his injuries. However, a young mother in an SUV died. Her four-year-old son is in critical condition. In addition, the driver of an old Toyota has several broken bones. Many people are grieving today asking questions and confronting some terrible guilt. I am one of them. To please

Richie I used to attend regular street races late at night on lonely stretches of highway.

I cheered his victories and found his driving exciting daring and heroic. I never

dreamed that his love of speed would lead him to a busy street in rush hour. I never

dreamed that his daring would lead to so much death and destruction.

Other Ways to Use a Comma

Besides the four main ways, there are other ways to use a comma. Reviewing these uses will help you feel more confident as a writer.

1. **Use commas with quotations.** Use a comma to set off direct quotations from the rest of the sentence.

   examples:
   Sylvia warned me, "Don't swim there."
   "I can give you a ride," Alan said.
   Note that the comma that introduces the quotation goes before the quotation marks. But once the quotation has begun, commas (or periods) go inside the quotation marks.

2. **Use commas with dates and addresses.** Put commas between the items in dates and addresses.

   examples:
   August 29, 1981, is the day we were married.
   I had an apartment at 2323 Clover Avenue, Houston, Texas, until I was transferred to California.
   Notice the comma after the year in the date, and the comma after the state in the address. These commas are needed when you write a date or an address within a sentence.

3. **Use commas in numbers.** Use commas in numbers of one thousand or larger.

   examples:
   He owed me $1,307.
   That wall contains 235,991 bricks.

4. **Use commas for clarity.** Use a comma when you need to make something clear.

   examples:
   She waltzed in, in a stunning silk gown.
   Whatever you did, did the trick.
   I don't have to apologize, but I want to, to make things right between us.
   Not long after, the party ended.

Exercise 15   **Other Ways to Use a Comma**

Add commas where they are needed in the following sentences.

1. When Nathan lived in Topeka Kansas he worked at a furniture warehouse.

2. "Money isn't everything" my grandmother used to say.

3. We lived at 307 Orchard Avenue Jackson Mississippi when my father was in the army.

4. A spokesperson from the police department said "We have no suspects at this time."

5. When you meet her her expensive jewelry will be the first thing you notice.

6. In Chicago Illinois you would pay rent of $2500 a month for this apartment.

7. Shortly before a man had been seen entering the building.

8. Priscilla paid $1279 for her living room furniture, but I got similar furniture on sale for $960.

9. "Someone took the last piece of pizza"my roommate complained.

10. Richard encouraged me to visit the flea market but said "If you go go early."

Exercise 16 **Punctuating with Commas: A Comprehensive Exercise**

Add commas where they are needed in the following sentences.

1. "Don't walk on the wet floor" my mother warned Joel but he paid no attention.

2. Sergei met Gina at a party and was instantly attracted to her.

3. After all we've dealt with plenty of bad luck over the years.

4. Amy who would be sending us a package from 770 Taft Boulevard Tulsa Oklahoma?

5. Todd met Dina's brother he spent time with her best friends he visited her cousins yet he never met her parents.

6. Teenagers who have nothing to do are likely to find dangerous ways to pass the time.

7. My parents got engaged on December 25 1979 but didn't get married until June 15 1981 because they waited to get married until my mother had finished school.

8. Michelle Rodriguez who rides the bus with me always has a joke for me in the morning.

9. No one likes to hurt another person's feelings but you need to to clear up a misunderstanding.

10. The little dog never barked nor did it chew on the furniture.

Exercise 17 **Punctuating with Commas: Another Comprehensive Exercise**

Add commas where they are needed in the following sentences.

1. Since Ron got his own apartment he's learned to do his own laundry and shop for groceries.

2. Once Tamika got her phone bill she swore "I will never again stay on the phone for more than ten minutes."

3. Jon and Barbara spent $2700 on their trip to Cancun for they wanted a vacation that would remain in their minds forever.

4. Whenever I get tired of studying I think of the opportunities an education will bring and I feel better.

5. After Andrew tasted my homemade barbecue sauce he wanted the recipe.

6. The person who taught me how to swim is my uncle.

7. Sammy likes training to be a chef although he has a hard time dealing with the steaming kitchens the long hours and the hectic pace that are part of the job.

8. The Coffee Corner which is open all night is a favorite with college students who want to study with friends.

9. People are attracted to you Josh by your sense of fun.

10. Red white and blue streamers flew from the fence posts and the street lamps.

Exercise 18 **Punctuating with Commas**

Collaborate

Working alone, write a paragraph that is at least six sentences long. The paragraph should require at least five commas, but leave the commas out. Then give your paragraph to a partner; let your partner add the necessary commas. Meanwhile, you punctuate your partner's paragraph. When you are both finished, check each other's answers.

Write your paragraph in the lines below, using the sentence given to you as the topic sentence.

Of all the places I remember from my childhood, one place stands out. _____

_____

_____

_____

_____

_____

_____

_____

_____

_____

_____

_____

_____

Connect

Exercise 19 **Punctuating with Commas: A Comprehensive Exercise**

Add commas where they are needed in the following paragraph. Do not add or change any other punctuation; just add commas.

Everyone seems to be short of cash these days and many people are looking for ways to save a few dollars. My cousin Sam, for instance, found a way to save money while he also made some money. Sam is a coffee lover and his weakness is a fancy coffee drink made with cream, foam, special flavors, and a price tag of $5.00. Because his daily trip to a coffee shop was cutting into his budget Sam reluctantly decided to sacrifice his high-priced coffee. After three bad days without his latte, Sam searched for another solution. He applied for and was offered a part-time job at a coffee shop that serves his favorite beverage. Although Sam already had one part-time job he decided the offer was extremely inviting. His decision was based on some new information about the coffee shop. Employees at the place he learned, are permitted free coffee during their working hours. If Sam works at the shop for two years and drinks one latte each day of his three-day workweek, he will save $1450 in coffee expenses. Best of all, Sam says "Not many jobs pay a salary and give free drinks, too!"

THE APOSTROPHE

Use the apostrophe in the following ways:

1. Use an apostrophe in contractions to show that letters have been omitted.

   examples:

do not	=	don't
she will	=	she'll
he would	=	he'd
is not	=	isn't
will not	=	won't

   Use an apostrophe to show that numbers have been omitted, too.

   the winter of 1999 = the winter of '99

   > **Note:** Your instructor may want you to avoid contractions in formal assignments. Be sure to follow his or her instructions.

2. Use an apostrophe to show possession. If a word does not end in *s*, show ownership by adding an apostrophe and *s*.

   examples:

the car belongs to Maria	=	Maria's car
the toy is owned by my cousin	=	my cousin's toy
the hat belongs to somebody	=	somebody's hat

If two people own something, put the *'s* on the last person's name.
Jack and Joe own a dog   =   Jack and Joe's dog

If a word already ends in *s* and you want to show ownership, just add an apostrophe.

examples:
The doll belongs to Dolores   =   Dolores' doll
two girls own a cat   =   the girls' cat
Mr. Ross owns a house   =   Mr. Ross' house

3. Use an apostrophe for special uses of time and to create a plural of numbers mentioned as numbers, letters mentioned as letters, and words that normally do not have plurals.

> **special use of time:** It took a *month's* work.
> **numbers mentioned as numbers:** Add the *7's*.
> **letters mentioned as letters:** Dot your *i's*.
> **words that normally do not have plurals:** Give me some more *thank you's*.

Caution: Be careful with apostrophes. Possessive pronouns like *his, hers, theirs, ours, yours,* and *its* do not take apostrophes.

> **not this:** I was sure the dress was ~~her's~~.
> **but this:** I was sure the dress was hers.

> **not this:** The movie has ~~it's~~ flaws.
> **but this:** The movie has its flaws.

Do not add an apostrophe to a simple plural.
> **not this:** The pudding comes in three ~~flavor's~~.
> **but this:** The pudding comes in three flavors.

Exercise 20 **Punctuating with Apostrophes**

Add apostrophes where they are needed in the following sentences.

1. One mans lifelong dream of helping others came true when a mens counseling center opened at the hospital.

2. Wed never interfere in other peoples private quarrels.

3. Its silly to buy an expensive hair product just because its advertising is glamorous.

4. The winter of 98 was so cold that my parents thought about moving to Nevada.

5. Frances little boy has trouble writing his *p*s.

6. My sisters knew that theyd have a long ride ahead of them before they got to Manny and Frank's house.

7. You shouldnt have asked Jessica about her job; thats a subject she doesnt want to discuss.

8. Theres a pile of books on the table; you can take the ones that are yours.

9. Mrs. Rivera is planning for her grandchildrens education; she is saving money in a special bank account.

10. You never listen to anybodys advice, and I think youd better start paying attention to your friends.

Exercise 21 **More on Punctuating with Apostrophes**

Add apostrophes where they are needed in the following sentences.

1. On Saturday, Jareds taking me to see the monkeys at the Animal Sanctuary for Apes in Trentwood.

2. You still print your *t*s instead of writing them, but that habit doesnt make your writing difficult to read.

3. Ernie and Annabella both drive 2007 Mustangs, but his is a sportier model than hers.

4. Molly is taking care of Luke and Lucys cat over the weekend.

5. Im going to need everybodys help clearing out the weeds behind the house and planting flowers.

6. Patrick apologizes so often that his *sorry*s are starting to sound insincere.

7. Texas huge expanses of open land and its cowboys impressed the visitors from Japan.

8. If Desmond comes with us on our trip to Memphis, hell pay for our gas, but he wont let us take his car.

9. Jane and Catalina have years of experience in carpentry; theyll help you build a simple bookcase.

10. Tyler spent a months salary on a diamond ring for Julie, so its unfortunate that Julie doesnt care for the rings style.

Connect

Exercise 22 **Punctuating with Apostrophes**

Edit the following paragraph, correcting the errors related to apostrophes. You need to add some apostrophes and eliminate the unnecessary apostrophes.

In a time when everybodys complaining about doctors, I was lucky enough to find a great doctor. Since I am rarely sick, I didnt know any doctor's to call when I got a bad case of bronchitis. I asked all my friends about their doctors, but all I heard were horror stories about long hours spent in the waiting room, days spent trying to get an appointment, and one or two minutes spent with a hurried and distracted doctor. Feeling worse, I turned to my mother. "Go to Dr. Morano," she said. "Dr. Moranos wonderful." Within ten minutes, I had reached the doctors office and made an appointment for the next day. The voice on the phone was warm and kind. Still, I was prepared for an hours wait in a room packed with unhappy patients. Thats not what I got. My time in the waiting room was about thirty minutes, for I had to fill out a form for new patient's. Then I prepared myself to sit alone in an examining room while the doctor tended to two or three other patients stacked up in other rooms. Dr. Morano appeared within ten minutes, and she actually sat down to talk.

Id never met a doctor like Dr. Morano, and she left only after she had explored my medical history, checked me carefully, and prescribed some medication for my cough. I realized that its possible to find a kind and human atmosphere inside a doctor's office.

Exercise 23   **Punctuating with Apostrophes**

Connect

Punctuate the following paragraph, correcting the errors related to apostrophes. You need to add some apostrophes and eliminate the unnecessary apostrophes.

When I was child, my grandparents had some old sayings that were a mystery to me. For instance, when a stressful incident occurred, my grandfather would say, "Well, its all in a days work." Year's later, I began to understand that the saying was his way of accepting the stress and moving past it. My grandmother had several sayings about food. One that I have never been able to understand is "You cant make an omelet without breaking a few eggs." It seems obvious to me that egg's get broken when someone makes an omelet, but I don't see how the saying applies to work, or sports, or love, or anything else. Another egg saying became easier for me to comprehend as I grew up. I learned that "Don't put all your eggs in one basket" was a warning about counting too much on one solution to a problem or investing too much of one's resources in one area such as a quest for fame. The strangest effect of my grandparents proverbs is the way they linger in my brain. Even today, when I am twenty-five year's old, I become startled when a saying such as "The early bird catches the worm" pop's into my head. At that moment, I am back in my childhood again, safe in my grandmother and grandfathers wise and loving company.

THE COLON

A colon is used at the end of a complete statement. It introduces a list or explanation.

colon introducing a list:
When my father went to the Bahamas, he brought me back some lovely gifts: a straw bag, a shell necklace, and some Bahamian perfume.

colon introducing an explanation:
The salesperson was very helpful: he told us about special discounted items and the free gift-wrap service.

Remember that the colon comes after a complete statement. What comes after the colon explains or describes what came before the colon. Look once more at the two examples, and you'll see the point.

When my father went to the Bahamas, he brought me back some lovely gifts: a straw bag, a shell necklace, and some Bahamian perfume. (The words after the colon, *a straw bag, a shell necklace, and some Bahamian perfume,* describe the lovely gifts.)

The salesperson was very helpful: he told us about special discounted items and the free gift-wrap service. (The words after the colon, *he told us about special discounted items and the free gift-wrap service,* explain what the salesperson did to be helpful.)

Some people use a colon every time they put a list in a sentence, but this is not a good rule to follow. Instead, remember that a colon, even one that introduces a list, must come after a complete statement.

> **not this:** ~~If you are going to the drugstore, remember to pick up: toothpaste, dental floss, and mouthwash.~~
>
> **but this:** If you are going to the drugstore, remember to pick up these items: toothpaste, dental floss, and mouthwash.

A colon may also introduce a long quotation.

> **colon introducing a long quotation:**
> In a speech to the alumni at Columbia University, Will Rogers joked about what a big university it was and said: "There are 3,200 courses. You spend your first two years in deciding what course to take, the next two years in finding the building that these courses are given in, and the rest of your life in wishing you had taken another course."

Exercise 24   Punctuating with Colons

Add colons where they are needed in the following sentences.

1. After my first day of class at the college, I felt bewildered by the crowds of students, the fast pace of the instructors' lectures, and the long lines at the bookstore.

2. After my first day of class at the college, I felt bewildered by three experiences the crowds of students, the fast pace of the instructors' lectures, and the long lines at the bookstore.

3. My niece's bed is piled with bears teddy bears, bears dressed in bride and groom outfits, bears in football jerseys, and even talking bears.

4. To be sure I had enough clothes for the weekend at the Water Adventure amusement park, I packed everything sweaters, swimsuits, jeans, fancy dresses, tee shirts, sweatshirts, sneakers, and high heels.

5. When my mother told my brother to clean out his closet, he stuffed shoes, socks, empty soda cans, ancient bags of cookies, old magazines, and a broken lightbulb under his bed.

6. With a big grin on his face, my boyfriend said he had won fifty dollars in a radio contest.

7. My supervisor's desk was always immaculate all the paper stacked neatly, the pencils placed in a china mug, the computer lined up with the mouse pad, and one personal photograph framed in shiny metal.

8. Since Wednesday is a long day for me at the college, I always bring snacks an apple, a candy bar, and a large bottle of water.

9. If you have more party guests than you expected, you can always send Phil out to get tortilla chips, salsa, crackers, and cheese.

10. The student who spoke at the student government meeting seemed nervous he kept looking at the floor and forgetting what he wanted to say.

Exercise 25 **Punctuating with Colons**

Connect

Edit the following paragraph, correcting the errors related to colons. You need to add some colons and eliminate any unnecessary colons.

Buying furniture can be tricky because so-called bargains can turn out to be deceptive. The other day I saw a newspaper advertisement for a bedroom set that looked like a good deal. It offered a five-piece set for a sale price of $900. The photograph showed an attractive group of furniture a large, queen-sized bed, two nightstands, a large dresser with a mirror, and a tall bureau. Because I desperately needed some new bedroom furniture, I visited the furniture showroom during the sale. The bedroom set was quite impressive the bed was large and sturdy, the dresser and bureau seemed solid, and the nightstands were a good size. I quickly found a salesperson and told him that I wanted to get: the bed, two nightstands, the bureau, and the dresser for the sale price. I was shocked by his reply: the sale price applied to five pieces of furniture, but the pieces were not the ones I had expected. I had failed to read the small print in the advertisement. It said that the five pieces were: the bed, the bed rails, the headboard, the dresser, and its mirror. The other pieces, the bureau and the nightstands, were sold separately and cost between $250 and $400 apiece. Feeling tricked and disappointed, I went home to my decrepit bedroom furniture.

THE EXCLAMATION MARK

The exclamation mark is used at the end of sentences that express strong emotion.

appropriate: Mr. Zimmerman, you've just become the father of triplets!

inappropriate: The dance was fabulous! (*Fabulous* already implies excitement and enthusiasm, so you don't need the exclamation mark.)

Be careful not to overuse the exclamation mark. If your choice of words is descriptive, you should not have to rely on the exclamation mark for emphasis. Use it sparingly, for it is easy to rely on exclamation marks instead of using better vocabulary.

THE DASH

Use a dash to interrupt a sentence; use two dashes to set off words in a sentence. The dash is somewhat dramatic, so be careful not to overuse it.

> **examples:**
> Helena's frustration at her job made her an angry woman—a mean, angry woman.
> My cousins Celia and Rick—the silly fools—fell off the dock when they were clowning around.

PARENTHESES

Use parentheses to set off words in a sentence.

> **examples:**
> The movies he rented (Kung Fu Panda, Blades of Glory, and The Happening) were all too silly for me.

> **Note:** In student essays, movie titles are underlined.

Simon nominated Justin Lewis (his best friend) as club treasurer.

> **Note:** Commas in pairs, dashes in pairs, and parentheses are all used as inserters. They set off inserted material that interrupts the flow of the sentence. The least dramatic and smoothest way to insert material is to use commas.

THE HYPHEN

A hyphen joins two or more descriptive words that act as a single word.

> **examples:**
> Mr. Handlesman was wearing a custom-made suit.
> My great aunt's hair is a salt-and-pepper color.

Exercise 26 **Punctuating with Exclamation Marks, Dashes, Parentheses, and Hyphens**

In the following sentences, add exclamation marks, dashes, parentheses, or hyphens where they are needed. Answers may vary because some writers may use dashes instead of parentheses.

1. Artie used to be a good ballplayer one of the best at our college.

2. My old car once known as the Broken Beast has been running fairly well recently.

3. My parents encouraged me to spend the summer at a workshop for student leaders; they called it a once in a lifetime opportunity.

4. Rebecca Richman my former best friend is spreading a nasty rumor about me.

5. The Kennerly Lodge a first rate hotel is hiring extra staff for the summer season.

6. I've just seen a ghost

7. If you are self conscious, you may have a hard time speaking in public.

8. Patrice Green who was once a homeless mother of two has just completed her second year of work as a paralegal at a large law firm.

9. There's an alligator in your swimming pool

10. Eric put on some old clothes a ratty looking sweater and filthy jeans to clean the trash out of the cellar.

| Exercise 27 | Punctutating with Exclamation Marks, Dashes, Parentheses, and Hyphens |

Connect

Edit the following paragraph, correcting the errors related to exclamation marks, dashes, parentheses, and hyphens. You can add, change, or eliminate punctuation. Answers may vary because dashes in pairs and parentheses are both used as inserters. Also, try to use only one exclamation mark in your edited version of the paragraph.

My visit to a fancy and expensive restaurant was not at all what I had expected. A new friend wanted to impress me and took me to Palm Breeze the most popular restaurant in town last Saturday night. We sat in a courtyard decorated with an elegant, bubbling fountain and lush foliage. Bright tropical flowers peeked from behind green palm fronds! The sights and sounds were enticing, but some unpleasant surprises followed! First, my friend ordered oysters for us both. I love seafood and expected a tasty dish of baked, broiled, or steamed shellfish. I recoiled in horror when I realized that the oysters were raw a gooey mess of gray, jelly like tissue. The main course was somewhat better, but the portions were tiny. Because Palm Breeze charges so much, I expected it to serve generous helpings that would cover the plate. Instead, my plate contained a tiny portion of roast pork, thin slivers of red, yellow, and green peppers, and a spoonful of rice. Unfortunately, my biggest surprise was yet to come. For dessert, I ordered a Palm Breeze speciality a tropical fruit salad filled with guava, pineapple, mangoes, and berries. This dessert called Passion at Sunset was famous for the delicious orange sauce covering the fruit. However, one other item was also covered by that sauce. It was a large, green, scaly lizard. That lizard was a little more of the tropics than I wanted. Clearly, my first visit to Palm Breeze will also be my last.

QUOTATION MARKS

Use quotation marks for direct quotes, for the titles of short works, and for other, special uses.

1. Put quotation marks around direct quotations (a speaker or writer's exact words).

   quotation marks around direct quotations:
   Ernest always told me, "It is better to give than to receive."
   "Nobody goes to that club," said Ramon.
   "We could go to the movies," Christina offered, "but we'd better hurry."
   My mother warned me, "Save your money. You'll need it for a rainy day."

Look carefully at the preceding examples. Note that a comma is used to introduce a direct quotation, and that, at the end of the quotation, a comma or a period goes inside the quotation marks.

   Ernest always told me, "It is better to give than to receive."

Notice how direct quotations of more than one sentence are punctuated. If the quotation is written as one unit, quotation marks go before the first quoted word and after the last quoted word:

   My mother warned me, "Save your money. You'll need it for a rainy day."

But if the quote is not written as one unit, the punctuation changes:

   "Save your money," my mother warned me. "You'll need it for a rainy day."

   Caution: Do *not* put punctuation marks around indirect quotations.

   indirect quotation: Tyree asked if the water was cold.
   direct quotation: Tyree asked, "Is the water cold?"

   indirect quotation: She said that she needed a break from work.
   direct quotation: She said, "I need a break from work."

2. Put quotation marks around the titles of short works. If you are writing the title of a short work like a short story, an essay, a newspaper or magazine article, a poem, or a song, put quotation marks around the title.

   quotation marks around the titles of short works:
   My father's favorite poem is "The Raven" by Edgar Allan Poe.
   When I was little, I used to sing "Twinkle, Twinkle, Little Star."
   I couldn't think of a good title, so I just called my essay "How I Spent My Summer Vacation."

If you are writing the title of a longer work like a book, movie, magazine, play, television show, or music album, underline the title.

   underlining the titles of longer works:
   My favorite childhood movie was Star Wars.
   For homework, I have to read an article called "Children and Reading Skills" in Time magazine.

Note: In printed publications such as books or magazines, titles of long works are put in italics. But when you are writing by hand, or typing, underline the titles of long works.

---

3. There are other, special uses of quotation marks. You use quotation marks around special words in a sentence.

   quotation marks around special words:
   When you say "sometimes," how often do you mean?
   People from Boston say "frappe" when they mean "milkshake."

If you are using a quotation within a quotation, use single quotation marks.

   a quotation within a quotation:
   Janey said angrily, "You took my car without permission, and all you can say is, 'It's no big deal.' "
   Aunt Mary said, "You need to teach that child to say 'please' and 'thank you' more often."

Exercise 28 **Punctuating with Quotation Marks**

Add quotation marks where they are needed in the following sentences.

1. There are so many meanings to the word love that it is hard to define.

2. Rena told her boyfriend, Unless you are willing to say I was wrong, we have no future together.

3. A British child may call his or her mother Mummy, but an American child is likely to say Mommy.

4. I have got to save some money, my sister said. I will have to cut back on expensive haircuts and manicures.

5. I have got to save some money. I will have to cut back on expensive haircuts and manicures, said my sister.

6. We were all shocked when Tara said she was quitting her job and moving out of the state.

7. The Wind Beneath My Wings is a popular song at weddings and at banquets that honor a special person.

8. Did you remember to turn off the stove? Mrs. Bethel asked her husband as they left for work.

9. Yesterday, Linda called to ask if I knew anyone who wanted to work as a babysitter.

10. I can tell that you're not eating right, my Aunt Rita scolded, because you look like skin and bones.

Exercise 29 **More on Punctuating with Quotation Marks**

Add quotation marks where they are needed in the following sentences.

1. Sonya isn't sure whether she has to work late next weekend.

2. I've had enough of your nagging, she said. I'm not going to listen to it any longer, she added.

3. Stephanie once said, I wish my father had been able to say I love you to me at least once.

4. Groovy used to be a popular slang term in the 1960s; in fact, there was even a hit song called Feelin' Groovy about feeling happy.

5. My girlfriend sometimes says she loves a particular gift from me when I know she is just trying not to hurt my feelings.

6. Good idea, my roommate said when I asked him if he wanted to order a pizza.

7. I'm hungry, my five-year-old nephew complained. When can we get out of the car and get something to eat?

8. Sandra questioned why so many turning points in her life seemed to be the result of pure luck.

9. After I become a ballerina, my six-year-old daughter declared, I'm going to be a superhero.

10. The Legend of Sleepy Hollow is an old story about one man's encounter with a ghost called The Headless Horseman.

CAPITAL LETTERS

There are ten main situations when you capitalize.

1. Capitalize the first word of every sentence.

   examples:
   Sometimes we take a walk on the beach.
   An apple is a healthy snack.

2. Capitalize the first word in a direct quotation if the word begins a sentence.

   examples:
   Jensina said, "Here is the money I owe you and a little something extra."
   "Here is the money I owe you," Jensina said, "and a little something extra." (Notice that the second section of this quotation does not begin with a capital letter because it does not begin a sentence.)

3. Capitalize the names of people.

   examples:
   Ingrid Alvorsen and Sean Miller invited me to their wedding.
   I asked Father to visit me.

Do not capitalize words like *mother*, *father*, or *aunt* if you put a possessive in front of them.

   names with possessives:
   I asked my father to visit me.
   She disliked her aunt.

4. Capitalize the titles of people.

   examples:
   I worked for Dr. Mabala.
   She is interviewing Dean Richards.

Do not capitalize when the title is not connected to a name.

> **a title not connected to a name:**
> I worked for that doctor.
> She is interviewing the dean.

5. Always capitalize nationalities, religions, races, months, days of the week, documents, organizations, holidays, and historical events or periods.

> **examples:**
> In eighth grade, I did a project on the American Revolution.
> At my son's nursery school, the students presented a program to
>   celebrate Thanksgiving.
> Every Tuesday night, he goes to meetings at the African American Club.

Use small letters for the seasons.

> **a season with a small letter:**
> I always look forward to the coming of winter.

6. Capitalize the names of particular places.

> **examples:**
> I used to attend Hawthorne Middle School.
> My friends like to stroll through City Center Mall.

Use small letters if a particular place is not given.

> **small letter for no particular place:**
> My friends like to stroll through the mall.

7. Use capital letters for geographic locations.

> **examples:**
> Lisa wanted to attend a college in the South.
> I love autumn in the Midwest.

But use small letters for geographic directions.

> **small letter for a geographic direction:**
> The easiest way to find the airport is to drive south on the freeway.

8. Capitalize the names of specific products.

> **examples:**
> I need some Tylenol for my headache.
> Melanie eats a Snickers bar every day.

But use small letters for a general type of product.

> **small letter for a general product:**
> Melanie eats a candy bar every day.

9. Capitalize the names of specific school courses.

> **examples:**
> My favorite class is Ancient and Medieval History.
> Alicia is taking Introduction to Computers this fall.

But use small letters for a general academic subject.

> **small letter for a general subject:**
> Before I graduate, I have to take a computer course.

10. Capitalize the first and last words in the titles of long or short works, and capitalize all other significant words in the title.

examples:
I loved the movie <u>Fifty First Dates</u>.
There is a beautiful song called "You Are the Sunshine of My Life."

(Remember that the titles of long works, like movies, are underlined; the titles of short works, like songs, are placed in quotation marks.)

Exercise 30   **Punctuating with Capital Letters**

Add capital letters where they are needed in the following sentences.

1. My cousin is a captain in the police department of a large city in the west.

2. I have recently become aunt Hannah to my sister's newborn baby, but I am not really sure what an aunt does.

3. In our introduction to american government class, we studied the parts of the constitution of the united states of america.

4. I have a bad cold, so I can't go anywhere without a box of kleenex and some cough drops.

5. The new professor who teaches education courses is not as friendly as professor Schaeffer.

6. On memorial day my family is going to a ceremony that will commemorate the American soldiers who died in the Vietnam war.

7. "you would make me very happy," my girlfriend said, "if you would wash my car."

8. The caribbean art center, north of Miami, is exhibiting a fine collection of haitian art.

9. Amanda got a job working at the john parker auditorium near chestnut street.

10. The manager at the service station is making me work on thanksgiving.

Exercise 31 **Punctuating with Capital Letters: Creating
Your Own Examples**

Do this exercise with a partner or group. Below is a list giving situations when
you should—or should not—use capital letters. Write a sentence at least five
words long as an example for each item on the list.

1. Capitalize the names of particular places.

   example: _____

   _____

2. Use capital letters for geographic locations.

   example: _____

   _____

3. Use small letters for geographic directions.

   example: _____

   _____

4. Capitalize historic events or periods.

   example: _____

   _____

5. Capitalize nationalities.

   example: _____

   _____

6. Capitalize the names of persons.

   example: _____

   _____

7. Do not capitalize words like *mother*, *father*, or *uncle* if you put a possessive in front of them.

   example: _____

   _____

8. Capitalize the titles of persons.

   example: _____

   _____

9. Don't capitalize when the title is not connected to a name.

   example: _____

   _____

10. Capitalize the names of specific products.

    example: _____

    _____

Exercise 32	Punctuating with Quotation Marks, Underlining, and Capital Letters

Following is a paragraph with some blank spaces. Fill in the blanks, remembering the rules for using quotation marks, underlining, and capital letters. When you have completed the exercise, be ready to share your responses with members of the class.

When I think about last year, I remember some very specific details. I remember

that one song I was always listening to was called _____

_____, and the singer I admired most was _____ The one

movie I remember best is _____, and a television show I

recall watching is _____ There are several places I associ-

ate with last year, also. Among them is a store called _____, the

school nearest to my home, called _____, and a place I always

wanted to go to, but never visited, called _____ When I think of

last year, I realize that I spent many hours eating or socializing at a fast-food restau-

rant named _____ My favorite cold drink was _____

_____ Today, I realize that some of my habits and tastes have changed, yet I am still

very much connected to the places and things of the past.

Exercise 33	Punctuating with Quotation Marks, Underlining, and Capital Letters

Edit the following paragraph, correcting the errors related to quotation marks, underlining, and capital letters. You need to add some quotation marks, underlining, and capital letters, and eliminate the unnecessary or incorrect quotation marks, underlining, and capital letters.

I have recently become interested in ghosts. My interest began when I was flipping

through the television channels and then stopped at a grainy black-and-white image

of two men in a shadowy room. The men were walking quietly and carefully, and one

held a light. The other had a camera. The scene was silent. When the image was

replaced by a commercial break, I discovered the show I had been watching was

"Ghost Hunters," and this episode was about ghosts in new england. After watching

one or two more episodes of this show, I learned that the hunters were believers in

ghosts or scientists trying to investigate the reality of ghosts. I have also learned some new vocabulary. The hunters focus on what they call sightings of spirits, or incidents of paranormal activity. Nobody on the show ever seems to wonder "if ghosts are real." I have an open mind on the subject but have become more curious. Recently, I went to my town's Library and asked a librarian "if she would help me search for books and articles about ghosts." I was surprised to find several books about hauntings in my area: "The Spirits Of Western Ghost Towns," "Mountain Mysteries," and "The haunted Mines of Colorado." In fact, I even discovered an article called Paranormal Denver, about the ghosts in my hometown. So far, my ghost-hunting has been limited to the library, and unless there is a spirit hiding among the book shelves, I will never see a ghost.

NUMBERS

Spell out numbers that take one or two words to spell out.

> **examples:**
> The coat cost seventy dollars.
> Bridget sent two hundred invitations.

Use hyphens to spell out compound numbers from twenty-one to ninety-nine.

> **examples:**
> Clarissa, twenty-three, is the oldest daughter.
> I mailed sixty-two invitations.

Use numerals if it takes more than two words to spell out a number.

> **examples:**
> The company sold 367 toy trains.
> The price of the car was $15,629.

Also use numerals to write dates, times, and addresses.

> **examples:**
> You can visit him at 223 Sailboat Lane.
> I received my diploma on June 17, 2004.
> We woke up at 6:00 a.m., bright and early.

Use numbers with *a.m.* and *p.m.*, but use words with *o'clock.*

> **example:**
> We woke up at six o'clock, bright and early.

ABBREVIATIONS

Although you should spell out most words rather than abbreviate them, you may use common abbreviations like *Mr., Mrs., Ms., Jr., Sr.,* and *Dr.* when they are used with a proper name. Abbreviations may also be used for references to time and for organizations widely known by initials.

> **examples:**
> I gave Dr. Lambert my medical records.
> The phone rang at 3:00 a.m. and scared me out of a sound sleep.
> Nancy got a job with the FBI.

Spell out the names of places, months, days of the week, courses of study, and words referring to parts of a book.

> **not this:** I visited a friend in Philadelphia, ~~Penn.~~
> **but this:** I visited a friend in Philadelphia, Pennsylvania.

> **not this:** My brother skipped his ~~phys. ed.~~ class yesterday.
> **but this:** My brother skipped his physical education class yesterday.

> **not this:** Last week, our garbage was not picked up on ~~Weds.~~ or ~~Sat.,~~ so I called the ~~Dept.~~ of Sanitation.
> **but this:** Last week, our garbage was not picked up on Wednesday or Saturday, so I called the Department of Sanitation.

Exercise 34   Punctuating with Numbers and Abbreviations

Correct the errors in punctuating with numbers and abbreviations in the following sentences.

1. Pres. Thurman closed Salton U. yesterday after heavy rains flooded parts of the campus.

2. I couldn't sleep last night, so I watched a movie about the CIA until one twenty-five a.m.

3. My sister got a scholarship to Penn. State U., and she leaves for her first semester on Weds.

4. You can find 5 or 6 topics for your psych. paper if you look on p. 323 of the text.

5. I spent ninety five dollars on a blood test, but the doc. couldn't find anything wrong with me.

6. The last chapt. of our Intro. to Business textbook has a helpful section on writing a resumé.

7. Jan. 15, 2005, is the day I moved into Carlton Apts. in New Bedford, Mass.

8. Thomas started volunteering at the Red Cross during his sr. year in high school.

9. My father used to dream about becoming a scientist and working in one of the labs at NASA.

10. My neighbors had to wait 15 minutes for somebody from the police dept. to arrive.

Exercise 35   Punctuation: A Comprehensive Exercise

In the following sentences, add punctuation where it is needed and correct any punctuation errors.

1. After I pay off my college loans Sam said I can start saving for a house.

2. Macaroni and cheese which is my childrens favorite food is an easy meal to make when youre in a hurry.

3. Helena doesnt like to fly instead she drives long distances to see her son and daughter in law.

4. Lester had a hard time dealing with his puppies energy so he enrolled them in an obedience class for young dogs.

5. Prof. Marcus asked Does anyone want to do some work for extra credit

6. Prof. Marcus asked if anyone wanted to do some work for extra credit

7. After she moved to Los Angeles Sally considered a career in three fields computers health and education.

8. My boyfriend knows all about Jefferson community hospital because he spent two months there last Feb.

9. My father wants me to read a book called The purpose-driven life he loved it and wants to pass it on.

10. Boris used to call me from work then his supervisor warned him about making too many personal calls.

Exercise 36   Punctuation: Another Comprehensive Exercise

In the following sentences, add punctuation where it is needed and correct any punctuation errors.

1. Until Mitchell gets rid of that broken down truck I wont go anywhere with him.

2. My toddler dragged me out of bed at 7 a.m. consequently I got an early start on my chores on Sat. morning.

3. If you see Chelsea tell her to return my black dress gold sandals and hoop earrings before the weekend.

4. This summer, I found a box full of my grandparents old photographs their wedding pictures baby pictures and birthday celebrations.

5. No I don't have a boyfriend Mom but I don't want to meet Mrs. Youngs lovely nephew from Texas.

6. A movie that my two little boys love is The Wizard of Oz

7. I was born on Sept 29 1985 in Boulder, Col. but spent most of my childhood with my grandmother in the east.

8. A few years ago aunt Marlene's favorite song was I hope you Dance.

9. After I saw dozens of cockroaches in my kitchen I spent one hundred and thirty-three dollars for pest control.

10. You like an active social life and Rick likes to stay home but both of you will be satisfied if you learn to compromise.

Connect

Exercise 37 **Editing a Paragraph for Errors in Punctuation**

Edit the following paragraph for errors in punctuation. You may have to add, omit, or change punctuation.

I am a receptionist in the office of a large Physical Therapy Center. My job has brought me many new friends; and each one has a special quality. Among these friends are Lynne Povitch, the manager of the center, Andrew Falzone, an experienced thera-pist specializing in back injuries, Kristin Wing, a therapist specializing in hand and wrist therapy, Alicia nardello, a therapy student training at the center, and Arthur Con-nolly, the office custodian. I know when Lynne Povitch has arrived at the office because she always sings the same song; You Had A Bad Day. Although her choice of song is a bit negative, Lynne sings it in a cheery voice. Andrew Falzone arrives each day in worn jeans and a hawaiian shirt; however, he carries a top of the line leather briefcase. He is a serious person dedicated to his work but he has a new joke for me every day. Kristin Wing loves to bake, and brings homemade cookies, muffins, or Banana bread to the office every Friday. Alicia Nardello, the trainee therapist spends most of her day assisting the other therapists. She runs from one piece of equipment to another. Sometimes she distributes fresh, hot towels or lotion at other times, she finds files or charts. Alicia is a tiny woman who scurries like a mouse and always smiles. Everyones favorite staff member is Arthur Connolly. he is respected because he can repair anything without losing his cheerful, calm personality. However, he is loved for his generosity. He has time to listen to every member of the office. I have confided in him many times. Arthur never proposes a solution to my problems but his willingness to listen to my stories allows me to think through my worries and find my own way to deal with them. When I think about the kindness, humor, and spirit of my office friends, I know that I am lucky to work in an environment, with so many special people.

Quick Question

Does the following sentence contain a spelling error? Yes/No

Ryan has been conserveing gas by checking his gas receipts carefully, cutting back on trips to the mall, and remaining on campus between classes instead of leaving for lunch.

(After you study this chapter, you will be confident of your answer)

Spelling

No one is a perfect speller, but there are ways to become a better speller. If you can learn a few spelling rules, you can answer many of your spelling questions.

VOWELS AND CONSONANTS

To understand the spelling rules, you need to know the difference between vowels and consonants. **Vowels** are the letters *a, e, i, o, u,* and sometimes *y.* **Consonants** are all the other letters.

The letter *y* is a vowel when it has a vowel sound.

examples:

silly (The *y* sounds like *ee,* a vowel sound.)
cry (The *y* sounds like *i,* a vowel sound.)

The letter *y* is a consonant when it has a consonant sound.

examples:

yellow (The *y* has a consonant sound.)
yesterday (The *y* has a consonant sound.)

SPELLING RULE 1: DOUBLING A FINAL CONSONANT

Double the final consonant of a word if all three of the following are true:

1. the word is one syllable, or the accent is on the last syllable,
2. the word ends in a single consonant preceded by a single vowel, and
3. the ending you are adding starts with a vowel.

examples:

begin	+	ing	=	beginning
shop	+	er	=	shopper
stir	+	ed	=	stirred
occur	+	ed	=	occurred
fat	+	est	=	fattest
pin	+	ing	=	pinning

Exercise 1 **Doubling a Final Consonant**

Add *-ed* to the following words by applying the rules for double consonants.

1. pad _____
2. scatter _____
3. scan _____
4. track _____
5. offer _____

6. defer _____
7. strand _____
8. wander _____
9. cover _____
10. repel _____

SPELLING RULE 2: DROPPING THE FINAL *E*

Drop the final *e* before you add an ending that starts with a vowel.

examples:

observe	+	ing	=	observing
excite	+	able	=	excitable
fame	+	ous	=	famous
create	+	ive	=	creative

Keep the final *e* before an ending that starts with a consonant.

examples:

love	+	ly	=	lovely
hope	+	ful	=	hopeful
excite	+	ment	=	excitement
life	+	less	=	lifeless

Exercise 2 **Dropping the Final *e***

Combine the following words and endings by following the rule for dropping the final *e*.

1. adore + able _____
2. home + less _____

3.	active	+	ly	_____
4.	name	+	ing	_____
5.	adore	+	ing	_____
6.	encourage	+	ment	_____
7.	promote	+	ion	_____
8.	expense	+	ive	_____
9.	genuine	+	ness	_____
10.	inflate	+	able	_____

SPELLING RULE 3: CHANGING THE FINAL *Y* TO *I*

When a word ends in a consonant plus *y*, change the *y* to *i* when you add an ending.

examples:

try	+	es	=	tries
silly	+	er	=	sillier
rely	+	ance	=	reliance
tardy	+	ness	=	tardiness

> **Note:** When you add *-ing* to words ending in *y*, always keep the *y*.

examples:

cry	+	ing	=	crying
rely	+	ing	=	relying

Exercise 3 **Changing the Final *y* to *i***

Combine the following words and endings by applying the rule for changing the final *y* to *i*.

1.	sloppy	+	er	_____
2.	hardy	+	ness	_____
3.	cry	+	er	_____
4.	pity	+	less	_____
5.	try	+	ing	_____
6.	marry	+	ed	_____
7.	apply	+	ance	_____
8.	plenty	+	ful	_____
9.	apply	+	es	_____
10.	convey	+	ed	_____

SPELLING RULE 4: ADDING *-S* OR *-ES*

Add *-es* instead of *-s* to a word if the word ends in *ch*, *sh*, *ss*, *x*, or *z*. The *-es* adds an extra syllable to the word.

examples:

box	+	es	=	boxes
witch	+	es	=	witches
class	+	es	=	classes
clash	+	es	=	clashes

Exercise 4 Adding *-s* or *-es*

Add *-s* or *-es* to the following words by applying the rule for adding *-s* or *-es*.

1. astonish _____
2. perch _____
3. glass _____
4. bunch _____
5. fix _____

6. fetch _____
7. wonder _____
8. block _____
9. fizz _____
10. splash _____

SPELLING RULE 5: USING *IE* OR *EI*

Use *i* before *e* except after *c*, or when the sound is like *a*, as in *neighbor* and *weigh*.

examples of *i* before *e*:

relief   field   friend   piece

examples of *e* before *i*:

conceive   sleigh   weight   receive

Exercise 5 Using *ie* or *ei*

Add *ie* or *ei* to the following words by applying the rules for using *ie* or *ei*.

1. bel _ _ ve
2. dec _ _ t
3. cr _ _ d
4. th_ _f
5. _ _ ght

6. misch _ _ f
7. r _ _ ns
8. gr _ _ f
9. perc _ _ ve
10. n _ _ ce

Exercise 6 Spelling Rules: A Comprehensive Exercise

Combine the following words and endings by applying the spelling rules.

1. coax   + s *or* es   _____
2. toy   + s *or* es   _____
3. deny   + s *or* es   _____
4. bounty   + ful   _____
5. conserve   + ing   _____
6. shape   + less   _____

7. force	+	ful	_____
8. force	+	ing	_____
9. confer	+	ed	_____
10. plan	+	er	_____

Exercise 7   **Spelling Rules: Another Comprehensive Exercise**

Combine the following words and endings by applying the spelling rules.

1. ready	+	ness	_____
2. commit	+	ment	_____
3. commit	+	ed	_____
4. forget	+	ing	_____
5. hatch	+	s *or* es	_____
6. harass	+	s *or* es	_____
7. filthy	+	er	_____
8. sleigh	+	s *or* es	_____
9. carry	+	ed	_____
10. rumor	+	ed	_____

Collaborate

Exercise 8   **Creating Examples for the Spelling Rules**

Working with a partner or group, write examples for the following rules.

Spelling Rule 1: Doubling the Final Consonant
Double the final consonant of a word if all three of the following are true:

1. the word is one syllable, or the accent is on the last syllable,
2. the word ends in a single consonant preceded by a single vowel, and
3. the ending you added starts with a vowel.

example:

1. Write a word that is one syllable (or the accent is on the last syllable), and that ends in a consonant preceded by a single vowel: _____
2. Write an ending that starts with a vowel: _____
3. Combine the word and the ending: _____

Spelling Rule 2: Dropping the Final *e*
Drop the final *e* before you add an ending that starts with a vowel.

example:

1. Write a word that ends with an *e:* _____
2. Write an ending that starts with a vowel: _____
3. Combine the word and the ending: _____

Spelling Rule 3: Changing the Final *y* to *i*
When a word ends in a consonant plus *y*, change the *y* to *i* when you add an ending. (Note: When you add -*ing* to words ending in *y*, always keep the *y*.)

example:

1. Write a word that ends in a consonant plus *y:* _____
2. Write an ending (not an *-ing* ending): _____
3. Combine the word and the ending: _____

Spelling Rule 4: Adding *-s* or *-es*

Add *-es* instead of *-s* to a word if the word ends in *ch, sh, ss, x,* or *z.* The *-es* adds an extra syllable to the word.

example:

1. Write a word that ends in *ch, sh, ss, x,* or *z:* _____
2. Add *-es* to the word: _____

Spelling Rule 5: Using *ie* or *ei*

Use *i* before *e,* except after *c,* or when the sound is like *a,* as in *neighbor* and *weigh.*

example:

1. Write three words that use *i* before *e:* _____, _____, _____
2. Write one word that uses *ei:* _____

Exercise 9   **Editing a Paragraph for Spelling Errors**

Connect

Correct the ten spelling errors in the following paragraph. Write your corrections above each error.

Last night, when my neice Ella asked me to help her with her homework, I suddenly

realized how bad my spelling truly is. Here I was, triing hard to help a nine-year-old

child with an essay she had written about a beautyful day at the beach. While I know

something about beachs, I don't know much about puting a paper together. In fact, I

think my writing is hopless, and I will not be surprised if someday soon Ella catchs me

in a mistake or two, especially in spelling. I am almost ready to spend some time learn-

ing to be a better speller. Not only would Ella respect me more, but I also beleive that

all my written work—business letters, job applications, reports, and forms—would be

more convinceing if I could remove the sloppyness of bad spelling. In addition, learn-

ing to spell could be my first step to better writing.

Exercise 10   **Editing a Paragraph for Spelling Errors**

Correct the eight spelling errors in the following paragraph. Write your corrections above each error.

I have had few experiences worse than the sudden suspicion of a problem with my

car. The worrys may begin when I sense a slight hesitation as I begin a turn. At that moment, I fear that the car will stall and I will be hit by the car behind me. After I feel this hesitation once, I wait for it anxiously each time I turn. Another occurence that sends me into a panic is a strange sound that suddenly joins the usual car noises. The sound can be a clicking, wheezing, grinding, or spining noise. At first, I am likely to pretend that the noise was a one-time event, such as a pebble hiting the underside of the car or a sound completly unrelated to the car, such as the sound of a large truck comeing to a stop. Eventually, I percieve the reality of the situation and admit that the noise is now constant. It makes no difference what event causes me to expect a car problem, for each incident has that same effect on me. Any slight change in my car's behavior brings me the kind of excitment I don't need in my life.

HOW DO YOU SPELL IT? ONE WORD OR TWO?

Sometimes you can be confused about certain words. You are not sure whether to combine them to make one word or to spell them as two words. The lists below show some commonly confused words.

Words That Should Not Be Combined

a lot	even though	home run
all right	every time	in front
dining room	good night	living room
each other	high school	no one

Words That Should Be Combined

another	nevertheless
bathroom	newspapers
bedroom	playroom
bookkeeper	roommate
cannot	schoolteacher
downstairs	southeast, northwest, etc.
good-bye, goodbye, or good-by	throughout
grandmother	worthwhile
nearby	yourself, myself, himself, etc.

Words Whose Spelling Depends on Their Meaning

one word: *Already* means "before."
He offered to do the dishes, but I had *already* done them.
two words: *All ready* means "ready."
My dog was *all ready* to play Frisbee.

one word: *Altogether* means "entirely."
That movie was *altogether* too confusing.
two words: *All together* means "in a group."
My sisters were *all together* in the kitchen.

one word: *Always* means "every time."
My grandfather is *always* right about baseball statistics.
two words: *All ways* means "every path" or "every aspect."
We tried *all ways* to get to the beach house.
He is a gentleman in *all ways*.

one word: *Anymore* means "any longer."
I do not want to exercise *anymore*.
two words: *Any more* means "additional."
Are there *any more* pickles?

one word: *Anyone* means "any person at all."
Is *anyone* home?
two words: *Any one* means "one person or thing in a special group."
I'll take *any one* of the chairs on sale.
He offered *any one* of the students a ride home.

one word: *Apart* means "separate."
Liam stood *apart* from his friends.
two words: *A part* is a piece or section.
I read *a part* of the chapter.

one word: *Everyday* means "ordinary."
Tim was wearing his *everyday* clothes.
two words: *Every day* means "each day."
Sam jogs *every day*.

one word: *Everyone* means "all the people."
Everyone has bad days.
two words: *Every one* means "all the people or things in a specific group."
My father asked *every one* of the neighbors for a donation to the Red
    Cross.

one word: *Maybe* means "perhaps."
Maybe you can go to a college near your home.
two words: *May be* means "might be."
Sam *may be* the right person for the job.

one word: *Thank-you* is an adjective that describes a certain kind of
    note or letter.
Heather wrote her grandfather a *thank-you* note.
two words: We state our gratitude by saying, "*Thank you*."
"*Thank you* for lending me your car," Kyle said.

Exercise 11 How Do You Spell It? One Word or Two?

Circle the correct word in the following sentences.

1. It was an (everyday / every day) kind of luncheon; (nevertheless /
   never the less), I was glad to have been invited.

2. Steve saw (apart / a part) of the movie, but he left after ten minutes
   because the story didn't seem (worthwhile / worth while).

3. In my mother's apartment, the (livingroom / living room) is large and
   comfortable, but the (bedroom / bed room) is tiny and cramped.

4. I (cannot / can not) figure out how (everyone / every one) of my
   shirts got stained with blue ink.

5. My best friend lives (nearby / near by), and we see each other (alot / a lot).

6. My son was (already / all ready) to spend more time in the (playroom / play room) at the local mall.

7. Years after he graduated from college, Alonzo sent a (thank-you / thank you) letter to the (schoolteacher / school teacher) who had helped him learn to read.

8. You (always / all ways) nag me about putting gas in the car, (even-though / even though) you know I have never let the gauge get to "Empty."

9. I waited for a phone call (throughout / through out) the day, but (no one / noone) called with the results of my blood test.

10. Often my local (newspaper / news paper) is full of depressing stories of crime, natural disasters, and war, but yesterday the paper reported an (altogether / all together) inspiring story about a lost boy rescued by a search party of volunteers.

Connect

Exercise 12 **How Do You Spell It? One Word or Two?**

The following paragraph contains ten errors in word combinations. Correct the errors in the space above each line.

   I have always been interested in numbers, and math has been my favorite subject

for years, so a career in accounting has been my goal for years. My mother, who had

only a highschool education, has worked as a book keeper for many years. However, I

have a higher goal for my self and want to be an accountant. I have all ready applied to

several colleges near by and I hope that I will be accepted into one with a good

accounting program. Eventhough I would like to experience college life on my own,

I can not afford the cost of my own apartment, even if I shared with a room mate.

Living in a dormitory would also be expensive. As a person who likes to account for

every penny, I am all ways looking for the most economical way to reach my goal,

even if it means sleeping in my old bed room at home for a few more years.

A LIST OF COMMONLY MISSPELLED WORDS

Below is a list of words you use often in your writing. Study this list and use it as a reference.

1. absence	6. acquire	11. a lot
2. absent	7. across	12. all right
3. accept	8. actually	13. almost
4. ache	9. advertise	14. always
5. achieve	10. again	15. amateur

16. American
17. answer
18. anxious
19. apology
20. apparent
21. appetite
22. appreciate
23. argue
24. argument
25. asked
26. athlete
27. attempt
28. August
29. aunt
30. author
31. automobile
32. autumn
33. avenue
34. awful
35. awkward
36. balance
37. basically
38. because
39. becoming
40. beginning
41. behavior
42. belief
43. believe
44. benefit
45. bicycle
46. bought
47. breakfast
48. breathe
49. brilliant
50. brother
51. brought
52. bruise
53. build
54. bulletin
55. bureau
56. buried
57. business
58. busy
59. calendar
60. cannot
61. career
62. careful
63. catch
64. category
65. caught
66. cemetery
67. cereal
68. certain

69. chair
70. cheat
71. chicken
72. chief
73. children
74. cigarette
75. citizen
76. city
77. college
78. color
79. comfortable
80. committee
81. competition
82. conscience
83. convenient
84. conversation
85. copy
86. cough
87. cousin
88. criticism
89. criticize
90. crowded
91. daily
92. daughter
93. deceive
94. decide
95. definite
96. dentist
97. dependent
98. deposit
99. describe
100. desperate
101. development
102. different
103. dilemma
104. dining
105. direction
106. disappearance
107. disappoint
108. discipline
109. disease
110. divide
111. doctor
112. doesn't
113. don't
114. doubt
115. during
116. dying
117. early
118. earth
119. eighth
120. eligible
121. embarrass

122. encouragement
123. enough
124. environment
125. especially
126. etc.
127. every
128. exact
129. exaggeration
130. excellent
131. except
132. excite
133. exercise
134. existence
135. expect
136. experience
137. explanation
138. factory
139. familiar
140. family
141. fascinating
142. February
143. finally
144. forehead
145. foreign
146. forty
147. fourteen
148. friend
149. fundamental
150. general
151. generally
152. goes
153. going
154. government
155. grammar
156. grateful
157. grocery
158. guarantee
159. guard
160. guess
161. guidance
162. guide
163. half
164. handkerchief
165. happiness
166. heavy
167. height
168. heroes
169. holiday
170. hospital
171. humorous
172. identity
173. illegal
174. imaginary

175. immediately
176. important
177. independent
178. integration
179. intelligent
180. interest
181. interfere
182. interpretation
183. interrupt
184. irrelevant
185. irritable
186. iron
187. island
188. January
189. jewelry
190. judgment
191. kindergarten
192. kitchen
193. knowledge
194. laboratory
195. language
196. laugh
197. leisure
198. length
199. library
200. listen
201. loneliness
202. lying
203. maintain
204. maintenance
205. marriage
206. mathematics
207. meant
208. measure
209. medicine
210. million
211. miniature
212. minute
213. muscle
214. mysterious
215. naturally
216. necessary
217. neighbor
218. nervous
219. nickel
220. niece
221. ninety
222. ninth

223. occasion
224. o'clock
225. often
226. omission
227. once
228. operate
229. opinion
230. optimist
231. original
232. parallel
233. particular
234. peculiar
235. perform
236. perhaps
237. permanent
238. persevere
239. personnel
240. persuade
241. physically
242. pleasant
243. possess
244. possible
245. potato
246. practical
247. prefer
248. prejudice
249. prescription
250. presence
251. president
252. privilege
253. probably
254. professor
255. psychology
256. punctuation
257. pursue
258. quart
259. really
260. receipt
261. receive
262. recognize
263. recommend
264. reference
265. religious
266. reluctantly
267. remember
268. resource
269. restaurant
270. rhythm

271. ridiculous
272. right
273. sandwich
274. Saturday
275. scene
276. schedule
277. scissors
278. secretary
279. seize
280. several
281. severely
282. significant
283. similar
284. since
285. sincerely
286. soldier
287. sophomore
288. strength
289. studying
290. success
291. surely
292. surprise
293. taught
294. temperature
295. theater
296. thorough
297. thousand
298. tied
299. tomorrow
300. tongue
301. tragedy
302. trouble
303. truly
304. twelfth
305. unfortunately
306. unknown
307. until
308. unusual
309. using
310. variety
311. vegetable
312. Wednesday
313. weird
314. which
315. writing
316. written
317. yesterday

Exercise 13   **A Comprehensive Exercise on Spelling**

The following exercise contains ten spelling errors, including errors related to the spelling rules, one- or two-word errors, and errors related to commonly misspelled words. Correct the errors in the space above each line.

My brother is the only member of our family who reads for pleasure. I can read, but

I am more intrested in math than in English. I don't read books or magazines for enjoy-

ment. In addition, I never read the news paper becose I use the Internet if I need to

find information. My sister is not much of a reader, either. She wants to be a graphic

designer and spends more time looking at cartoons, games, and videos than enjoying

books. However, Adam, my older brother, reads all the time. In fact, he will read any-

thing, including the cerial box as he eats breakfast. He is the happyest when he comes

home from the library with an armful of books. On many weekends, I have seen him

sit on his bed for hours, piles of books stackked around him. Adam's favorite books

are about the unknown or the imaginery. He dreams of becomming an author who

specializes in tales of fantasy and the supernatural. If reading is good training for that

type of writeing, then Adam should be a tremendous sucess.

Words That Sound Alike/Look Alike

WORDS THAT SOUND ALIKE/LOOK ALIKE

Words that sound alike or look alike can be confusing. Here is a list of some of the confusing words. Study this list, and make a note of any words that give you trouble.

a, an, and
A is used before a word beginning with a consonant or consonant sound.
>   Jason bought *a* car.
An is used before a word beginning with a vowel or vowel sound.
>   Nancy took *an* apple to work.
And joins words or ideas.
>   Pudding *and* cake are my favorite desserts.
>   Fresh vegetables taste delicious, *and* they are nutritious.

accept, except
Accept means "to receive."
>   I *accept* your apology.
Except means "excluding."
>   I'll give you all my books *except* my dictionary.

addition, edition

An *addition* is something that is added.

>My father built an *addition* to our house in the form of a porch.

An *edition* is an issue of a newspaper or one of a series of printings of a book.

>I checked the latest *edition* of the <u>Daily News</u> to see if my advertisement is in it.

advice, advise

Advice is an opinion offered as a guide; it is what you give someone.

>Betty asked for my *advice* about finding a job.

Advise is what you do when you give an opinion offered as a guide.

>I couldn't *advise* Betty about finding a job.

affect, effect

Affect means "to influence something."

>Getting a bad grade will *affect* my chances for a scholarship.

Effect means "a result" or "to cause something to happen."

>Your kindness had a great *effect* on me.

>The committee struggled to *effect* a compromise.

aloud, allowed

Aloud means "out loud."

>The teacher read the story *aloud.*

Allowed means "permitted."

>I'm not *allowed* to skateboard on those steps.

all ready, already

All ready means "ready."

>The dog was *all ready* to go for a walk.

Already means "before."

>David had *already* made the salad.

altar, alter

An *altar* is a table or place in a church.

>They were married in front of the *altar.*

Alter means "to change."

>My plane was delayed, so I had to *alter* my plans for the evening.

angel, angle

An *angel* is a heavenly being.

>That night, I felt an *angel* guiding me.

An *angle* is the shape formed by two intersecting points.

>The road turned at a sharp *angle.*

are, our

Are is a verb, the plural of *is.*

>We *are* friends of the mayor.

Our means "belonging to us."

>We have *our* family quarrels.

beside, besides

Beside means "next to."

>He sat *beside* me at the concert.

Besides means "in addition."

> I would never lie to you; *besides*, I have no reason to lie.

brake, break

Brake means "to stop," or "a device for stopping."

> That truck *brakes* at railroad crossings.
>
> When he saw the animal on the road, he hit the *brakes*.

Break means "to come apart," or "to make something come apart."

> The eggs are likely to *break*.
>
> I can *break* the seal on that package.

breath, breathe

Breath is the air you take in, and it rhymes with "death."

> I was running so fast that I lost my *breath*.

Breathe means "to take in air."

> He found it hard to *breathe* in high altitudes.

buy, by

Buy means "to purchase something."

> Sylvia wants to *buy* a shovel.

By means "near," "by means of," or "before."

> He sat *by* his sister.
>
> I learn *by* taking good notes in class.
>
> *By* ten o'clock, Nick was tired.

capital, capitol

Capital means "a city" or "wealth."

> Albany is the *capital* of New York.
>
> Jack invested his *capital* in real estate.

A *capitol* is a building.

> The city has a famous *capitol* building.

cereal, serial

Cereal is a breakfast food or type of grain.

> My favorite *cereal* is Cheerios.

Serial means "in a series."

> Look for the *serial* number on the appliance.

choose, chose

Choose means "to select." It rhymes with "snooze."

> Today I am going to *choose* a new sofa.

Chose is the past tense of *choose*.

> Yesterday I *chose* a new rug.

close, clothes, cloths

Close means "near" or "intimate." It can also mean "to end or shut something."

> We live *close* to the train station.
>
> James and Margie are *close* friends.
>
> Noreen wants to *close* her eyes for ten minutes.

Clothes are wearing apparel.

> Eduardo has new *clothes*.

Cloths are pieces of fabric.

> I clean the silver with damp *cloths* and a special polish.

coarse, course

Coarse means "rough" or "crude."

> The top of the table had a *coarse* texture.
>
> His language was *coarse.*

A *course* is a direction or path. It is also a subject in school.

> The hurricane took a northern *course.*
>
> In my freshman year, I took a *course* in drama.

complement, compliment

Complement means "complete" or "make better."

> The colors in that room *complement* the style of the furniture.

A *compliment* is praise.

> Trevor gave me a *compliment* about my cooking.

conscience, conscious

Your *conscience* is your inner, moral guide.

> His *conscience* bothered him when he told a lie.

Conscious means "aware" or "awake."

> The accident victim was not fully *conscious.*

council, counsel

A *council* is a group of people.

> The city *council* meets tonight.

Counsel means "advice" or "to give advice."

> I need your *counsel* about my investments.
>
> My father always *counsels* me about my career.

decent, descent

Decent means "suitable" or "proper."

> I hope Mike gets a *decent* job.

Descent means "the process of going down, falling, or sinking."

> The plane began its *descent* to the airport.

desert, dessert

A *desert* is a dry land. To *desert* means "to abandon."

> To survive a trip across the *desert*, people need water.
>
> He will never *desert* a friend.

Dessert is the sweet food we eat at the end of a meal.

> I want ice cream for *dessert.*

do, due

Do means "perform."

> I have to stop complaining; I *do* it constantly.

Due means "owing" or "because of."

> The rent is *due* tomorrow.
>
> The game was canceled *due* to rain.

does, dose

Does is a form of *do.*

> My father *does* the laundry.

A *dose* is a quantity of medicine.

> Whenever I had a cold, my mother gave me a *dose* of cough syrup.

fair, fare

Fair means "unbiased." It can also mean "promising" or "good."

The judge's decision was *fair*.

José has a *fair* chance of winning the title.

A *fare* is a fee for transportation.

My subway *fare* is going up.

farther, further

Farther means "at a greater physical distance."

His house is a few blocks *farther* down the street.

Further means greater or additional. Use it when you are not describing a physical distance.

My second French class gave me *further* training in French conversation.

flour, flower

Flour is ground-up grain, an ingredient used in cooking.

I use whole-wheat *flour* in my muffins.

A *flower* is a blossom.

She wore a *flower* in her hair.

forth, fourth

Forth means "forward."

The pendulum on the clock swung back and *forth*.

Fourth means "number four in a sequence."

I was *fourth* in line for the tickets.

hear, here

Hear means "to receive sounds in the ear."

I can *hear* the music.

Here is a place.

We can have the meeting *here*.

heard, herd

Heard is the past tense of *hear*.

I *heard* you talk in your sleep last night.

A *herd* is a group of animals.

The farmer has a fine *herd* of cows.

hole, whole

A *hole* is an empty place or opening.

I see a *hole* in the wall.

Whole means "complete" or "entire."

Silvio gave me the *whole* steak.

isle, aisle

An *isle* is an island.

We visited the *isle* of Capri.

An *aisle* is a passageway between sections of seats.

The flight attendant came down the *aisle* and offered us coffee.

its, it's

Its means "belonging to it."

The car lost *its* rear bumper.

It's is a shortened form of *it is* or *it has.*
>   *It's* a beautiful day.
>   *It's* been a pleasure to meet you.

knew, new
Knew is the past tense of *know.*
>   I *knew* Teresa in high school.
New means "fresh, recent, not old."
>   I want some *new* shoes.

know, no
Know means "to understand."
>   They *know* how to play soccer.
No is a negative.
>   Carla has *no* fear of heights.

Exercise 1   Words That Sound Alike/Look Alike

Circle the correct word in the following sentences.

1. When I first saw the (desert / dessert) in a Tucson sunset, the sight was so beautiful that I had to catch my (breath / breathe).

2. Ron and Sandy were (conscience / conscious) of the fact that they would need more (capital / capitol) to start their own business.

3. Marcy hoped that, (buy / by) working extra hours, she would save enough money to (buy / by) her brother a special wedding present.

4. After graduation, the students felt that they could go (forth / fourth) into the world and face (knew / new) challenges.

5. I (heard / herd) that (hole / whole)-grain bread is better for people than white bread.

6. I hate to read (allowed / aloud); (beside / besides), I have a cold today, and my voice is weak.

7. Lee Anne had (all ready / already) eaten all the leftover macaroni and cheese by the time I got home; the only thing left in the refrigerator was a box of (cereal / serial).

8. Martin (choose / chose) to make his (decent / descent) into a world of violence and despair instead of fighting for a better life.

9. The design of the building is all sharp (angles / angels); the (affect / effect) is cold and intimidating.

10. Let's stop this arguing; we (are / our) wasting (are / our) time over silly disagreements.

Exercise 2   Words That Sound Alike/Look Alike

Collaborate

With a partner or a group, write one sentence for each of the words below. When you have completed this exercise, exchange it with another group's completed exercise for evaluation.

1. a. its _____

    b. it's _____

2. a. addition　　_____

　　　b. edition　　_____

3. a. accept　　_____

　　　b. except　　_____

4. a. brake　　_____

　　　b. break　　_____

5. a. close　　_____

　　　b. clothes　　_____

　　　c. cloths　　_____

6. a. farther　　_____

　　　b. further　　_____

7. a. hear　　_____

　　　b. here　　_____

8. a. isle　　_____

　　　b. aisle　　_____

9. a. fair　　_____

　　　b. fare　　_____

10. a. its　　_____

　　　b. it's　　_____

Connect

| Exercise 3 | **Correcting Errors in Words That Sound Alike/Look Alike** |

The following paragraph has ten errors in words that sound alike or look alike. Correct the errors in the space above each error.

　　If someone asked me to chose a perfect day, I would not altar one moment of yesterday. Twenty-four hours ago, my brother returned from months of military duty in Iraq. Once I had been informed of his return, I spent the final days of his overseas service holding my breathe. I was conscience of the many stories of soldiers being wounded or killed days before their tours of duty were over. Every time I herd a knock at the door, I feared bad news. Yet the day came when Carleton was supposed to arrive, and my sisters and I were already to meet are hero at the airport. Seeing Carleton was better than I had expected. He looked strong, healthy, and happy. Being able to hug him was pure joy. I felt as if a whole in my heart had been filled with happiness. Fear had lost it's power over me, and I new real peace at last.

Exercise 4   **Correcting Errors in Words That Sound Alike/Look Alike**

Connect

The following paragraph has eight errors in words that sound alike or look alike. Correct the errors in the space above each error.

Traveling by plane lost its appeal for me after a terrible experience last week. I and the two hundred other passengers on my flight boarded the aircraft on time. The weather seemed fine, but none of us new that we would be stuck on the ground for hours because of terrible storms at are destination. After we had been sitting on the runway with the engines running for about fifty minutes, the plane suddenly turned back to the terminal. Soon the pilot announced that we would be remaining at the airport until the blizzard-like weather cleared in Chicago, our destination. I could here the entire cabin begin to groan and moan. People realized that we could expect a long delay before we took off for Chicago. However, no one expected to spend seven hours on the grounded aircraft. We never returned to an airport building but sat in our seats. During that time, the air in the plane became stifling hot, it was difficult to breath, and the flight attendants ran out of snacks and beverages. In edition, the toilets overflowed. Most of the passengers complained and begged to be returned to the airline terminal. Although babies cried and older people felt weak, the airline choose to keep the passengers on the aircraft. Most of the passengers found it difficult to except this decision. They felt that the airline had deserted them. After two or three hours of thirst, hunger, and toxic air, I came to a bitter decision. I swore to limit my future flying to absolute necessities.

MORE WORDS THAT SOUND ALIKE/LOOK ALIKE

lead, led
When *lead* rhymes with *need*, it means "to give direction, to take charge." When *lead* rhymes with *bed*, it is a metal.
　　The marching band will *lead* the parade.
　　Your bookbag is as heavy as *lead.*
Led is the past form of *lead* when it means "to take charge."
　　The cheerleaders *led* the parade last year.

loan, lone
A *loan* is something you give on the condition that it be returned.
　　When I was broke, I got a *loan* of fifty dollars from my aunt.

Lone means "solitary, alone."

> A *lone* shopper stood in the checkout line.

loose, lose

Loose means "not tight."

> In the summer, *loose* clothing keeps me cool.

To *lose* something means "to be unable to keep it."

> I'm afraid I will *lose* my car keys.

moral, morale

Moral means "upright, honorable, connected to ethical standards."

> I have a *moral* obligation to care for my children.

Morale is confidence or spirit.

> After the game, the team's *morale* was low.

pain, pane

Pain means "suffering."

> I had very little *pain* after the surgery.

A *pane* is a piece of glass.

> The girl's wild throw broke a window *pane*.

pair, pear

A *pair* is a set of two.

> Mark has a *pair* of antique swords.

A *pear* is a fruit.

> In the autumn, I like a *pear* for a snack.

passed, past

Passed means "went by." It can also mean "handed to."

> The happy days *passed* too quickly.
>
> Janice *passed* me the mustard.

Past means "a time before the present." It can also mean "beyond" or "by."

> The family reunion was like a trip to the *past*.
>
> Rick ran *past* the tennis courts.

patience, patients

Patience is calm endurance.

> When I am caught in a traffic jam, I should have more *patience*.

Patients are people under medical care.

> There are too many *patients* in the doctor's waiting room.

peace, piece

Peace is calmness.

> Looking at the ocean brings me a sense of *peace*.

A *piece* is a part of something.

> Norman took a *piece* of coconut cake.

personal, personnel

Personal means "connected to a person." It can also mean "intimate."

> Whether to lease or own a car is a *personal* choice.
>
> That information is too *personal* to share.

Personnel are the staff in an office.

> The Digby Electronics Company is developing a new health plan for its *personnel*.

plain, plane
Plain means "simple," "clear," or "ordinary." It can also mean "flat land."
> The restaurant serves *plain* but tasty food.
> Her house was in the center of a windy *plain*.
A *plane* is an aircraft.
> We took a small *plane* to the island.

presence, presents
Your *presence* is your attendance, your being somewhere.
> We request your *presence* at our wedding.
Presents are gifts.
> My daughter got too many birthday *presents*.

principal, principle
Principal means "most important." It also means "the head of a school."
> My *principal* reason for quitting is the low salary.
> The *principal* of Crestview Elementary School is popular with students.
A *principle* is a guiding rule.
> Betraying a friend is against my *principles*.

quiet, quit, quite
Quiet means "without noise."
> The library has many *quiet* corners.
Quit means "stop."
> Will you *quit* complaining?
Quite means "truly" or "exactly."
> Victor's speech was *quite* convincing.

rain, reign, rein
Rain is wet weather.
> We have had a week of *rain*.
To *reign* is to rule; *reign* is royal rule.
> King Arthur's *reign* in Camelot is the subject of many poems.
A *rein* is a leather strap in an animal's harness.
> When Charlie got on the horse, he held the *reins* very tight.

right, rite, write
Right is a direction (the opposite of left). It can also mean "correct."
> To get to the gas station, turn *right* at the corner.
> On my sociology test, I got nineteen out of twenty questions *right*.
A *rite* is a ceremony.
> I am interested in the funeral *rites* of other cultures.
To *write* is to set down words.
> Brian has to *write* a book report.

sight, site, cite
A *sight* is something you can see.
> The truck stop was a welcome *sight*.
A *site* is a location.
> The city is building a courthouse on the *site* of my old school.
Cite means to quote an authority. It can also mean to give an example.
> In her term paper, Christina wanted to *cite* several computer experts.
> When my father lectured me on speeding, he *cited* the story of my best
> friend's car accident.

sole, soul

A *sole* is the bottom of a foot or shoe.

My left boot needs a new *sole*.

A *soul* is the spiritual part of a person.

Some people say meditation is good for the *soul*.

stair, stare

A *stair* is a step.

The toddler carefully climbed each *stair*.

A *stare* is a long, fixed look.

I wish that woman wouldn't *stare* at me.

stake, steak

A *stake* is a stick driven into the ground. It can also mean "at risk" or "in question."

The gardener put *stakes* around the tomato plants.

Keith was nervous because his career was at *stake*.

A *steak* is a piece of meat or fish.

I like my *steak* cooked medium rare.

stationary, stationery

Stationary means "standing still."

As the speaker presented his speech, he remained *stationary*.

Stationery is writing paper.

For my birthday, my uncle gave me some *stationery* with my name
     printed on it.

than, then

Than is used to compare things.

My dog is more intelligent *than* many people.

Then means "at that time."

I lived in Buffalo for two years; *then* I moved to Albany.

their, there, they're

Their means "belonging to them."

My grandparents donated *their* old television to a women's shelter.

There means "at that place." It can also be used as an introductory word.

Sit *there*, next to Simone.

There is a reason for his happiness.

They're is a short form of *they are*.

Jaime and Sandra are visiting; *they're* my cousins.

thorough, through, threw

Thorough means "complete."

I did a *thorough* cleaning of my closet.

Through means "from one side to the other." It can also mean "finished."

We drove *through* Greenview on our way to Lake Western.

I'm *through* with my studies.

Threw is the past form of *throw*.

I *threw* the moldy bread into the garbage.

to, too, two

To means "in a direction toward." It is also a word that can go in front of a verb.

I am driving *to* Miami.

Selena loves *to* write poems.

Too means "also." It also means "very."

> Anita played great golf; Adam did well, *too*.
> It is *too* kind of you to visit.

Two is the number.

> Mr. Almeida owns *two* clothing stores.

vain, vane, vein

Vain means "conceited." It also means "unsuccessful."

> Victor is *vain* about his dark, curly hair.
> The doctor made a *vain* attempt to revive the patient.

A *vane* is a device that moves to indicate the direction of the wind.

> There was an old weather *vane* on the barn roof.

A *vein* is a blood vessel.

> I could see the *veins* in his hands.

waist, waste

The *waist* is the middle part of the body.

> He had a leather belt around his *waist*.

Waste means "to use carelessly." It also means "thrown away because it is useless."

> I can't *waste* my time watching trashy television shows.
> That manufacturing plant has many *waste* products.

wait, weight

Wait means "to hold oneself ready for something."

> I can't *wait* until my check arrives.

Weight means "heaviness."

> He tested the *weight* of the bat.

weather, whether

Weather refers to the conditions outside.

> If the *weather* is warm, I'll go swimming.

Whether means "if."

> *Whether* you help me or not, I'll paint the hallway.

were, we're, where

Were is the past form of *are*.

> Only last year, we *were* scared freshmen.

We're is the short form of *we are*.

> Today *we're* confident sophomores.

Where refers to a place.

> Show me *where* you used to play basketball.

whined, wind, wined

Whined means "complained."

> Paula *whined* about the weather because the rain kept her indoors.

Wind (if it rhymes with *find*) means "to coil or wrap something" or "to turn a key."

> *Wind* that extension cord or you'll trip on it.

Wind (if it rhymes with *sinned*) is air in motion.

> The *wind* blew my cap off.

If someone *wined* you, he or she treated you to some wine.

> My brother *wined* and dined his boss.

who's, whose

Who's is a short form of *who is* or *who has*.

> *Who's* driving?
>
> *Who's* been stealing my quarters?

Whose means "belonging to whom."

> I wonder *whose* dog this is.

woman, women

Woman means "one female person."

> A *woman* in the supermarket gave me her extra coupons.

Women means "more than one female person."

> Three *women* from Missouri joined the management team.

wood, would

Wood is the hard substance in the trunks and branches of trees.

> I have a table made of a polished *wood*.

Would is the past form of *will*.

> Albert said he *would* think about the offer.

your, you're

Your means "belonging to you."

> I think you dropped *your* wallet.

You're is the short form of *you are*.

> *You're* not telling the truth.

Exercise 5 **Words That Sound Alike/Look Alike**

Circle the correct word in the following sentences.

1. (Your / You're) not looking at the good parts of (your / you're) job.

2. Al (wood / would) like to know (weather / whether) Caitlin is selling her car.

3. (Were / We're / Where) at the spot (were / we're / where) that great seafood restaurant used to be.

4. King Henry VIII of England (rained / reigned / reined) for many years and (lead / led) his people during a time of great change.

5. I have to get some good (stationary / stationery) so I can (right / rite / write) letters of application to potential employers.

6. (Their / There / They're) house has a bright and cheerful kitchen, but (their / there / they're) is something gloomy about our small kitchen.

7. Every time Irving (whined / wind / wined) about the long (wait / weight) at the ticket line, Sheila wanted to shout at him.

8. I'm not sure (who's / whose) been making those prank phone calls, but I know (who's / whose) idea it was.

9. It seems as if my boss' (sole / soul) purpose in life is to get me to (quiet / quit / quite) my job.

10. If you find out that Damon is making more money (than / then) you are, (than / then) you should ask for a raise.

Exercise 6 **Words That Look Alike/Sound Alike**

With a partner or group, write one sentence for each of the words below. When you have completed this exercise, exchange it for another group's completed exercise for evaluation.

1. a. waist _____
   b. waste _____
2. a. principal _____
   b. principle _____
3. a. quiet _____
   b. quit _____
   c. quite _____
4. a. passed _____
   b. past _____
5. a. patience _____
   b. patients _____
6. a. stake _____
   b. steak _____
7. a. loan _____
   b. lone _____
8. a. pair _____
   b. pear _____
9. a. than _____
   b. then _____
10. a. loose _____
    b. lose _____

Exercise 7 **Correcting Errors in Words That Sound Alike/Look Alike**

Connect

The following paragraph has twelve errors in words that sound alike or look alike. Correct the errors in the space above each error.

Amanda is very self-conscious when people stair at her. Her first reaction is to

assume that strangers are looking at her because something is wrong with her. She

wonders if she's wearing to much make-up, or if her outfit is too plane, or if a peace of

spinach is stuck to her teeth. Amanda is not a vane person; in fact, it's her insecurity

that puts her thorough the pane of examining herself for her flaws. To try to improve

her moral, I tell her that others are not staring because her presents is unattractive.

I advise her that everyone enjoys the site of a women with personnel style.

Connect

Exercise 8 **Correcting Errors in Words That Sound Alike/Look Alike**

The following paragraph has eight errors in words that sound alike or look alike. Correct the errors in the space above each error.

A constant complainer can become a difficult companion. When I first met Andrew, he had a tendency to comment on every small annoyance in his day. He wined about the traffic, or the heat, or the cold, or his bad luck with women. Andrew interpreted even the slightest gesture, such as a waitress in a hurry to clear a table, as an insult specifically designed to injure his sole. At first I excused his perpetual misery as a small flaw in his personality, but eventually I lost patients with Andrew. Instead of enjoying my time with him, I spent it weighting for another complaint. I eventually concluded that he was to much of a pessimist for me to tolerate. Instead of waisting my time with someone who seemed to enjoy being in a bad mood, I ended the friendship. Once I was threw with Andrew, I felt like a person who's life was suddenly brighter.

Exercise 9 **Words That Sound Alike/Look Alike: A Comprehensive Exercise**

Circle the correct word in the following sentences.

1. When I am trying to find the (right / rite / write) way to handle a big problem, my brother sometimes (councils / counsels) me.

2. I wonder if my warning had (a / an / and) (affect / effect) on Simon.

3. In my paper on the (rain / reign / rein) of Queen Victoria, I have to (sight / site / cite) at least three historians.

4. Hundreds of years ago, people wore (close / clothes / cloths) made of (coarse / course) wool (close / clothes / cloths).

5. Drive a little (farther / further) down the street, and you will see the (capital / capitol) building in the distance.

6. The doctor told the patient to increase her (does / dose) of the (pain / pane) medicine.

7. Train (fair / fare) has increased so much that (its / it's) forced many people to walk to work.

8. Above the (altar / alter) was a huge painting of an (angel / angle).

9. Whenever I go to the supermarket, I avoid the snack food (isle / aisle); all those Fritos, Doritos, salsa, and dips can add inches to my (waist / waste).

10. Every day, my grandfather rides his (stationary / stationery) bike; he gets many (complements / compliments) on his trim body.

Exercise 10 **Words That Sound Alike/Look Alike: Another Comprehensive Exercise**

Circle the correct word in the following sentences.

1. (Weather / Whether) we make it to class on time depends on you: you have to be (all ready / already) to leave when I pick you up.

2. I think a kitten (wood / would) be a welcome (addition / edition) to our family.

3. Every time I walk (passed / past) my old girlfriend's house, I find it hard to (accept / except) her decision to leave me.

4. We were wondering (who's / whose) (knew / new) car is parked in the driveway.

5. You should have a little more (patience / patients) when your father tries to give you (advice / advise).

6. Laurie is an understanding (woman / women); (beside / besides), she can keep a secret.

7. The chances for (peace / piece) in that part of the world can be improved by (farther / further) negotiations between the warring nations.

8. The amber beads you are wearing (compliment / complement) the color of (your / you're) eyes.

9. While Zack and I consumed a large pizza with three extra toppings, he (whined / wind / wined) about his struggle to (loose / lose) (wait / weight).

10. Yesterday was the (forth / fourth) time I tried to practice my speech (allowed / aloud).

Exercise 11 **Correcting Errors in Words That Sound Alike/Look Alike: A Comprehensive Exercise**

Connect

The following paragraph has eleven errors in words that sound alike or look alike. Correct the errors in the space above each line.

    One big difference between me and my parents is in the role music plays in there

lives and in mine. I want music to be everywhere in my life. When I am at home, music

channels like MTV or BET are on constantly; they are the background music for my

meals, my studies, my chores, and my free time. If I am not listening to the music on

television, I drown out the quite with CDs. In the car, I have programmed the radio

with the stations that are my favorites, and I blast the music as I drive. My parents, on

the other hand, may go threw an entire day without music. My mother and father

wood never think of turning on a music channel like VH1, which appeals to older people. My mother sometimes listens to music on the car radio, but my father tunes in to talk radio as he drives. To my parents, the principle purpose of music seems to be to act as a background at large gatherings like weddings or dances. Perhaps people our destined to brake the habit of living with music as they grow older. Still, its hard for me to except the idea that one day I, to, may loose my need for music in every part of the day and night.

Exercise 12 **Correcting Errors in Words That Sound Alike/Look Alike: A Comprehensive Exercise**

The following paragraph has eleven errors in words that sound alike or look alike. Correct the errors in the space above each line.

Color is a powerful element in our lives. Color effects our moods and behavior; our choice of colors can also make a personnel statement about the image we want to convey to others. Anyone who has ever been in a hospital remembers the muted colors of beige, green, and gray-blue that cover the walls, floors, and fabrics. These colors are supposed to be calming, but many people believe they create sadness rather then piece. Bright neon colors and flashing bars of light create excitement and invite people to video arcades, tattoo parlors, and nightclubs. Warm colors of red, gold, and green attract diners to restaurants serving home-style food such as pizza, quesadillas, and barbecued ribs. Colors matter even more when a person's identity is involved in a color choice. Women can spend hours debating the right color for a special dress or a shade of makeup. Both men and women are very conscience of the power of color in major purchases. No one wants to by a car in an unpopular shade, and a cell phone in the rite color offers more status then one in a dull color. Each season, the fashion industry introduces one or two colors that will rein as the most important shades for anyone who longs to dress stylishly. Meanwhile, home improvement stores and home design television channels advice homeowners about the latest shades for walls, carpets, and tile. Because color has a powerful influence on our mood, behavior, and self-image, choosing the rite color for one's hair, house, or hot-dog stand can be quiet a challenge.

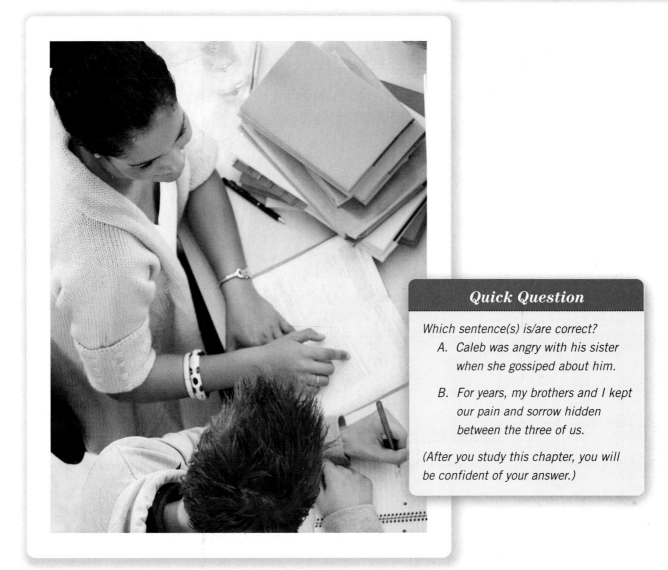

Using Prepositions Correctly

Prepositions are usually short words that often signal a kind of position, possession, or other relationship. The words that come after the preposition are part of a **prepositional phrase.** You use prepositions often because there are many expressions that contain prepositions.

Sometimes it is difficult to decide on the correct preposition. The following pages explain kinds of prepositions and their uses, and list some common prepositions.

PREPOSITIONS THAT SHOW TIME

At a specific time means "then."
> I will meet you *at* three o'clock.
> *At* 7:00 p.m., he closes the store.

By a specific time means "no later than" that time.
> You have to finish your paper *by* noon.
> I'll be home *by* 9:30 p.m.

Until a specific time means "continuing up to" that time.

> I talked on the phone *until* midnight.
> I will wait for you *until* 7:00 p.m.

In a specific time period is used with hours, minutes, days, weeks, months, or years.

> *In* a week, I'll have my diploma.
> My family hopes to visit me *in* August.

> **Note:** Write *in* the morning, *in* the afternoon, *in* the evening, but *at* night.

For a period of time means "during" that time period.

> James took music lessons *for* five years.
> I studied *for* an hour.

Since means "from then until now."

> I haven't heard from you *since* December.
> Juanita has been my friend *since* our high school days.

On a specific date means "at that time."

> I'll see you *on* March 23.
> The restaurant will open *on* Saturday.

During means "within" or "throughout" a time period.

> The baby woke up *during* the night.
> Robert worked part-time *during* the winter semester.

PREPOSITIONS TO INDICATE PLACE

On usually means "on the surface of," "on top of."

> Put the dishes *on* the table.
> They have a house *on* Second Avenue.

In usually means "within" or "inside of."

> Put the dishes *in* the cupboard.
> They have a house *in* Bolivia.

At usually means "in," "on," or "near to."

> I'll meet you *at* the market.
> The coffee shop is *at* the corner of Second Avenue and Hawthorne Road.
> Jill was standing *at* the door.

EXPRESSIONS WITH PREPOSITIONS

angry about: You are *angry about* a thing.

> Suzanne was *angry about* the dent in her car.

angry at: You are *angry at* a thing.

> Carl was *angry at* the cruel treatment of the refugees.

angry with: You are *angry with* a person.

> Richard became *angry with* his mother when she criticized him.

approve of, disapprove of: You *approve* or *disapprove* of a thing, or of a person or group's actions.

> I *approve of* the new gun law.
> I *disapprove of* smoking in public places.

argue about: You *argue about* some subject.
>   We used to *argue about* money.

argue for: You *argue for* something you want.
>   The Student Council *argued for* more student parking.

argue with: You *argue with* a person.
>   When I was a child, I spent hours *arguing with* my little sister.

arrive at: You *arrive at* a place.
>   We will *arrive at* your house tomorrow.

between, among: You use *between* with two. You use *among* with three or more.
>   It will be a secret *between* you and me.
>   We shared the secret *among* the three of us.

bored by, bored with: You are *bored by* or *bored with* something. Do *not* write *bored of*.
>   The audience was *bored by* the long movie.
>   The child became *bored with* her toys.
>   **not this:** ~~I am bored of school~~.

call on: You *call on* someone socially or to request something of a person.
>   My aunt *called on* her new neighbors.
>   Our club will *call on* you to collect tickets at the door.

call to: You *call to* someone from a distance.
>   I heard him *call to* me from the top of the hill.

call up: You *call up* someone on the telephone.
>   When she heard the news, Susan *called up* all her friends.

differ from: You *differ from* someone, or something *differs from* something.
>   Roberta *differs from* Cheri in hair color and height.
>   A van *differs from* a light truck.

differ with: You *differ with* (disagree with) someone about something.
>   Theresa *differs with* Mike on the subject of food stamps.

different from: You are *different from* someone; something is *different from* something else. Do *not* write *different than*.
>   Carl is *different from* his older brother.
>   The movie was *different from* the book.
>   **not this:** ~~The movie was different than the book.~~

grateful for: You are *grateful for* something.
>   I am *grateful for* my scholarship.

grateful to: You are *grateful to* someone.
>   My brother was *grateful to* my aunt for her advice.

interested in: You are *interested in* something.
>   The children were *interested in* playing computer games.

look at: You *look at* someone or something.
　　My sister *looked at* my haircut and laughed.

look for: You *look for* someone or something.
　　David needs to *look for* his lost key.

look up: You *look up* information.
　　I can *look up* his address in the phone book.

made of: Something or someone is *made of* something.
　　Do you think I'm *made of* money?
　　The chair was *made of* plastic.

need for: You have a *need for* something.
　　The committee expressed a *need for* better leadership.

object to: You *object to* something.
　　Lisa *objected to* her husband's weekend plans.

obligation to: You have an *obligation to* someone.
　　I feel an *obligation to* my parents, who supported me while I was in
　　　college.

opportunity for: You have an *opportunity for* something; an *opportunity*
exists *for* someone.
　　The new job gives her an *opportunity for* a career change.
　　A trip to China is a wonderful *opportunity for* Mimi.

pay for: You *pay* someone *for* something.
　　I have to *pay* the plumber *for* the repairs to my sink.

pay to: You *pay* something *to* someone.
　　Brian *paid* fifty dollars *to* the woman who found his lost dog.

popular with: Something or someone is *popular with* someone.
　　Jazz is not *popular with* my friends.

prefer . . . to: You *prefer* something *to* something.
　　I *prefer* jazz *to* classical music.

prejudice against: You have a *prejudice against* someone or something.
　　My father finally conquered his *prejudice against* women drivers.

> **Note:** Remember to add *-ed* when the word becomes an adjective.
> 　　He is *prejudiced* against scientists.

protect against: Something or someone *protects against* something or
someone.
　　A good raincoat can *protect* you *against* heavy rain.

protect from: Something or someone *protects from* something or someone.
　　A good lock on your door can *protect* you *from* break-ins.

qualification for: You have a *qualification for* a position.
  André is missing an important *qualification for* the job.

qualified to: You are *qualified to* do something.
  Tim isn't *qualified to* judge the paintings.

quote from: You *quote* something *from* someone else.
  The graduation speaker *quoted* some lines *from* Shakespeare.

reason for: You give a *reason for* something.
  He offered no *reason for* his rude behavior.

reason with: You *reason with* someone.
  Sonny tried to *reason with* the angry motorist.

responsible for: You are *responsible for* something.
  Luther is *responsible for* the mess in the kitchen.

responsible to: You are *responsible to* someone.
  At the restaurant, the waiters are *responsible to* the assistant manager.

rob of: You *rob* someone *of* something.
  His insult *robbed* me *of* my dignity.

similar to: Someone or something is *similar to* someone or something.
  Your dress is *similar to* a dress I had in high school.

succeed in: You *succeed in* something.
  I hope I can *succeed in* getting a job.

superior to: Someone or something is *superior to* someone or something.
  My final paper was *superior to* my first paper.

take advantage of: You *take advantage of* someone or something.
  Maria is going to *take advantage of* the fine weather and go to the
    beach.

take care of: You *take care of* someone or something.
  Rick will *take care of* my cat while I'm away.

talk about: You *talk about* something.
  We can *talk about* the trip tomorrow.

talk over: You *talk over* something.
  The cousins met to *talk over* the plans for the anniversary party.

talk to: You *talk to* someone.
  I'll *talk to* my father.

talk with: You *talk with* someone.
  Esther needs to *talk with* her boyfriend.

tired of: You are *tired of* something.
Sylvia is *tired of* driving to work.

wait for: You *wait for* someone or something.
Jessica must *wait for* Alan to arrive.

wait on: You use *wait on* only if you wait on customers.
At the diner, I have to *wait on* too many people.

Exercise 1   **Choosing the Correct Preposition**

Circle the correct preposition in each of the following sentences.

1. With flowers or cookies in her hands, my aunt (calls on / calls to / calls up) lonely or housebound neighbors.

2. Paul likes shrimp, but he prefers a large steak (over / to) most seafood.

3. You have to be at work (by / during) 8:00 a.m. tomorrow.

4. Mark was never interested (at / in) going to college.

5. Hang your jacket (on / in) the closet.

6. Leo likes to work (in / at) night.

7. My boss said I had all the qualifications (for / to) a promotion to assistant manager.

8. A child who is abused is robbed (from / of) his or her innocence.

9. Emilio soon became bored (of / with) the silly game.

10. When it comes to the subject of teenage marriage, Kristin differs (from / with) me.

Exercise 2   **Choosing the Correct Preposition**

Circle the correct preposition in each of the following sentences.

1. If you go to the mall, be sure to (look up / look for) a cheap raincoat.

2. My uncle works in a restaurant (in / at) the north end of Mill Road.

3. I have been waiting (on / for) you (since / for) twenty minutes.

4. Bruce was riding (in / on) a new pickup truck yesterday.

5. My college English class is different (from / than) my senior English class in high school.

6. At the school board meeting, several parents came to argue (with / for) smaller class sizes in the elementary grades.

7. After he saw the movie about starvation in Africa, John became angry (at / with) the hopeless situation of millions.

8. My grandmother wanted to divide her small collection of jewelry (between / among) her three daughters.

9. Yasar lived (on / in) Turkey before he came to the United States.

10. You are so angry that no one can reason (for / with) you.

Exercise 3 **Writing Sentences Using Expressions with Prepositions**

Collaborate

Do this exercise with a partner or group. Below are pairs of expressions with prepositions. Write a sentence that contains each pair. The first one is done for you.

1. a. argue with   b. object to

   sentence: *In college, I used to argue with my roommate whenever he* _____

   would object to my loud music. _____

2. a. take advantage of   b. arrive at

   sentence: _____

   _____

3. a. grateful for   b. wait on

   sentence: _____

   _____

4. a. between   b. similar to

   sentence: _____

   _____

5. a. popular with   b. bored by

   sentence: _____

   _____

6. a. look for   b. qualified to

   sentence: _____

   _____

7. a. prejudice against   b. reason for

   sentence: _____

   _____

8. a. superior to   b. opportunity for

   sentence: _____

   _____

9. a. need for   b. made of

   sentence: _____

   _____

10. a. protect from   b. rob of

    sentence: _____

    _____

Collaborate

Exercise 4 **Writing Sentences Using Expressions with Prepositions**

Do this exercise with a partner. Review the list of expressions with prepositions in this chapter. Select five expressions that you think are troublesome for writers. Write the expressions below. Then exchange your list for a partner's list. Your partner will write a sentence for each expression on your list; you will write sentences for his or her list. When you have completed the exercises, check each other's sentences.

1. expression: _____

   sentence: _____

2. expression: _____

   sentence: _____

3. expression: _____

   sentence: _____

4. expression: _____

   sentence: _____

5. expression: _____

   sentence: _____

Connect

Exercise 5 **Using Prepositions Correctly**

The following paragraph has ten errors in prepositions. Correct the errors in the space above each error.

My roommate Bill has a habit of becoming angry with some minor incident, and then it is impossible to reason for him. Last week, for example, he told me that he and I needed to talk with my careless behavior. Until the time I was able to figure out what "behavior" Bill was describing, he had already turned into a red-faced, shouting monster. He was ranting about my leaving the door unlocked while I went down the hall to check our mailbox. "Someday, you'll be responsible to a burglary when someone sees the unlocked door and walks right on!" he complained. "You'll have to pay to the missing items when some criminal robs the apartment!" Because our apartment door is about twenty feet from the mailboxes, I refused to argue for Bill. I am getting tired by listening to Bill's tantrums. So, instead of arguing, I am going to look on "Roommate Wanted" ads in the newspaper. Maybe I'll find someone calmer than Bill.

Connect

Exercise 6 **Using Prepositions Correctly**

The following paragraph has eleven errors in prepositions. Correct the errors in the space above each error.

Our dog Annabelle was terrified of thunderstorms, and for a long time, we couldn't do anything to help her. At the first distant rumble of thunder, Annabelle looked up, with her ears raised, and listened. Then she would look at the family (my father, my mother, and me) as if to beg us for some comfort. Annabelle wanted the storm to go away. By the time the lightning and thunder had reached our home, the dog was hiding under the bed or on a closet. Often she began to wail. Since years, Annabelle suffered. We didn't know what to do. We couldn't reason for a dog by explaining that the storm would be gone soon. Between the three of us, we tried many remedies for Annabelle's pain. My mother sat near the bed or closet, called up the dog and, by holding a treat, tried to lure Annabelle out of hiding. Using the Internet, my father looked on information about dogs and thunderstorms, but he couldn't find much. I tried dragging the dog out of her hiding place, but she shook so pitifully that I let her go back to her safe spot. We felt extremely sorry for our dog and knew that we could not protect her about inevitable summer storms. Eventually, we did succeed on helping, but not curing, Annabelle. Our neighbor told us about an herb that helps to calm anxiety in pets. We found the herb, in capsule form, at a local pet store. The next time we heard a faint roll of thunder, we slipped the herbal pill into a spoonful of canned dog food and fed the mixture to our dog. On that thunderstorm, Annabelle remained anxious, but she was not frightened enough to hide and cry. Until the day we first gave our dog the herbal remedy, we have continued to rely on it to calm Annabelle when a storm threatens. We will always be grateful for our neighbor for helping us to ease our dog's suffering.

Exercise 7   **Recognizing Prepositional Phrases in a Famous Speech**

Collaborate

Do this exercise with a group. Following is part of famous speech by Winston Churchill, prime minister of Great Britain during World War II. When Churchill gave this speech in 1940, the Nazis had just defeated the British troops at Dunkirk, France. In this speech, Churchill explained the events at Dunkirk and then rallied the nation to keep fighting.

To do this exercise, have one member of your group read the speech aloud while the other members listen. Then underline all the prepositional phrases in it. Be ready to share your answers with another group.

We shall not flag* nor fail. We shall go on to the end. We shall fight in France and on the seas and oceans; we shall fight with growing confidence and growing strength in the air.

We shall defend our island whatever the cost may be; we shall fight on beaches, on landing grounds, in fields, in streets and on the hills. We shall never surrender and even if, which I do not for a moment believe, this island or a large part of it were subjugated* and starving, then our empire beyond the seas, armed and guarded by the British Fleet*, would carry on the struggle until in God's good time the New World, with all its power and might, sets forth to the liberation and rescue of the Old.

*flag means to lose energy
*subjugated means conquered by the enemy
*the fleet is a group of warships

Writing in Steps:
The Process Approach

INTRODUCTION

Learning by Doing

Writing is a skill, and like any skill, writing improves with practice. This part of the book provides you with ample practice to improve your writing through a variety of individual and group activities. Whether you complete assignments at home or in the classroom, just remember that *good writing takes practice:* you can learn to write well by writing.

Steps Make Writing Easier

Writing is easier if you *do not try to do too much at once.* To make the task of writing easier, this section breaks the process into four major parts:

PREWRITING

In this stage, you think about your topic, and you *gather ideas.* You *react* to your own ideas and add even more thoughts. You can also react to other people's ideas as a way of expanding your own writing.

PLANNING

In this stage, you examine your ideas and begin to *focus* them around one main idea or point. Planning involves combining, categorizing, and even eliminating some ideas. Placing your specific details in a logical order often involves *outlining*.

DRAFTING

In this stage, the thinking and planning begins to take shape as a piece of writing. You complete a draft of your work, a *rough version* of the finished product. Then you examine the draft and consider ways to *revise* it, a process that may require extensive editing and several versions of your original draft.

POLISHING

In this stage, you give the final draft of your writing one last, careful *review* when you are rested and alert. You *proofread* and concentrate on identifying and correcting any mistakes in spelling, mechanics, punctuation, or word choice you may have missed. This stage is the *final check* of your work to make your writing the best it can be.

These four stages in the writing process—**prewriting, planning, drafting,** and **polishing**—may overlap. You may be changing your plan even as you work on the draft of your paper. There is no rule that prevents you from returning to an earlier stage. In these writing chapters, you will have many opportunities to become familiar with the stages of effective writing. Working individually and with your classmates, you can become a better writer along *all* lines.

Contents Page

CHAPTER 20

Jumping In

*Where do you get your ideas for writing? Do they seem to come at you all at once? Working with a jumble of ideas is a natural part of the writing process. Fortunately, there are several ways to draw on your imagination, experiences, beliefs, and opinions as you sort through these ideas and begin a **paragraph** that focuses on one idea or point.*

Writing a Paragraph: Prewriting—Generating Ideas

The **paragraph** is the basic building block of most writing. It is a group of sentences focusing on one idea or one point. Keep this concept in mind: *one idea for each paragraph*. Focusing on one idea or one point gives a paragraph *unity*. If you have a new point, start a new paragraph.

You may ask, "Doesn't this mean a paragraph will be short? How long should a paragraph be, anyway?" To convince a reader of one main point, you need to make it, support it, develop it, explain it, and describe it. There will be shorter and longer paragraphs, but for now, you can assume your paragraph will be between seven and twelve sentences long.

This chapter guides you through the first stage of the writing process, the **prewriting** stage, where you generate ideas for your paragraph.

BEGINNING THE PREWRITING

Suppose your instructor asks you to write a paragraph about family. To write effectively, you need to know your *purpose* and your *audience.* In this case, you already know your purpose: to write a paragraph that makes some point about family. You also know your audience since you are writing this paragraph for your instructor and classmates. Often, your purpose is to write a specific type of paper for a class. However, you may have to write with a different purpose for a particular audience. Writing instructions for a new employee at your workplace, or writing a letter of complaint to a manufacturer, or composing a short autobiographical essay for a scholarship application are examples of different purposes and audiences.

Freewriting, Brainstorming, Keeping a Journal

Once you have identified your purpose and audience, you can begin by finding some way to *think* on paper. To gather ideas, you can use the techniques of freewriting, brainstorming, or keeping a journal.

Freewriting Give yourself ten minutes to write whatever comes into your mind on the subject. If you can't think of anything to write, just write, "I can't think of anything to write," over and over until you think of something else. The main goal of **freewriting** is to *write without stopping*. Don't stop to tell yourself, "This is stupid," or "I can't use any of this in a paper." Just write. Let your ideas flow. Write freely. Here's an example:

Freewriting about Family

Family. Family. Whose family? What is a family? What does she want me to write about? I'm not married. I don't have a family. Sure, my mother. I guess I have a big <u>other</u> family, too. Cousins, aunts, uncles. But my basic family is my mother and brother, Tito. Is that a family? She's a good mom. Always takes care of me. Family ties. Family matters. How a family treats children.

Brainstorming **Brainstorming** is like freewriting because you write whatever comes into your head, but it is a little different because you can *pause to ask yourself questions* that will lead to new ideas. When you brainstorm alone, you "interview" yourself about a subject. Or you can brainstorm within a group.

If you are brainstorming about family, alone or with a partner or group, you might begin by listing ideas and then add to the ideas by asking and answering questions. Here's an example:

Brainstorming about Family

Family.
Family members.

Who is your favorite family member?
I don't know. Uncle Ray, I guess.

Why is he your favorite?
He's funny. Especially at those family celebrations.

What celebrations?
Birthdays, anniversaries, dinners. I hated those dinners when I was little.

Why did you hate them?

I had to get all dressed up.

What else did you hate about them?

I had to sit still through the longest, most boring meals.

Why were they boring?

All these grown-ups talking. My mother made me sit there, politely.

Were you angry at your mother?

Yes. Well, no, not really. She's strict, but I love her.

If you feel like you are running out of ideas in brainstorming, try to form a question out of what you've just written. For example, if you write, "Families are changing," you could form these questions:

What families? How are they changing? Are the changes good? Why? Why not?

Forming questions helps you keep your thoughts flowing, and you will eventually arrive at a suitable focus for your paragraph.

Keeping a Journal A **journal** is a notebook of your personal writing, a notebook in which you write regularly and often. *It is not a diary, but it is a place to record your experiences, reactions, and observations.* In it, you can write about what you've done, heard, seen, read, or remembered. You can include sayings that you'd like to remember, news clippings, snapshots—anything that you'd like to recall or consider. Journals are a great way to practice your writing and a great source of ideas for writing.

If you were asked to write about family, for example, you might look through entries in your journal in search of ideas, and you might see something like this:

Journal Entry about Family

I was at Mike's house last night. We were just sitting around, talking and listening to CDs. Then we were bored, so we decided to go to the movies. When we left, we walked right past Mike's mother in the kitchen. Mike didn't even say goodbye or tell her where we were going. Mike is so rude to his mother. He can't stand her. Lots of my friends hate their parents. I'm lucky. I'm close to my mother.

Finding Specific Ideas

Whether you freewrite, brainstorm, or consult your journal, you end up with something on paper. Follow these first ideas; see where they can take you. You are looking for specific ideas, each of which can focus the general one you started with. At this point, you do not have to decide which specific idea you want to write about. You just want to narrow your range of ideas.

You might ask, "Why should I narrow my ideas? Won't I have more to say if I keep my topic big?" But remember that a paragraph has one idea. You want to say one thing clearly, and you want to use convincing details that support your main idea. If you write one paragraph on the broad topic of family, for example, you will probably make only general statements that say very little and that bore your reader.

General ideas are big, broad ones. Specific ideas are narrow. If you scanned the freewriting example on family, you might underline many specific ideas that could be topics.

Family. Family. Whose family? What is a family? What does she want me to write about? I'm not married. I don't have a family. Sure, <u>my mother.</u> I guess I have a <u>big other family,</u> too. Cousins, aunts, uncles. But <u>my basic family</u> is my mother and brother, Tito. Is that a family? <u>She's a good mom.</u> <u>Always takes care of me.</u> Family ties. Family matters. How a family treats children.

Consider the underlined parts. Many of them are specific ideas about family. You could write a paragraph about one underlined item or about several related items.

Another way to find specific ideas is to make a list after brainstorming, underlining specific ideas. Here is an underlined list about family:

Family.
Family members.
<u>Uncle Ray.</u>
He's funny. Especially at those <u>family celebrations.</u>
<u>Birthdays, anniversaries, dinners. I hated those dinners when I was little.</u>
<u>I had to get all dressed up.</u>
I had to sit still through the <u>longest, most boring meals.</u>
All these grown-ups, talking. My mother made me sit there, politely.
<u>She's strict, but I love her.</u>

These specific ideas could lead you to specific topics.

If you reviewed the journal entry on family, you would be able to underline many specific ideas:

I was at Mike's house last night. We were just sitting around, talking and listening to CDs. Then we were bored, so we decided to go to the movies. When we left, we walked right past Mike's mother in the kitchen. <u>Mike didn't even say goodbye or tell her where we were going.</u> <u>Mike is so rude to his mother. He can't stand her.</u> <u>Lots of my friends hate their parents. I'm lucky. I'm close to my mother.</u>

Remember, following the steps can lead you to specific ideas. Once you have some specific ideas, you can pick one idea and develop it.

Exercise 1 **Brainstorming Questions and Answers**

Following are several general topics. For each one, brainstorm by writing three questions and answers related to the topic that could lead you to specific ideas. The first topic is done for you.

1. general topic: home computers

Question 1. *Do I need my home computer?*

Answer 1. *Sure. I use it all the time.*

Question 2. *But what do I use it for?*

Answer 2. *Games. Going online to MySpace and YouTube. E-mail.*

Question 3. *So I don't use it for anything serious, do I?*

Answer 3. *It helps me do research and type my papers.*

2. general topic: exercise

Question 1. Is exercise a good thing?

Answer 1. well yeah, It keeps to stay fit + healthy

Question 2. well do I need to exercise?

Answer 2. It probably would help.

Question 3. _____

Answer 3. _____

3. general topic: memories

Question 1. what kind of memories are there?

Answer 1. good memories + bad memories

Question 2. Do I remember my childhood?

Answer 2. well some of it I do.

Question 3. why do you only remember some memories and not others?

Answer 3. some might not be important

4. general topic: television contests

Question 1. Do you enjoy watching them?

Answer 1. some of them,

Question 2. _____

Answer 2 _____

Question 3. _____

Answer 3. _____

5. general topic: relationships

Question 1. _____

Answer 1. _____

Question 2. _____

Answer 2. _____

Question 3. _____

Answer 3. _____

Exercise 2 **Finding Specific Ideas in a List**

Following are general topics; each general topic is followed by a list of words or phrases about the general topic. It is the kind of list you could make after brainstorming. Underline the phrases that are specific and that could lead you to a specific topic. The first list is done for you.

1. **general topic:** sleeping habits
   how people sleep
   <u>snoring all night</u>
   everyone sleeps
   <u>why people toss and turn</u>
   ways of sleeping

2. **general topic:** nature
snorkeling on a reef
<u>preserving the environment</u>
pleasures of a bird feeder
how to plant a tree
<u>endangered species</u>

3. **general topic:** employment
my terrible boss
bad jobs
<u>office gossip</u>
working the night shift
<u>finding and keeping a suitable job</u>

4. **general topic:** meals
<u>big meals</u>
<u>disgusting fast food</u>
<u>preparing food</u>
the best breakfast in town
eating on the run

5. **general topic:** money
<u>financial problems</u>
banking online
saving spare change
regular investing
<u>people and finances</u>

Exercise 3 **Finding Specific Ideas in Freewriting**

Following are two samples of freewriting. Each is a written response to a different topic. Read each sample, and then underline any words or phrases that could become the focus of a paragraph.

Freewriting on the Topic of Cooking

What do I know about cooking? I'm a guy. I never cook. My mom cooks really well. My girlfriend cooks, too. She can't cook like my mother. I did cook, once. It was a disaster. Nearly set my apartment on fire when I tried to cook a turkey. I love turkey. My mother makes a great turkey dinner. Home cooking. Nothing like it. It's great. That's cooking. Home cooking is better than a restaurant any day.

Freewriting on the Topic of Comfort

I like a comfortable chair. Those stiff, straight-backed wooden chairs are awful. Comfortable room temperature. My mother's house is always too warm. I feel most comfortable when the windows are open. Even in winter. Some kinds of blankets called comforters. They're great on a cold night. Comfortable shoes. For old people. Maybe for sensible people.

Exercise 4 **Finding Topics through Freewriting**

Begin this exercise alone; then complete it with a partner or group. First, pick one of the topics and freewrite on it for ten minutes. Then read your freewriting to your partner or group. Ask your listener(s) to jot down any words or phrases that lead to a specific subject for a paragraph.

Your listener(s) should read the jotted-down words or phrases to you. You will be hearing a collection of specific ideas that came from *your* writing. As you listen, underline the words in your freewriting.

Freewriting Topics (pick one):

a. rules

b. health

c. pleasure

Freewriting on _____ (name of topic chosen)

_____

_____

_____

_____

_____

_____

_____

Selecting an Idea

After you have a list of specific ideas, you must pick one and try to develop it by adding details. To pick an idea about family, you could survey the ideas you gathered through freewriting. Review the following freewriting in which the specific ideas are underlined:

Family. Family. Whose family? What is a family? What does she want me to write about? I'm not married. I don't have a family. Sure, <u>my mother.</u> I guess I have <u>a big other family,</u> too. Cousins, aunts, uncles. But <u>my basic family</u> is my mother and brother, Tito. Is that a family? <u>She's a good mom. Always takes care of me.</u> Family ties. Family matters. How a family treats children.

Here are the specific ideas (the underlined ones) in a list:

my mother	*She's a good mom.*
a big other family	*Always takes care of me.*
my basic family	

Looking at these ideas, you decide to write your paragraph on this topic: My Mother.

Now you can begin to add details.

Adding Details to an Idea

You can develop the one idea you picked in a number of ways:

1. *Check your list* for other ideas that seem to fit the one you've picked.
2. *Brainstorm*—ask yourself more questions about your topic, and use the answers as details.
3. *List any new ideas* you have that may be connected to your first idea.

One way to add details is to go back and check your list for other ideas that seem to fit with the topic of My Mother. You find these entries:

She's a good mom. Always takes care of me.

Another way to add details is to brainstorm some questions that will lead you to more details. These questions do not have to be connected to each other; they are just questions that could lead you to ideas and details.

Question: What makes your mom a good mom?

Answer: She works hard.

Question: What work does she do?

Answer: She cooks, cleans.

Question: What else?

Answer: She has a job.

Question: What job?

Answer: She's a nurse.

Question: How is your mother special?

Answer: She had a rough life.

Another way to add details is to list any ideas that may be connected to your first idea of writing about your mother. The list might give you more specific details:

makes great chicken casserole
good-looking for her age
lost her husband
went to school at night

If you tried all three ways of adding details, you would end up with this list of details connected to the topic of My Mother:

She's a good mom.   *She had a rough life.*
Always takes care of me.   *makes great chicken casserole*
She works hard.   *good-looking for her age*
She cooks, cleans.   *lost her husband*
She has a job.   *went to school at night*
She's a nurse.

You now have details that you can work with as you move into the next stage of writing a paragraph.

This process may seem long, but once you have worked through it several times, it will become nearly automatic. When you think about ideas before you try to shape them, you are off to a good start.

INFO BOX: Beginning the Prewriting: A Summary

The prewriting stage of writing a paragraph enables you to gather ideas. This process begins with four steps:

1. *Think on paper and write down any ideas that you have about a general topic.* You can do this by freewriting, brainstorming, or keeping a journal.

2. *Scan your writing for specific ideas that have come from your first efforts.* List these ideas.

3. *Pick one specific idea.* This idea will be the topic of your paragraph.

4. *Add details to your topic.* You can add details by reviewing your early writing, by questioning, and by thinking further.

FOCUSING THE PREWRITING

Once you have a topic and some ideas about the topic, your next step is to *focus* your topic and ideas around some point.

Two techniques that you can use are:

- marking a list of related ideas
- mapping related ideas

Marking Related Ideas

To develop a marked list, take a look at the following marked list developed under the topic My Mother. In this list, you'll notice some of the items have been marked with letters that represent categories for related items.

H marks ideas about your mother at *home.*

J marks ideas about your mother's *job.*

B marks ideas about your mother's *background.*

Following is a marked list of ideas related to the topic My Mother.

H She's a good mom.	*B She had a rough life.*
H Always takes care of me.	*H makes great chicken casserole*
H&J She works hard.	*good-looking for her age*
H She cooks and cleans.	*B lost her husband*
J She has a job.	*B went to school at night*
J She's a nurse.	

You have probably noticed that one item, *She works hard,* is marked with two letters, H and J, because your mother works hard both at home and on the job. One item on the list, *good-looking for her age,* isn't marked. Perhaps you can come back to this item later, or perhaps you will decide you don't need it in your paragraph.

To make it easier to see what ideas you have and how they are related, try *grouping related ideas,* giving each list a title, like this:

my mother at home

She's a good mom.	*Always takes care of me.*
She works hard.	*She cooks, cleans.*
makes great chicken casserole	

my mother at her job

She has a job.	*She's a nurse.*
She works hard.	

my mother's background

She had a rough life.	*lost her husband*
went to school at night	

Mapping

Another way to focus your ideas is to mark your first list of ideas and then cluster the related ideas into separate lists. You can *map* your ideas like this:

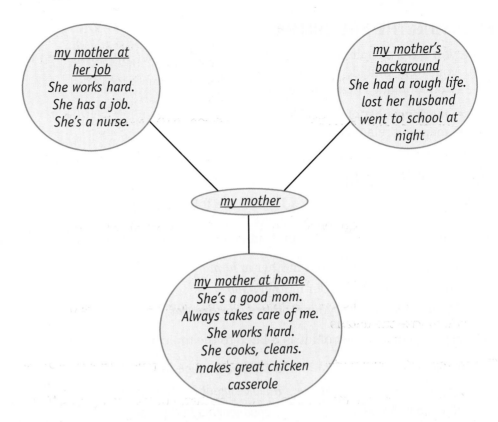

Whatever way you choose to examine and group your details, you are working toward a focus, a point. You are asking and beginning to answer the question, "Where do the details lead?" The answer will be the main idea of your paragraph, which will be stated in the topic sentence.

Grouping Related Items in Lists of Details

Following are lists of details. In each list, circle the items that seem to fit in one group; then underline the items that seem to belong to a second group. Some items may not belong in either group. The first list is done for you.

1. **topic:** my favorite aunt
   always cheerful   unusual appearance
   tells jokes   orange hair
   gives me compliments   an accountant
   laughs at her troubles   outrageous hats
   dresses in wild colors   drives a jeep

2. **topic:** a hurricane
   fallen trees   weather reports
   flooding   beach erosion
   bottled water   flashlights
   summer season   batteries
   hurricane shutters   power outages

3. **topic:** carpooling
   highway patrol   save on daily tolls
   less wear and tear on car   make friends
   share the driving stress   road rage
   develop a support system   speed traps
   save on gas   highway patrol

4. topic: my first day at college

got lost	buying text books
proud of myself	the student center
waited in long lines	class schedule problems
felt grown up	kind counsellor
parking was impossible	tired and hot from walking

5. topic: my brother's tattoo

shocked my mother	eagle in design carries an arrow
done in blue and gold	I want a tattoo
tattoos are fashionable	tattoo done at the mall
covering up tattoos	father upset
small eagle design on shoulder	tattoo shows on television

Forming a Topic Sentence

To form a topic sentence, do the following:

1. Review your details and see if you can form some general idea that will summarize the details.
2. Write that general idea in one sentence.

The sentence that summarizes the details is the *topic sentence*. It makes a general point, and the more specific details you have gathered will support this point.

To form a topic sentence about your mother, you can ask yourself questions about the details. First, there are many details about your mother. You can ask yourself, "What kinds of details do I have?" You have details about your mother's background, about her job, and about her role as a mother. You might then ask, "Can I summarize those details?" You might then summarize those details to get the topic sentence:

My mother survived difficult times to become a good parent and worker.

Check the sentence against your details. Does it cover your mother's background? Yes, it mentions that she survived *difficult times*. Does it cover her job? Yes, it says she is a *good worker*. Does it cover her role as a mother? Yes, it says she is a *good parent*. The topic sentence is acceptable; it is a general idea that summarizes the details.

Hints About Topic Sentences

1. Be careful. *Topics are not the same as topic sentences. A topic is the subject you will write about. A topic sentence states the main idea you have developed on a topic.* Consider the differences between the following topics and topic sentences:

topic:	my mother
topic sentence:	My mother survived difficult times to become a good parent and worker.

topic:	effects of drunk driving
topic sentence:	Drunk driving hurts the victims, their families, and friends.

Exercise 6 Turning Topics into Topic Sentences

Do this exercise with a partner or group. The following list contains some topics and some topic sentences. Have someone read the list aloud. As the list is read, decide which items are topics. Put an *X* by those items. On the lines following the list, rewrite the topics into topic sentences.

1. __✗__ A short road trip *can be*

2. __✗__ Why too much sugar is bad for you

3. _____ Family quarrels ruined the picnic

4. __✗__ How to write a thank-you note

There are many ways on how to write a thank-you note.

5. __✗__ My father is my best friend

6. _____ I learned compassion at my job

7. __✗__ A wonderful place to live

8. _____ Speeding is foolish and selfish

9. __✗__ The misery and pain of a sore throat

10. _____ Voice mail can be irritating

Rewrite the topics. Make each one into a topic sentence.

1. A short road trip can be fun when your with friends

2. Too much sugar is bad for you because it rot your teeth

4. There are many ways on how to write a thank-you note.

7. Hawaii is a wonderful place to live because of its climate and senery

2. *Topic sentences do not announce;* they make a point. Look at the following sentences and notice the differences between sentences that announce and topic sentences.

announcement:	The subject of this paper will be my definition of a bargain.
topic sentence:	A bargain is a necessary item that I bought at less than half the regular price.
announcement:	I will discuss the causes of depression in my best friend.
topic sentence:	My best friend's depression was caused by stress at home, work, and school.

Exercise 7   Turning Announcements into Topic Sentences

Do this exercise with a partner or group. The following list contains some topic sentences and some announcements. Have someone read this list aloud. As the list is read, decide which items are announcements. Put an *X* by those items. On the lines following the list, rewrite the announcements, making them topic sentences.

1. _____ I learned to be a good tennis player by practicing regularly.

2. _____ How to make friends at work is the subject of this paper.

3. _____ The worries of a single parent will be explained.

4. _____ Working students feel stressed at home, at work, and in school.

5. _____ I will explain the reasons for shopping online.

6. _____ Buying at thrift shops can save you money and give you quality merchandise.

7. _____ Why our street needs a stop sign is the issue to be discussed.

8. _____ The three characteristics of a good preschool are the topic of this essay.

9. _____ A real leader is responsible, confident, and generous.

10. _____ This essay will tell you why people buy lottery tickets.

Rewrite the announcements. Make each one a topic sentence.

_____

_____

_____

_____

_____

_____

_____

_____

_____

_____

3. *Topic sentences should not be too broad to develop in one paragraph.* A topic sentence that is too broad may take many pages of writing to develop. Look at the following broad sentences and then notice how they can be narrowed.

too broad:	Television violence is bad for children. (This sentence is too broad because "television violence" could include anything from bloody movies to nightly news, and "children" could mean anyone under eighteen. Also, "is bad for children" could mean anything from "causes nightmares" to "provokes children to commit murder."
a narrower topic sentence:	Violent cartoons teach preschoolers that hitting and hurting is fun.
too broad:	Education changed my life. (This sentence is so broad that you would have to talk about your whole education and your whole life to support it.)
a narrower topic sentence:	Studying for my high-school equivalency diploma gave me the confidence to try college.

Exercise 8   **Revising Topic Sentences That Are Too Broad**

Do this exercise with a partner or group. Following is a list of topic sentences. Some are too broad to support in one paragraph. Have someone read this list aloud. As the list is read, decide which sentences are too broad. Put an *X* by those sentences. On the lines following the list, rewrite those sentences, focusing on a limited idea—a topic sentence—that could be supported in one paragraph.

1. __×__   Performing can be very frustrating.

2. _____   Getting children to go to bed is the hardest part of babysitting.

3. __×__   College opened my eyes to new ideas.

4. __×__   Television has too much influence on people.

5. __×__   Their peers can be very hard on children.

6. _____   Beer advertising on television makes drinking seem like a way to be popular.

7. __×__   My brother grew up when he started working.

8. _____   A college math class forced me to learn how to study.

9. _____   Christopher developed self-confidence when he joined a boxing club.

10. _____   When parents argue, teenagers can feel torn and confused.

Rewrite the broad sentences. Make each one more limited.

1) Performing on broadway can be very frustrating.

3) College opened my eyes to the new idea of growing

4) Television violence has too much influence op people

5) Bullies can be very hard on children.

4. *Topic sentences should not be too narrow* to develop in one paragraph. A topic sentence that is too narrow can't be supported by details. It may be a fact, which can't be developed. A topic sentence that is too narrow leaves you with nothing more to say.

too narrow:	We had fog yesterday.
a better, expanded topic sentence:	Yesterday's fog made driving difficult.
too narrow:	I moved to Nashville when I was twenty.
a better, expanded topic sentence:	When I moved to Nashville at age twenty, I learned to live on my own.

Exercise 9   **Revising Topic Sentences That Are Too Narrow**

Do this exercise with a partner or group. Following is a list of topic sentences. Some of them are too narrow to be developed in a paragraph. Have someone read the list aloud. As the list is read, decide which sentences are too narrow. Put an *X* by those sentences. On the lines following the list, rewrite those sentences as broader topic sentences that could be developed in a paragraph.

1. _X_ Cathy got a studio apartment.

2. _____ A compact car is a more practical car than a sport utility vehicle.

3. _X_ We have a new kitten.

4. _____ Living in the center of town has three advantages.

5. _X_ The beach in front of our hotel was crowded. For a picnic.

6. _X_ My sister made me a cake for my twenty-fifth birthday.

7. _____ Mr. Rodriguez's offer of a ride was generous and thoughtful.

8. _____ When Dana visited me in the hospital, she showed me her love.

9. _X_ Levar's haircut at the new hair salon cost fifty dollars.

10. _____ Betty asked to borrow $115, but I had reasons for refusing her request.

Rewrite the narrow sentences. Make each one broader.

(1) Cathy got a studio apartment which has a great view, of the city.

(3) we have a new kitten which is very hyper.

(5) ↑

(6) ↑

_____

_____

_____

Once you have a topic sentence, you have completed the prewriting stage of writing. This stage begins with free, unstructured thinking and writing. As you work through the prewriting process, your thinking and writing will become more focused.

INFO BOX: Focusing the Prewriting: A Summary

The prewriting stage of writing a paragraph enables you to develop an idea into a topic sentence and related details. You can *focus* your thinking by working in steps.

1. Try marking a list of related details or mapping to group your ideas.

2. Write a topic sentence that summarizes your details.

3. Check your topic sentence. Be sure that it makes a point and focuses the details you have developed. Be sure that it is a sentence (not a topic), is not too broad or too narrow, and is not an announcement.

Exercise 10 Recognizing and Writing Good Topic Sentences

Some of the following are good topic sentences. Others are not; they are topics (not topic sentences) or announcements, or they are too broad or too narrow. Put an *X* next to the ones that are not good topic sentences and rewrite them on the lines following the list.

1. ___X___ How you can make extra money in college.

2. _____ Hitchhiking is a dangerous form of transportation.

3. ___X___ Relationships have always been difficult for me.

4. ___X___ After 8:00 p.m., the local bakery sells doughnuts at half price.

5. ___X___ Sources of protein in a healthy diet.

6. ___X___ Many teenagers are endangering their health.

7. ___X___ Several risks associated with skydiving will be the subject of this paper.

8. _____ Vitamin C can be found in many popular foods.

9. ___X___ An old remedy for boredom and apathy.

10. _____ A twenty-four-hour pharmacy is a neighborhood asset.

Rewrite the faulty topic sentences:

_____

_____

_____

_____

_____

_____

_____

_____

Exercise 11 Writing Topic Sentences for Lists of Details

Following are lists of details that have no topic sentences. Write an appropriate topic sentence for each one.

1. **topic sentence:** *There are many different reasons for walking instead of driving.*

> Walking is good exercise.
> Walking saves money spent on gas for a car.
> Walkers don't get stuck in traffic.
> Walkers get to enjoy their surroundings.
> Cars pollute the air but walkers don't.
> Walking is less stressful than driving.

2. topic sentence: _____

_____

Professor Spinetti is a patient teacher.
He is willing to answer questions.
He gives extra help after class.
He has many office hours for student conferences.
He demands students' best work.
Professor Spinetti is very strict about deadlines.
He gives many assignments.

3. topic sentence: There are many different types of mugs.

coffee mugs
soup mugs
mugs with sayings on them
plastic mugs
mugs with cartoon characters
beer mugs
china mugs
mugs with college names
glass mugs

4. topic sentence: _____

_____

My mother truly cares about me.
She checks on me every day.
She does my laundry.
She gives me food to take home to my house.
My mother worries when I don't return her calls.
She wants to know all about my friends.
She constantly questions me about my social life.

5. topic sentence: _____

_____

Spends time with his children every weekend
Tries to be home to tuck them in at night
Works overtime to support his family
Shares household chores with his wife
Gives his wife love and respect
Arrives at work early
Volunteers for work projects so he may be promoted

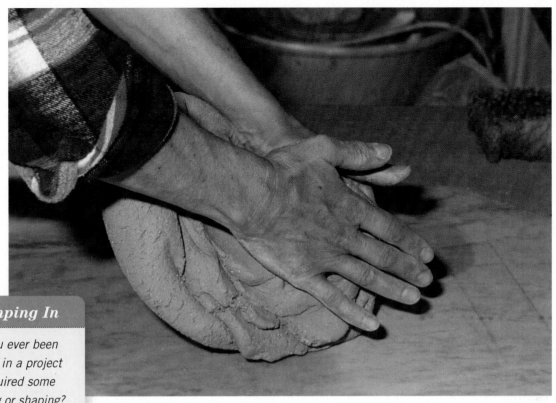

CHAPTER 21

Jumping In

*Have you ever been involved in a project that required some planning or shaping? For example, have you ever painted a room? Worked with clay? Designed a Web page? Writers often begin with a range of ideas and details. Later, they find a way to sort, shape, and focus them. Part of the planning and shaping process involves devising a **topic sentence and an outline**.*

Writing a Paragraph: Planning—Devising a Plan

Once you have a topic sentence, you can begin working on an *outline* for your paragraph. The outline is a *plan* that helps you stay focused in your writing. The outline begins to form when you write your topic sentence and the details beneath it.

CHECKING YOUR DETAILS

You can now look at your list and ask yourself an important question: "Do I have enough details to support my topic sentence?" Remember, your goal is to write a paragraph of seven to twelve sentences.

Consider this topic sentence and list of details:

topic sentence:	Fresh fruit is a good dessert.
details:	tastes good
	healthy
	easy

Does the list contain enough details for a paragraph of seven to twelve sentences? Probably not.

Adding Details When There Are Not Enough

To add details, try brainstorming. Ask yourself some questions:

What fruit tastes good?
What makes fruit a healthy dessert?
Why is it easy? How can you serve it?

By brainstorming, you may come up with these details:

topic sentence: Fresh fruit is a good dessert.
details: tastes good
a ripe peach or a juicy pineapple tastes delicious
crunchy apples are always available and satisfying
plump strawberries are great in summer
healthy
low in calories
rich in vitamins and fiber
easy
served as it is
in a fruit salad
mixed with ice cream or sherbet
no cooking necessary

Keep brainstorming until you feel you have enough details for a paragraph with seven to twelve sentences. Remember, it is better to have too many details than to have too few, for you can always edit the extra details later.

Exercise 1   Adding Details to Support a Topic Sentence

Collaborate

Do this exercise with a partner or group. The following topic sentences have some—but not enough—details. Write sentences to add details to each list.

1. topic sentence: Renting a movie on a DVD has many advantages over seeing a movie in a theater.

   details: **1.** You don't have to get dressed up to see a DVD at home.

   2. You can stop the DVD to get a snack or answer the phone.

   3. renting online saves gas

   4. is more relaxing

   5. more people can watch the DVD

   6. you can watch it whenever

2. topic sentence: I find amazing objects in the pockets of my jeans and jackets.

   details: **1.** Once I found a wrinkled apple in my raincoat.

   2. There was a toothbrush in my hoodie.

3. _____

_____

4. _____

_____

5. _____

_____

6. _____

_____

3. topic sentence: People hold garage sales for a number of reasons.

details: 1. Some people want to clear the clutter out of their house.

2. Others want to make a little money.

3. Other people can find some nice + cheap things.

4. They might not want to throw their stuff away.

5. _____

_____

6. _____

_____

4. topic sentence: I listen to some kind of music nearly all day.

details: 1. I hear soft background music at the supermarket.

2. I jog with an iPod that plays my favorite music.

3. When I wake up, my son is singing a song that he learned in first grade.

4. _____

_____

5. _____

_____

6. _____

_____

5. topic sentence: Not all fast-food restaurants offer the same kinds of food.

details: 1. Some offer pizza.

2. Others sell deli subs.

3. _____

_____

4. _____

_____

5. _____

_____

6. _____

_____

Eliminating Details That Do Not Relate to the Topic Sentence

Sometimes, what you thought were good details don't relate to the topic sentence because they don't fit or support your point. Eliminate details that don't relate to the topic sentence. For example, the following list contains details that don't relate to the topic sentence. Those details are crossed out.

topic sentence: My neighbors are making my home life unbearable.
details: play their music loud at 3:00 a.m.
I can't sleep
leave garbage all over the sidewalk
~~come from Philadelphia~~
sidewalk is a mess
insects crawl all over their garbage
~~I carefully bag my garbage~~
they argue loudly and bang on the walls
my privacy is invaded
park their van in my parking space

Exercise 2   **Eliminating Details That Do Not Fit**

Following are topic sentences and lists of details. Cross out the details that do not fit the topic sentence.

1. **topic sentence:** Some professional athletes set a bad example for the children who admire them.
   details: One basketball player choked a coach.
   ~~I think basketball has become more of a business than a sport.~~
   A baseball player spit at an umpire.
   Several football players have been charged with spousal abuse.
   ~~I used to collect autographs of famous players.~~
   Some hockey players are notorious for fighting on the ice.
   Children see this behavior and think it is acceptable.

2. **topic sentence:** Caps are worn by all kinds of people in all kinds of places.
   details: Truckers wear caps when they drive.
   Men on tractors wear caps with the name of the tractor company.
   ~~Caps are inexpensive.~~
   Children in Little League wear baseball caps.
   There are caps to protect fishermen from the sun.
   Servers in some restaurants have to wear caps.

Some ladies wear baseball caps covered in sequins to match their fancy clothes.

College bookstores sell caps printed with the name of the college, for students.

~~Years ago, businessmen used to wear hats to work.~~

Teens wear caps when they're having a bad hair day.

3. topic sentence: Daniella is known for bringing something whenever she visits.

details: If she visits someone in the hospital, she always brings flowers.

Fresh flowers are really expensive.

Daniella brings dessert when you invite her for dinner.

She brings me candy when she stops by.

When Celeste had a baby, Daniella brought the baby a knitted blanket.

I invited her to a picnic, and she came with an extra bag of ice.

Daniella always takes an extra pencil to class for the person who forgot one.

4. topic sentence: For a number of reasons, most children enjoy teasing their siblings.

details: Bored children can find teasing exciting.

Teasing a brother or sister makes a child feel powerful.

By teasing, a child can release a little anger or envy.

Some adults enjoy teasing other adults and children.

A child enjoys getting a reaction from a sister or brother.

Teasing a sibling can also win a parent's attention.

Nothing is worse than children fighting in a car.

5. topic sentence: The new movie theater was very glamorous.
details: The exterior was made to look like a rock-and-roll drive-in restaurant.

Neon lights were shaped like guitars and musical notes.

Rock music blasted outside the ticket booths.

The ticket prices were reasonable.

The movies showing were the same as the ones at the theater down the block.

The concessions area sold gourmet pizza as well as popcorn and candy.

It also had a coffee bar with cappuccino.

From List to Outline

Take another look at the topic sentence and list of details on the topic of My Mother:

topic sentence: My mother survived difficult times to become a good parent and worker.

details: She's a good mom.

Always takes care of me.

She works hard.

> She cooks, cleans.
> makes a great chicken casserole
> She has a job.
> She's a nurse.
> She had a rough life.
> lost her husband
> went to school at night

After you scan the list, you will be ready to develop the outline of a paragraph.

The outline is a plan for writing, and it can be a kind of draft in list form. It sketches what you want to write and the order in which you want to present it. An organized, logical list will make your writing unified because each item on the list will relate to your topic sentence.

When you plan, keep your topic sentence in mind:

My mother <u>survived difficult times</u> to become <u>a good parent</u> and <u>worker.</u>

Notice that the key words are underlined and lead to key phrases:

> *survived difficult times*
> *a good parent*
> *a good worker*

Can you put the details together so that they connect to one of these key phrases?

survived difficult times

She had a rough life, lost her husband, went to school at night

a good parent

She's a good mom, Always takes care of me, She cooks, cleans, makes a great chicken casserole

a good worker

She works hard, She has a job, She's a nurse

With this kind of grouping, you have a clearer idea of how to organize a paragraph. You may have noticed that the details grouped under each phrase explain or give examples that are connected to the topic sentence. You may also have noticed that the detail "She works hard" is placed under the phrase "a good worker." It could also be placed under "a good parent," so it would be your decision where to place it.

Now that you have grouped your ideas with key phrases and examples, you can write an outline:

An Outline for a Paragraph on My Mother

topic sentence:	My mother survived difficult times to become a good parent and worker.
details:	⎧ She had a rough life.
difficult times	⎨ She lost her husband.
	⎩ She went to school at night.
	⎧ She's a good mom and always takes care of me.
a good parent	⎨ She cooks and cleans.
	⎩ She makes a great chicken casserole.
a good worker	⎧ She works hard at her job.
	⎩ She's a nurse.

As you can see, the outline combines some details from the list. Even with these combinations, the details are very rough in style. As you reread the list of details, you may notice places that need more combining, places where ideas need more explaining, and places that are repetitive. Keep in mind that an outline is merely a rough organization of your paragraph.

As you work through the steps of devising an outline, you can check for the following:

Checklist: A Checklist for an Outline

✓ **Unity:** Do all the details relate to the topic sentence? If they do, the paragraph will be unified.

✓ **Support:** Do I have enough supporting ideas? Can I add to those ideas with more specific details?

✓ **Coherence:** Are the ideas listed in the right order? If the order of the points is logical, the paragraph will be coherent.

Coherence

Check the sample outline again; you'll notice that the details are grouped in the same order as in the topic sentence: first, details about your mother's difficult life; next, details about your mother as a parent; finally, details about your mother as a worker. Putting details in an order that matches the topic sentence is logical for this paragraph. It makes the paragraph *coherent*.

Determining the Order of Details

Putting the details in a logical order makes the ideas in the paragraph easier to follow. The most logical order for a paragraph depends on the subject of the paragraph. If you are writing about an event, you might use **time order** (such as telling what happened first, second, and so forth); if you are arguing some point, you might use **emphatic order** (such as saving your most convincing idea for last); if you are describing a room, you might use **space order** (such as describing from left to right or from top to bottom).

Exercise 3 Coherence: Putting Details in the Right Order

These outlines have details that are in the wrong order. In the space provided, number the sentences so that they are in the proper order: *1* would be the number for the first sentence, and so on. (Put the sentences in time order, from first to last.)

1. topic sentence: My last day at my job was sadder than I had expected.

_____ Everyone went through the morning routine as usual.

_____ I spent my afternoon feeling hurt and insulted.

_____ At lunchtime, no one even asked me out for a farewell lunch.

_____ When I first came in, no one acted as if he or she remembered it was my last day.

_____ Just as we were closing the store, my boss and coworkers surprised me with a big cake and other treats.

_____ I left feeling grateful for their thoughtfulness.

_____ I was also sad to leave these kind people.

2. **topic sentence:** As a result of the car accident, David suffered multiple injuries. (Put the sentences in space order, from top to bottom.)

_____ His eye sockets were black and blue.

_____ David had cracked several ribs.

_____ Broken glass from the windshield had cut his neck.

_____ His jaw was dislocated.

_____ He suffered a broken ankle.

_____ His nose was broken.

3. **topic sentence:** Driving while texting is foolish and dangerous. (Put the sentences in emphatic order, from the least important reason to the most important.)

_____ You can be killed.

_____ In some states, you can be ticketed.

_____ You can be bumped and bruised in a minor fender bender.

_____ You can be severely hurt in a more serious accident.

4. **topic sentence:** The speech was long, boring, and confusing. (Put the sentences in the same order as in the topic sentence.)

_____ The speaker jumped from topic to topic.

_____ One minute he was talking about pollution; then he was telling a joke.

_____ He spoke in a monotone.

_____ He was putting me to sleep.

_____ I checked my watch after thirty minutes.

_____ He went on for another forty minutes.

Where the Topic Sentence Goes

The outline format helps you organize your ideas. The topic sentence is written above the list of details. This position helps you remember that the topic sentence is the main idea and that the details that support it are written under it. You can easily check each detail on your list against your main idea. You can also check the unity (relevance) and coherence (logical order) of your details.

When you actually write a paragraph, the topic sentence does not necessarily have to be the first sentence in the paragraph. Read the following paragraphs, and notice where each topic sentence is placed.

Topic Sentence at the Beginning of the Paragraph

<u>Dr. Chen is the best doctor I have ever had.</u> Whenever I have to visit him, he gives me plenty of time. He does not rush me through a physical examination and quickly hand me a prescription. Instead, he takes time to chat with me and encourages me to describe my symptoms. He examines me carefully and allows me to ask as many questions as I want. After I am dressed, he discusses his diagnosis, explains what medicine he is prescribing, and tells me exactly how and when to take the medication. He tells me what results to expect from the medication and how long it should take for

me to get well. Dr. Chen acts as if he cares about me. I believe that is the most important quality in a doctor.

Topic Sentence in the Middle of the Paragraph

The meal was delicious, from the appetizer of shrimp cocktail to the dessert of strawberry tarts. Marcel had even taken the time to make home-baked bread and fresh pasta. <u>Marcel had worked hard on this dinner, and his hard work showed.</u> Everything was served on gleaming china placed on an immaculate tablecloth. There were fresh flowers in a cut glass bowl at the center of the table, and there was a polished goblet at every place setting. The pale green napkins had been carefully ironed and folded into precise triangles.

Topic Sentence at the End of the Paragraph

I woke up at 5 a.m. when I heard the phone ringing. I rushed to the phone, thinking the call was some terrible emergency. Of course, it was just a wrong number. Then I couldn't get back to sleep because I was shaken by being so suddenly awakened and irritated by the wrong number. The day got worse as it went along. My car stalled on the freeway, and I had to get towed to a repair shop. The repair cost me $250. I was three hours late for work and missed an important training session with my boss. On my way out of work, I stepped into an enormous puddle and ruined a new pair of shoes. <u>Yesterday was one of those days when I should have stayed in bed.</u>

> **Note:** Be sure to follow your own instructor's directions about placement of the topic sentence.

Exercise 5   **Identifying the Topic Sentence**

Underline the topic sentence in each of the following paragraphs.

1. Last week I had just gotten out of bed when I had an unpleasant surprise. I was in the kitchen, making myself some instant coffee, when I ran my hand through my tangled hair. I suddenly realized that one of my earrings, a small gold ball, was gone. Since I knew I had been wearing it when I went to bed, I figured it was somewhere in the apartment. I crawled on the floor, checked the corners and crannies, and shook out the bedsheets and pillows. I looked everywhere. I couldn't find it. The next day, I looked again but once more found nothing except dust and crumbs. Finally, I was forced to give up. Then, yesterday, I was again making coffee. As I spooned the last of the coffee granules out of the jar, a small gold ball appeared at the bottom. It was my earring. I have now realized that sometimes objects get lost in the strangest places.

2. Larry is addicted to cookies. He keeps a bag of chocolate chip cookies in his car, and he has been known to drive with one hand on the wheel and one in the cookie bag. At the food court in the mall, he will skip the tacos and burgers and head straight for the freshly baked cookies. Everyone at the local bakery knows Larry. For his birthday, the staff makes Larry a giant cookie, the size of a flat cake, and writes "Happy Birthday" on it, in icing. The local Girl Scouts also know Larry well, for he is their biggest buyer of Girl Scout cookies.

3. Uncle Mike never forgets birthdays and always sends a card on time. He knows how to lighten the mood of someone having a bad day or some bad luck. He also knows hundreds of jokes guaranteed to make anyone smile. His nieces and nephews adore him, and his four sisters and two brothers consider him their best friend. The man is welcome at every family gathering, in good times and bad. If an aunt, uncle, or cousin is sick, he calls and offers to run errands or bring some chicken soup. If someone is in the hospital, he is the first to visit, and if the patient's hospital stay is long, he visits regularly. He is also available when a person needs sympathy. He will attend a funeral but, unlike many family members, he continues to help grieving relatives by visiting, listening, running errands, and just being there.

Jumping In

*Once a project begins to take shape, what comes next? If you were creating a piece of sculpture or writing a song, would you try to rush the project to completion, or would you concentrate on further shaping and refining? Such questions relate to **drafting and revising,** the next phase of the writing process.*

CHAPTER 22

Writing a Paragraph: Drafting— Writing and Revising the Drafts

An outline is a draft of a paragraph in list form. Once you have an outline, you are ready to write the list in paragraph form, to create a first draft of your assignment.

DRAFTING

The drafting stage of writing is the time to draft, revise, edit, and draft again. You may write several drafts or versions of the paragraph in this stage. Writing several drafts is not an unnecessary chore or a punishment. It is a way of taking pressure off yourself. By revising in steps, you are telling yourself, "The first try doesn't have to be perfect."

Review the outline on the topic of My Mother. You can create a first draft of this outline in the form of a paragraph. (Remember that the first line of each paragraph is indented.) In the draft of the following paragraph, the first sentence of the paragraph is the topic sentence.

A First Draft of a Paragraph on My Mother

My mother survived difficult times to become a good parent and worker. She had a rough life. She lost her husband. She went to school at night. She's a good mom and always takes care of me. She cooks and cleans. She makes a great chicken casserole. She works hard at her job. She's a nurse.

Revising the Draft

Once you have a first draft, you can begin to think about revising and editing it. Revising means rewriting the draft to change the structure, the order of the sentences, and the content. Editing includes making changes in the choice of words, in the selection of the details, in the punctuation, and in the patterns and kinds of sentences. It may also include adding transitions—words, phrases, or sentences that link ideas.

Below is a list of some common transitional words and phrases and the kind of connections they express.

INFO BOX: Common Transitions

To join two ideas

again	another	in addition	moreover
also	besides	likewise	similarly
and	furthermore		

To show a contrast or a different opinion

but	instead	on the other hand	still
however	nevertheless	or	yet
in contrast	on the contrary	otherwise	

To show a cause-and-effect connection

accordingly	because	for	therefore
as a result	consequently	so	thus

To give an example

for example	in the case of	such as	to illustrate
for instance	like		

To show time

after	first	recently	subsequently
at the same time	meanwhile	shortly	then
before	next	soon	until
finally			

One easy way to begin the revising and editing process is to read your work aloud to yourself. As you do so, listen carefully to your words and concentrate on their meaning. Each question in the following checklist will help you focus on a specific part of revising and editing. The name (or key term) for each part is in parentheses.

Checklist: A Checklist for Revising the Draft of a Paragraph (with key terms)

✔ Am I staying on my point? (unity)

✔ Should I eliminate any ideas that do not fit? (unity)

✔ Do I have enough to say about my point? (support)

✔ Should I add any details? (support)

✔ Should I change the order of my sentences? (coherence)

✔ Is my choice of words appropriate? (style)

✔ Is my choice of words repetitive? (style)

✔ Are my sentences too long? Too short? (style)

✔ Should I combine any sentences? (style)

✔ Am I running sentences together? (grammar)

✔ Am I using complete sentences? (grammar)

✔ Can I link my ideas more smoothly? (transitions)

If you apply the checklist to the draft of the paper on My Mother, you will probably find these rough spots:

- The sentences are very short and choppy.
- Some sentences could be combined.
- Some words are repeated often.
- Some ideas need more details for support.
- The paragraph needs transitions: words, phrases, or sentences that link ideas.

Consider the following revised draft of the paragraph, and notice the changes, underlined, that have been made in the draft:

A Revised Draft of a Paragraph on My Mother

topic sentence:

sentences combined, transition

details added, transition

details added,

details added,

details added,

details added

transition

details added

My mother survived difficult times to become a good parent and worker. <u>Her hard times began when she lost her husband. At his death, she was only nineteen and had a baby, me, to raise. She survived by</u> going to school at night <u>to train for a career. Even though she lives a stressful life,</u> she is a good mom. She always takes care of me. <u>She listens to my problems, encourages me to do my best, and praises all my efforts. She cleans our apartment until it shines, and she makes dinner every night.</u> She makes a great chicken casserole. <u>In addition,</u> she works hard at her job. She is a nurse <u>at a home for elderly people, where she is on her feet all day and is still kind and cheerful.</u>

When you are revising your own paragraph, you can use the checklist to help you. Read the checklist several times; then reread your draft, looking for answers to the questions on the list. If your instructor agrees, you can work with your classmates. You can read your draft to a partner or group. Your listener(s) can react to your draft by applying the questions on the checklist and by making notes about your draft as you read. When you are finished reading aloud, your partner(s) can discuss their notes about your work.

> **Note:** You can also revise a draft of your paragraph by working with a partner and using the Peer Review Form for a Paragraph at the end of Chapter 23.

Exercise 1   Revising a Draft for Unity

Some of the sentences in the following paragraph do not fit the topic sentence. (The topic sentence is the first sentence in the paragraph.) Cross out the sentences that do not fit.

My husband any I finally found a way to handle our child's nightmares. Our five-year-old son, Enrique, used to sleep peacefully through the night in his own room, but recently he has been waking up, screaming. He claims that there is a ghost in his room. Once he is awake, he cannot go back to sleep and instead becomes frightened at every ordinary sound. I remember when the sound of tree branches against the window used to terrify my little sister. At first we took Enrique into our bed, and he slept fairly well. However, he began to wake up, startled, and listen for "ghosts." Soon all three of us were awake for most of the night. The "ghosts" seemed to get worse. Comic books and cartoons often contain ghosts, but they don't always frighten small children. My husband realized that Enrique spent each night listening for ghosts, so our son might feel safer if he couldn't hear strange noises. Enrique returned to his own room where we played soft music all night. He sleeps much better now.

Exercise 2   Adding Support to a Draft

Collaborate

Do this exercise with a partner or group. The following paragraph needs more details to support its point. Add the details in the blank spaces provided.

Our trip to Florida was a disappointment. First of all, the weather was terrible.

(Add two sentences of details.) _____

_____

In addition, the amusement park we visited was too crowded for us to enjoy. For

example, the parking lots were so full, we had to wait thirty minutes for a parking

space. (Add one sentence of details about the crowding.) _____

_____

Worst of all, I got sick on our trip. (Add two sentences of details.)   _____

_____

_____ I'm glad I got to see Florida, but I wish

my visit had been more enjoyable.

Exercise 3 Revising a Draft for Coherence

In the following paragraph, one sentence is in the wrong place. Move it to the right place in the paragraph by drawing an arrow from the sentence to its proper place.

Damien's gift to his mother was dazzling. He handed her an elegantly wrapped box. Inside the tissue paper was a beautiful silver and turquoise necklace. On top of the box was a blue silk rose tied with shiny blue ribbon. The ribbon covered blue wrapping paper dotted with silver stars. When she tore off the wrapping paper and opened the lid of the box, Damien's mother saw a nest of silver and blue tissue paper. She plunged her hands into the soft tissue paper to discover her gift.

Collaborate

Exercise 4 Revising a Draft for Style

Do this exercise with a partner or a group. The following paragraph is repetitive in its word choice. Replace each underlined word with a word that is less repetitive. Write the new word above the underlined one.

My friend Isaac's tropical pets are all ugly. I expected some of them to be pretty, but I was disappointed to find each one <u>uglier</u> than the next. For example, Isaac has a pet iguana that lives in the yard, and I thought it would be a <u>pretty</u> lizard. Instead, it was a large, <u>ugly</u> lizard with <u>ugly</u> scales on its back. Isaac also rescued an abandoned parrot who had been left in a cage. People usually think of parrots as <u>pretty</u> birds with <u>pretty</u> feathers, but Isaac's parrot is <u>ugly</u>. Isaac's tropical fish were the worst disappointment. They were the <u>ugliest</u> tropical fish I had ever seen. I know Isaac must love his pets, but I wish Isaac had found at least one <u>pretty</u> one.

Exercise 5 Revising a Draft by Combining Sentences

The following paragraph has many short, choppy sentences that are underlined. Wherever you see two or more underlined sentences clustered next to each other, combine them into one clear, smooth sentence. Write your revised version of the underlined sentences in the spaces above the lines. To review ways to combine sentences, see Chapter 5.

José loves mysteries. <u>He visits every used bookstore in our town. He looks for mysteries he hasn't read yet.</u> He is a member of the Mystery Book Club. <u>On weekends, he works with a drama group. The group stages mystery plays. The plays are staged at local restaurants.</u> The plays are part of a dinner theater show that involves the audience in solving the mystery. <u>In addition to reading mysteries and acting in them,</u>

<u>José enjoys watching mysteries on television. He sees them at the movies. He enjoys</u>

<u>them on video.</u> Someday, José will write a mystery of his own. I am sure it will be

excellent because José already knows everything there is to know about dark crimes,

dangerous secrets, and suspenseful endings.

Exercise 6   Revising a Draft by Correcting Run-Together Sentences

The following paragraph has some run-together (run-on) sentences. Correct
the run-ons by writing in the spaces above the lines. To review ways to correct
run-on sentences, see Chapter 3.

I love to watch the dogs in my neighborhood when they are being taken for a walk.

One large boxer I know walks calmly and slowly, his head held proudly. Other dogs are

so emotional they can hardly suppress their excitement. One terrier pulls at his leash

he has to sniff every tree and inspect every inch of sidewalk. A big black Labrador jumps

up to greet every passerby. Then there are the happy dogs every day I see a big golden

retriever smiling, with her tennis ball in her mouth. She knows she is on her way to the

park to play fetch. A tiny Yorkshire terrier trots proudly as she displays a tiny pink satin

bow in her topknot. I love dogs however, I do not have a pet of my own. Therefore, I rely

on the dogs in my neighborhood to bring me amusement, entertainment, and joy.

Exercise 7   Editing a Paragraph for Complete Sentences

The following paragraph has some incomplete sentences (sentence fragments).
Correct the fragments by writing in the spaces above the lines. To review ways
to correct sentence fragments, see Chapter 6.

Food can be a source of disagreement in my family. My mother insists on serving

large, elaborate meals even when nobody is very hungry. She becomes angry and hurt

by our indifference to all her hard work. My father also likes to cook. Such food as

barbecued ribs and grilled fish. My sister, who is a vegetarian, refuses to eat either my

mother's or my father's cooking. Instead, she buys her own food. Preferring to eat

yogurt and organic vegetables. When I come to visit with a bag full of gourmet meats,

salads, and cakes, I cause an argument. My mother is upset. Because I didn't let her do

the cooking. While my sister won't eat the meat, the nonorganic salads full of

pesticides, or the cakes full of refined sugar. Meanwhile, my father wants to know why

we couldn't have a barbecue.

CHAPTER 23

Jumping In

*Do you know anyone who is extremely careful about applying the finishing touches to a task such as personalizing a Web page, designing a landscape, or even waxing a car? Do you apply the same degree of care when you check your writing, or do you become frustrated and end up rushing the process just to meet a deadline? What approach do you take toward **polishing** your writing?*

Writing a Paragraph: Polishing and Proofreading

The final version of your paragraph is the result of careful thinking, planning, and revising. After many drafts and much editing, and when you are satisfied with the result, read the final draft aloud to *polish* and *proofread*. You can avoid too many last-minute corrections if you check your last draft carefully for the following:

- spelling errors
- punctuation errors
- mechanical errors
- word choice
- a final statement

CORRECTING THE FINAL DRAFT OF A PARAGRAPH

Take a look at the following final draft of the paragraph on My Mother. The draft has been corrected directly above the crossed out material. You will notice corrections in spelling, punctuation, mechanics, and word choice. You'll notice that the slang term *mom* has been changed to *mother*. At the end, you'll notice that a final statement has been added to unify the paragraph.

A Corrected Final Draft of a Paragraph on My Mother

My mother survived difficult ~~time's~~ *times* to become a good ~~parrent~~ *parent* and worker. Her

hard times began when she lost her husband. At his death, ~~She~~ *she* was only nineteen

and had a baby, me, to raise. ~~she~~ *She* survived by going to school at ~~nite~~ *night* to train for a

career. Even though she lives a stressful life, she is a good ~~mom~~ *mother*. She ~~allways take~~ *always takes*

care of me. She listens to my ~~prolems, encourage~~ *problems encourages* me to do my best, and praises all

my efforts. She cleans our apartment until it ~~shine~~ *shines*, and she makes dinner every

night. She makes a ~~great~~ *delicious* chicken casserole. In addition, she works hard at her job.

She is a nurse at a home for elderly people, where she is on her feet ~~allday~~ *all day* and is

still kind and cheerful. At work or at home, my mother is an inspiration to me.

Exercise 1   **Correcting the Errors in the Final Draft of a Paragraph**

Proofread the following paragraph, looking for errors in word choice, spelling, punctuation, and mechanics. Correct the twelve errors by crossing out each mistake and writing the correction above it.

If I had listened to my classmates' opinion of one boy in our fifh-grade class, I would

of missed a strong friendship. His name was Matthew and no body ever talked to him. He

always wore the same clothes and sat alone in the same place in the lunch room. After

school, I sometimes saw him fighting with bigger boys. One day, I was sitting out side the

Principal's office, waiting to pick up a form for my Mother to sign, when Matthew showed

up. I figured he was in some kind of trouble. We waited a long time, and talked a little. He

was very shy but also very funny. The next day, I sat next to Matthew at lunch

eventhough some students stared at me. That year, I learned more about Matthew. He

allways wore the same clothes because he was poor. He and his mother lived in a shelter.

Matthew was no troublemaker; he fought to defend himself against bullies. When we first

talked outside the principle's office, he had been there to sign up for a free lunch pro-

gram. I learned all this because Matthew become my best friend.

Exercise 2 More on Correcting the Errors in the Final Draft of a Paragraph

Proofread the following paragraph, looking for errors in word choice, spelling, punctuation, and mechanics. Correct the thirteen errors by crossing out each mistake and writing the correction above it.

Paper is constantly giveing me problems. I don't mean the kind of paper that I can write or print on, but the other varieties of paper that feel my life. Wrapping paper is on of my worst enemies. I have to fight it, in order to get it to fit around a gift in a box. It, wrinkles in the wrong places; it winds up in big, ugly clumps at the end's of the box. Paper towels are another problem. They are purforated so that it is easy to tear one piece of paper towel from a roll. Unfortunately, one piece of paper towel is useless, if I want to wipe up some spilled juice or clean the crumbs off a counter. Consequently, I rip too many sheets of paper towels at a time, just too be safe. another kind of paper seems to be cheating me. I am convinced that tissues are getting smaller all the time. One tissue is definately not enough to cover a sneeze or catch a sniffle. The price of tissues goes up, but the size of tissues shrinks. Clearly, paper goods are not as good as I wood like them to be.

Giving Your Paragraph a Title

When you prepare the final version of your paragraph, you may be asked to give it a title. The title should be short and should fit the subject of the paragraph. For example, an appropriate title for the paragraph on your mother could be "My Wonderful Mother" or "An Inspiring Mother." Check with your instructor to see if your paragraph needs a title. (In this book, the paragraphs do not have titles.)

Exercise 3 Creating a Title

With a partner or group, create a title for the following paragraph.

Title: _____

My family left New Jersey when I was seven years old, and I am very happy living in Florida. However, sometimes I feel homesick for the North. At Christmas, especially, I wish I could see the snow fall and then run outdoors to make a snowman. In December, it feels strange to string outdoor lights on palm trees. I also miss the autumn when the leaves on the trees turn fiery red and gold. Sometimes my aunt in New Jersey sends me an envelope of autumn leaves, and I remember the crackle of leaves beneath my feet and the smell of the burning leaves in the fall bonfires. Life is different in Florida where we enjoy sunshine all year. We are spared the icy gray days of a Northern winter, the slush of melting snow, and the gloomy rain of early spring. I now live in a place that is always warm and bright, but sometimes I miss the changing seasons of my first home.

Reviewing the Writing Process

In four chapters, you have worked through *four important stages* in writing. As you become more familiar with the stages and with working through them, you will be able to work more quickly. For now, try to remember the four stages:

INFO BOX: The Stages of the Writing Process

Prewriting: gathering ideas, thinking on paper through freewriting, brainstorming, or keeping a journal

Planning: planning the paragraph by grouping details, focusing the details with a topic sentence, listing the support, and devising an outline

Drafting: drafting the paragraph, then revising and editing it

Polishing: preparing the final version of the paragraph, with one last proofreading check for errors in spelling, punctuation, and mechanics

---

Following are an outline, revised draft, and final version of the paragraph on My Mother. Notice how the assignment evolved through the stages of the writing process.

An Outline for a Paragraph on My Mother

topic sentence: My mother survived difficult times to become a good parent and worker.

details: She had a rough life.
She lost her husband.
She went to school at night.
She's a good mom and always takes care of me.
She cooks and cleans.
She makes a great chicken casserole.
She works hard at her job.
She's a nurse.

A Revised Draft of a Paragraph on My Mother

My mother survived difficult times to become a good parent and worker. Her hard times began when she lost her husband. At his death, she was only nineteen and had a baby, me, to raise. She survived by going to school at night to train for a career. Even though she lives a stressful life, she is a good mom. She always takes care of me. She listens to my problems, encourages me to do my best, and praises all my efforts. She cleans our apartment until it shines, and she makes dinner every night. She makes a great chicken casserole. In addition, she works hard at her job. She is a nurse at a home for elderly people, where she is on her feet all day and is still kind and cheerful.

A Final Version of a Paragraph on My Mother
(Changes from the draft are underlined.)

My mother survived difficult times to become a good parent and worker. Her hard times began when she lost her husband. At his death, she was only nineteen and had a baby, me, to raise. She survived by going to school at night to train for a career. Even though she <u>still</u> lives a stressful life <u>today</u>, she is a good <u>mother.</u> She always takes care of me. She listens to my problems, encourages me to do my best, and praises all my efforts. She cleans our apartment until it shines, and she makes dinner every night. She makes a delicious chicken casserole. In addition, she works hard at her job. She is a nurse at a home for elderly people, where she is on her feet all day and is still kind and cheerful. <u>At work or at home, my mother is an inspiration to me.</u>

Lines of Detail: A Walk-Through Assignment

Write a paragraph about a friend. To write this paragraph, follow these steps:

Step 1: For fifteen minutes, freewrite or brainstorm about a friend.

Step 2: Survey your freewriting or brainstorming and underline any specific ideas you can find. Put these ideas in a list.

Step 3: Pick one idea from your list; it will be your topic. Try to develop it by adding details. Get details by going back to your list for other ideas that fit your topic, by brainstorming for more ideas, and by listing new ideas.

Step 4: Put the ideas on your list into categories by marking them or by mapping them.

Step 5: Write a topic sentence and list your ideas below it.

Step 6: Draft your paragraph by writing the topic sentence and all the ideas on your list in paragraph form. Revise, draft, and edit until you are satisfied with your paragraph.

Step 7: Proofread your final draft; then prepare your good copy of your paragraph.

Writing Your Own Paragraph

When you write on any of these topics, be sure to go through the stages of the writing process in preparing your paragraph.

Collaborate

1. This assignment involves working with a group. First, pick a topic from the following list:

    bad drivers
    keeping secrets
    powerful music

    Next, join a group of other students who picked the same topic you did. Brainstorm in a group. Discuss questions that could be asked to get ideas for your paragraph.

    For the drivers topic, sample questions could include "What kind of driver is the worst?" or "How can you avoid being a bad driver?"

    For the secrets topic, sample questions could include "When is it permissible to reveal a secret?" or "Have you ever asked someone to keep your secret?"

    For the music topic, sample questions could include "Is music most powerful at sad occasions or at happy ones?" or "Do the words or the rhythm make music powerful?"

    As you brainstorm, write the questions down. Keep them flowing. Don't stop to answer the questions. Don't stop to say, "That's silly," or "I can't answer that." Try to generate at least twelve questions.

Twelve Brainstorming Questions:

1. _____

2. _____

3. _____

4. _____

5. _____

6. _____

7. _____

8. _____

9. _____

10. _____

11. _____

12. _____

Once you have the questions, split up. Begin the prewriting step by answering as many questions as you can. You may also add more questions or freewrite. Then pick a specific topic, list the related details, and write a topic sentence.

Work through the planning stage by developing an outline with sufficient details.

After you've written a draft of your paragraph, read it to your writing group, the same people who met to brainstorm. Ask each member of your group to make one positive comment and one suggestion for revision.

Finally, revise and edit your draft, considering the group's ideas for improvement. When you are satisfied with your revised draft, prepare a final version of the paragraph.

2. Following are some topic sentences. Select one and use it to write a paragraph.

> Parents should always remember that adult children need _____ and _____.
>
> Learning a new language is hard because _____.
>
> I still have two unanswered questions about college; they are _____ and _____.
>
> Some people enjoy _____ because it is an escape from their problems.

3. This assignment requires you to interview a partner. Your final goal is to write a paragraph that will inform the class about your partner. Your paragraph should use this topic sentence:

Collaborate

> _____ (fill in your partner's name) has had three significant experiences.

Step 1: Before you write the paragraph, prepare to interview a classmate. Make a list of six questions you want to ask. They can be questions such as, "Have you ever had any interesting experiences?" or "Have you ever been in danger?" Write at least six questions *before* you begin the interview. List the questions below, leaving room to fill in short answers later.

Interview Form

1. Question: _____

   Answer: _____

2. Question: _____

   Answer: _____

3. Question: _____

   Answer: _____

4. Question: _____

   Answer: _____

5. Question: _____

   Answer: _____

6. Question: _____

   Answer: _____

Additional questions and answers:

_____

_____

_____

Step 2: As you interview your partner, ask the questions on your list and jot down brief answers. Ask any additional questions you can think of as you are talking; write down the answers in the additional lines at the end of the interview form.

Step 3: Change places. Let your partner interview you.

Step 4: Split up. Use the list of questions and answers about your partner as the prewriting part of your assignment. Work on the outline and draft steps.

Step 5: Ask your partner to read the draft version of your paragraph, to write any comments or suggestions for improvement below the paragraph, and to mark any spelling or grammar errors in the paragraph itself.

Step 6: Revise your draft. When you have completed a final version of your paragraph, read the paragraph to the class.

4. Select one of the following topics. Then narrow it to one aspect of the topic and write a paragraph on that aspect. If you choose the topic of old movies, for example, you might want to narrow it by writing about your favorite old movie.

clothing styles	college rules	junk food
holidays	national heroes	habits
old movies	viral videos	ambitions
college sports	diets	transportation

5. Look carefully at Photograph A. In it, a student is working with a media program that looks a little outdated. Consider the technology that you use (at school, at work, or in your personal life) and write about one item you would like to upgrade.

Photograph A

6. Study Photograph B. Use this silhouette as a prompt to write a paragraph about the most significant relationship in your life.

Photograph B

Name: _____   Section: _____

Peer Review Form for a Paragraph

After you have written a draft version of your paragraph, let a writing partner read it. When your partner has completed the following form, discuss it. Then repeat the same process for your partner's paragraph.

The topic sentence of this paragraph is _____

_____

_____

_____

The detail that I liked best begins with the words _____

The paragraph has enough/too many/too few [circle one] details to support the topic sentence.

A particularly good part of the paragraph begins with the words _____

_____

I have questions about _____

_____

_____

_____

_____

Other comments on the paragraph: _____

_____

_____

_____

_____

_____

_____

_____

_____

Reviewer's name: _____

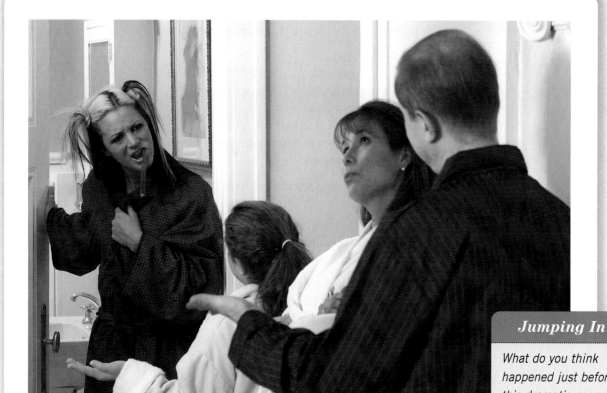

CHAPTER 24

Jumping In

What do you think happened just before this dramatic scene? Can you imagine what led to the expressions of frustration? There must be a story behind this picture, and if you write the story, you will be writing a **narrative** *paragraph.*

Writing a Narrative Paragraph

Paragraphs use different methods to make their points. One kind of paragraph uses *narration.*

WHAT IS NARRATION?

Narration means telling a story. Everybody tells stories; some people are better storytellers than others. When you write a **narrative** paragraph, you can tell a story about something that happened to you or to someone else, or about something that you saw or read.

A narrative covers events in a time sequence because it is always about happenings: events, actions, incidents. However, interesting narratives do more than just tell what happened. They help the reader become involved in the story by providing vivid details. These details come from your memory, your observation, or your reading. Using good details, you don't just tell the story; you *show* it.

Give the Narrative a Point

We all know people who tell long stories that seem to lead nowhere. These people talk on and on; they recite an endless list of activities and soon become boring. Their narratives have no point.

The difficult part of writing a narrative is making sure that it has a point. That point will be included in the topic sentence. The point of a narrative is the meaning of the incident or incidents you are writing about. To get to the point of your narrative, ask yourself questions like these:

What did I learn?
What is the meaning of this story?
What is my attitude toward what happened?
Did it change me?
What emotion did it make me feel?
Was the experience a good example of something (like unfairness, or kindness, or generosity)?

The answers to such questions can lead you to a point. An effective topic sentence for a narrative is

not this: This paper will be about the time I found a wallet on the sidewalk. (This is an announcement; it does not make a point.)
but this: When I found a wallet on the sidewalk, my honesty was tested.

not this: Last week my car alarm wouldn't stop screeching. (This identifies the incident but does not make a point. It is also too narrow to be a good topic sentence.)
but this: I lost my faith in fancy gadgets when my car alarm wouldn't stop screeching.

Exercise 1 Recognizing Good Topic Sentences for Narrative Paragraphs

If a sentence is a good topic sentence for a narrative paragraph, write *OK* on the line provided.

1. _____ Losing my car keys sent me into a foolish panic.

2. _____ A strange encounter will be the subject of this paragraph.

3. _____ Two kittens appeared on our doorstep yesterday.

4. _____ I want to tell you about my first rock-climbing experience.

5. _____ A bad car accident made me grateful to be alive.

6. _____ Auditioning for a local play helped me become more confident.

7. _____ The discovery of a mouse in my closet will be discussed here.

8. _____ When Simon was accused of a crime, he learned about patience.

9. _____ Last night, someone stole my mountain bike.

10. _____ This is the story of an argument between friends.

Collaborate

Exercise 2 Writing the Missing Topic Sentences in Narrative Paragraphs

Following are three paragraphs. Working with a partner or group, write an appropriate topic sentence for each one. Be ready to share your answers with another group or with the class.

1. topic sentence: _____

_____

_____

Yesterday was my day off, so I decided to get some fresh air and sunshine in my backyard. I grabbed an old lawn chair, turned on my CD player, and stretched out in the hot sun. At first, the sun was strong, almost overpowering, and I resolved to go inside before I roasted. But soon I was dozing in the sun, and I felt the comfort of a breeze. Every few minutes, I woke up enough to glance at the sky and see clouds forming. After about a half hour of napping, I became conscious of a distant rumbling. Then the breeze developed into a wind. Suddenly I felt cooler, even cold. However, it felt so good to lie in the chilly current that I fell asleep again. I quickly woke to what sounded like a gunshot right next to me. I jumped up, terrified. The tree two feet away from me had been torn in half by lightning. Shaking with fear, I ran into my house.

2. topic sentence: _____

_____

_____

My favorite television game show was coming to my town, and the producers were giving away free tickets on a first-come, first-served basis. I was determined to get those tickets and be in the audience for a taping of the show. When I told my best friend about the show, he wanted to go, too. "Let's camp out in front of the theater overnight," he said, "and be the first in line to get tickets." We went to the theater at midnight, carrying our backpacks full of snacks, CDs, and video games. As we arrived, we were stunned to see that two hundred people had arrived before us, all with the same idea. We joined the end of the line and spent the night making friends, swapping music, and talking about our favorite parts of the show. The time went quickly because we were having so much fun. When morning came, the tickets ran out just before we got to the front of the line. It was a disappointment, but we didn't feel the night had been totally wasted.

3. topic sentence: _____

_____

_____

A huge music festival called Summer Fun was scheduled for the last weekend in August. Admission was inexpensive, and the park where the event would be held was nearby, so I agreed to go with two friends. Our first challenge was finding a parking space. We wound up parking in a dusty field transformed into an overflow parking lot. After a twenty-minute walk, we arrived at the crowded festival. Thousands of people were standing around three sound stages. Each stage had its own performers, and the noise of one band carried to the music of a second stage. It was hard to hear much. Smart people had brought their own lawn chairs or blankets, but we stood for a long time. The sun was baking our bodies, and we got thirsty. Unfortunately, a bottle of water cost $5.00 at one of the refreshment stands. Even if we had wanted to pay the price, we would have had to wait for twenty or thirty minutes to get the head of the line. After an hour of trying to enjoy the festival, we left, sunburned, hot, and tired.

HINTS FOR WRITING A NARRATIVE PARAGRAPH

Everyone tells stories, but some people tell stories better than others. When you write a story, be sure to

- Be clear.
- Be interesting.

- Stay in order.
- Pick a topic that is not too big.

1. **Be clear.** Put in all the information the reader needs in order to follow your story. Sometimes you need to explain the time, or place, or the relationships of the people in your story in order to make the story clear. Sometimes you need to explain how much time has elapsed between one action and another. This paragraph is not clear:

> Getting the right textbooks from the campus bookstore was a frustrating experience. First of all, I missed the first two days of classes, so José had to give me the list of books, and I really couldn't understand his writing. Then, when I got there, they didn't have all the books I needed. The book I needed the most, the workbook for my Intermediate Algebra class, wasn't on the shelves, and they said they had run out and wouldn't get more until next week. In addition, I couldn't use a Mastercard, only a Visa card, to pay, and I didn't have a Visa card. I left with only one of my required textbooks.

What is wrong with the paragraph? It lacks all kinds of information. Who is José? Is he a classmate? Someone who works in the bookstore? And what list is *the* list of books? The writer talks about getting "there," but is "there" the campus bookstore or another bookstore, and who are "they"?

2. **Be interesting.** A boring narrative can make the greatest adventure sound dull. Here is a dull narrative:

> Volunteering with the homebuilders club was great. Last weekend I helped the club members fix up an old house. First, we did some things outside. Then we worked on the inside and cleaned up the kitchen. We did a little painting, too. I particularly liked the end of the project, when the family who owned the house saw the improvements. They were happy.

Good specific details are the difference between an interesting story and a dull one.

3. **Stay in order.** Put the details in a clear order so that the reader can follow your story. Usually, time order is the order you follow in narration. This narrative has a confusing order:

> Celia was really upset with me yesterday. But that was before I explained about the car accident. Then she forgave me and felt guilty about being so mean. She was angry because I had promised to take her to the movies last night. When I didn't show up, she started calling me on my cell phone. She claims she called seven times and never got an answer. What Celia didn't know was that, on my way to her house, I skidded on a wet road and hit a tree. I wasn't badly hurt, but the paramedics insisted on taking me to the emergency room. My cell phone was in my car while I rode in an ambulance. By the time I left the hospital and made it to Celia's house, it was midnight, and Celia was not in a good mood.

There's something wrong with the order of events here. Tell the story in the order it happened: first, I promised to take Celia to the movies. Second, I had a car accident. Third, Celia tried to call many times. Fourth, I was taken to the emergency room and then released. Fifth, I went to Celia's house, where she was angry. Sixth, I told my story and she forgave me. A clear time sequence helps the reader follow your narrative.

4. **Pick a topic that is not too big.** If you try to write about too
many events in a short space, you risk being superficial. You cannot
describe anything well if you cover too much. This paragraph covers
too much:

> Visiting New York City was like exploring a new world for me. It
> started with a ride on the subway, which was both frightening and exciting.
> Then my cousin, a native New Yorker, introduced me to Times Square,
> where I saw people dressed like aliens in a science fiction movie and I
> learned to navigate through thousands of people all trying to cross the
> street. After that, we went to a famous New York deli where I ate Greek,
> Korean, and Italian food. The next day, we walked to Central Park and
> heard a free concert. That night, we went to a club where the music was
> modern and wild.

This paragraph would be better if it discussed one shorter time period in
greater depth and detail. For example, it could cover one incident—the subway
ride, the visit to Times Square, the deli meal, the concert, or the club—more
fully.

Using a Speaker's Exact Words in Narrative

Some of the examples of narrative that you have already seen have included the
exact words someone said. You may want to include part of a conversation in
your narrative. To do so, you need to know how to punctuate speech.

A person's exact words get quotation marks around them. If you change
the words, you do not use quotation marks.

> **exact words:** "You're acting strangely," he told me.
> **not exact words:** He told me that I was acting strangely.

> **exact words:** My father said, "I can get tickets to the soccer match."
> **not exact words:** My father said he could get tickets to the soccer
>   match.

There are a few other points to remember about punctuating a person's exact
words. Once you've started quoting a person's exact words, periods and commas generally go inside the quotation marks. Here are two examples:

> Marcelline said, "My car needs new tires."
> "Eat your breakfast," my grandmother told me.

When you introduce a person's exact words with phrases like "She said," or
"The police officer told us," put a comma before the quotation marks. Here are
two examples:

> She said, "Take your umbrella."
> The police officer told us, "This road is closed."

If you are using a person's exact words and have other questions about punctuation, check the section on quotation marks in Chapter 16.

WRITING THE NARRATIVE PARAGRAPH IN STEPS

PREWRITING   Gathering Ideas: Narration

Suppose your instructor asks you to write a narrative paragraph on this
topic:

My Last _____

You might begin by *freewriting:*

Freewriting on My Last _____

My last _____. *My last what? Last chance? Last dance? My last chance at passing Algebra. My last cup of coffee. My last day of high school. That was wild. Seniors are crazy sometimes. Coffee—I love coffee. Quit it suddenly. Last cup of morning coffee. Needed my morning coffee.*

You scan your freewriting and realize that you have three possible topics: My Last Day of High School, My Last Chance at Passing Algebra, and My Last Cup of Coffee. Since you do not have any details on passing algebra, and the last day of high school seems like a topic that many students might write about, you decide to be original and work with My Last Cup of Coffee.

Exercise 3 Finding Topics in Freewriting

Each of the freewriting examples that follow contains more than one possible topic for a paragraph. In the spaces below each freewriting, write the possible topics, and write the one that you think would be the best topic for a narrative paragraph. Briefly explain why it would be the best topic: Is it the one with the most details? Is it the most original topic? Or is it the one that would be the easiest to develop with specific details?

1. Freewriting on this Topic: My Only _____

   My only. Only the lonely. Only what? My only afternoon in student detention. My only win at gambling. Those silly Lotto cards you scratch off and see the amount underneath. What a surprise. I never win anything. My only car accident. But it was minor. My only plane trip. Never again, after that experience. Too much waiting around.

   possible topics: _____

   _____

   your choice of the best topic: _____

   reason for your choice: _____

2. Freewriting on This Topic: My Best _____

   My best dress. A beautiful satin dress. Emerald green. My best day. The best day ever. Hard to tell. I guess the day I met Antonio. Antonio was so handsome. I miss him now. It's hard to break up. The day we met, he was so funny. I thought he was wild. A friend. My best friend. I could write about how I met my best friend. My best birthday. The one when I got a surprise party was excellent. I was truly surprised.

   possible topics: _____

   _____

   your choice of the best topic: _____

   reason for your choice: _____

Listing Ideas

Now that you have a specific topic, you can scan your freewriting for all your ideas on that topic. You put all those ideas into a list:

My Last Cup of Coffee

I love coffee.
Quit it suddenly.
Last cup of morning coffee.
Needed my morning coffee.

Adding Specific Details by Brainstorming

To add ideas to your list, try brainstorming. Add questions that will lead you to more details. You can start with questions that are based on the details you already have. See where the questions—and their answers—lead you.

Question: **Why do you love coffee?**

Answer: *I love the taste.*

Question: **Is that the only reason?**

Answer: *It picks me up. Gives me energy.*

Question: **Why did you quit it suddenly?**

Answer: *I figured quitting suddenly would be the best way. Don't drag it out.*

Question: **Why was your last cup drunk in the morning? Why not the afternoon or evening?**

Answer: *My first cup in the morning was the one I needed the most. To wake up.*

Question: **Were there any other times you needed it?**

Answer: *I needed it all day.*

Question: **Can you be more specific?**

Answer: *I craved coffee around 10:00 a.m., and then again around 3:00 or 4:00 p.m., and also after dinner.*

Question: **How did you feel after you quit?**

Answer: *I felt terrible at first. The next day I felt better.*

Question: **What do you mean by saying you felt terrible?**

Answer: *I was irritable. Shaky. I had bad headaches.*

As you can see, questions can lead you to more details and can help you to decide whether you will have enough details to develop a paragraph on your topic or whether you need to choose another topic. In this case, the details in the answers are sufficient for writing a paragraph.

Exercise 4   **Brainstorming for Details**

Collaborate

Following are topics and lists of details. With a partner or group, brainstorm at least five questions and answers, based on the existing details, that could add more details. The first one is partly done for you.

1. **topic:** A Power Failure

   The electricity went off.

   It was a very hot day.

We had no air conditioning or fans.
The ice in the freezer was melting.
I tried to cool off.
I couldn't do a lot of things because there was no electricity.

Brainstorming Questions and Answers:

Question 1: *How long did the power stay off?*

Answer 1:   *About four hours.*

Question 2: *What was the temperature?*

Answer 2:   *Ninety degrees.*

Question 3: _____

Answer 3:   _____

Question 4: _____

Answer 4:   _____

Question 5: _____

Answer 5:   _____

2. **topic:** An Accident on the School Bus
   I was in fifth grade.
   We were riding to school one morning.
   The driver yelled.
   Our bus flipped into a ditch.
   Everyone was screaming.
   No one was badly hurt.

Brainstorming Questions and Answers:

Question 1: _____

Answer 1:   _____

Question 2: _____

Answer 2:   _____

Question 3: _____

Answer 3:   _____

Question 4: _____

Answer 4:   _____

Question 5: _____

Answer 5:   _____

3. **topic:** A Special Gift
   Dave gave it to me.
   It was a framed picture.

He was very thoughtful.

The picture was special.

He really surprised me.

It happened a long time ago.

Brainstorming Questions and Answers:

Question 1: _____

Answer 1:   _____

Question 2: _____

Answer 2:   _____

Question 3: _____

Answer 3:   _____

Question 4: _____

Answer 4:   _____

Question 5: _____

Answer 5:   _____

Focusing the Prewriting

To begin focusing your topic and details around some point, list your topic and all the details you have gathered so far. The list that follows includes all of the details gathered from freewriting and brainstorming.

My Last Cup of Coffee

I love coffee.

Quit it suddenly.

Last cup of morning coffee.

Needed my morning coffee.

I love the taste of coffee.

It picks me up.

Gives me energy.

I figured quitting suddenly would be the best way.

Don't drag it out.

My first cup in the morning was the one I needed the most.

To wake up.

I needed it all day.

I craved coffee around 10:00 a.m., and then again around 3:00 or 4:00 p.m., and also after dinner.

I felt terrible at first.

The next day I felt better.

First I was irritable. Shaky. I had bad headaches.

Coherence: Grouping the Details and Selecting a Logical Order

If you survey the list, you can begin to group the details:

List of Details on My Last Cup of Coffee

Why I Love Coffee

I love the taste.
It picks me up.
Gives me energy.

The Morning I Quit

I quit it suddenly.
I figured quitting suddenly would be the best way.
Don't drag it out.
Drank my last cup in the morning.
My first cup in the morning was the one I needed most.
To wake up.

The Afternoon

I needed it all day.
Around 3:00 or 4:00 p.m., I craved coffee.
I felt terrible at first.
I was irritable and shaky.

The Evening

I craved coffee after dinner.
I was more irritable.
I had a bad headache.

The Next Day

I felt better.

Looking at these groups, you notice one, Why I Love Coffee, is background for your narrative. Three groups, The Morning I Quit, The Afternoon, and The Evening, tell about the *stages* of your quitting. And the last group tells how you felt *after* you had your last cup. These groups seem to lead to a *logical order* for the paragraph: a *time order*. A logical order will give your paragraph coherence.

Unity: Selecting a Topic Sentence

To give the paragraph unity, you need a point, a topic sentence. Surveying your topic and detail, you might decide on this topic sentence:

My last cup of coffee was in the morning.

To be sure that your paragraph has *unity*, check your topic sentence. It should (1) make a point and (2) relate to all your details.

Does it make a point? No. It says your last cup of coffee was in the morning. That isn't much of a point. It is too narrow to develop into a paragraph. Does the topic sentence relate to all your details? No. You have details about why you love coffee, when you needed it, how you quit, and how you felt afterward. But with your topic sentence, you can talk only about the morning you quit.

You need a better topic sentence. To find it, ask yourself questions like,

Did I learn anything from this experience?
Did the experience hurt me?
Did it help me?
Was it a sad experience?
Was it a joyful one?
Were the results good or bad?
Is there a lesson in this experience?

Surveying your details, you might realize that they tell of someone who drank a great deal of coffee and who feels better after he or she quit. You might decide on a better topic sentence:

My last cup of coffee was the beginning of better health.

This topic sentence relates to many of the details you have. You can mention why you love coffee and when you drank it so that you can give some background on how hard it was to quit. You can explain quitting and discuss how you felt afterward. This topic sentence will give your paragraph unity.

To check your topic sentence for unity, ask the following questions:

Checklist: Unity and the Topic Sentence: A Checklist

✔ Does the topic sentence make a point?

✔ Is the point broad enough to cover all the details?

✔ Do the details relate to the topic sentence?

If the answer to these questions is yes, you are helping to unify your paragraph.

Now that you have a topic sentence and a list of details, you are ready to begin the planning stage of writing.

Exercise 5 **Grouping Details**

Below are topics and lists of details. Group the details of each list, writing them under the appropriate headings. Some details may not fit under any of the headings.

1. **topic:** A Day at the Beach
    details: I came home with a bad sunburn and thoughts of my new friend.
    It had been raining for weeks last summer.
    I was dying to go to the beach.
    I set up my beach chair and unpacked my sunblock, water bottle, and CD player.
    On my first vacation day, the sun suddenly shone, and I was off to the beach.
    After listening to one song on my CD player, I fell asleep.
    My friend Manny woke me up by sprinkling sand on my back.
    Alex and I talked for hours.
    Manny was with his handsome friend Alex.
    Manny introduced Alex and left.
    People on the beach were playing Frisbee.
    Alex and I didn't leave the beach until sundown.

List details about the background of the day: _____

_____

_____

_____

List details about the first part of the day at the beach, when you were

alone: _____

_____

_____

_____

List details about Manny and Alex's arrival: _____

_____

_____

_____

List details about your time with Alex: _____

_____

_____

_____

List details about leaving: _____

_____

_____

_____

2.   **topic:** A True Friend's Courage
   details: Salvatore always lent me money.
        One day in my senior year, I was taken in for questioning
        about an armed robbery.
        I met Salvatore when we were both in the sixth grade.
        Sal was much smaller than any of the guys in the hall that day.
        We were friends through high school.
        The word of the police questioning got around at my school.
        The day after the police questioned me, I was in the hall at
        school.
        Some tough members of a school clique started taunting me,
        pushing me against the hallway wall.
        Salvatore came up to my tormentors.
        After Sal's challenge, no one threatened or teased me.
        Salvatore came between me and the group and raised his fists.
        He told them to back off.

A month later, when the real armed robbers were arrested, Sal's faith
in me was justified.

List details about the writer's and Salvatore's background: _____

_____

_____

_____

List details about the writer's trouble with the police and the spread of

the story at school: _____

_____

_____

_____

List details about the writer's confrontation with a group of students:

_____

_____

_____

List details about what Salvatore did and its effects: _____

_____

_____

_____

List details about what happened a month after the incident in the

hall: _____

_____

_____

3.   **topic:** A Surprise
     details: Cato was nowhere to be found, indoors or out.
               My dog always wants to be in the room that I am in.
               One busy Saturday, I began by running from room to room,
               taking out the trash and doing other chores.
               I dumped some clothes in my tiny laundry room on my way to
               make the bed.
               In my bedroom, I noticed that Cato wasn't with me.
               I checked the rooms in my house, but it was no use.
               Panicked, I feared that he might haven gotten outside.
               I checked the backyard.
               I ran to the front yard and called his name.
               Feeling guilty and stupid, I hugged my dog tight.
               I checked the dark garage in the backyard.
               Just as I was about to give up hope, I had an idea.
               My idea was to check the one place I had forgotten: my tiny
               laundry room.
               There was Cato, waiting quietly to be freed from the small
               space.
               My dog Cato loves to be with people.

List details about Cato's personality: _____

_____

_____

List details about what the narrator was doing before Cato disappeared on Saturday: _____

_____

_____

List details about the realization that Cato was missing and the search indoors: _____

_____

_____

List details about the search outdoors: _____

_____

_____

List details about finding Cato: _____

_____

_____

_____

Collaborate

Exercise 6   **Creating Topic Sentences**

Do this exercise with a partner or a group. Following are lists of details. For each list, write two appropriate topic sentences.

1. **topic sentence 1:** _____

_____

   topic sentence 2: _____

_____

   details: Last weekend my boyfriend and I nearly had a serious argument.
   It started when he asked me if I wanted to go bowling on Sunday night.
   I was furious because Sunday was my birthday.
   I was expecting him to take me to a more romantic place for my special day.
   I was also hurt because I thought he had forgotten my birthday.
   My first reaction to his question was to say I hated bowling.
   He said, "But you always want to go bowling. You're in a league."
   Then I cried and called him inconsiderate.
   He just said he couldn't figure me out.
   He got up to leave.
   Finally I said, "You are so selfish, you even forgot that Sunday is my birthday!"
   That was when he told me he had planned a big surprise party for me at the bowling lanes.

2. **topic sentence 1:** _____

_____

topic sentence 2: _____

_____

details: Last week my mother decided to clean out her bed-room closet.

Her first step was to get me to help her.

As we started packing up old shoes, sweaters, and dresses, I was counting the hours until I could escape this chore.

Then we began clearing the shelves at the top of the closet.

Pretty soon my mother was sighing over old pictures of my father and faded Valentine's Day cards he had given her.

Now I was extremely bored.

Next she pulled down a dusty shoe box.

In it were hundreds of photos of an adorable baby and a handsome little boy.

"Who's that?" I said, only half interested.

"Why, it's you," my mother said.

Suddenly I was extremely interested.

As I looked through the photos, the minutes seemed to fly by.

3. topic sentence 1: _____

_____

topic sentence 2: _____

_____

details: I am always in a hurry, and yesterday was particularly hectic for me.

I was on my way home after a long day at work and school.

I realized that I had nothing to eat in my house.

Driving past a local supermarket, I swung into the parking lot to pick up something from the deli.

I left my cell phone on the front passenger seat.

I locked my car doors.

I raced into the market and went straight to the deli.

Within ten minutes, I left with a huge sandwich, some chips, and a bottle of lemonade.

I walked purposefully to my car.

The front passenger window was in pieces on the ground.

My cell phone was gone.

PLANNING   **Devising a Plan: Narration**

Once you have a topic sentence and a list of details, you can write them in outline form. Below is an outline for a paragraph on My Last Cup of Coffee. As you read the outline, you will notice that some of the items on the earlier list have been combined and the details have been grouped into logical categories.

Outline on My Last Cup of Coffee

topic sentence:	My last cup of coffee was the beginning of better health.
details:	
why I love coffee	I love the taste of coffee. Coffee picks me up and gives me energy.
the morning I quit	I quit it suddenly. I figured quitting suddenly would be the best way. Don't drag it out. Drank my last cup in the morning. My first cup in the morning was the one I needed most. I needed it to wake up.
the afternoon	I needed it all day. Around 3:00 or 4:00 p.m., I craved coffee. I felt terrible at first. I was irritable and shaky.
the evening	I craved coffee after dinner. I was more irritable. I had a bad headache.
the next day	I felt better.

Once you prepare your outline, check it for these qualities, using the following checklist.

Checklist: A Checklist for a Narrative Outline

✔ Do all the details connect to the topic sentence?

✔ Are the details in a clear order?

✔ Does the outline need more details?

✔ Are the details specific enough?

With a good outline, you are ready to write a rough draft of a narrative paragraph.

Exercise 7 Finding Details That Do Not Fit

Following are outlines. In each outline, there are details that do not relate to the topic sentence. Cross out the details that do not fit.

1. topic sentence: After one incident, I stopped buying clothes that need ironing.

details: One day I had an important job interview.
To look my best, I decided to wear a freshly ironed white shirt.
I searched my closet, but everything I owned was wrinkled.
I hate ironing, so I often put it off.
Desperate, I set up the ironing board and turned on the iron.

I was frantically trying to press the creases out of a cotton shirt as the minutes ticked by.
Then the phone rang.
I put down the iron and dashed to the phone.
I was stuck on the phone, arguing with my landlord, for ten minutes.
When I hung up the phone, I noticed a strange smell.
I realized I had placed the iron face down and it had burned a hole in my shirt and in the ironing board.
Smoke was fogging the room.
Now there are irons with an automatic "off" switch for such emergencies.

2. topic sentence: One evening, we had an unexpected visitor from the natural world.

details: My husband and I live in a first-floor apartment.
Although it is a large modern complex, it is close to a nature preserve.
The complex has a large pool and patio area.
One night after dinner, we were sitting outdoors on our small, screened porch.
We like to relax as the sun goes down.
Suddenly, we saw a small creature about fifteen feet away.
"It's a cat," I said.
The creature came closer.
It was a small fox.
We were thrilled to see the wild fox so close to us.
We've seen many squirrels, but never a fox.

3. topic sentence: Last Friday was one of those days when everything goes right.

details: First, my computer class was cancelled, so I had some free time.
At work, I got paid.
After work, I met my friends at our favorite club.
There are three places I like to visit.
We listened to music and had a great meal.
After dinner, the place became crowded with people singing, dancing, flirting, and laughing.
There's a new dance I don't know yet.
Sometimes it seems Friday night is just as popular as Saturday night.
I could stay out late and dance because I didn't have class or work on Saturday.
I felt rich, carefree, and excited.

Exercise 8   Recognizing Details That Are Out of Order

Each outline below has one detail that is out of order. Indicate where it belongs by drawing an arrow from it to the place where it should go.

1. topic sentence: My brother's carelessness cost me my job yesterday.
details: Tom was supposed to drive me to work.
I got up on time, but he overslept.

I had to rush him through breakfast so he would not be late.
He had forgotten to put the spare tire in the car.
We got in the car, and the gas gauge was on "Empty."
The night before, Tom had forgotten to put gas in the car.
We made it to the gas station, riding on gas fumes.
Getting gas made me fifteen minutes late for work.
A mile past the gas station, we had a flat tire.
I was ready to scream.
"No problem," said Tom.
Then he looked embarrassed.
Waiting for the tow truck took an hour.
I was so late, my boss fired me.

2. topic sentence: Two children turned my long wait at the doctor's office into an amusing afternoon.

details: I arrived on time for my 2:00 p.m. doctor's appointment.
When I arrived, there were four other people in the waiting room.
"The doctor is running a little late," said the receptionist a few minutes later when a sixth person arrived.
At 2:30 p.m., a mother with a little girl arrived.
The little girl sat next to her mother but soon began to fidget.
By 2:45, the mother had warned the little girl, scolded, and even grabbed the child when the little girl began to wander.
The receptionist replied that the doctor had been handling an emergency.
At about ten minutes past three, a little boy and his mother entered the waiting room. For the little boy, one look at the little girl led to instant love.
He ran to the little girl and kissed her.
Everyone in the room laughed.
After an hour of waiting, I asked the receptionist why no one had been called in to see the doctor.
For a few minutes, all of us in the waiting room forgot to be impatient as we watched the toddlers play together.

3. topic sentence: Listening to the words "I dare you" can be foolish and dangerous.

details: When my brother was eighteen, he got his own car.
The first thing he did with his car was ride around, showing it to all his friends.
Then he decided to take three of his buddies for a ride.
Fortunately, no one was hurt when my brother learned a hard lesson.
"How fast can this car go?" his friend Leroy asked.
"Pretty fast," said my brother.
My brother pushed the gas pedal hard.
"Oh, come on," said Leroy. "That's nothing. Hit it hard. Come on. I dare you."

My brother didn't want to go any faster, but the other two friends were watching and grinning.

They were waiting to see what he would do.

He hit the gas; the car skidded into a light pole.

The front end of the car was destroyed.

Exercise 9 **Putting Details in the Correct Order**

Collaborate

Do this exercise with a partner or a group. In each of the outlines below, the list of details is in the wrong order. Number the details in the correct order, writing *1* next to the detail that should be listed first, and so on.

1. topic sentence: Samantha's plan for giving a surprise birthday party showed her talent for organizing.

details: _____ She invited Tyrone, the guest of honor, for a quiet dinner at her house on the day she wanted to have the party.

_____ Once she knew Tyrone would come for dinner, she mailed the invitations, clearly marked "Surprise Party."

_____ When her guests arrived, she hid them all on the gaily decorated back porch.

_____ Tyrone entered the porch and saw all his friends in a room decorated for a party.

_____ On the day of the party, she called each guest to remind him or her to be early.

_____ When Tyrone arrived, Samantha led him to the porch.

_____ The guests and Tyrone had a wonderful time.

2. topic sentence: Getting my son to preschool yesterday morning was a terrible chore.

details: _____ My son had been up late the night before because I had taken him to a special children's show at the community center.

_____ He was very tired and cranky the next morning.

_____ I had to go back to his bedroom at least twice.

_____ He said "Yes" when I asked him if he was awake, but he buried his head under the covers.

_____ I came in early and woke him gently.

_____ He raced to my car but resisted wearing his car seat.

_____ He wouldn't wear the clothes I put out for him.

_____ He came to breakfast wearing one green and one blue sneaker and a torn sweatshirt.

_____ At breakfast, he couldn't decide what to eat.

_____ I finally gave him Cheerios, but he played with them.

_____ Once he was out of bed, we fought about his clothes.

_____ I finally gave up and let him wear whatever he wanted; meanwhile, I made breakfast.

_____ It got late, so we rushed to leave.

3. topic sentence: Yesterday, I began learning how to stand up for myself.

details: _____ The supervisor said that one staff member was going to take two days of sick leave.

_____ Mr. Ricci asked all of the remaining staff to pick up a few extra hours to cover for the missing person.

_____ The remaining block of time was the late Saturday night time slot.

_____ On Friday, my supervisor, Mr. Ricci, called a meeting to set the schedule for next week's work.

_____ Everyone cooperated until only one block of time remained empty.

_____ "Dan will take it," my coworker said. "Dan's a good guy."

_____ After those kind words, I was about to accept the time slot when suddenly I changed my mind.

_____ Everyone was silent when Mr. Ricci asked for a volunteer for Saturday night.

_____ Then the silence was broken by one of my coworkers.

_____ Instead of accepting the Saturday night hours, I said, "I've filled that slot too often; it's time for someone else to pitch in."

_____ The silence in the group was astonishment at my assertiveness.

DRAFTING Drafting and Revising: Narration

Once you have a good outline, you can write a draft of your paragraph. Once you have a first draft, you can begin to think about revising and editing. The checklist below may help you revise your draft.

Checklist: A Checklist for Revising the Draft of a Narrative Paragraph

✔ Is my narrative vivid?

✔ Are the details clear and specific?

✔ Does the topic sentence fit all the details?

✔ Are the details written in a clear order?

✔ Do the transitions make the narrative easy to follow?

✔ Have I made my point?

Transitions

Transitions are *words*, *phrases*, or even *sentences* that link ideas. Sometimes they tell the reader what he or she has just read and what is coming next. Every kind of writing has its own transitions. When you tell a story, you have to be sure that your reader can follow you as you move through the steps of your story. Most of the transitions in narration have to do with time. Below is a list of transitions writers often use in writing narratives.

INFO BOX: **Transitions for a Narrative Paragraph**

after	finally	now
again	first (second, etc.)	soon
always	frequently	soon after
at first	immediately	still
at last	in the meantime	suddenly
at once	later	then
at the same time	later on	until
before	meanwhile	when
during	next	while

Following is a draft created from the outline on My Last Cup of Coffee. As you read it, you will notice that it combines some of the short sentences from the outline, adds some details, and adds transitions.

A Revised Draft of a Paragraph on My Last Cup of Coffee

sentences combined,
added details
sentences combined,
added details,
transition added
details added

detail added,
transition added

  My last cup of coffee was the beginning of better health. It was hard for me to stop drinking coffee because I love the taste of coffee. In addition, coffee picks me up and gives me energy. I quit it suddenly because I figured that a sharp break from my habit would be better than dragging out the process. I drank my last cup in the morning. It was the cup I needed most, to wake up, so I decided to allow myself that cup. By afternoon, I saw how much I needed coffee all day. Around 3:00 or 4:00 p.m., I craved it. I felt terrible. I was shaky and irritable. After dinner, my coffee craving was worse. I was more irritable, and I had a pounding headache. The next day, I felt better.

Exercise 10 **Recognizing Transitions**

Underline all the transitions—words and phrases—in the paragraphs below.

  1. Yesterday I learned the dangers of trying to perform two tasks at the same time.

My girlfriend was coming over for dinner, and I had promised I would make the dinner myself. Of course, my idea of cooking is boiling water for spaghetti and throwing on a jar of sauce. I had just begun to heat a pot of water when I realized the kitchen was filthy. Immediately, I rushed to mop the floor and clean the counters. While I frantically washed the floor, the water on the stove boiled over. Now I had to turn down the heat under the pot and clean the stove. Meanwhile, I was tracking dirty footsteps over the part of the floor I had just wiped clean. At the same time, I dumped some spaghetti into the pot and popped a jar of spaghetti sauce into the microwave. Then I went back to re-cleaning the floor and swabbing the remaining spills off the stove. Suddenly, I heard a "pop" from the microwave. I had covered the jar of sauce too tightly. After a few seconds, the bubbling tomato mixture had exploded, coating the entire microwave with a hot, sticky red mess. While I struggled to clean up this latest disaster, my girlfriend arrived and quickly suggested that we call out for pizza.

2. My mother has always been a fan of Ricky Martin, the singer, and dreamed of seeing him perform. When Martin began a new tour, my mother checked the Internet and discovered that he was coming to our city. Immediately, she begged me to accompany her to the Martin concert and even offered to pay for my ticket. At first, I provided several reasons for refusing her request, but later on I gave in. When the night of the concert came, we arrived early at the auditorium. At the same time, so did thousands of adoring fans. After nearly an hour of waiting in line, we entered the lobby and soon found our seats. I was tired and a bit irritated by the crowds and the waiting. Then I saw the joy in my mother's eyes; at once, I realized how much this trip meant to her. Her happiness was my reward for accompanying her to the concert.

Exercise 11   Adding the Appropriate Transitions

In the paragraphs below, transitions are shown in parentheses. Circle the appropriate transitions.

1. An ordinary day for my father would be an impossible one for most people. His day starts at 5:30 a.m. (when / after) he wakes up and makes breakfast for me and my two sisters, Amber, two, and Tiffany, four. (Soon after / At the same time), he helps the girls dress and checks that their backpacks have their favorite toys and school

supplies. (Then / Until) he takes them to preschool and drives to his own classes at a school where he is studying to be a chef. (Later / Meanwhile), he picks up the girls, plays with them, and makes an early dinner for us all. (Finally / Suddenly), he leaves for work. My father has a night job as a security guard. (After / Immediately), he puts in his eight hours at work, he comes home, grabs a few hours of sleep, and begins another day of family life, classes, and work.

2. After last weekend's experience, I will never again be a passenger in my Aunt Jennifer's car. (As soon as / At once) we got in the car, Aunt Jennifer opened a pack of cigarettes. She backed out of the driveway with one hand (now / while) she was taking out a cigarette and lighting it with the other hand. She waved this cigarette as she drove; (at last / meanwhile), she sat sideways, half facing me and maintaining a non-stop conversation. (Then / Still) her cell phone rang. She picked it up and talked, holding her cigarette in one hand and the phone in the other. (Before / During) this time, she was steering the car with her elbows and even her knees. (Until / Frequently), she narrowly missed hitting a light pole or a street sign. (At the same time / Again), I prayed that we would arrive alive. (When / Soon) we finally reached our destination, I promised myself never again to get into an automobile with this distracted driver.

Exercise 12 **Using Transitions**

Collaborate

Do this exercise with a partner or a group. Write a sentence for each item below. Be ready to share your answers with another group or with the entire class.

1. Write a sentence with *frequently* in the middle of the sentence

   _____

2. Write a sentence that begins with *Before.*

   _____

3. Write a sentence with *at last* in the middle of the sentence.

   _____

4. Write a sentence that begins with *At first.*

   _____

5. Write a sentence with *later on* in the middle of the sentence.

   _____

6. Write a sentence with *when* in the middle of the sentence.

   _____

7. Write a sentence with *always* in the middle of the sentence.

   _____

8. Write a sentence that begins with *Then.*

   _____

9. Write a sentence that begins with *Suddenly.*

   _____

10. Write a sentence with *in the meantime* in the middle of the
    sentence.

   _____

POLISHING   Polishing and Proofreading: Narration

The draft of the paragraph on My Last Cup of Coffee has some rough spots:

- One idea is missing from the paragraph: Why did you decide to give up coffee? How was it hurting your health?
- Added details could make it more vivid.
- The paragraph needs transitions to link ideas.
- To make its point, the paragraph needs a final sentence about better health.

Following is the final version of the paragraph on My Last Cup of Coffee. As you review the final version, you will notice several changes:

- A new idea, about why you wanted to stop drinking coffee, has been added.
- To avoid repetition, one use of the word "coffee" has been replaced with "it."
- More transitions have been added, including words, phrases, and clauses.
- Some vivid details have been added.
- The verbs in the first few sentences of the paragraph have been changed to the past tense because those sentences talk about the time when you drank coffee.
- A final sentence about better health has been added.

A Final Version of a Paragraph on My Last Cup of Coffee

(Changes from the draft are underlined.)

   My last cup of coffee was the beginning of better health. It was hard for me to stop drinking coffee because I loved the taste of it. In addition, I thought that coffee picked me up and gave me energy. However, I decided to quit drinking coffee when I realized how much I needed it to keep going and to keep from feeling low. I quit it suddenly because I figured that a sharp break from my habit would be better than dragging out the process. I drank my last cup in the morning. It was the cup I needed most, to wake up, so I decided to allow myself that final cup. By afternoon, I saw how much I needed coffee all day. Around 3:00 or 4:00 p.m., I craved it. I felt terrible. I was shaky, nervous, and irritable. After dinner, when I used to have two or three cups of strong coffee, my craving was worse. I was more irritable, I was ready to snap at anyone who asked me a question, and I had a pounding headache. Soon, the worst was over, and by the next day, I felt better. Now, free of my coffee-drinking habit, I have a steady flow of energy, few crashing lows, and pride in my achievement.

Before you prepare your final copy of your paragraph, check it for any places where grammar, word choice, and style need revision. Check also for any errors in spelling and punctuation.

Exercise 13   **Correcting Errors in the Final Draft of a Narrative Paragraph**

Proofread the following paragraphs. Correct any errors in spelling, punctuation, or word choice. There are eleven errors in the first paragraph and twelve in the second paragraph. Write your corrections in the space above each error.

1. Although my Sister is usually my biggest critic, yesterday she gave me some needed support. I had just came home from work when Jennifer noticed the tears in my eyes. "What's the matter"? she asked, in an irritated tone. "What's bothering you now?" I was to tired to fight back, so I just left the living room and locked myself in the bathroom to cry in private. After about five minute of quiet tears, I washed my face with cold water, and opened the door. Jennifer was sitting on the floor, silently waiting for me. "Tell me about it," she said. This time her voice was soft and I poured out the story of my struggles with my boss. Jennifer didnt scold me for handling the situation bad, nor did she give me her tuff version of advice. Instead, she just hugged me. At that moment, I felt that I had someone to help me thru this rough time.

2. Frustration and anxiety, filled my morning when I got stuck in a traffic jam. I was driving to school on Miller highway when I was suddenly forced to slow down. Both lanes ahead of me were a solid mass of cars and truck. At first, we crawld down the road, but soon we wasn't moving at all. Alls I could see were cars, trucks, and the flashing lights of emergency vehicles way ahead. I tried to be patience. Looking for a station with a traffic report, I punched all the buttons on the car radio. I got out and stood beside the car until I coudn't take the heat of the sun and the smell of the car exhaust fumes The minutes turned into a half hour. There was no thing I could do accept think about the quiz I was missing in my speech class. 10 minutes later, traffic began to move again, and my mood improved.

Lines of Detail: A Walk-Through Assignment

For this assignment, write a paragraph on My First _____. (You fill in the blank. Your topic will be based on how you complete Step 1 below.)

Step 1: To begin the prewriting part of writing this paragraph, complete the following questionnaire. It will help you think of possible topics and details.

Collaborative Questionnaire for Gathering Topics and Details

Answer the following questions as well as you can. Then read your answers to a group. The members of the group should then ask you follow-up questions, based on your answers. For example, if your answer is "I felt nervous," a group member might ask, "Why were you nervous?" or "What made you nervous?" Write your answers on the lines provided; the answers will add details to your list.

Finally, share your answers by asking each member of your group to circle one topic or detail that could be developed into a paragraph. Discuss the suggestions.

Repeat this process for each member of the group.

Questionnaire

1. Have you ever been interviewed for a job? When? _____

   _____

   Write four details you remember about the interview:

   a. _____

   b. _____

   c. _____

   d. _____

   Additional details to add after working with the group:

   _____

   _____

   _____

2. Do you remember your first day of school (in elementary school, middle school, high school, or college)? Write four details about that day.

   a. _____

   b. _____

   c. _____

   d. _____

   Additional details to add after working with the group:

   _____

   _____

   _____

3. Do you remember your first visit to a special place? Write four details about that place.

   a. _____

   b. _____

   c. _____

   d. _____

   Additional details to add after working with the group:

   _____

   _____

   _____

Step 2: Select a topic from the details and ideas on the questionnaire. Brainstorm and list ideas about the topic.

Step 3: Group your ideas in time order.

Step 4: Survey your grouped ideas and write a topic sentence. Check that your topic sentence makes a point and is broad enough to relate to all the details.

Step 5: Write an outline of your paragraph, putting the grouped details below the topic sentence. Check your outline. Be sure that all the details relate to the topic sentence and that the details are in a clear and logical order.

Step 6: Write a first draft of your paragraph. Then revise and edit; check that you are sticking to your point, that all your details relate to your point, that your ideas are easy to follow, and that you are using effective transitions.

Step 7: Before you prepare the final copy of your paragraph, check your last draft for errors in punctuation, spelling, and word choice.

Writing Your Own Narrative Paragraph

When you write on any of the following topics, be sure to follow the stages of the writing process in preparing your paragraph.

1. Write about the best or the worst day of your life. Begin by freewriting. Then read your freewriting, looking for both the details and the focus of your paragraph.

   Collaborate

   If your instructor agrees, ask a writing partner or a group to (a) listen to your freewriting, (b) help you focus it, (c) help you add details by asking you questions.

2. Interview a family member or friend who is older than you. Ask the person about a significant event in his or her childhood. Ask questions as the person speaks. You can ask questions like, "Why do you think you remember this incident?" or "How did you feel at the time?" Take notes. If you have a recording device, you can record the interview. But take notes as well.

   When you have finished the interview, review the information with the person you've interviewed. Would he or she like to add anything? If you wish, ask follow-up questions.

Next, on your own, find a point to the story. Use that point in your topic sentence. In this paragraph, you will be writing about another person, not about yourself.

3. Write about a time when you were afraid. Begin by brainstorming questions about what frightened you, why you were afraid, how you dealt with the situation, and so forth. In the planning stage, focus on some point about the incident: Did you learn from it? Did it change you? Did it hurt or help you? Answering such questions can help you come to a point.

Connect

4. Visit the Web site of your local newspaper and find a news story about an unusual crime. Summarize the details of the story in time order and focus your summary with a topic sentence that states what type of crime was committed as well as the most unusual aspect of the crime. Be aware that newspaper accounts of a crime are not always written in time order, so you may have to determine the sequence of events.

5. Following are some topic sentences. Complete one of them and use it to write a paragraph.
When _____, I became angry because _____.
Saying goodbye to _____ was one of the hardest things I have ever done.
One day at _____ taught me _____.
My greatest success came when I _____.
The longest day of my life was the day I _____.

6. To write on this topic, begin with a partner. Ask your partner to tell you about a day that turned out unexpectedly. It can be a day that included a good or bad surprise.

As your partner speaks, take notes. Ask questions. When your partner has finished speaking, review your notes. Ask your partner if he or she has anything to add.

On your own, outline and draft a paragraph on your partner's day. Read your draft to your partner, adding comments and suggestions.

Check the final draft of your paragraph for errors in punctuation, spelling, and word choice.

Your partner can work through this same process to write a paragraph about a day that turned out unexpectedly for you.

7. Write a paragraph that tells a story based on Photograph A. In the photo, the couple appears to be arguing. Create an incident from this photo. To develop your narrative, consider what they are arguing about, why they are so angry, what the children are thinking, and what will happen next.

Photograph A

8. Write a paragraph that tells a story based on Photograph B. To get started, imagine who the hooded person is, where he or she has been, what he or she may have done, what he or she is thinking, and where he or she is headed.

Photograph B

Name: _____   Section: _____

Peer Review Form for a Narrative Paragraph

After you have written a draft of your paragraph, let a writing partner read it. When your partner has completed the following form, discuss the responses. Then repeat the same process for your partner's paragraph.

The topic sentence for this paragraph is _____

_____

I think the topic sentence (a) states the point well or (b) could be revised.

The part of the narrative I liked best begins with the words _____

_____

The part that could use more or better details begins with the words _____

_____

One effective transition is _____

(Write the words of a good transition.)

I would like to see something added about _____

_____

I would like to take out the part about _____

_____

I think this paragraph is (a) easy to follow or (b) a little confusing [choose one].

Other comments: _____

_____

_____

_____

_____

_____

_____

_____

Reviewer's name: _____

Jumping In

*What is your strongest impression of this scene? Does the scene stir up feelings of power? Excitement? Fear? Examining the scene carefully, along with your reactions, will help you **describe** it effectively.*

CHAPTER 25

Writing a Descriptive Paragraph

WHAT IS DESCRIPTION?

Description shows a reader what a person, place, thing, or situation is like. When you write description, you try to *show, not tell*, about something. You want to make the reader see that person, place, or situation, and then, perhaps, to make the reader think about or act on what you have shown.

HINTS FOR WRITING A DESCRIPTIVE PARAGRAPH

Using Specific Words and Phrases

Your description will help the reader see if it uses specific words and phrases. If a word or phrase is *specific*, it is *exact and precise*. The opposite of specific language is language that is vague, general, or fuzzy. Think of the difference between specific and general in this way:

> Imagine that your mother asks you what gift you want for your birthday.
> "Something nice," you say.
> "What do you mean by nice?" your mother asks.
> "You know," you say. "Not the usual stuff."
> "What stuff?" she asks.

"Like the usual things you always give me," you reply. "Don't give me that kind of stuff."

"Well, what would you like instead?" she asks.

The conversation could go on and on. You are being very general in saying that you want "something nice." Your mother is looking for specific details: What do you mean by "nice?" What is "the usual stuff?" What are "the usual things?"

In writing, if you use words like "nice" or "the usual stuff," you will not have a specific description or a very effective piece of writing. Whenever you can, try to use a more precise word instead of a general term. To find a more explicit term, ask yourself such questions as "What type?" or "How?" The examples below show how a general term can be replaced by a more specific one.

> **general word:** sweater (Ask "What type?")
> **more specific words:** pullover, vest, cardigan
>
> **general word:** vegetables (Ask "What type?")
> **more specific words:** broccoli, carrots, peas
>
> **general word:** walked (Ask "How?")
> **more specific words:** stumbled, strutted, strode
>
> **general word:** funny (Ask "How?")
> **more specific words:** strange, comical, entertaining

Exercise 1 Identifying General and Specific Words

Below are lists of words. Put an X by the one term in each list that is a more general term than the others. The first one is done for you.

List 1

_X_ silverware

____ knife

____ soup spoon

____ teaspoon

____ fork

List 2

____ suitcase

____ garment bag

____ trunk

____ overnight bag

_X_ luggage

List 3

____ guitar

____ saxophone

_X_ musical instrument

____ violin

____ flute

List 4

____ aspirin

____ cough syrup

_X_ medicine

____ antacid

____ cold pills

List 5

____ apples

____ strawberries

____ mangoes

_X_ fruit

____ bananas

List 6

____ sports cars

_X_ cars

____ convertibles

____ sedans

____ luxury cars

Exercise 2   **Ranking General and Specific Items**

Below are lists of items. In each list, rank the items from the most general (*1*) to the most specific (*4*).

List 1

___1___ dogs

___2___ trained dogs

___3___ dogs in police work

___4___ search and rescue dogs

List 2

___1___ food

___3___ Thanksgiving food

___2___ holiday food

___4___ Thanksgiving turkey

List 3

___1___ medical worker

___3___ surgeon

___2___ physician

___4___ brain surgeon

List 4

___2___ cookies

___3___ cookies with chocolate

___1___ baked goods

___4___ chocolate chip macadamia cookies

Exercise 3   **Interviewing for Specific Answers**

Collaborate

To practice being specific, interview a partner. Ask your partner to answer the questions below. Write his or her answers in the spaces provided. When you have finished, change places. In both interviews, your goal is to find specific answers, so both you and your partner should be as explicit as you can in your answers.

Interview Questions

1. What is your favorite kind of pet? grey & white short hair tabby cat

2. Name three objects that are in your wallet or purse right now. photo I.D. Indiana money,

3. What is your favorite television commercial? Dont have one

4. What actor or actress do you most dislike? _____

5. If you were buying a car, what color would you choose? blue

6. What sound do you think is the most irritating? when people crack their necks

7. When you think of a beautiful woman or man, who comes to mind? __

8. When you think of a vacation getaway, what place do you picture? ___ the bahamas on a chruis

9. When you are at home and want to relax, what kind of chair do you sit on? recliner

Exercise 4 **Finding Specific Words or Phrases**

List four specific words or phrases beneath each general one. The first word on
List 1 is done for you.

List 1:

general word: green

specific word or phrase: *olive green*

                               dark green

                               light green

                               hunter green.

List 2:

general word: student

specific word or phrase: _____

_____

_____

_____

List 3:

general word: entertainment

specific word or phrase: CMA awards

_____

_____

_____

List 4:

general word: happy

specific word or phrase: _____

_____

_____

_____

List 5:

general word: house

specific word or phrase: _____

_____

_____

_____

Exercise 5 **Identifying Sentences That Are Too General**

Below are lists of sentences. In each group put an *X* by one sentence that is general and vague.

    1. **a.** _____ José has some issues with his father.

       b. _____ José and his father do not agree about José's decision to leave college.

       c. _____ José's father dislikes José's wife.

2. a. _____ She constantly complains about her salary.

   b. _____ She loves to gossip about other people's misery.

   c. _____ She is a negative person.

3. a. _____ Michael is a great guy.

   b. _____ Michael lends me money often.

   c. _____ Michael volunteers at a homeless shelter.

4. a. _____ Most of the movie showed cars crashing.

   b. _____ There was no real plot.

   c. _____ The movie I saw last night was stupid.

5. a. _____ I want to be the best that I can be.

   b. _____ I want to work with disabled children.

   c. _____ I want to play in the Super Bowl.

Using Sense Words in Your Descriptions

One way to make your description specific and vivid is to use **sense words.** As you plan a description, ask yourself,

What does it **look** like?
What does it **sound** like?
What does it **smell** like?
What does it **taste** like?
What does it **feel** like?

The sense details can make the description vivid. Try to include details about the five senses in your descriptions. Often you can brainstorm sense details more easily if you focus your thinking.

INFO BOX: Devising Sense Details

For the sense of	think about
sight	colors, light and dark, shadows, or brightness.
hearing	noise, silence, or the kinds of sounds you hear.
smell	fragrance, odors, scents, aromas, or perfume.
taste	bitter, sour, sweet, or compare the taste of one thing to another.
touch	the feel of things: texture, hardness, softness, roughness, smoothness.

Exercise 6 **Brainstorming Sense Details for a Description Paragraph**

With a partner or a group, brainstorm the following ideas for a paragraph. That is, for each topic, list at least six questions and answers that could help you find sense details. Be prepared to read your completed exercise to another group or to the class.

1. topic: Eric has the most cluttered workstation in the office.
Brainstorm questions and answers:

Question: _____

Answer: _____

Question: _____

Answer: _____

Question: _____

Answer: _____

Question: _____

Answer: _____

Question: _____

Answer: _____

Question: _____

Answer: _____

2. topic: The car hit by a truck was a total loss.
Brainstorm questions and answers:

Question: _____

Answer: _____

Question: _____

Answer: _____

Question: _____

Answer: _____

Question: _____

Answer: _____

Question: _____

Answer: _____

Question: _____

Answer: _____

3. topic: The Halloween party turned into a nightmare.
Brainstorm questions and answers:

Question: _____

Answer: _____

Question: _____

Answer: _____

Question: _____

Answer: _____

Question: _____

Answer: _____

_____

Question: _____

Answer: _____

Question: _____

Answer: _____

Exercise 7   Writing Sense Words

Write sense descriptions for the items below.

1. Write four words or phrases to describe what a new pair of sneakers feels like:

_____

_____

2. Write four words or phrases to describe what a squirrel looks like:

_____

_____

3. Write four words or phrases to describe the sounds of a traffic jam:

_____

_____

4. Write four words or phrases to describe the taste of a slice of lemon:

_____

_____

WRITING THE DESCRIPTIVE PARAGRAPH IN STEPS

PREWRITING   Gathering Ideas: Description

Suppose your instructor asks you to write about this topic: An Outdoor Place. You might begin by *brainstorming*.

Sample Brainstorming on an Outdoor Place

Question: What place?

Answer: Outside somewhere.

Question: Like the outside of a building?

Answer: Maybe.

Question: The beach?

Answer: That would be OK. But everybody will write on that.

Question: How about a park?

Answer: Yes. A park would be good.

Question: How about the park near your workplace—the city park?

Answer: I could do that. I go there at lunchtime.

You scan your brainstorming and realize you have three possible topics: the outside of a building, the beach, or a city park. You decide that you can write the most about the city park, so you brainstorm further:

Brainstorming on a Specific Topic: A City Park

Question: What does the park look like?

Answer: It's small.

Question: How small?

Answer: Just the size of an empty lot.

Question: What's in it?

Answer: Some trees. Benches.

Question: What else is in it?

Answer: A fountain. In the middle.

Question: Any swing sets or jungle gyms?

Answer: No, it's not that kind of park. Just a green space.

Question: Why do you like this park?

Answer: I just like it. It's near the store where I work. I go there at lunchtime.

Question: But why do you go there?

Answer: It's nice and green. It's not like the rest of the city.

Question: What's the rest of the city like?

Answer: The rest of the city is dirty, gray, and noisy.

By asking and answering questions, you can (1) choose a topic, and (2) begin to develop ideas on that topic. Each answer can lead you to more questions and thus to more ideas.

Exercise 8   Identifying Topics in Brainstorming

Following are examples of early brainstorming. In each case, the brainstorming is focused on selecting a narrow topic from a broad one. Imagine that the broad topic is one assigned by your instructor. Survey each example of brainstorming and list all the possible narrower topics within it.

1. **broad topic:**   Describe an outdoor gathering you attended.

   brainstorming:

   Question: **What kind of outdoor gathering?**

   Answer: *I can't think of any.*

   Question: **Don't you get together with people outdoors?**

   Answer: *Sure. At the lake. My friends and I fish.*

   Question: **Do you go fishing on a boat?**

   Answer: *Yes. My friend's old boat.*

   Question: **Or could you write about another outdoor gathering?**

   Answer: *A barbecue at my cousin's house. Over the Labor Day weekend.*

   Question: **Did you enjoy it?**

   Answer: *Yes, but I don't know what I'd write about it.*

   Question: **Do you get together with people and play any outdoor sports?**

   Answer: *I play on a softball team on weekends.*

   possible topics: _____

   _____

   _____

2. **broad topic:**   Write about a powerful person.

   brainstorming:

   Question: **Who is powerful?**

   Answer: *A president. A sports star. A rich person.*

   Question: **Can it be a different kind of power?**

   Answer: *Somebody with a powerful personality.*

   Question: **What's a powerful personality?**

   Answer: *A strength that can change lives. Or maybe someone who just changed his or her life.*

   Question: **What do you mean when you say "changed"?**

   Answer: *Changed attitudes, changed bad habits, or maybe just improved life for one or more people.*

   possible topics: _____

   _____

   _____

Collaborate

Exercise 9 **Developing Ideas through Further Brainstorming**

Following are examples of brainstorming. Each example brainstorms a single, narrow topic. Working with a group, write four more questions and answers based on the ideas already listed.

1. **topic:** My Favorite Cap

   brainstorming:

   Question: **What can you say about your favorite cap?**
   Answer: It's comfortable.

   Question: **Why is it comfortable?**
   Answer: It's broken in.

   Question: **What does that mean?**
   Answer: It's old and soft.

   Question: **How did it get soft?**
   Answer: I sat on it, threw it on the floor.

   Question: **Deliberately?**
   Answer: No, I'm just very careless.

   Four additional questions and answers:

   Question: _____

   Answer: _____

   Question: _____

   Answer: _____

   Question: _____

   Answer: _____

   Question: _____

   Answer: _____

2. **topic:** My Favorite Meal: A Burger and Fries

   brainstorming:

   Question: **Why do you like burgers and fries so much?**
   Answer: I like crispy fries and juicy burgers.

   Question: **Why? Is it the taste?**
   Answer: Sure.

   Question: **What do you like about the taste of a burger?**
   Answer: I guess I like the pickles and onions and the chewy taste of ground meat.

   Question: **What else?**
   Answer: I like beef.

   Four additional questions and answers:

   Question: _____

   Answer: _____

Question: _____

Answer: _____

Question: _____

Answer: _____

Question: _____

Answer: _____

Focusing the Prewriting

To begin focusing your topic and details around some point, list the topic and all the details you've gathered so far. The following list includes all the details you've gathered from both sessions of brainstorming on A City Park.

> *topic: A City Park*
> *park near my workplace*
> *I go there at lunchtime.*
> *It's small.*
> *just the size of an empty lot*
> *Some trees. Benches.*
> *A fountain. In the middle.*
> *a green space*
> *I like it.*
> *It's near the store where I work.*
> *It's nice and green.*
> *It's not like the rest of the city.*
> *The rest of the city is dirty, gray, and noisy.*

Grouping the Details

If you survey the list, you can begin to group the details:

What It Looks Like	*Where It Is*
It's small.	*park near my workplace*
just the size of an empty lot	*It's near the store where I work.*
it's nice and green.	
a green space	
Some trees. Benches.	
A fountain. In the middle.	

How I Feel About It
I like it.
I go there at lunchtime.
It's not like the rest of the city.
The rest of the city is dirty, gray, and noisy.

Surveying the details, you notice that they focus on the look and location of a place you like. You decide on this topic sentence:

A small city park is a nice place for me because it is not like the rest of the city.

You check your topic sentence to decide whether it covers all your details. Does it cover what the park looks like and its location? Yes, the words "small" and "city" relate to what it looks like and its location. Does it cover how you feel about the park? Yes, it says the park is "a nice place for me because it is not like the rest of the city."

Now that you have a topic sentence and a list of details, you are ready to begin the planning stage of writing.

Exercise 10   **Grouping Details**

Following are topics and lists of details. Group the details of each list, writing them under the appropriate headings. Some details may not fit under any of the headings.

1. topic: A Great Front Porch

details: It got a constant breeze from the nearby river.
The wood floor and railings were painted white.
Oak trees shaded it on three sides.
Flower pots of fragrant jasmine lined the edges of the railings.
White wicker chairs sat on the porch.
Hanging plants smelled fresh and clean.
Each chair had a soft pillow for a seat.

List details about the temperature: _____

_____

_____

_____

List details about the colors related to the porch: _____

_____

_____

_____

List details about the scents and smells related to the porch: _____

_____

_____

_____

2. topic: A Cheap Motel Room

details: There were cracks in the bathroom sink.
The bedroom smelled moldy.
The hairdryer didn't work.
Two small holes in the drapes allowed light to penetrate into the bedroom.
The coffeemaker was missing the carafe.
The bedroom carpet was worn and shiny.
The people in the next room were noisy.
The bathtub was stained.

List details about the bathroom: _____

_____

_____

_____

List details about the appliances: _____

_____

_____

_____

List details about the bedroom: _____

_____

_____

_____

3. topic: An Antique Book

details: It had a green leather cover.
The title of the book was pressed into the cover in faded gold letters.
The pages were yellow.
The book smelled musty.
Several pages were loose.
Two pages had stains.
The corners of the leather cover were frayed.
The title page was missing.

List details about the cover of the book: _____

_____

_____

_____

List details about the inside of the book: _____

_____

_____

_____

Exercise 11   Writing Appropriate Topic Sentences

Collaborate

Do this exercise with a partner or a group. Following are lists of details. For each list, write two appropriate topic sentences.

1. topic sentence 1: _____

_____

_____

topic sentence 2: _____

_____

_____

details: The abandoned factory had once employed most of the townspeople.

The impressive entrance showed traces of white trim on gray stone.

Inside, debris covered the floors.

Large stone counters, now cracked, ran in parallel lines.

Long, high windows cast the only light.

Dust shimmered in the beams of light.

An elaborate molding at the top of the walls still survived.

A high ceiling gave a touch of style.

2. topic sentence 1: _____

_____

_____

topic sentence 2: _____

_____

_____

details: The man in the dentist's waiting room had sweat trickling down his face.

He kept looking at the clock.

His eyes were full of misery.

His jaw was clenched.

His hands trembled as he tried to flip through a magazine.

He sat on the edge of his chair.

When the nurse called his name, he jumped.

3. topic sentence 1: _____

_____

_____

topic sentence 2: _____

_____

_____

details: I had always resisted my friends' attempts to get me to try frozen yogurt.

I imagined the sour taste of regular yogurt with an ice cream texture.

One day, my cousin dragged me to a frozen yogurt store.

"Try the white chocolate mousse," she said.

I gave in to her urging.

The taste was not at all sour.

It hinted at white chocolate but also at vanilla.

The yogurt was softer than ice cream.

It was more like the ice cream products that are swirled onto a cone.

The light texture felt smooth on my tongue.

I wanted more of this tasty treat.

4. topic sentence 1: _____

_____

_____

topic sentence 2: _____

_____

_____

details: The thunder roared while the lightning crashed and crackled, coming closer and closer.

Rain gushed into the streets.

The wind became stronger.

Leaves and tree branches flew in the air.

Doors blew shut and windows flew open.

Cars pulled over to the side of the road.

Pedestrians ran for cover.

PLANNING   ## Devising a Plan: Description

Once you have a topic sentence, a list of details, and some grouping of the details, you can write them in outline form. Before you write your details in outline form, check their order. Remember, when you write a description, you are trying to make the reader *see*. It will be easier for the reader to imagine what you see if you put your description in a simple, logical order. You might want to put descriptions in order by **time sequence** (first to last), by **spatial position** (for example, top to bottom, right to left, or outside to inside), or by **similar types** (for example, all about the flowers, then all about the trees in a garden).

If you are describing a house, for instance, you may want to start with the outside of the house and then describe the inside. You do not want the details to shift back and forth, from outside to inside and back to outside. If you are describing a person, you might want to group all the details about his or her face before you describe the person's body. You might want to describe a meal from the first course to dessert.

Look again at the grouped list of details on a city park. To help make the reader see the park, you decide to arrange your details in *spatial order*: First, describe where the park is located; second, describe the edges and the middle of the park. The final lines of your paragraph can describe your feelings about the park. The following outline follows this order.

Outline for a Paragraph on A City Park

topic sentence:	A small city park is a nice place for me because it is not like the rest of the city.
details:	
location	{ It is near the store where I work.
appearance	It is just the size of an empty lot.
from edges	It is nice.
	It is a green space.
to the middle	It has some trees and benches.
	It has a fountain in the middle.
	I like it.
how I feel	I go there at lunchtime.
about it	It is not like the rest of the city.
	The rest of the city is dirty, gray, and noisy.

Once you have an outline, you can begin writing a description paragraph.

Exercise 12 **Putting Details in Order**

Following are lists that start with a topic sentence. The details under each topic sentence are not in the right order. Put the details in the right order by labeling them, with *1* being the first detail, *2* the second, and so forth.

1. topic sentence: The children's choir quickly found its rhythm.
(Arrange the details in time order.)

details: _____ By their second selection, they and their audience were having fun.

_____ As they entered the stage, the children awkwardly stumbled into their places.

_____ The music director calmly extended his hands to the children as they stood waiting to sing.

_____ Family and friends waited eagerly for the children to appear.

_____ They began their first number a little hesitantly.

_____ The children's power grew until they left the stage with a standing ovation.

2. topic sentence: The old house had been well cared for.
(Arrange the details from outside to inside.)

details: _____ The white wooden fence was freshly painted.

_____ The front hall had a gleaming tile floor.

_____ Every tree in the front yard had been trimmed.

_____ The front door had a polished door knob.

_____ Not a speck of dust could be found in the living room.

3. topic sentence: The painting of the old man's face showed an angry person. (Arrange the details from forehead to chin.)

details: _____ The wrinkles on the forehead led to scowling eyebrows.

_____ The chin jutted out defiantly.

_____ The old man's eyes were dark slits.

_____ There were deep lines around the sides of his nose.

_____ These lines extended below his mouth, pulling downward.

Collaborate

Exercise 13 **Creating Details Using a Logical Order**

The following lists include a topic sentence and indicate a required order. With a partner or group, write five sentences of details in the required order.

1. topic sentence: The medicine cabinet in my bathroom is full of everything except medicine.
(Describe the contents of the cabinet from top shelf to bottom shelf.)

a. _____

b. _____

c. _____

d. _____

e. _____

2. topic sentence: The movie was filled with suspenseful encounters.
(Describe these encounters from the beginning of the
movie to the end.)

a. _____

b. _____

c. _____

d. _____

e. _____

3. topic sentence: Both the players and the crowd at the baseball game
behaved badly.
(First describe the players' behavior; then describe the
crowd's behavior.)

a. _____

b. _____

c. _____

d. _____

e. _____

4. topic sentence: My little sister looked like a model.
(Describe the person from head to foot.)

a. _____

b. _____

c. _____

d. _____

e. _____

DRAFTING Drafting and Revising: Description

After you have an outline, the next step is creating a rough draft of the paragraph. Once you have the first draft, look it over, using the following checklist:

Checklist: A Checklist for Revising a Descriptive Paragraph

✓ Are there enough details?

✓ Are the details specific?

✓ Do the details use sense words?

✓ Are the details in order?

✓ Is the description easy to follow?

✓ Have I made my point?

If you look at the outline for A City Park, you'll notice that it has some problems:

- The details are not very specific. Words like "nice" do not say much, and "nice" is used twice, in the topic sentence and in the details.

- Some parts of the outline need more support. The description of the inside of the park needs more details.

- The description would also be easier to follow if it had some effective transitions.

These weak areas can be improved in the drafting and revising stage of the writing process.

Transitions

As you revise your description paragraph, you may notice places in the paragraph that seem choppy or abrupt. That is, one sentence may end, and another may start, but the two sentences don't seem to be connected. Reading your paragraph aloud, you may sense that it is not very smooth. Good transitions can help to make smooth connections between your ideas. Here are some transitions you may want to use in writing a description:

INFO BOX: Transitions for a Descriptive Paragraph

To show ideas brought together

and	also	in addition	next

To show a contrast

although	however	on the contrary	unlike
but	in contrast	on the other hand	yet

To show a similarity

all	each	like	similarly
both			

To show a time sequence

after	first	next	then
always	second (etc.)	often	when
before	meanwhile	soon	while

To show a position in space

above	between	in front of	over
ahead of	beneath	inside	there
alongside	beyond	near	toward
among	by	nearby	under
around	close	next to	up
away	down	on	underneath
below	far	on top of	where
beside	here	outside	

There are many other transitions you can use, depending on what you need to link your ideas.

Below is a revised draft of the paragraph on A City Park. When you read it, you will notice the added details and more precise words. You will also notice that some short, choppy sentences have been combined and that transitions have been added. In addition, a final sentence of details has been added to the end of the paragraph.

A Revised Draft of a Paragraph on A City Park

specific detail	A small city park is a <u>pleasant</u> place for me because it is not like the rest of the city. The park is near the
added details, sentences combined, specific detail, transition added, sense detail, transition, added details	store where I work; <u>in fact, it is only a ten-minute walk.</u> <u>It is just the size of an empty lot, yet it is an attractive green space.</u> <u>Under</u> the trees are <u>weathered</u> <u>wooden</u> benches <u>where people of every age sit and</u>
sense detail	<u>enjoy the calm.</u> The only sound is the <u>splash</u> of the
sentences combined	fountain at the center of the park. <u>I enjoy the park and visit it at lunchtime.</u> It is not like the rest of the city,
sense words specific details	which is dirty, gray, and <u>filled with the noise of</u> <u>screeching brakes, rumbling trucks, and blaring</u>
final sentence transition, sense words	<u>horns.</u> <u>The park is a quiet, clean spot where the sun filters through the leaves of trees.</u>

Although it is important to work on specific details and sense words in each stage of your writing, it is easiest to focus on revising for details in the drafting stage, when you have a framework for what you want to say. With that framework, you can concentrate on the most vivid way to express your ideas.

Exercise 14 **Recognizing Transitions**

Underline the transitions in the paragraph below.

My sister's one-room apartment was a college student's dream. It was on the second floor of an old house converted into small apartments. Inside the door was a small room painted a cheerful yellow. The walls were covered with black-and-white photographs in red, yellow, and blue frames. My sister, who was majoring in photography, had placed bookcases made of bricks and boards below the photos. On every bookshelf, piles of books about famous photographers and their works were mixed with cameras, lenses, and photographic prints. Between two bookcases, my sister had placed an old single bed disguised to look like a sofa. Nearby was an old oak table; on top of the table, shiny green plants reached out to the sun coming from a large window above the table. Two old oak stools under the table completed the room. Beyond this room were a tiny kitchen alcove and a small bathroom. When I, a sixteen-year-old, saw my older sister's college apartment, I couldn't wait to finish high school and have my own sophisticated place.

Exercise 15 **Adding the Appropriate Transitions**

In the paragraph below, transitions are shown in parentheses. Circle the appropriate transitions.

Mrs. Gallagher served me and her son an unforgettable breakfast. (First / Before) she gave each of us a huge glass of fresh-squeezed orange juice. (After / While) we were enjoying the juice, she was whisking a huge bowl of raw eggs, milk, and spices into a frothy mix for scrambled eggs. (Soon / Often), the egg mixture was slowly cooking in a buttered pan. As it cooked, Mrs. Gallagher focused on popping some homemade cinnamon buns into the oven. (Always / When) the scrambled eggs began to gel, Mrs. Gallagher stirred them softly with a wooden spoon. (Then / Second), the scent of cinnamon filled the room. With perfect timing, Mrs. Gallagher pulled the buns from the oven and spooned the scrambled eggs onto our plates. The eggs were the creamiest I had ever tasted. (Until / In addition), the cinnamon buns were the softest, sweetest, and most cinnamon-infused of my life. (After / Before) my first taste of Mrs. Gallagher's breakfast, I had no idea how good breakfast could be.

Exercise 16 **Revising for Specific Details or Sense Words**

In the following paragraph, replace each underlined word or phrase with more specific details or sense words. Write your changes in the space above the underlined items.

I had a difficult time selecting a special shirt for Calvin, my boyfriend. I wanted him to look <u>nice</u> at his cousin's graduation party, but I couldn't find a shirt that <u>would look right on Calvin.</u> I looked at <u>lots of</u> shirts in <u>a bunch of</u> stores but most of the shirts were either <u>funny-looking</u> or <u>wrong.</u> One came in <u>a weird color,</u> another had a <u>stupid</u> stripe, and another <u>wouldn't fit him right</u>. I became <u>fed up with</u> looking at <u>stuff</u> that I would never want Calvin to wear. Just as I was leaving the mall, I saw one <u>nice</u> shirt

on a sale rack. I grabbed the shirt, paid for it, and left the mall, feeling <u>good</u>.

POLISHING   **POLISHING AND PROOFREADING: DESCRIPTION**

Focus on Support and Details

Before you prepare the final version of your paragraph, check it again for any problems in support and details, and for any places where grammar, word choice, and style need revision. Check also for any errors in spelling and punctuation.

Following is the final version of the paragraph on A City Park. As you review it, you'll notice several changes:

- The name of the park has been added to make the details more specific.

- More sense details have been added.

- There were too many repetitions of "it" in the paragraph, so "it" has frequently been changed to "the park," "Sheridan Park," and so forth.

- An introductory sentence has been added to make the beginning of the paragraph smoother.

A Final Version of a Paragraph on A City Park

(Changes from the draft are underlined.)

<u>Everyone has a place where he or she can relax.</u> A small city park is a pleasant place for me because it is not like the rest of the city. <u>Sheridan Park</u> is near the store where I work; in fact, it is only a ten-minute walk. <u>The park</u> is just the size of an empty lot, yet it is an attractive green space <u>ringed with maple trees.</u> Under the trees are weathered wooden benches where people of every age sit and enjoy the calm. The only sound is the splash of the fountain at the center of the park. I enjoy the park and visit it at lunchtime. <u>This special place</u> is not like the rest of the city, which is dirty, gray, and filled with the noise of screeching brakes, rumbling trucks, and blaring horns. The park is a clean, quiet spot where the sun filters through the leaves of trees.

Exercise 17   **Correcting Errors in the Final Draft of a Descriptive Paragraph**

Proofread the following paragraphs. Correct any errors in spelling, punctuation, or word choice. There are eleven errors in each paragraph. Write your corrections in the space above the errors.

1. Last week, I endured the torture of a long wait at the airport. My flight was

delayed for three hour, and I had to sit on a hard plastic airport chair and wait. I tried

to sleep the time away, but their was no way to realax my body against the metal arms

that devided my seat from the others in the row. Every time I tried closing my eyes

and daydreaming about a more pleasant scene a loudspeaker blasted a garbled announcement Each time, I snapped into awareness because i was hoping to hear good news about my flight. all around me, I heard the sounds of passengers picking up their carry-on luggage, and I watched them get into long, hopeful lines. However, I had to wait and be patient, until I feel like apart of the airport seats.

2. My granmother's kitchen was a happy little room where I learned about family love. I spent most of my first five years at my grandmother house cause both my parents worked long hours. Since my grandmother spent most of her time in her kitchen, I grow up in that room. The kitchen was cluttered with pots, pans, and piles of dirty dishes. Nothing was easy to find. The hot pepper could be under frying pan or in the refrigerator. The garbage can, always overflowed. Yet the room was the center of the universe for me, and my extended family. Two or there cousins, aunts, great-uncles, or nephews were always sitting at the table, drinking coffee, gossiping, and arguing about what some other cousin or neighbor had done. Everynight, my grand-mother cooked huge quantities of beans and rice, chicken, or pork chops for the eight or ten family members who crowded into the small house. I liked the loud laughter and grew hungry when I smell the meet sizzling in the hot oil. Most of all, I loved the hot, cramped kitchen where my grandmother dished out large portions of love.

Lines of Detail: A Walk-Through Assignment

For this assignment, write a paragraph about your classroom, the one in which you take this class.

Step 1: To begin, freewrite about your classroom for ten minutes. In your freewriting, focus on how you would *describe* your classroom.

Step 2: Next, read your freewriting to a partner or a group. Ask your listener(s) to write down any ideas in your freewriting that could lead to a specific topic for your paragraph. (For example, maybe your freewriting has several ideas about how you feel when you are in the classroom, how others behave, or how the furniture and decor of the room create a mood.)

Step 3: With a specific topic in mind, list all the ideas in your freewriting that might fit that main topic.

Step 4: Now, brainstorm. Write at least ten questions and answers based on your list of ideas.

Step 5: Group all the ideas you've found in freewriting and brainstorming. Survey them and write a topic sentence for your paragraph. Your topic sentence may focus on the atmosphere of the classroom, the look of the classroom, how you feel in the classroom, the activity in the classroom, and so forth.

Step 6: Write an outline. Be sure that your outline has enough supporting points for you to write a paragraph of seven to twelve sentences.

Step 7: Write and revise your paragraph. Check each draft for support, and work on using specific details and sense words.

Step 8: Share your best draft with a partner or the group. Ask for suggestions or comments. Revise once more.

Step 9: Prepare the final copy of your paragraph, checking for errors in punctuation, spelling, or word choice.

Writing Your Own Description Paragraph

When you write on any of the following topics, be sure to follow the stages of the writing process in preparing your paragraph.

1. Visit your school's home page and describe its appearance. Consider such questions as what is attractive or unattractive about the page, whether the photographs on it are striking or plain, whether the descriptions of your school are accurate, and whether the page will attract a potential student's attention. Pay close attention to such details as the use of color, size and style of print, and use of space.

Computer

2. Write about your most comfortable piece of clothing. In your topic sentence, focus on what makes it so comfortable.

3. Interview a partner so that you and your partner can gather details and write separate paragraphs with the title "My Dream Vacation."

Collaborate

First, prepare a list of at least six questions to ask your partner. Write down your partner's answers and use these answers to ask more questions. For example, if your partner says she wants a trip to the Caribbean, ask her what part of the Caribbean she would like to visit. If your partner says he would like to go to the Super Bowl, ask him what teams he would like to see.

When you have finished the interview, switch roles. Let your partner interview you.

Finally, give your partner his or her interview responses; take your own responses and use them as the basis for gathering as many details as you can. In this way, you are working through the prewriting stage of your paragraph. Then go on to the other stages. Be prepared to read your completed paragraph to your partner.

4. Write a paragraph that describes one of the following: *topic sentence ?*

    a pet you own or know well   *My sister Trisha's cat is very*
    the contents of your refrigerator   *playful and entertaining.*
    any people riding the subway
    people in the express lane at the supermarket
    children riding the school bus
    a toddler in a car seat or stroller
    the contents of your wallet
    what you ate for breakfast

Be sure to focus your paragraph with a good topic sentence.

5. Write a paragraph about the messiest room you've ever seen.

6. Imagine a place that would bring you a sense of peace. In a paragraph, describe that place.

7. Following are some topic sentences. Complete one of them and use it to write a paragraph.

   The happiest place I know is _____.

   _____ is the most comfortable place in my home.

   Whenever I visit _____, I feel a sense of _____.

   Between classes, the halls of the college seem _____.

   I like to spend time alone at _____ because _____.

8. Write about the sensations of riding in a crowded elevator. You might begin by brainstorming all the details you recall.

9. Look carefully at Photograph A or Photograph B. In a paragraph, describe the face in either photograph. To write this description, consider how you can use specific details and sense descriptions to express what you see and what impression the photograph conveys.

Photograph A   **Photograph B**

10. Write a paragraph about Photograph C. Describe the scene; be sure to include a description of the weather, the circumstances, the body language, and the man in the foreground.

Photograph C

Name: _____   **Section:** _____

Peer Review Form for a Descriptive Paragraph

After you have written a draft version of your paragraph, let a writing partner read it. When your partner has completed the following form, discuss the responses. Then repeat the same process for your partner's paragraph.

The part of this paragraph that I like best begins with the words _____

_____

This paragraph uses some sense words and phrases. Among these sense words and phrases are _____

_____

_____

The part of the paragraph that could use more specific details or sense words begins with the words

_____

The topic sentence of this paragraph is _____

_____

_____

I think there is (enough/too little) [circle one] support for the topic sentence.

I have questions about _____

_____

_____

Other comments on the paragraph: _____

_____

_____

_____

_____

_____

_____

_____

_____

Reviewer's name: _____

CHAPTER 26

Writing an Illustration Paragraph

Jumping In

*Love of country can be exhibited in a number of ways, including parades and celebrations of national holidays. Are there other ways to express a love of one's country? Are they public or personal? Do some involve a long-term commitment? By answering such questions, you will be **illustrating** ways that people express their love of country.*

WHAT IS ILLUSTRATION?

Illustration uses specific examples to support a general point. In your writing, you often use illustration because you frequently want to explain a point with a specific example.

HINTS FOR WRITING AN ILLUSTRATION PARAGRAPH

Knowing What Is Specific and What Is General

A *general statement* is a broad point. The following statements are general:

> College students are constantly short of money.
> Bronson Avenue is in a bad neighborhood.
> Pictures can brighten up a room.

You can support a general statement with specific examples:

general statement: College students are constantly short of money.
specific examples: They need gas money, or bus or subway fare.
                         They need cash for snacks, lunch, or dinner.

general statement: Bronson Avenue is in a bad neighborhood.
specific examples: It has burned out and abandoned buildings.
There are drug dealers on the corners.

general statement: Pictures can brighten up a room.
specific examples: I love to look at my grandmother's family photos, which cover a whole living room wall.
My dentist has framed cartoons on the walls of his waiting room.

When you write an illustration paragraph, be careful to support a general statement with specific examples, not with more general statements:

not this: general statement: Essay tests are difficult.
more general statements: ~~I find essay tests to be hard.~~
~~Essay tests present the most challenges.~~

but this: general statement: Essay tests are difficult.
specific examples: They test organizational skills.
They demand a true understanding of the subject.

If you remember to illustrate a broad statement with specific examples, you will have the key to this kind of paragraph.

Exercise 1 **Recognizing Broad Statements**

Each list below contains one broad statement and three specific examples. Underline the broad statement.

1. On Thanksgiving, there are football games on many television channels.

   If the weather is good, my cousins and I play hockey.

   Thanksgiving means sports to me.

   Everyone talks sports as we eat our turkey.

2. Small children have short attention spans.

   Toddlers like to explore, not to sit in one place.

   Kindergartners don't like to play any game for an hour.

   Five-year-olds can't listen to music for long unless they can sing or dance.

3. Some teens film their crimes of violence and put the videos online.

   Today many crimes are solved because of videos.

   Most stores have cameras that record all in-store activity.

   Some cities have installed cameras on all their streets.

4. I called the cable company and was put on hold for ten minutes.

   Trying to get information from my cable television company was a frustrating experience.

   The person at the end of the line told me she would not answer a question about my bill.

   She said I had to come to the cable office in person, even though the office is open only from 9:00 a.m. to 5:00 p.m., when I work.

5. My sister spends sixty percent of her salary on child care.

   I pay less, but my child's babysitter is an untrained teen.

   There is a waiting list for subsidized preschool care.

   Parents are desperate for quality, affordable childcare.

Exercise 2   **Distinguishing the General Statement from the Specific Example**

Each general statement below is supported by three items of support. Two of these items are specific examples; one is too general to be effective. Underline the one that is too general.

1. **general statement:** Most television-reality programs focus on contests.
   support: Contestants often compete to be the best model.
   Competition is at the heart of most television-reality shows.
   Some contestants fight to become the most outstanding chef.

2. **general statement:** We should think of what our bodies can do, not what they look like.
   support: The appearance of our bodies is not as important as the way our bodies function.
   A person may not have a perfectly shaped body but may be in great physical condition.
   As we age, we may look older than we would like, but we can stay as fit as many young people.

3. **general statement:** A night at the movies is an expensive one.
   support: A movie ticket can cost ten dollars or more.
   Popcorn and a Coke can cost as much as a movie ticket.
   Going to the movies isn't cheap.

4. **general statement:** Other people's music can be irritating.
   support: Teens tend to hate their parents' favorite songs.
   Neighbors will complain about loud music next door.
   Only our kind of music pleases us.

5. **general statement:** I rarely use stamps these days.
   support: I write my friends by e-mail.
   I don't buy stamps very often.
   I pay my bills online.

Exercise 3   **Adding Specific Examples to a General Statement**   Collaborate

With a partner or group, add four specific examples to each general statement below.

1. **general statement:** High school cafeteria food can be awful.

   examples: Some of the food is cold.

   the breadsticks are hard as a rock.

   Pizza tastes like cardboard

2. general statement: Animals are used in many television advertisements.

    examples: Geico comercal

               Benefulld

               Meowmix

3. general statement: People perform many activities while they drive a car.

    examples: talk on the phone _or the tet_

               eat

               makeup

               radio

4. general statement: Today's drugstores sell more than medicine and toothpaste.

    examples: Shampoo

               beer

               magazines

               makeup

WRITING THE ILLUSTRATION PARAGRAPH IN STEPS

PREWRITING Gathering Ideas: Illustration

Suppose your instructor asks you to write a paragraph about some aspect of **cars.** You can begin by listing ideas about your subject to find a focus for your paragraph. Your first list might look like the following:

Listing Ideas About Cars

cars in my neighborhood
my brother's car
car prices
drag racing
cars in the college parking lot
parking at college
car insurance

This list includes many specific ideas about cars. You could write a paragraph about one item or about two related items on the list. Reviewing the list, you decide to write your paragraph on cars in the college parking lot.

Adding Details to an Idea

Now that you have a narrowed topic for your paragraph, you decide to write a list of ideas about cars in the college parking lot:

Cars in the College Parking Lot: Some Ideas

vans
cars with strollers and baby seats
beat-up old cars, some with no bumpers
few new sports cars, gifts from rich parents
some SUVs
older people's cars, Volvos and Cadillacs
racing cars, modified, brightly striped
elaborate sound systems
bumper stickers
some stickers have a message
some brag

Creating a Topic Sentence

If you examine this list and look for *related ideas*, you can create a topic sentence. The ideas on the list include (1) details about the kinds of cars, (2) details about what is inside the cars, and (3) details about the bumper stickers. Not all the details fit into these categories, but many do.

Grouping the related ideas into the three categories can help you focus your ideas into a topic sentence.

Kinds of Cars

beat-up old cars, some with no bumpers

vans

few new sports cars, gifts from rich parents

some SUVs

older people's cars, Volvos and Cadillacs

racing cars, modified, brightly striped

Inside the Cars

elaborate sound systems

strollers and baby seats

Bumper Stickers

some stickers have a message

some brag

You can summarize these related ideas in a topic sentence:

Cars in the college parking lot reflect the diversity of people at the school.

Check the sentence against your details. Does it cover the topic? Yes. The topic sentence begins with "Cars in the college parking lot." Does it make some point about the cars? Yes. It says the cars "reflect the diversity of people at the school."

Because your details are about old and new cars, what is inside the cars, and what is written on the bumper stickers, you have many details about differences in cars and some hints about the people who drive them.

Exercise 4 Finding Specific Ideas in Lists

Following are two lists. Each is a response to a broad topic. Read each list, and then underline any words that could become a more specific topic for a paragraph.

Topic: business

big business success	computers in business
running a business	business law class
working for yourself	business ethics
the stock market	collecting unemployment
the dress code at a bank	writing a good resumé

Topic: health

getting a flu shot	home remedies for a cold
health insurance	heart attacks
nursing around the world	healthy snacks for children
staying healthy	a silly high-school health class
mental illness	medical school

Exercise 5 Grouping Related Ideas in Lists of Details

Following are lists of details. In each list, circle the items that seem to fit into one group; then underline the items that seem to fit into a second group. Some items may not fit into either group.

1. **topic:** marrying young

emotional closeness	financial stresses
role of friends	new demands on each person's time
constant source of support	coping with another person's needs
increased responsibilities	wedding anniversaries
sharing new adventures	freedom from parental control

2. **topic:** a true friend

won't betray a confidence	laughs at your jokes
listens to your worries	hard to find
never gossips about you	gives honest advice
respects your dreams	celebrates your success
like a family member	doesn't hold a grudge

3. **topic:** ways to exercise

hire a personal trainer	walk in your neighborhood
join a private health club	jog on the beach
run in a park	buy expensive equipment
burning calories	ride a bike to work
play basketball with friends	take the stairs, not elevators

4. **topic:** fighting the flu

wads of tissue	chicken soup
aspirin	antibiotics
tea with lemon and honey	high fever and body aches
cough medicine	orange juice
decongestant tablet	cough drops

Exercise 6 Writing Topic Sentences for Lists of Details

Following are lists of details that have no topic sentences. Write an appropriate topic sentence for each one.

1. **topic sentence:** _The care that is being sold is in mint condition._

details: The car for sale has a perfectly clean engine.

It also has low mileage.

The interior is well-maintained.

It has air bags.

The tires have very little tread left.

There is a dent in the driver's side door.

The car radio is broken.

The car needs a new battery.

2. topic sentence: _____

_____

details: A young family owns the Pine Tree Café.

The father and mother manage the place.

The panels behind the counter are covered with children's art.

Sometimes the owners' children, ages six and eight, help their parents.

The children get to push the buttons on the cash register.

The children hand the bags of take-out food to the customers.

Families with small children like to come to the café for weekend breakfasts.

The restaurant gives a free cookie to each child.

3. topic sentence: _____

_____

details: When I was suspended from kindergarten, Uncle Tomas brought me a gift to console me.

He said I was just an independent child.

When Uncle Tomas was my babysitter, he let me stay up late and watch scary movies on television.

He also let me eat ice cream just before dinner.

He said it was full of calcium and other nutrients.

He took me to my first professional baseball game.

When I was a teenager, he took me to big empty parking lots and taught me how to drive.

At my high school graduation, he was in the front row, cheering for me.

4. topic sentence: _____

_____

details: Each week, my parents go to the hospital to hold and comfort newborn babies with AIDS.

My brother is a volunteer with Habitat for Humanity.

I volunteer at the Boys and Girls Club, teaching the elementary school students how to use computers.

My grandfather is part of a motorcycle club that rides together to aid Toys for Tots, a charity for children.

Even my sister's dog is a trained therapy dog.

My sister and her dog Sky visit nursing homes, where Sky lets people pet and cuddle him.

| Exercise 7 | **Choosing the Better Topic Sentence** |

Following are lists of details. Each list has two possible topic sentences. Underline the better topic sentence for each list.

1. possible topic sentences:

   a. Laura and Tyler don't get along.

   b. Laura is bullying Tyler, her boyfriend.

   details: Laura constantly teases her boyfriend Tyler about his weight.

   She criticizes him for eating dessert or fattening snacks.

   Tyler looks miserable when Laura scolds him.

   He tries to please her by giving her small gifts.

   Laura doesn't seem impressed by his efforts.

   She makes him return many of the gifts.

   As a result, Tyler tries harder.

   He often asks Laura what would make her happy.

   She says that he ought to know.

2. possible topic sentences:

   a. Humor can hide a person's dark side.

   b. The ability to make people laugh is a true talent.

   details: Sean was always the joker in our group.

   He was lively, cheerful, and quick with a witty comment.

   He could make me break into laughter during the most serious movie.

   His smart remarks caused me to laugh in many classes.

   When I got scolded for laughing, Sean would sit, looking very serious.

   His expression made me laugh even more.

   Sean was always the center of fun and good times.

Then one day I saw him sitting alone in the college cafeteria.

He didn't know anyone was looking at him.

His expression was sad and lonely.

3. possible topic sentences:

a. It's impossible to know what a person will like for a gift.

b. A perfect gift starts with thoughtfulness, not money.

details: Mrs. Garcia knew that her sons would give her gifts on her birthday.

She wasn't surprised when her older son, Mike, handed her a beautifully wrapped box of expensive chocolates.

Covered in pale blue velvet ribbon and pink silk flowers, the box was almost too pretty to open.

When she opened it, she saw two layers of the finest chocolates: dark chocolate, milk chocolate, and white chocolate.

She knew that two pounds of this chocolate must have cost Mike at least thirty dollars.

Then Danny, her younger son, gave her a small box, badly wrapped in wrinkled tissue paper.

Inside the box was a cheap plastic frame with a faded snapshot in it.

It was an old photo of Mrs. Garcia as a beautiful young girl.

The chocolates were the same gift that Mike gave her every year on her birthday and on Mother's Day.

They were available in every luxury mall.

The picture was one Mrs. Garcia had stashed away years ago and forgotten.

It became her favorite gift.

PLANNING **Devising a Plan: Illustration**

When you plan your outline, keep your topic sentence in mind:

Cars in the college parking lot reflect the diversity of people at the school.

Remember the three categories of related details:

Kinds of Cars
Inside the Cars
Bumper Stickers

These three categories can give you an idea for how to organize the outline.

Following is an outline for a paragraph on cars in the college parking lot. As you read the outline, you will notice that details about the insides of the cars and about bumper stickers and license plates have been added. Adding details can be part of the outlining stage.

An Outline on Cars in the College Parking Lot

topic sentence: Cars in the college parking lot reflect the diversity of people at the school.

details:

kinds of cars
- There are beat-up old cars.
- Some have no bumpers.
- There are vans.
- There are a few new sports cars.
- Maybe these are gifts from rich parents.
- There are some SUVs.
- Older people's cars, like Volvos and Cadillacs, are there.
- There are a few racing cars, modified and brightly striped.

inside the cars
- Some cars have elaborate sound systems.
- Some have a baby stroller or baby seat.
- Some have empty paper cups and food wrappers.

bumper stickers
- Some have stickers for a club.
- There are stickers with a message.
- There are stickers that brag.

As you can see, the outline used the details from the list and included other details. You can add more details, combine some details to eliminate repetition, or even eliminate some details as you draft your essay.

Collaborate

Exercise 8   **Adding Details to an Outline**

Below are three partial outlines. Each has a topic sentence and some details. Working with a partner or group, add more details that support the topic sentence.

1. **topic sentence:** There are many foods that we eat without knives, forks, or spoons.

   details:
   a. Fruits like apples and grapes are finger foods.

   b. You don't need a knife and fork for doughnuts.

   c. Many people eat fried chicken without utensils.

   d. _____

   e. _____

   f. _____

   g. _____

2. **topic sentence:** For a number of reasons, parents may give their child an unusual first name.

   details:
   a. Some parents choose an old family name.

   b. Some parents pick the name of a celebrity.

   c. Other parents name their child after a wealthy relative.

   d. _____

e. _____

f. _____

g. _____

3. topic sentence: Many college students have the same complaints.

details: **a.** The college food is terrible.

b. They can't get into the classes they want.

c. There are not enough holidays.

d. _____

e. _____

f. _____

g. _____

Exercise 9   **Eliminating Details That Are Repetitive**

In the following outlines, some details use different words to repeat an example given earlier on the list. Cross out the repetitive details.

1. topic sentence: Many hungry students on a budget rely on a few inexpensive foods.

details: Toaster pastries are popular at any time of day.

Microwave popcorn can fill an empty stomach.

Cereal makes up a large part of many students' diet.

Frozen pizzas fill many students' freezers.

Frozen dinners, such as chicken pot pies and beef with rice, satisfy student appetites.

If a product such as popcorn can be microwaved, it is attractive.

Students also buy ramen noodles.

Some students resort to the sugary cereals they enjoyed as children.

No student can resist potato chips.

Dinners that can be reheated are often stacked in students' freezers.

2. topic sentence: The cheapest product is not always the best buy.

details: I bought cheap cellophane tape, but it never held anything together.

Cheap dishwashing liquid is weaker than the more expensive, concentrated kind.

My cheap umbrella lasted through one rainy day.

Expensive cellophane tape is more effective than the low-priced brand.

Big bags of bargain cookies can taste stale and dry.

I bought a bag of sale-priced ballpoint pens, and they leaked all over my clothes.

I was proud of my $2.99 shirt, but it fell apart after one washing.

What good is a bargain umbrella that turns inside-out when the weather is breezy?

3. topic sentence: My father has more courage than anyone I know.

details: He fought against cancer and survived.

He never complained about chemotherapy.

He calmed his family's fears before his surgery.

When he was in the military, he was a Navy Seal.

He endured rigorous training under miserable and dangerous conditions.

He lost his job when he was forty-five.

He had the courage to go back to school and train for a new career.

He was terrified of computers.

Now he is learning to use technology as part of his career training.

My father faced a life-and-death cancer operation.

He survived some of the U. S. Navy's most challenging physical tests to become a Navy Seal.

DRAFTING **Drafting and Revising: Illustration**

Review the outline on Cars in the College Parking Lot on pages 372. You can create a first draft of this outline in the form of a paragraph. At this point, you can combine some of the short, choppy sentences of the outline, add details, and add transitions to link your ideas. You can revise your draft using the following checklist.

Checklist: A Checklist for Revising an Illustration Paragraph

✔ Should some of the sentences be combined?

✔ Do I need more or better transitions?

✔ Should I add more details to support my points?

✔ Should some of the details be more specific?

Transitions

As you revise your illustration paragraph, you may find places where one idea ends and another begins abruptly. This problem occurs when you forget to add **transitions,** the words, phrases, or sentences that connect one idea to another. When you write an illustration paragraph, you will need (1) some transitions that link one example to another and (2) other transitions to link one section of your paragraph to another section. Here are some transitions you may want to use in writing an illustration paragraph.

INFO BOX: **Transitions for an Illustration Paragraph**

another example	one instance
a second example	other examples
for example	other kinds
for instance	such as
in addition	the first instance
in the case of	another instance
like	to illustrate
one example	

Look carefully at the following draft of the paragraph on Cars in the College Parking Lot, and note how it combines sentences, adds details, and uses transitions to transform the outline into a clear and developed paragraph.

A Revised Draft of a Paragraph on Cars in the College Parking Lot

details added,

sentences combined

sentences combined

details added,

transition added

transition added

transition added

details added

details added

details added

transition,

details added

details, transition added

details added

details added

details added

Cars in the college parking lot reflect the diversity of people at the school. <u>There are beat-up old cars, some with no bumpers, near several vans.</u> <u>There are one or two sports cars like BMWs; they might belong to the few lucky students with rich and generous parents.</u> Other kinds include SUVs and older people's cars <u>such as</u> Volvos and Cadillacs. <u>In addition,</u> the parking lot holds a few racing cars, modified and brightly striped. Some cars have elaborate sound systems for <u>music lovers. Others must belong to parents</u> because they have a baby stroller or baby seat inside. Many are filled with empty paper cups or food wrappers <u>since busy students have to eat on the run. Many cars also have bumper stickers;</u> some are for clubs, <u>like Morristown Athletic Club,</u> while others have a message <u>such as "Give Blood, Save Lives" or "Animals: It's Their World, Too."</u> Some stickers brag that <u>the driver is the "Proud Parent of an Honor Roll Student at Grove Elementary" or is "Single—and Loving It."</u>

Exercise 10 **Revising a Draft by Combining Sentences**

The paragraph below has many short, choppy sentences, which are underlined. Wherever you see two or more underlined sentences clustered next to each other, combine them into one clear, smooth sentence. Write your revised versions of the sentences in the spaces above the lines.

My aunt's backyard is ideal for someone like me. <u>First of all, it has plenty of shade.</u>

<u>Shade is essential on hot summer days in our state.</u> Three large leafy trees are clustered

near the house. <u>They block the rays of the afternoon sun. They lower the temperature</u>

about ten degrees. Another pleasant feature of this yard is the patio. <u>I love to sit</u> <u>outside. I like to read there. I also like to sleep. In addition, I love to listen to music.</u> My aunt's large, paved patio is the perfect place to relax. Finally, this backyard appeals to my lazy nature. <u>Most of the yard is filled by the patio. It is also filled by</u> <u>trees and plants. It has barely any lawn.</u> This is my ideal yard because there is hardly any lawn to mow.

Exercise 11 **Revising a Draft by Adding Transitions**

The paragraph below needs some transitions. Add appropriate transitions (words or phrases) to the blanks.

Sometimes I feel that I have too many choices and that they only confuse me. _____ my brother wanted a sweater for his birthday. When I asked him what color he wanted, he said blue. At my local mall, I found sweaters in many shades of blue. _____ there were navy blue, powder blue, royal blue, turquoise blue, and gray blue sweaters. _____ my mother asked me to pick up some milk at the store. But did she want skimmed milk, low-fat milk, acidophilus milk, chocolate milk, or whole milk? I didn't know what to buy. _____ of too much variety occurred when I had to pick a long-distance calling plan. I was trapped in a maze of plans _____ Cingular, Sprint, and Verizon. I know I should value my freedom to choose, but all these choices are cutting into my free time.

Collaborate

Exercise 12 **Adding Details to a Draft**

The paragraph below lacks the kind of details that would make it more interesting. Working with a partner or group, add details to the blank spaces provided. When you are finished, read the revised paragraph to the class.

Even a person who rents a furnished apartment needs to make many purchases for his or her new home. For example, he or she will have to get _____, _____, and _____ for the kitchen. A furnished apartment may come with a basic sofa, chairs, and a lamp or two, but the new resident needs to get _____ and _____ to make the living room livable. A bedroom may offer a bed, a mattress, a chest of drawers, and a ceiling lamp, but does it have _____, _____, or _____? The bathroom will also need a few items. Few rental units come with _____, _____, or

_____. Clearly, moving into a furnished apartment can save a person con-

siderable money and frustration, but it still requires some spending.

POLISHING   Polishing and Proofreading: Illustration

As you prepare the final version of your illustration paragraph, make any
changes in word choice or transitions that can refine your writing. Following is
the final version of the paragraph on Cars in the College Parking Lot. As you
read it, you will notice a few more changes:

- Some details have been added.
- Several long transitions have been added. The paragraph needed to
  signal the shift in subject from the kinds of cars to what was inside the
  cars; then it needed to signal the shift from the interior of the cars to
  bumper stickers.
- A concluding sentence has been added to reinforce the point of the
  topic sentence: A diverse college population is reflected in its cars.

A Final Version of a Paragraph on Cars in the College Parking Lot

(Changes from the draft are underlined.)

Cars in the college parking lot reflect the diversity of people at the school.
There are beat-up old cars, some with no bumpers, near several vans. There are one
or two new sports cars like BMWs; they might belong to the few lucky students with
rich and generous parents. Other kinds include SUVs and older people's cars such
as Volvos and Cadillacs. In addition, the parking lot holds a few racing cars, modified and brightly striped. <u>What is inside the cars is as revealing as the cars themselves.</u> Some cars have elaborate sound systems for music lovers <u>who can't drive
without pounding sound.</u> Others must belong to parents because they have a baby
stroller or baby seat inside. Many are filled with empty paper cups or food wrappers
since busy students have to eat on the run. <u>Bumper stickers also tell a story.</u> Many
cars have stickers; some are for clubs, like Morristown Athletic Club, while others
have a message, such as "Give Blood, Save Lives" or "Animals: It's Their World,
Too." Some stickers brag that the driver is the "Proud Parent of an Honor Student at
Grove Elementary School" or is "Single—and Loving It." <u>A walk through the parking
lot hints that this college is a place for all ages, backgrounds, and interests.</u>

Before you prepare the final version of your illustration paragraph, check your
latest draft for errors in spelling or punctuation and for any errors made in typing and copying.

Exercise 13   Correcting the Errors in the Final Draft of an
Illustration Paragraph

Following are two illustration paragraphs with the kind of errors it is easy to
overlook when you prepare the final version of an assignment. Correct the
errors by writing above the lines. There are eleven errors in the first paragraph
and nine errors in the second paragraph.

1. A stranger would be amazed at what college students carry to school. I am always impress when I see people, usually older woman, arrive with a small suitcase on wheel's. These suitcases are the kind people take to the airport because the luggage can fit into the overhead compartments on airplanes. At my college, older students pack the cases full of textbooks, notebooks, folders, spell-checkers, calculators, dictionaries, highlighters, pencils, and pens. These students are highly prepared for class. Most students is more like me and come with a backpack that contains a note-book or two, a couple of textbooks, a pencil, a bottle of water, a piece of fruit, and maybe a sandwitch. This students are likely to have forgotten the book they need for English Class or left their homework at home. Of course, there are a few students who arrive at school as if they are just visiting, and they carry no thing at all. One student in my sociology class, for example, always borrows a pencil and paper from me I have never seen him carrying the textbook for the class. Viewing my campus, a stranger might wonder what "school supplies" means to college student.

2. The best fathers are not always biological fathers. For example I never knew my biological father. He left my mother and I when I was a baby. Fortunately, my mother married a wonderful men when I was 3 years old, and he is my true father. He was the one who walked me to kindergarten each day, cooked me dinner when my mother worked a night shift, and red me a story at night. He was the proudest person in the room when I got my high School diploma. Another true father is my uncle. Uncle Eddie never had children of his own, but he and my Aunt Elise fostered more then twenty children over the years. Aunt Elise died a few years ago, but every year, grown-up foster children return to my uncle house to celebrate the holidays with him. Some bring their own little children, so my Uncle is not only a father, but also a grandfather to the family he loves.

Lines of Detail: A Walk-Through Assignment

Your assignment is to write an illustration paragraph about change.

Step 1: List all your ideas on this broad topic for ten minutes. You can list ideas on any aspect of change, such as a change of attitude, changing schools, a new job, a change in a daily routine, and so forth.

Step 2: Review your list. Underline any parts that are specific ideas related to the broad topic: change.

Step 3: List all the specific ideas. Choose one as the narrowed topic for your paragraph.

Step 4: Add related ideas to your chosen, narrowed topic. Do this by reviewing your list for related ideas and by brainstorming for more related ideas.

Step 5: List all your related ideas and review their connection to your narrowed topic. Then write a topic sentence and an outline for your paragraph.

Step 6: Write a first draft of your paragraph.

Step 7: Revise your first draft. Be sure it has enough details and clear transitions. Combine any choppy sentences.

Step 8: After a final check for any errors in punctuation, spelling, and word choice, prepare the final version of the paragraph.

Writing Your Own Illustration Paragraph

When you write on any of these topics, be sure to work through the stages of the writing process in preparing your paragraph.

1. Select one of the topics listed. Narrow the topic and write a paragraph on it. If you choose the topic of money, for example, you might narrow it by writing about credit cards for college students or about paying bills.

basketball	money	jobs
driving	exercise	sleep
the Internet	movies	children
photographs	spam	rumors
crime	weather	fashion
books	celebrities	boxing
time	lies	travel

2. Following are topic sentences. Select one and use it to write a paragraph.

The best advice I've ever been given is _____.

There are several parts of my daily routine that I dislike.

There are several parts of my daily routine that I enjoy.

The most hurtful word in the language is _____.

The most beautiful word in the language is

_____.

The most frustrating part of relying on a computer is

_____.

An empty room makes me think of _____.

Three teams represent the best in _____

(baseball, football, basketball, hockey, soccer—choose one).

Several people illustrate what it means to be a hero.

3. If you were asked to give the motto you live by, what would it be? For example, do you live by the words, "Treat other people the way you would like to be treated" or "Always do your best"? Write a paragraph that illustrates why you believe that your motto is a good one. You can begin with a topic sentence such as

I live by the motto "_____" because it has been

proven true many times.

In the paragraph, give examples of times when this motto has been shown to be true.

4. Look carefully at Photographs A, B, and C, and use these photos to think about this topic sentence: *Tired people can fall asleep anywhere.* In a paragraph, support this topic sentence with your own examples.

Photograph A

Photograph B

Photograph C

5. Look carefully at Photographs D, E, and F. Use them as a way to begin thinking about a paragraph with this topic sentence: The best kind of pet is a _____. Draw on your experience with any kind of pet (from a cat to an iguana) to write an illustration paragraph.

Photograph D

Photograph E

Photograph F

Name: _____ Section: _____

Peer Review Form for an Illustration Paragraph

After you have written a draft version of your paragraph, let a writing partner read it. When your partner has completed the following form, discuss the responses. Then repeat the same process for your partner's paragraph.

The topic sentence of the paragraph is _____

_____

_____

The details that I liked best begin with the words _____

_____

The paragraph has _____ (enough, too many, too few) details to support the topic sentence.

A particularly good part of the paragraph begins with the words _____

_____

I have questions about _____

_____

_____

I noticed several transitions in the paragraph. They include the following: _____

_____

Other comments on the paragraph: _____

_____

_____

_____

_____

_____

_____

_____

Reviewer's name: _____

Writing a Process Paragraph

WHAT IS PROCESS?

Process writing explains how to do something or describes how something happens or is done. When you tell the reader how to do something (a **directional process**), you speak directly to the reader and give him or her clear, specific instructions about performing some activity. Your purpose is to explain an activity so that a reader can do it. For example, you may have to leave instructions telling a new employee how to close the cash register or use the copy machine.

When you describe how something happens or is done (an **informational process**), your purpose is to explain an activity without telling a reader how to do it. For example, you can explain how a boxer trains for a fight or how the special effects for a movie were created. Instead of speaking directly to the reader, an informational process speaks about "I," "he," "she," "we," "they," or about a person by his or her name. A directional process uses "you" or, in the way it gives directions, the word "you" is understood.

A Process Involves Steps in Time Order

Whether a process is directional or informational, it describes something that is done in steps, and these steps are in a specific order: a **time order.** The process

> ### *Jumping In*
>
> *Could you teach someone how to swim faster or more efficiently? How would you start your explanation? Would you have to demonstrate as well as explain? Teaching in steps, and emphasizing the importance of each step, is one kind of **process**.*

383

can involve steps that are followed in minutes, hours, days, weeks, months, or even years. For example, the steps in changing a tire may take minutes, whereas the steps taken to lose ten pounds may take months.

You should keep in mind that a process involves steps that *must follow a certain order*, not just a range of activities that can be placed in any order. This sentence *signals a process:*

> Planting a rose garden takes planning and care. (Planting a rose garden involves following steps in order; that is, you cannot put a rose bush in the ground until you dig a hole.)

This sentence *does not signal a process:*

> There are several ways to build your confidence. (Each way is separate; there is no time sequence here.)

Telling a person in a conversation how to do something or how something is done gives you the opportunity to add important points you may have overlooked or to throw in details you may have skipped at first. Your listener can ask questions if he or she does not understand you. Writing a process, however, is more difficult. Your reader is not there to stop you, to ask you to explain further, or to question you. In writing a process, you must be organized and very clear.

Hints for Writing a Process Paragraph

1. **In choosing a topic, find an activity you know well.** If you write about something familiar to you, you will have a clearer paragraph.

2. Choose a topic that includes steps that must be done in a specific time sequence.

   not this: I find lots of things to do with old photographs.
   but this: I have a plan for turning an old photograph into a special gift.

3. **Choose a topic that is fairly small.** A complicated process cannot be covered well in one paragraph. If your topic is too big, the paragraph can become vague, incomplete, or boring.

   too big: There are many steps in the process of an immigrant becoming an American citizen.
   smaller and manageable: Persistence and a positive attitude helped me through the stages of my job search.

4. **Write a topic sentence that makes a point.** Your topic sentence should do more than announce. Like the topic sentence for any paragraph, it should have a point. As you plan the steps of your process and gather details, ask yourself some questions: What point do I want to make about this process? Is the process hard? Is it easy? Does the process require certain tools? Does the process require certain skills, like organization, patience, endurance?

   an announcement: This paragraph is about how to change the oil in your car.
   a topic sentence: You do not have to be a mechanic to change the oil in your car, but you do have to take a few simple precautions.

5. **Include all of the steps.** If you are explaining a process, you are writing for someone who does not know the process as well as you do.

Keep in mind that what seems clear or simple to you may not be clear or simple to the reader, and be sure to tell what is needed before the process starts. For instance, what ingredients are needed to cook the dish? Or what tools are needed to assemble the toy?

6. **Put the steps in the right order.** Nothing is more irritating to a reader than trying to follow directions that skip back and forth. Careful planning, drafting, and revision can help you get the time sequence right.

7. **Be specific in the details and steps.** To be sure you have sufficient details and clear steps, keep your reader in mind. Put yourself in the reader's place. Could you follow your own directions or understand your steps?

If you remember that a process explains, you will focus on being clear. Now that you know the purpose and strategies of writing a process, you can begin the prewriting stage of writing one.

Exercise 1 **Recognizing Good Topic Sentences for Process Paragraphs**

If a sentence is a good topic sentence for a process paragraph, put *OK* on the line provided. If a sentence has a problem, label that sentence with one of these letters:

> **A** This is an announcement; it makes no point.
>
> **B** This sentence covers a topic that is too big for one paragraph.
>
> **S** This sentence describes a topic that does not require steps.

1. _____ I've found a system for doing the laundry that saves me time and stress.

2. _____ The best way to clean bathroom tile will be the subject of this paragraph.

3. _____ There are several places to look for previously owned lamps.

4. _____ The steps involved in liver transplants are complicated.

5. _____ Finding a bargain on a digital camera means knowing where to look and what to look for.

6. _____ This paper shows the method of deep-frying a turkey.

7. _____ The Constitution of the United States evolved in several stages.

8. _____ A few hints can help you make a good impression at a job interview.

9. _____ If you learn just a few techniques, you can paint a room like the professionals do.

10. _____ Gabriella discovered the correct way to repair a tear in wallpaper.

Exercise 2 **Including Necessary Materials in a Process**

Below are three possible topics for a process paragraph. For each topic, work with a partner or a group and list the items (materials, ingredients, tools, utensils, supplies) the reader would have to gather before he or she began the process. When you've finished the exercise, check your lists with another group to see if you've missed any items.

1. **topic:** polishing a pair of leather shoes

   needed items: _____

   _____

2. **topic:** waxing a car

   needed items: _____

   _____

3. **topic:** doing your laundry

   needed items: _____

   _____

WRITING THE PROCESS PARAGRAPH IN STEPS

PREWRITING   Gathering Ideas: Process

The easiest way to start writing a process paragraph is to pick a small topic, one that you can cover well in one paragraph. Then you can gather ideas by listing or freewriting or both.

If you decided to write about how to adopt a shelter dog, you might begin by freewriting.

Then you might check your freewriting, looking for details that have to do with the process of adopting a shelter dog. You can underline those details, as in the example that follows.

Freewriting for a Process Paragraph

Topic: How to Adopt a Shelter Dog
<u>What kind of dog do you want?</u> <u>It's difficult to walk through an animal shelter</u> and see all those dogs begging for a home. Be realistic. A purebred or a mixed breed? A puppy? <u>Can you afford it?</u> <u>There's a fee at the shelter.</u> <u>You have to be willing to take care of a dog for a long time.</u>

Next, you can **put what you've underlined into a list, in correct time sequence:**

before you decide on any dog

Can you afford it?
You have to be willing to take care of a dog for a long time.

considering the right dog

What kind of a dog do you want?
A purebred or a mixed breed. A puppy?
Be realistic.

at the shelter

It's difficult to walk through a shelter.
A fee at the shelter.

Check the list. Are some details missing? Yes. A reader might ask, "How do you decide what kind of dog is best for you? What's so expensive about getting a dog at a shelter? And how much does it cost to own a dog, anyway?" Answers to questions like these can give you the details needed to write a clear and interesting informational process.

Writing a Topic Sentence for a Process Paragraph

Freewriting and a list can now help you focus your paragraph by identifying the point of your process. You already know that the subject of your paragraph is how to adopt a shelter dog. But what's the point? Is it easy to adopt a shelter dog? Is it difficult? What does it take to find the right dog?

Looking at your list of steps and details, you notice that most of the steps come before you actually select a dog. Maybe a topic sentence could be

You have to do your homework if you want to find the shelter dog that's right for you.

Once you have a topic sentence, you can think about adding details that explain your topic sentence, and you can begin the planning stage of writing.

Exercise 3 **Finding the Steps of a Process in Freewriting**

Read the following freewriting, then reread it, looking for all the words, phrases, or sentences that have to do with steps. Underline all those items. Then once you've underlined the freewriting, put what you've underlined into a list in a correct time sequence.

How to Make Brewed Coffee: Freewriting

I love coffee in the morning. Especially brewed. Instant tastes awful once you've had brewed coffee. Don't forget to fill the glass carafe with the right amount of water for the number of cups. Start it all with a clean carafe. Use a spoon or plastic scoop to put the coffee in the brew basket. After you put a clean paper filter in the brew basket, get ready to add coffee. Don't turn on the coffeemaker until all the other steps have been completed. If you forget the paper filter, you'll have a mess. Make sure you measure out the right amount of coffee. The tempting smell of coffee brewing. Pour the water from the carafe into the water-heating compartment. Coffee tastes funny if it comes from a dirty carafe. Decide how many cups of coffee you want to make.

Your List of Steps in Time Sequence

_____

_____

_____

_____

_____

_____

_____

_____

_____

_____

PLANNING Devising a Plan: Process

Using the freewriting and topic sentence on how to adopt a shelter dog, you could make an outline. Then you could revise it, checking the topic sentence and improving the list of details where you think they could be better. A revised outline on adopting a shelter dog is shown below.

An Outline for a Paragraph on How to Adopt a Shelter Dog

topic sentence: You have to do your homework if you want to find the shelter dog that's right for you.

details:

before you decide on any dog
Decide whether you can afford a dog.
Dogs cost money for food, regular veterinary care, and grooming.
Decide if you are willing to take care of a dog for a long time.
Dogs can live ten to fifteen years.
They need exercise, attention, and training.

considering the right dog
Think carefully about what kind of dog you want.
You have to decide whether you want a purebred or mixed breed.
You can get both types at a shelter.
Puppies are adorable and fun.
They need more training and attention.
The size and temperament of the dog are important, too.
Do some research and talk to friends who own dogs.

at the shelter
It is difficult to walk through an animal shelter and see all the dogs begging for a home.
But remember the kind of dog you've decided to adopt.
Look around carefully.
Make your selection, pay the adoption fee, and look forward to giving your dog the best years of its life.

You probably noticed that the outline follows the same stages as the list but has many new details. These details can be added as you create your plan.

The following checklist may help you revise an outline for your own process paragraph.

Checklist: A Checklist for Revising a Process Outline

✔ Is my topic sentence focused on some point about the process?

✔ Does it cover the whole process?

✔ Do I have all the steps?

✔ Are they in the right order?

✔ Have I explained clearly?

✔ Do I need better details?

Exercise 4   **Revising the Topic Sentence in a Process Outline**

The topic sentence below doesn't cover all the steps of the process. Read the outline several times; then write a topic sentence that covers all the steps of the process and has a point.

topic sentence: You can buy a unique gift at a flea market if you look around.

details: First, decide what you're looking for: a dish, a framed poster, candle holders.

Decide how much you are willing to pay.

At the market, survey all the stalls before you make a choice.

Even if you see the perfect gift at the first stall, keep looking.

If you show too much interest too soon, the price may go up.

On the second tour of the market, return to the objects you liked and narrow your choice to one.

Casually ask the price.

Then offer much less.

If your offer is not accepted, act as if you are leaving.

You will most likely get a new price, and the bargaining will begin.

When you and the seller can reach a compromise, you have your gift.

revised topic sentence: _____

_____

Exercise 5   **Revising the Order of Steps in a Process Outline**

The steps in each of these outlines are out of order. Put numbers in the spaces provided, indicating what step should be first, second, and so forth.

1. topic sentence: Every night, my dog Captain Crunch has the same bedtime routine.

details: _____ At first he stretches out on the living room rug while I lie on the couch and watch television.

_____ Captain Crunch is not a night person, so he doesn't want to spend too much time in front of the television.

_____ He follows me into my bedroom.

_____ When I am nearly asleep, Captain Crunch jumps on my bed and sleeps on my feet.

_____ He settles on the bedroom carpet while I climb into bed.

_____ To signal me it is time for bed, he starts to yawn in front of the television.

_____ When the yawns don't work, he starts to sigh.

_____ Then I feel a wet nose under my hand, and I finally get up and turn off the television.

2. topic sentence: In less than ten minutes, I can make my room look clean.

details: _____ I now have a clean-looking room with a new pillow, full of garbage, on my bed.

_____ First, I take all the major junk (like a basketball, a bunch of smelly sneakers) and throw it in the closet.

_____ I want to cram all this food garbage into a big bag.

_____ Suddenly I realize I have no bag.

_____ I have a sudden inspiration for a bag substitute.

_____ I snatch a pillowcase off one of the pillows on my newly made bed.

_____ Once the major junk is in the closet, I take the smaller junk (like dirty socks and shirts) and put it under the sheets of my bed.

_____ I proceed to make my bed, concealing all the dirty clothes.

_____ Last comes the minor food garbage: Pepsi cans, candy wrappers, leftover cookies.

_____ I fill the pillowcase with the cans, wrappers, and cookies.

3. topic sentence: My best friend Mary has a system for coping with the stress of too many responsibilities.

details: _____ The next morning, Mary's list of duties and chores seems more manageable.

_____ As it gets later in the evening, Mary thinks of more responsibilities and adds them to her list.

_____ It starts in the evening when Mary has a tendency to worry about the demands of the next day.

_____ On the page, she lists all her responsibilities for the next day.

_____ Now that her worries are put away, Mary gets a good night's sleep.

_____ Before she goes to bed, she puts her notebook back in her purse.

_____ As soon as she begins to worry, she reaches for a small notebook in her purse.

_____ She opens her notebook to a new page.

Exercise 6   **Listing All the Steps in an Outline**

Following are three topic sentences for process paragraphs. Write all the steps needed to complete an outline for each sentence. After you've listed all the steps, number them in the correct time order.

1. topic sentence: There are a few simple steps for buying your college textbooks.

steps: _____

_____

_____

_____

_____

_____

_____

2. topic sentence: Anyone can make a delicious salad.

steps: _____

_____

_____

_____

_____

_____

_____

_____

_____

_____

3. topic sentence: At registration time, you can develop a plan for getting
the classes you want.

steps: _____

_____

_____

_____

_____

_____

_____

_____

_____

DRAFTING Drafting and Revising: Process

You can take the outline and write it in paragraph form, and you'll have a first
draft of the process paragraph. As you write the first draft, you can combine
some of the short sentences from the outline. Then you can review your draft
and revise it for organization, details, clarity, grammar, style, and word choice.

Using the Same Grammatical Person

Remember that the *directional* process speaks directly to the reader, calling
him or her "you." Sentences in a directional process use the word "you," or they
imply "you."

> **directional:** *You* need a good skillet to get started.
>
> Begin by cleaning the surface. ("You" is implied.)

Remember that the *informational* process involves somebody doing the process. Sentences in an informational process use words such as "I" or "we" or "he" or "she" or "they" or a person's name.

> **informational:** *Dave* needed a good skillet to get started.
>
> First, *I* can clean the surface.

One problem in writing a process is shifting from describing how somebody did something to telling the reader how to do an activity. When that shift happens, the two kinds of processes get mixed. That shift is called a **shift in person.** In grammar, the words "I" and "we" are considered to be in the first person, "you" is the second person, and "he," "she," "it," and "they" are in the third person.

If these words refer to one, they are *singular*; if they refer to more than one, they are *plural*. The following list may help.

INFO BOX: **A List of Persons**

1st person singular:	I
2nd person singular:	you
3rd person singular:	he, she, it, or a person's name
1st person plural:	we
2nd person plural:	you
3rd person plural:	they, or the names of more than one person

---

In writing your process paragraph, decide whether your process will be directional or informational, and stay with one kind.

Below are two examples of a shift in person. Look at them carefully and study how the shift is corrected.

> **shift in person:** After *I* preheat the oven to 350 degrees, *I* mix the egg whites and sugar with an electric mixer set at high speed. *Mix* until stiff peaks form. Then *I* put the mixture in small mounds on an ungreased cookie sheet. ("Mix until stiff peaks form" is a shift to the "you" person.)

> **shift corrected:** After *I* preheat the oven to 350 degrees, *I* mix the egg whites and sugar with an electric mixer set at high speed. *I* mix until stiff peaks form. Then *I* put the mixture in small mounds on an ungreased cookie sheet.

> **shift in person:** A *salesperson* has to be very careful when a customer tries on clothes. The *clerk* can't hint that a suit may be a size too small. *You* can insult a customer with a hint like that. (The sentences shifted from "salesperson" and "clerk" to "you.")

> **shift corrected:** A *salesperson* has to be very careful when a customer tries on clothes. The *clerk* can't hint that a suit may be a size too small. *He or she* can insult a customer with a hint like that.

Using Transitions Effectively

As you revise your draft, you can add transitions. Transitions are particularly important in a process paragraph because you are trying to show the steps in a *specific sequence,* and you are trying to show the *connections* between steps. Good transitions will also keep your paragraph from sounding like a choppy, boring list.

Following is a list of some of the transitions you can use in writing a process paragraph. Be sure that you use transitional words and phrases only when logical to do so, and try not to overuse the same transitions in a paragraph.

INFO BOX: Transitions for a Process Paragraph

after	during	later	then
afterward	eventually	meanwhile	to begin
as	finally	next	to start
as he/she is	first, second, etc.	now	until
as soon as	first of all	quickly	when
as you are	gradually	sometimes	whenever
at last	immediately	soon	while
at the same time	initially	suddenly	while I am
before	in the beginning	the first step	
begin by	last	the second step, etc.	

When you write a process paragraph, you must pay particular attention to clarity. As you revise, keep thinking about your audience to be sure your steps are easy to follow. The following can help you revise your draft.

Checklist: A Checklist for Revising a Process Paragraph

✔ Does the topic sentence cover the whole paragraph?

✔ Does the topic sentence make a point about the process?

✔ Is any important step left out?

✔ Should any step be explained further?

✔ Are the steps in the right order?

✔ Should any sentences be combined?

✔ Have I used the same person throughout the paragraph to describe the process?

✔ Have I used transitions effectively?

Exercise 7   **Correcting Shifts in Person in a Process Paragraph**

Below is a paragraph that shifts from being an informational to a directional process in several places. Those places are underlined. Rewrite the underlined parts, directly above the underlining, so that the whole paragraph is an informational process.

Eddie has an efficient system for sorting and organizing his mail. As soon as he picks up his mail, he begins sorting it. Any junk mail, such as advertisements and offers for credit cards or phone plans, never reaches the kitchen table. <u>You</u> immediately <u>toss</u> it into the garbage. Then Eddie sits at the table and sorts the remaining mail. Eddie opens all the bills. He puts the ones that <u>you need</u> to pay right away in one stack; he places the ones he can pay later in another stack. Next, Eddie places each stack in its own compartment in a plastic tray. Finally, he looks at what mail is left: cards from friends, a reminder from the dentist about his next appointment, a bank statement. By sorting his mail every day, Eddie never has to face a mountain of old mail that can take <u>you</u> hours to sort.

Exercise 8 Revising Transitions in a Process Paragraph

The transitions in this paragraph could be better. Rewrite the underlined transitions, directly above each one, so that the transitions are smoother.

Packing glassware for a move can be tricky, but a few steps can save you stress and broken glass. <u>First</u>, get a sturdy cardboard box that can be sealed across the top. <u>Second,</u> gather a stack of old newspapers or a pile of tissue paper. <u>Third</u>, place a roll of strong, wide packing tape and a pair of scissors near the box and the paper. <u>Fourth</u>, line the box with paper so that the glasses will be cushioned. <u>Fifth</u>, pick up one glass. Wrap it tightly in paper, making sure that the paper protects the inside, outside, and any stem or base on the glass. <u>Sixth</u>, place the first wrapped glass in the bottom of the box. <u>Seventh</u>, continue the packing process, using paper to separate each wrapped glass from the others. <u>Eighth</u>, close the box, cut large lengths of tape, and tape the top openings. <u>Ninth</u>, breathe deep, relax, and feel sure that your glasses will arrive intact at your destination.

Exercise 9 Combining Sentences in a Process Paragraph

The paragraph below has many short, choppy sentences, which are underlined. Wherever you see two or more underlined sentences clustered next to each other, combine them into one clear, smooth sentence. Write your revised version of the sentences in the spaces above the lines.

My uncle has come up with a smart way to avoid standing in line at popular restaurants. <u>His first step was to do a little research. He looked into which restaurants issue</u>

pagers to their waiting customers. Next, he drove around town and surveyed those restaurants. He was looking for specific ones. He wanted ones near a bookstore. He also wanted ones near a discount store. Once he was familiar with these restaurants, he began to put his plan into action. When he wants to eat at a restaurant, he always chooses one on his new list. If there is a long wait at the restaurant, my uncle knows what to do. He takes the pager. He leaves for the nearby bookstore. Sometimes he leaves for the nearby discount store. He browses in the bookstore or picks up a few items at the discount store. When his pager tells him his table is ready, he walks a few steps and has a good dinner.

The Draft

Below is a draft of the process paragraph on adopting a shelter dog. This draft has more details than the outline on page 388. Some short sentences have been combined, and transitions have been added.

A Draft of a Paragraph on How to Adopt a Shelter Dog

transition added
details added

transition added,
sentences combined
detail added
transition added

sentences combined

transition sentence
added
sentences combined

transition added,
sentences combined
transition added

You have to do your homework if you want to find the shelter dog that's best for you. Begin by deciding whether you can afford a dog. Most shelters spay and neuter their animals, but dogs cost money for food, regular veterinary care, and grooming. Then decide if you are willing to take care of a dog for the ten or fifteen years that is its likely life span. Remember that dogs need regular exercise, attention, and training. If you are ready to make the personal and financial commitment of owning a pet, you can begin thinking carefully about the kind of dog you want. You have to decide whether you want a purebred or a mixed breed, for you can get both types at a shelter. At the same time, think about the age of the dog you want. Puppies are adorable and fun, but they need more training and attention. The size and temperament of the dog are important, too. Do some research and talk to friends who own dogs. It is difficult to walk through an animal shelter and see all the dogs begging for a home. When you make your adoption visit, remember the kind of dog you've decided to adopt and look around carefully. Finally, make your selection, pay the adoption fee, and look forward to giving your dog the best years of its life.

POLISHING   **Polishing and Proofreading: Process**

Before you prepare the final copy of your process paragraph, you can check your latest draft for any places in grammar, word choice, and style that need revision.

Following is the final version of the process paragraph on adopting a shelter dog. It contains several changes from the draft on the previous page.

- A sentence of introduction has been added; it begins the paragraph and creates a smoother opening.
- Three more transitions have been added.
- "Look around" has been changed to "look" to emphasize that this is not a quick or casual glance but an examination.
- The second use of "carefully" has been changed to "thoroughly" to avoid repetition.

A Final Version of Paragraph on How to Adopt a Shelter Dog

(Changes from the draft are underlined.)

<u>Most people who love animals and have big hearts have thought about adopting a dog with no home, a shelter dog. However</u>, you have to do your homework if you want to find the shelter dog that's best for you. Begin by deciding whether you can afford a dog. Most shelters spay and neuter their animals, but dogs cost money for food, regular veterinary care, and grooming. Then decide if you are willing to take care of a dog for the ten or fifteen years that is its likely life span. Remember that dogs need regular exercise, attention, and training. If you are ready to make the personal and financial commitment of owning a pet, you can begin thinking carefully about the kind of dog you want. You have to decide whether you want a purebred or a mixed breed, for you can get both types at a shelter. At the same time, think about the age of the dog you want. Puppies are adorable and fun, but they need more training and attention. The size and temperament of the dog are important, too. <u>To make all these decisions,</u> do some research and talk to friends who own dogs. <u>Later, as you prepare to go to the shelter,</u> be aware that it is difficult to walk through an animal shelter and see all the dogs begging for a home. When you make your adoption visit, remember the kind of dog you've decided to adopt and <u>look thoroughly</u>. Finally, make your selection, pay the adoption fee, and look forward to giving your dog the best years of its life.

Before you prepare the final copy of your process paragraph, check your latest draft for errors in spelling, punctuation, and formatting .

Exercise 10   **Correcting Errors in the Final Draft of a Process Paragraph**

Following are two process paragraphs with the kind of errors it is easy to over-look when you prepare the final version of an assignment. Correct the errors, writing above the lines. There are ten errors in the first paragraph and ten in the second paragraph.

1. Their is a right way to brush your teeth, and brushing correctly can save you

many unpleasant moments in the dentists office. One of the first lessons I learned in the dental hygiene Program at my college is, that millions of people make mistakes during the simple process of brushing their teeth. You may be one of them. First of all, you need to brush with the proper toothbrush. Many people think a hard toothbrush is the best because it will be tough on tooth decay. However, a soft toothbrush is better at massaging your gums and covering the surface of your teeth. Second, don't waste your money on fancy new toothpasts. Most toothpastes contain the same cavity-fighting ingredients so a inexpensive one will do. Once you have put a small amount of toothpaste on your brush, you should brush gently. Don't scrub your teeth as if they were a dirty pot or pan. Softly massage them near the gum line. Last, brush for a long time. A long time don't mean hours, but it does mean two minutes. You may think that you all ready brush for two minutes, but you probably don't. The next time you brush, time yourself. Two minutes feels like a long time. However, if you spend thirty seconds one each part of your teeth (the upper teeth on the inner surface, the upper teeth on the outer surface, and so forth), you will be on your way to healthier teeth.

2. I have taken some important steps to overcome my paneful shyness. When I started college, I was terfied of sitting in the cafeteria alone. I felt sure that everyone would be starring at me, wondering why I didnt have any friends. For months, I avoided the place. Then, slowly, I began to practice being more confident. I began by simply setting down, alone, at a table in a corner. For a few minute's I sat there, my heart racing. After about a dozen of these short stays, I took the next step. I actually bought a Coke and some chips and ate them, alone, at a table. Two weeks after I recovered from this frightening experience, I repeated it, but this time I am brave enough to scan the people at the other tables. Noone seemed to notice me at all! Feeling encouraged, I took a big step soon after. I choosed a table in the middle of the room, not one in a distance corner. After a few moments, I experienced a major victory. I made eye contact with another student sitting alone, and I said, "Hi. How are you doing?" My steps may be small ones for other people, but for me, they are big strides.

Lines of Detail: A Walk-Through Assignment

Your assignment is to write an informational process on how you found the perfect gift for your best friend or parent. Follow these steps:

Step 1: Decide whether to write about a gift for your friend or for your parent. Then think about a time when you found a gift that made that person very happy.

Step 2: Now freewrite. Write anything you can remember about the gift, how you decided what to give, how you found it and gave it.

Step 3: When you've completed the freewriting, read it. Underline all the details that refer to steps in finding the gift. List the underlined details in time order.

Step 4: Add to the list by brainstorming. Ask yourself questions that can lead to more details. For example, if an item on your list is, "I realized my mother likes colorful clothes," ask questions like, "What colors does she like?" "What is her favorite color?" or "What kind of clothes does she like to wear?"

Step 5: Survey your expanded list. Write a topic sentence that makes some point about your finding this gift. To reach a point, think of questions like, "What made the gift perfect?" or "What did I learn from planning, finding, and giving this gift?"

Step 6: Use the topic sentence to prepare an outline. Be sure that the steps in the outline are in the correct time order.

Step 7: Write a first draft of the paragraph, adding details and combining short sentences.

Step 8: Revise your draft. Be careful to use smooth transitions, and check that you have included all the necessary steps.

Step 9: Proofread and prepare the final copy of your paragraph.

Writing Your Own Process Paragraph

When you write on one of these topics, be sure to work through the stages of the writing process in preparing your process paragraph.

1. Write a **directional** or **informational process** about one of these topics:

cleaning out a closet
setting a fancy table
painting a chair
training for a marathon
coloring your hair
choosing a roommate
using coupons to save on groceries
avoiding morning traffic jams
handling a customer's complaint
making a telemarketing call
getting to school on time
getting ready for moving day

asking a professor for help in a
    college course
getting children to eat vegetables
remembering the name of a
    person you've met recently
fixing a leaky pipe
installing speakers in a car
buying airline tickets online
quitting a job gracefully
getting or giving a manicure
fighting a traffic ticket
sticking to an exercise program

2. Imagine that a friend is about to register for classes at your college, but he cannot visit campus during regular business hours to register in person. This will be your friend's first term at the college. Write a paragraph giving your friend clear directions for registering online. Be sure to have an appropriate topic sentence.

3. Imagine that one of your relatives has never used a computer but wants to know how to use e-mail. Explain how to send an e-mail by describing the steps you use in sending one through your online service.

   Computer

4. Interview one of the counselors at your college. Ask the counselor to tell you the steps for applying for any available scholarships. Take notes or tape the interview, get copies of any forms that may be included in the application process, and ask questions about these forms.

   After the interview, write a paragraph explaining the process of applying for one specific scholarship. Your explanation is directed at a current student who has never applied for a scholarship.

5. Interview someone who always seems to be organized at school or at work. Ask that person to tell you how he or she manages to be so efficient. Narrow the question to something like how the person always manages to get all his work done at the store or how she always gets her assignments in on time. Ask whether the person has developed a system and what steps are involved in that system. Take notes or tape the interview.

   After the interview, write a paragraph about that system, explaining how to be organized for a particular task at college or at work. Your paragraph will explain the process to someone who needs to be more organized.

6. Look carefully at the people in Photograph A. They are socializing and having fun. Write a process paragraph on this related topic: how to get to know people you have just met.

Photograph A

7. The children in Photograph B are playing tug-of-war. Use the photograph to think about a childhood game you used to play. Write a paragraph explaining how to play that game.

Photograph B

Name: _____ Section: _____

Peer Review Form for a Process Paragraph

After you've written a draft of your process paragraph, let a writing partner read it. When your partner has completed the form below, discuss. Repeat the same process for your partner's paragraph.

The steps that are most clearly described are _____

_____

_____

I'd like more explanation about this step: _____

_____

This paragraph is a directional/informational process (choose one).

Some details could be added to the part that begins with the words _____

_____

A transition could be added to the part that begins with the words _____

_____

I have questions about _____

_____

When I finished a careful reading of this paragraph, I found the explanation of the process (1) clear and simple, (2) a little confusing (3) over my head (choose one.) Explain your choice: _____

_____

_____

Other comments on the paragraph: _____

_____

_____

_____

_____

Reviewer's name: _____

Jumping In

A well-built house begins with proper framing and quality building blocks. Similarly, a well-constructed **essay** relies on logical organization as its frame and on effective paragraphs as its building blocks. Keep this analogy in mind as you move from the paragraph to the essay.

CHAPTER 28

Moving from Paragraphs to Essays

WHAT IS AN ESSAY?

You write an essay when you have more to say than can be covered in one paragraph. An **essay** can consist of one paragraph, but in this book, we take it to mean a writing of more than one paragraph. An essay has a main point, called a *thesis*, supported by subpoints. The subpoints are the *topic sentences*. Each paragraph in the *body*, or main part, of the essay has a topic sentence. In fact, each paragraph in the body of the essay is like the paragraphs you've already written because each one makes a point and then supports it.

COMPARING THE SINGLE PARAGRAPH AND THE ESSAY

Read the paragraph and the essay that follow, both about sharing happy moments. You will notice many similarities.

A Single Paragraph

When I am happy, I want to share my happiness. When my wife gave birth to our son, for example, I couldn't wait to tell everyone. I started by calling my parents, my wife's parents, and every other relative I could think of. After I had run out of family members, I told friends, coworkers, and even a few total strangers. In another instance, I had to share the news about my dream of getting a college education. As soon as I opened the letter announcing my college loan, I wanted to spread the information. Just seeing the look on my wife's face increased my happiness. Later, telling my best friend, who had encouraged me to apply for the loan, was a pleasure. When good comes into my life, I figure, why not share it?

An Essay

Everybody has special moments of pure joy when a dream suddenly becomes a reality or a goal is finally in sight. These rare times mark the high points in life, and some people like to experience them alone. However, I am not one of these people. When I am happy, I want to share my happiness.

When my wife gave birth to our son, for example, I couldn't wait to tell everyone. I started by calling my parents, my wife's parents, and every other relative I could think of. By the time I found myself calling my second cousin in New Zealand, I realized I had run out of relatives. I prolonged my happiness by calling all my friends, the people at the bakery where I work, and even a few strangers. One poor man nearly tripped when I ran into him as he tried to get out of the hospital elevator. "Oh, I'm so sorry," I said, "but I've just had a baby boy." I even told the mail carrier on my street.

In another instance, I had to share the news about my dream of getting a college education. As soon as I opened the letter announcing my college loan, I wanted to spread the information. Just seeing the look on my wife's face increased my happiness. She knew what I was thinking: with the loan, I wouldn't have to take a second job in order to attend college. Later, telling my best friend, who had encouraged me to apply for the loan, was a pleasure. My getting the loan was his victory, too, for without him, I would have given up on going to college.

I suppose I could have told my friend about my financial aid a few days later, over lunch. As for the birth of my son, I could have saved hefty long-distance phone charges by sending birth announcements to aunts, uncles, and cousins who live far away. But I chose not to hold back. When good comes into my life, I figure, why not share it?

If you read the two selections carefully, you noticed that they make the same main point, and they support that point with two subpoints.

main point: When I am happy, I want to share my happiness.

subpoints: 1. When my wife gave birth to our son, I couldn't wait to tell everyone.
2. I had to share the news about my dream of getting a college education.

You noticed that the essay is longer because it has more details and examples to support the points.

ORGANIZING AN ESSAY

When you write an essay of more than one paragraph, the **thesis** is the focus of your entire essay; it is the major point of your essay. The other important points that relate to the thesis are in topic sentences.

Thesis: Working as a salesperson has changed my character.

Topic sentence: I have had to learn patience.

Topic sentence: I have developed the ability to listen.

Topic sentence: I have become more tactful.

Notice that the thesis expresses a bigger idea than the topic sentences below it, and it is supported by the topic sentences. The essay has an introduction, a body, and a conclusion.

1. **Introduction:** The first paragraph is usually the introduction. The thesis goes here.
2. **Body:** This central part of the essay is the part where you support your main point (the thesis). Each paragraph in the body of the essay has its own topic sentence.
3. **Conclusion:** Usually one paragraph long, the conclusion reminds the reader of the thesis. It can be shorter than a body paragraph.

WRITING THE THESIS

There are several characteristics of a thesis:

1. It is expressed in a sentence. A thesis is *not* the same as the topic of the essay or the title of the essay:

   topic: learning to ski
   title: Why I Learned to Ski
   thesis: I learned to ski because all my friends ski, I needed more exercise in the winter, and I wanted to meet girls.

2. A thesis **does not announce;** it makes a point about the subject.

   announcement: This essay will explain the reasons why street racing is popular with teens.
   thesis: Street racing is popular with teens because it gives them a sense of power and identity.

3. A thesis **is not too broad.** Some ideas are just too big to cover well in an essay. A thesis that tries to cover too much can lead to a superficial or boring essay.

   too broad: The world would be a better place if everyone would just be more tolerant.
   acceptable thesis: The diversity celebration at our school spread good feeling among many groups.

4. A thesis **is not too narrow.** Sometimes, writers start with a thesis that looks good because it seems specific and precise. Later, when they try to support such a thesis, they can't find anything to say.

   too narrow: Yesterday I spent five hours in a hospital emergency room, waiting for help.
   acceptable thesis: Because I have no health insurance, illness is always a crisis for me.

Hints for Writing a Thesis

1. Your thesis can **mention the specific subpoints** of your essay. For example, your thesis might be similar to the following:

Boundaries are important because they make children feel safe, connected, and loved.

With this thesis, you have indicated the three subpoints of your essay: (1) Boundaries make children feel safe, (2) Boundaries make children feel connected, and (3) Boundaries make children feel loved.

2. Another way to write your thesis is to **make a point** without listing your subpoints. For example, you can write a thesis like the following:

Children need boundaries in order to grow.

With this thesis, you can still use the subpoints stating that boundaries make children feel safe, boundaries make children feel connected, and boundaries make children feel loved. You just don't have to mention all your subpoints in the thesis.

Exercise 1   Recognizing Good Thesis Sentences

Following is a list of thesis statements. Some are acceptable, but others are too broad or too narrow. Some are announcements; others are topics, not sentences. Put a *G* next to the good thesis sentences.

1. _____ How rumors spread on college campuses will be discussed.

2. _____ On Saturday, a local police officer stopped my brother for speeding.

3. _____ Effective communication is the basis of all relationships.

4. _____ Cartoons with sophisticated humor appeal to many adults.

5. _____ Organized crime as an evil force spreading fear and corruption.

6. _____ Male college students are choosing a wide range of hairstyles.

7. _____ Discount stores do not always offer the best bargains.

8. _____ Brazil is a large South American nation with many natural resources.

9. _____ The advantages of working from a home office.

10. _____ Traffic congestion keeps many local people from visiting the city.

Exercise 2   Selecting a Good Thesis Sentence

In each pair of thesis statements below, put a *G* next to the good thesis sentence.

1. a. _____ The effects of music on young children.

   b. _____ Music is an effective tool for teaching young children.

2. a. _____ A high-speed train would take some of the traffic off our local highway.

   b. _____ Something must be done to solve the international crisis of overdevelopment and overloaded highways.

3. a. _____ The difficulties of learning English as a second language will be discussed in this essay.

   b. _____ Students learning English as a second language have difficulties with fast-talking native speakers and confusing grammar rules.

4. a. _____ What to do if a tornado threatens your neighborhood.

b. _____ If a tornado threatens your neighborhood, act fast and sensibly.

5. a. _____ I quit my job because the working conditions were terrible.

b. _____ The terrible working conditions and what I did about them will be the subject of this essay.

6. a. _____ Obedience training can help a young dog in several ways.

b. _____ What obedience training can do to help a young dog grow into a valued pet.

7. a. _____ The differences between a convertible and a car with a sunroof.

b. _____ A car with a sunroof is less likely to be vandalized or robbed than a convertible is.

8. a. _____ Fresh pizza has a better smell, taste, and texture than frozen pizza.

b. _____ Why fresh pizza is better than frozen pizza.

9. a. _____ The hidden story of bottled water and its origins.

b. _____ Bottled water can have the same risks and come from the same sources as tap water.

10. a. _____ Last year, Fernwood got its own suicide hotline.

b. _____ Fernwood's suicide hotline is helping to save lives.

Exercise 3 **Writing a Thesis That Relates to the Subpoints**

Following are lists of subpoints that could be discussed in an essay. Write a thesis for each list. Remember that there are two ways to write a thesis: you can write a thesis that includes the specific subpoints, or you can write one that makes a point without listing the subpoints. As an example, the first one is done for you, using both kinds of topic sentences.

1. **one kind of thesis:** *Children need to leave their computers and televisions and play some outdoor sports.*

another kind of thesis: *For children, playing sports outdoors burns more energy, creates more friendships, and stimulates more interest than playing indoors.*

subpoints: a. Sitting at a computer or in front of a television burns very little energy; playing sports burns more energy.
b. Playing indoors is often solitary; sports involve other children and may lead to friendships.
c. Children playing indoors can easily become bored, but outdoor sports require more involvement.

2. **thesis:** _____

_____

subpoints: a. Grandparents can be good listeners when grandchildren have a problem.

        b. Grandparents can be generous with their time when grandchildren need help.

3. thesis: _____

_____

   subpoints: **a.** Grandparents can be intolerant of grandchildren's appearance or lifestyle.

        b. Grandparents can be too free with their opinions and advice.

        c. Grandparents can be good listeners when grandchildren have a problem.

        d. Grandparents can be generous with their time when grandchildren need help.

4. thesis: _____

_____

   subpoints: **a.** People interviewing for a job should be appropriately dressed.

        b. Interviewers want people who are confident.

        c. People who are enthusiastic about the job are more likely to impress interviewers.

5. thesis: _____

_____

   subpoints: **a.** A house surrounded by large trees will stay cooler in the summer.

        b. Large trees around a house offer more privacy.

        c. A house circled by large trees may be expensive to heat in the winter.

        d. Large trees surrounding a house may make the house dark and gloomy.

WRITING THE ESSAY IN STEPS

In an essay, you follow the same steps you learned in writing a paragraph—prewriting, planning, drafting, and polishing—but you adapt them to the longer essay form.

PREWRITING   Gathering Ideas: An Essay

Often you begin by *narrowing a topic.* Your instructor may give you a large topic so you can find something smaller, within the broad one, that you would like to write about.

    Some students think that because they have several paragraphs to write, they should pick a big topic, one that will give them enough to say. But big topics can lead to boring, superficial, general essays. A smaller topic can challenge you to find the specific, concrete examples and details that make an essay effective.

    If your instructor asked you to write about student life, for instance, you might *freewrite* some ideas as you narrow the topic:

Narrowing the Topic of Student Life

Student activities—how boring!
*Maybe how to meet people at college, except, how <u>do</u> you meet people? I don't really
know. I have my friends, but I'm not sure how I met them.*
The food on campus. Everyone will do that topic.
The classrooms in college. The tiny chairs and the temperature.
Yes!

In your freewriting, you can consider your *purpose*—to write an essay about
some aspect of student life—and *audience*—your instructor and classmates.
Your narrowed topic will appeal to this audience because both college teachers
and students spend a good part of their time in classrooms.

Listing Ideas

Once you have a narrow topic, you can use whatever process works for you.
You can brainstorm by writing a series of questions and answers about your
topic, you can freewrite on the topic, you can list ideas on the topic, or you can
do any combination of these processes.

Following is a sample *listing of ideas* on the topic of classrooms.

College Classrooms: A List

the tiny chairs	the temperature
the awful desks	all the graffiti
the carving in the desks	too hot in the room
freezing on some days	cramped rooms
blinds on windows don't close	teacher's desk
no one cares	

By *clustering* related items on the list, you'll find it easier to see the connections between ideas. The following items have been clustered (grouped), and
they are listed under subtitles.

College Classrooms: Ideas in Clusters

the furniture	***student damage***
the tiny chairs	the carving in the desks
the awful desks	all the graffiti
teacher's desk	

the temperature
freezing on some days
too hot in the room
blinds on the windows don't close

When you surveyed the clusters, you probably noticed that some of the ideas from the original list were left out. These ideas—the cramped rooms and no one caring—could fit into more than one place and might not fit anywhere. You might come back to them later.

When you name each cluster by giving it a subtitle, you move toward a focus for each body paragraph of your essay. And by beginning to focus the body paragraphs, you start thinking about the main point, the thesis of the essay. Concentrating on the thesis and on focused paragraphs helps you to *unify* your essay.

Reread the clustered ideas. When you do so, you'll notice that each cluster is about a different kind of problem in the college classroom. You can incorporate that concept into a thesis with a sentence like this:

The typical classroom at my college is unwelcoming because of its tiny furniture, uncomfortable temperature, and student damage.

Once you have a thesis and a list of details, you can begin working on the planning part of your essay.

Exercise 4   **Narrowing Topics**

Collaborate

Working with a partner or a group, narrow these topics so that the new topics are related but smaller and suitable for short essays between four and six paragraphs long. The first topic is narrowed for you.

1. **topic:** health
   smaller, related topics:
   a. *fighting a cold* _____
   b. *the right vitamins to take* _____
   c. *getting a good night's sleep* _____

2. **topic:** law enforcement
   smaller, related topics:
   a. _____
   b. _____
   c. _____

3. **topic:** television
   smaller, related topics:
   a. _____
   b. _____
   c. _____

4. **topic:** homes
   smaller, related topics:
   a. _____
   b. _____
   c. _____

5. **topic:** athletes
   smaller, related topics:
   a. _____
   b. _____
   c. _____

Exercise 5   **Clustering Related Ideas**

Below are two topics, each with a list of ideas. Mark all the related items on the list with the same number (1, 2, or 3). Some items might not get any number.

When you've finished marking the list, write a title for each number that explains the cluster of ideas.

1. **topic:** what makes a relationship thrive

   _____ experts disagree on the importance of children

   _____ the partners are friends as well as lovers

   _____ there is a safe and pleasant home

   _____ the partners are mature

   _____ there is money coming in to pay the bills

   _____ friends provide a support system

   _____ the partners share mutual goals

   _____ family members accept and act kindly toward the partners

   _____ there are no major health problems

   _____ no friends or family try to control the partners' decisions

   The ideas marked 1 can be titled _____

   The ideas marked 2 can be titled _____

   The ideas marked 3 can be titled _____

2. **topic:** the first day of a new job

   _____ go home, breathe a sigh of relief, and relax

   _____ leave early for work

   _____ tell yourself you've just survived the hardest day of your new job

   _____ watch others carefully to see how things are done

   _____ get up extra early

   _____ don't lose any sleep worrying about how the day will go

   _____ lunch is an awkward time for new employees

   _____ keep your energy level up with your manager and coworkers

   _____ tune in to the rhythm and style of the workplace

   _____ lay your clothes out on the night before your first day

   _____ ask about anything you don't understand or know how to do

   The items marked 1 can be titled _____

   The items marked 2 can be titled _____

   The items marked 3 can be titled _____

PLANNING   **Devising a Plan: An Essay**

In the next stage of writing your essay, draft an outline. Use the thesis to focus your ideas. There are many kinds of outlines, but all are used to help a writer organize ideas. When you use a **formal outline,** you show the difference between a main idea and its supporting detail by _indenting_ the supporting detail. In a formal outline, Roman numerals (numbers) and capital letters are used. Each Roman numeral represents a paragraph, and the letters beneath the numeral represent supporting details.

The Structure of a Formal Outline

first paragraph	I. Thesis
second paragraph	II. Topic sentence
	A.
	B.
details	C.
	D.
	E.
third paragraph	III. Topic sentence
	A.
	B.
details	C.
	D.
	E.
fourth paragraph	IV. Topic sentence
	A.
	B.
details	C.
	D.
	E.
fifth paragraph	V. Conclusion

Hints for Outlining

Developing a good, clear outline now can save you hours of confused, disorganized writing later. The extra time you spend to make sure that your outline has sufficient details and that *each paragraph stays on one point* will pay off in the long run.

1. **Check the topic sentences.** Keep in mind that each topic sentence in each body paragraph should support the thesis sentence. If a topic sentence is not carefully connected to the thesis, the structure of the essay will be confusing. Here are a thesis and a list of topic sentences; the topic sentence that does not fit is crossed out:

thesis:	I. Designing a CD of a person's favorite songs is a creative act and a thoughtful gift.
topic sentences:	II. Selecting and purchasing the songs takes insight.
	III. Assembling the CD requires imagination.
	IV. ~~CD players are getting cheaper all the time.~~
	V. Whoever receives the CD will be flattered that someone took the time to design such a personal gift.
	VI. A personally crafted CD challenges the mind of the giver and opens the heart of the receiver.

Because the thesis of this outline is about the creative challenge of designing a personal CD as a gift and the pleasure of receiving one, topic sentence IV doesn't fit: it isn't about making the gift or receiving it. It takes the essay off track.

A careful check of the links between the thesis and the topic sentences will help keep your essay focused.

2. **Include enough details.** Some writers believe that they don't need many details in the outline. They feel they can fill in the details later, when they actually write the essay. Even though some writers do manage to add details later, others who are in a hurry or who run out of ideas run into problems.

   For example, imagine that a writer has included very few details in an outline such as in this outline for a paragraph:

II. Vandalism of cars takes many forms.
    A. Most cars suffer external damage.
    B. Some are hit in their interiors.

The paragraph created from that outline might be too short and lack specific details, like this:

> Vandalism of cars takes many forms. First of all, most cars suffer external damage. However, some are hit in their interiors.

If you have difficulty thinking of ideas when you write, try to tackle the problem in the outline. The more details you put into your outline, the more detailed and effective your draft essay will be. For example, suppose the same outline on the vandalism topic had more details, like this:

II. Vandalism of cars takes many forms.

more details about exterior damage
{
A. Most cars suffer external damage.
B. The most common damage is breaking off the car antenna.
C. "Keying" a car, scratching its surface with a key, is also widespread.
D. Some vandals slash or take the air out of the tires.
E. Others pour paint on the body of the car.
}

more details about interior damage
{
F. Some are hit in their interiors.
G. Interior damage ranges from ripped upholstery to torn carpet.
}

You will probably agree that the paragraph will be more detailed, too.

3. **Stay on one point.** It is a good idea to check the outline of each body paragraph to see if each paragraph stays on one point. Compare each topic sentence, which is at the top of the list for the paragraph, against the details indented under it. Staying on one point gives each paragraph unity.

   Below is the outline for a paragraph that has problems staying on one point. See if you can spot the problem areas.

III. Charles is a fun-loving and cheerful person.

    A. Every morning at work, he has a new joke for me.
    B. He even makes our boss, who is very serious, smile.
    C. One day when a customer was extremely rude to him, he kept his temper.
    D. On weekends, when our job gets hectic, Charles never becomes irritable.
    E. Most of our customers love him because he always greets them with, "How are you on this beautiful day?"
    F. When we all took a pay cut, he looked on the positive side.
    G. "At least we still have our jobs," he said.

The topic sentence of the paragraph is about Charles' love of fun and cheerfulness. But sentences C and D talk about Charles' ability to remain calm. When you have a problem staying on one point, you can solve the problem two ways:

1. Eliminate details that do not fit your main point.
2. Change the topic sentence to cover all the ideas in the paragraph.

For example, you could cut out sentences C and D about Charles' calm nature, getting rid of the details that do not fit. As an alternative, you could change the topic sentence in the paragraph so that it relates to all the ideas in the paragraph. A better topic sentence is "Charles is a fun-loving, even-tempered, and cheerful person."

Revisiting the Prewriting Stage

Writing an outline can help you identify skimpy places in your plan, places where your paragraphs will need more details. You can get these details in two ways:

1. Go back to the writing you did in the prewriting stage. Check whether items on a list or ideas from freewriting can lead you to more details for your outline.
2. Brainstorm for more details by using a question-and-answer approach. For example, if the outline includes "My little sister is greedy," you might ask, "When is she greedy? How greedy is she?" Or if the outline includes "There is nothing to do in this town," you might ask, "What do you mean? Sports? Clubs? Parties?"

The time you spend writing and revising your outline will make it easier for you to write an essay that is well-developed, unified, and coherently structured. The checklist below may help you to revise.

Checklist: A Checklist for Revising the Outline of an Essay

1. **Unity:** Do the thesis and topic sentences all lead to the same point? Does each paragraph make one, and only one, point? Do the details in each paragraph support the topic sentence? Does the conclusion unify the essay?

2. **Support:** Do the body paragraphs have enough supporting details?

3. **Coherence:** Are the paragraphs in the most effective order? Are the details in each paragraph arranged in the most effective order?

A sentence outline on college classrooms follows. It includes the thesis in the first paragraph. The topic sentences have been created from the titles of the ideas clustered earlier. The details have been drawn from ideas in the clusters and from further brainstorming. The conclusion has just one sentence that unifies the essay.

An Outline for an Essay

paragraph 1   I.   Thesis: The typical classroom at my college is unwelcoming because of its tiny furniture, uncomfortable temperature, and student damage.

continued

paragraph 2 **topic sentence** **details**	II. Child-size furniture makes it difficult to focus on adult-level classes. A. The student chairs are tiny. B. I am six feet tall, and I feel like I am crammed into a kindergarten chair. C. The chairs are attached to miniature desks which are just slightly enlarged armrests. D. I cannot fit my legs under the desk. E. I cannot fit my textbook and a notebook on the surface of the desk. F. In some classrooms, the teacher has no desk and is forced to use one of the miniature student versions.
paragraph 3 **topic sentence** **details**	III. The temperature in the classrooms is anything but pleasant. A. I have been at the college for both the fall and winter terms. B. In the early fall, the rooms were too hot. C. The air conditioning feebly pumped hot air. D. The sun beat through the glass windows because the blinds were broken. E. On some days in the winter, we froze. F. Two of my teachers have reported the problems to maintenance, but nothing changed. G. It is hard to concentrate when you are sweating or shivering.
paragraph 4 **topic sentence** **details**	IV. Student damage to the classrooms makes them seedy and ugly. A. There is graffiti all over the desks. B. There are messages, slogans, and drawings. C. They are all childish. D. Half the desks and chairs have gum stuck to their undersides. E. Some students carve into the desks and chairs. F. Others have stained the carpet with spilled coffee or soft drinks. G. It's depressing to think that my fellow students enjoy damaging the place where they come to learn.
paragraph 5 **conclusion**	V. When I started college, I knew I would face many challenges, but I didn't expect them to include squeezing into the chairs, dressing for a blizzard or a heat wave, and picking the gum off my desk.

Exercise 6   Completing an Outline for an Essay

Following is part of an outline that has a thesis and topic sentences, but no details. Add the details and write them in complete sentences. Write one sentence for each capital letter. Be sure that the details are connected to the topic sentence.

   I. **Thesis:** Money has a different meaning for different people.

  II. When some people think of money, they think of the freedom to spend it on whatever they want for themselves.

A. _____

B. _____

C. _____

D. _____

E. _____

III. To others, money means security.

   A. _____

   B. _____

   C. _____

   D. _____

   E. _____

IV. Some people think of money as something to share.

   A. _____

   B. _____

   C. _____

   D. _____

   E. _____

V. The way people perceive money reveals what matters to them.

Exercise 7   Focusing an Outline for an Essay

The outline below has a thesis and details, but it has no topic sentences for the body paragraphs. Write the topic sentences.

I. **Thesis:** My first visit to the Movieland Movie Theater will also be my last.

II. _____

   _____

   A. The place smelled moldy and sour.

   B. The first seat I tried to sit in had no back.

   C. The second one had no arms.

   D. When I finally found an intact seat, my shoes stuck to the floor as I sat down.

   E. The floor was coated with dried-up soda and candy.

   F. The projectionist forgot to start the movie.

   G. Someone from the audience had to find and remind him.

   H. Two of the speakers were broken.

III. _____

   _____

   A. People from the audience talked throughout the movie.

    B. Several talked on their cell phones.

    C. Four people sitting in the front row shouted to their friends, who had just arrived at the back of the theater.

    D. Two children ran up and down the aisles for an hour during the movie.

    E. Some teens started throwing popcorn.

    F. One man near me couldn't hear the dialogue on the screen, so his wife shouted it to him.

  IV. I never want to repeat the experience I had at Movieland.

> **DRAFTING** Drafting and Revising: An Essay

When you are satisfied with your outline, you can begin drafting and revising the essay. Start by writing a first draft of the essay, which includes these parts: introduction, body paragraphs, and conclusion.

WRITING THE INTRODUCTION

Where Does the Thesis Go?

The **thesis** should appear in the introduction of the essay, in the first paragraph. But most of the time it should not be the first sentence. In front of the thesis, write a few (three or more) sentences of introduction. Generally, the thesis is the *last sentence* in the introductory paragraph.

Why put the thesis at the end of the first paragraph? First of all, writing several sentences in front of your main idea gives you a chance to lead into it, gradually and smoothly. This will help you build interest and gain the reader's attention. Also, by placing the thesis after a few sentences of introduction, you will not startle the reader with your main point.

Finally, if your thesis is at the end of the introduction, it states the main point of the essay just before that point is supported in the body paragraphs. Putting the thesis at the end of the introduction is like putting an arrow pointing to the supporting ideas in the essay.

Hints for Writing the Introduction

There are a number of ways to write an introduction.

1. You can **begin with some general statements** that gradually lead to your thesis:

> **general statements**   My mother has two framed pictures in the living room. They are sketches of a town square. In the pictures, people are sitting and talking, shopping in the small stores around the square, and strolling through the friendly streets. I envy the people in these scenes, for they seem to enjoy a calm, central gathering place, far from busy highways and enormous parking lots. Unfortunately, my community
>
> **thesis at end**   has no such place. <u>My town needs a neighborly, accessible town center.</u>

2. You can **begin with a quote** that leads smoothly to your thesis. The quote can be a quote from someone famous, or it can be an old saying. It can be something your mother always told you, a slogan from an advertisement, or the words of a song.

quotation	A song tells us, "It's a small, small, small, small world." There are days when I wish my world were smaller. Sometimes I get sick of driving to a huge supermarket for my groceries, then dashing to a giant mall for new shoes, and finally making a quick stop at a drive-through restaurant for a hamburger. As I make this journey, I rarely meet anyone I know. At these times, I wish my life were different: I'd like to get off the highway, forget the fast food and the huge malls, and run into a few friends
thesis at end	as I do my errands. Then I realize that <u>my town needs a neighborly, accessible town center.</u>

> **Note:** You can add transition words or phrases to your thesis, as in the sample above.

3. You can **tell a story** as a way of leading into your thesis. You can open with the story of something that happened to you or to someone you know, a story you read about or heard on the news.

story	Yesterday my best friend called, and we got into a lengthy conversation. After we had talked for half an hour, we realized we wanted to continue our conversation face-to-face. "Let's meet for coffee," my friend said. He suggested a coffee shop near the interstate highway. I suggested another place, which he said was "in the middle of nowhere." Then we ran out of ideas. There was no easy, central place. At that
thesis at end	moment, it occurred to me that <u>my town needs a neighborly, accessible town center.</u>

4. You can **explain why this topic is worth writing about.** Explaining could mean giving some background on the topic, or it could mean discussing why the topic is an important one.

explain	Almost everyone feels lonely at some time. Teens feel left out by the many cliques that make up high-school society. Older people, often suffering the loss of a spouse, need human contact. Singles try to find a comfortable place in what seems to be a world of married couples. As for couples, each partner needs to feel part of a world outside of marriage. In my community, there is no friendly place where all types of people can feel
thesis at end	accepted. <u>My town needs a neighborly, accessible town center.</u>

5. You can **use one or more questions** to lead into your thesis. You can open with a question or questions that will be answered by your thesis. Or you can open with a question or questions that catch the reader's attention and move toward your thesis.

> **question**
>
> Have you ever seen an old movie called <u>It's a Wonderful Life</u>? It's about George Bailey, a small-town husband and father whose life changes on Christmas Eve when an angel visits to teach George a lesson. Although I enjoy the plot of the movie, what I like most about the film is the small town George lives in, where everyone seems to know everyone else and life centers on a few streets of stores, homes, and businesses. I sometimes wish that I had a little of that simple life. Then
>
> **thesis at end**
>
> I conclude that <u>my town needs a neighborly, accessible town center.</u>

6. You can **open with a contradiction** of your main point as a way of attracting the reader's interest and leading to your thesis. You can begin with an idea that is the opposite of what you will say in your thesis. The opposition of your opening and your thesis creates interest.

> **contradiction**
>
> My town appears to have every shopping and entertainment attraction of an ideal community. It has two giant malls, a movie theater with sixteen screens and stadium seating, cafés, restaurants, popular clubs, a water park, a skating rink, and a bowling alley. However, it doesn't offer what people want most: the comfort of a small-town gathering place that invites shoppers, strollers, people with their dogs, and people who like to sit, talk, and drink coffee. <u>My town needs a neighborly, accessible town center.</u>
>
> **thesis at end**

Exercise 8 **Writing an Introduction**

Below are five thesis sentences. Pick one. Then write an introductory paragraph on the lines provided. Your last sentence should be the thesis sentence. If your instructor agrees, read your introduction to others in the class who wrote an introduction to the same thesis, or read your introduction to the entire class.

Thesis Sentences

1. What men wear makes a statement about the image they want to convey.

2. Technology has revolutionized the music industry.

3. Today's tattoos can be art, fashion, or personal statements.

4. Many parents try to give their children what the parents never had.

5. A million dollars would/would not change the way I live my life.

(Write an introduction) _____

_____

_____

_____

_____

_____

_____

WRITING THE BODY OF THE ESSAY

In the body of the essay, the paragraphs *explain*, *support*, and *develop* your thesis. In this part of the essay, each paragraph has its own topic sentence. The topic sentence in each paragraph does two things:

1. It focuses the sentences in the paragraph.
2. It makes a point connected to the thesis.

The thesis and the topic sentences are ideas that need to be supported by details, explanations, and examples. You can visualize the connections among the parts of an essay like this:

Introduction with Thesis

Body
{
  Topic Sentence
  Details
  Topic Sentence
  Details
  Topic Sentence
  Details
}

Conclusion

When you write topic sentences, you can help to organize your essay by referring to the checklist below.

Checklist: A Checklist for the Topic Sentences of an Essay

✓ Does the topic sentence give the point of the paragraph?

✓ Does the topic sentence connect to the thesis of the essay?

How Long Are the Body Paragraphs?

Remember that the body paragraphs of an essay are the places where you explain and develop your thesis. Those paragraphs should be long enough to explain, not just list, your points. To do this well, try to make your body paragraphs *at least seven sentences* long. As you develop your writing skills, you may find that you can support your ideas in fewer than seven sentences.

Developing the Body Paragraphs

You can write well-developed body paragraphs by following the same steps you used in writing single paragraphs for the earlier assignments in this course. By working through the stages of gathering ideas, outlining, drafting, revising, editing, and proofreading, you can create clear, effective paragraphs.

To focus and develop the body paragraphs, ask the questions below as you revise:

Checklist: A Checklist for Developing Body Paragraphs for an Essay

✓   Does the topic sentence cover everything in the paragraph?

✓   Do I have enough details to explain the topic sentence?

✓   Do all the details in the paragraph support, develop, or illustrate the topic sentence?

Exercise 9   **Creating Topic Sentences**

Following are thesis sentences. For each thesis, write topic sentences (as many as indicated by the numbered blanks). The first one is done for you.

1. **Thesis:** Many families have traditions for celebrating special occasions.

    Topic sentence 1: *Family birthdays can involve special rituals.*
    _____

    Topic sentence 2: *At weddings, many family traditions appear.*
    _____

    Topic sentence 3: *Some families have customs for celebrating*
    New Year's Day.

2. **Thesis:** Daytime college classes are different from evening college classes.

    Topic sentence 1: _____
    _____

    Topic sentence 2: _____
    _____

3. **Thesis:** It is easy to spot the student who is falling behind in class.

    Topic sentence 1: _____
    _____

    Topic sentence 2: _____
    _____

    Topic sentence 3: _____
    _____

4. **Thesis:** My closest friends have several characteristics in common.

    Topic sentence 1: _____
    _____

    Topic sentence 2: _____
    _____

Topic sentence 3: _____

_____

5. **Thesis:** Working at night has its good and bad points for college students.

Topic sentence 1: _____

_____

Topic sentence 2: _____

_____

Topic sentence 3: _____

_____

Topic sentence 4: _____

_____

WRITING THE CONCLUSION

The last paragraph in the essay is the **conclusion.** It does not have to be as long as a body paragraph, but it should be long enough to tie the essay together and remind the reader of the thesis. You can use any of these strategies in writing the conclusion:

1. You can **restate the thesis in new words.** Go back to the first paragraph of your essay and reread it. For example, this could be the first paragraph of an essay:

introduction

> I recently moved to a city that is a thousand miles from my home town. I drove the long distance with only one companion, my mixed-breed dog Casey. Casey was a wonderful passenger: he kept me company, never asked to stop or complained about my driving, and was happy to observe the endless stretches of road. By the end of our trip, I loved Casey even more than I had when we started. Unfortunately, I found that landlords do not appreciate the bonds between dogs and their owners. In fact, <u>renting a decent apartment and keeping a dog is nearly impossible.</u>

thesis at end

The thesis, underlined above, is the sentence that you can restate in your conclusion. Your task is to _keep the point but put it in different words._ Then work that restatement into a short paragraph, like this:

> Most dogs can adapt to apartment living. They will not bark too much, destroy property, or threaten the neighbors. They can adjust to being alone indoors as long as their owners provide time for fun, exercise, and affection. But most landlords refuse to give dogs the benefit of the doubt. <u>The landlords pressure dog owners to make a choice between an apartment and a pet.</u>

restating the thesis

2. You can **make a judgment, valuation, or recommendation.** Instead of simply restating your point, you can end by making some comment on the issue you've described or the problem you've illustrated. If you were looking for another way to end the essay on finding an apartment that allows pets, for example, you could end with a recommendation.

<table>
<tr><td>ending with a
recommendation</td><td>I understand that landlords need to make a profit on their property and that some dogs and dog owners damage that property. However, not all dogs go wild, and not all dog owners let their pets destroy an apartment. <u>If landlords made an individual judgment about each applicant with a pet, instead of following a hard, cold, policy, they might realize that dogs can be model apartment dwellers.</u></td></tr>
</table>

3. You can **conclude by framing your essay.** You can tie your essay together neatly by *using something from your introduction* as a way of concluding. When you take an example, or a question, or even a quote from your first paragraph and refer to it in your last paragraph, you are "framing" the essay. Take another look at the introduction to the essay on finding an apartment that will allow a dog. The writer talks about driving a thousand miles away from home, about his or her dear companion, Casey. The writer also mentions the difficulties of finding a decent place to live when landlords will not allow dogs. Now consider how the ideas of the introduction are used in this conclusion:

<table>
<tr><td>frame
frame
frame

frame
frame
frame</td><td>When <u>I drove into this city a thousand miles from my home, I brought my dear friend and loyal companion with me.</u> That friend, <u>my dog Casey</u>, made me smile as he sat in the passenger seat, a tall, proud traveler. He fell asleep on my feet when I stopped at a lonely rest stop. <u>Many cruel landlords told me I would have to give Casey up if I wanted a comfortable place to live.</u> But I refused, for Casey brings me more comfort than any fancy apartment ever could.</td></tr>
</table>

Exercise 10 **Choosing a Better Way to Restate the Thesis**

Following are five clusters. Each cluster consists of a thesis sentence and two sentences that try to restate the thesis. Each restated sentence could be used as part of the conclusion to an essay. Put *B* next to the sentence in each pair that is a better restatement. Remember that the better choice repeats the same idea as the thesis but does not rely on too many of the same words.

1. **thesis:** If you want to eat healthy food, avoid sugar and sweets.

   restatement 1: _____ Sweets and sugar are not healthy food.

   restatement 2: _____ Controlling a sweet tooth is one way to a healthy diet.

2. **thesis:** The way a man treats his mother is a good indication of the way he will treat his wife.

   restatement 1: _____ A clue to how a man will relate to his wife is his relationship to his mother.

   restatement 2: _____ A good indication of the way a man will treat his wife is the way he treats his mother.

3. **thesis:** Martin has a gift for meeting people, putting them at ease, and persuading them to support his plans.

> **restatement 1:** _____ What Martin does best is meet people, put them at ease, and persuade them to support his plans.

> **restatement 2:** _____ Martin knows how to talk to strangers, relax their doubts, and persuade them to back his projects.

4. **thesis:** Every job has its drawbacks.

> **restatement 1:** _____ No job is perfect.

> **restatement 2:** _____ There are drawbacks to every job.

5. **thesis:** School children dream of summer vacation but can become bored or lonely in the long, unstructured days.

> **restatement 1:** _____ While every schoolboy or girl fantasizes about summer vacation, the reality may be more boring and empty than the fantasy.

> **restatement 2:** _____ Although many young students dream of summer vacation, they may become bored when the vacation days are long and unstructured.

Revising the Draft

Once you have a rough draft of your essay, you can begin revising it. The following checklist may help you to make the necessary changes in your draft.

Checklist: Checklist for Revising the Draft of an Essay

✓ Does the essay have a clear, unifying thesis?

✓ Does the thesis make a point?

✓ Does each body paragraph have a topic sentence?

✓ Is each body paragraph focused on its topic sentence?

✓ Are the body paragraphs roughly the same size?

✓ Do any of the sentences need combining?

✓ Do any of the words need to be changed?

✓ Do the ideas seem to be smoothly linked?

✓ Does the introduction catch the reader's interest?

✓ Is there a definite conclusion?

✓ Does the conclusion remind the reader of the thesis?

Transitions Within Paragraphs

In an essay, you can use two kinds of transitions: those within a paragraph and those between paragraphs.

Transitions that link ideas **within a paragraph** are the same kinds you've used earlier. Your choice of words, phrases, or even sentences depends on the kind of connection you want to make. Here is a list of some common transitions and the kind of connection they express.

INFO BOX: **Common Transitions Within a Paragraph**

To join two ideas

again	another	in addition	moreover
also	besides	likewise	similarly
and	furthermore		

To show a contrast or a different opinion

but	instead	on the other hand	still
however	nevertheless	or	yet
in contrast	on the contrary	otherwise	

To show a cause-and-effect connection

accordingly	because	for	therefore
as a result	consequently	so	thus

To give an example

for example	in the case of	such as	to illustrate
for instance	like		

To show time

after	first	recently	subsequently
at the same time	meanwhile	shortly	then
before	next	soon	until
finally			

Transitions Between Paragraphs

When you write something that is more than one paragraph long, you need transitions that link each paragraph to the others. There are several effective ways to link paragraphs and remind the reader of your main idea and of how the smaller points connect to it. Here are two ways:

   1. **Restate an idea** from the preceding paragraph at the start of a new paragraph. Look closely at the following two paragraphs and notice how the second paragraph repeats an idea from the first paragraph and provides a link.

Buying clothes for their designer labels is expensive. A tee shirt marked with the name of a popular designer can cost twenty or thirty dollars more than a similar tee shirt without the name. More expensive items like fleece jackets can be as much as seventy or eighty dollars higher if they carry a trendy name. For each designer jacket a person buys, he or she could probably buy two without a trendy logo or label. If a person decides to go all the way with fashion, he or she can spend a hundred dollars on designer socks and underwear.

transition
restating
an idea

<u>Creating a wardrobe of designer clothes is not only expensive; it is also</u> silly. While designers want buyers to think the designer label means quality, many trendy clothes are made in the same factories as less fashionable clothes. And after all, how much "design" can go into a pair of socks to make them worth four times what an ordinary pair costs? The worst part of spending money on designer labels has to do with style. The hot designer of today can be out of style tomorrow, and no one wants to wear that name across a shirt, a jacket, or a pair of socks.

2. Use synonyms and repetition as a way of reminding the reader of an important point. For example, in the two paragraphs below, notice how certain repeated words, phrases, and synonyms all remind the reader of a point about kindness and generosity. The repeated words and synonyms are underlined.

Often the kindest and most generous people are the ones who don't have much themselves. When I was evicted from my apartment, my Aunt Natalie, who has three children under ten, took me into her two-room apartment. Her heart was too big for her to leave me homeless. Another giving person is my best friend. He is a security guard trying to pay for college, but he regularly donates his time and money to the local Police Athletic League. One of the most compassionate people I know is a grandmother living on social security. Every day, she gets up at 5:00 a.m. to make sandwiches at the local food bank. She swears she isn't doing anything special, that she gets more than she gives by taking care of others.

Not everyone can be a hero working in a food bank at 5:00 a.m. But everyone can perform small acts of generosity and humanity, and most people do. Many are thoughtful and caring enough to leave a large tip for the server who lives on tips. Most people are decent on the highways; they let desperate drivers merge lanes. In the mall, shoppers routinely help lost children, hold the door for the shoppers behind them, and give directions to strangers. Without feeling at all heroic, people give blood at the blood drive, walk in the walk-a-thon, take in lost pets, and sell candy bars for their children's school. But even if they are not thinking about it, these people are acting for others and giving to others.

A Draft Essay

Following is a draft of the essay on college classrooms. As you read it, you'll notice many changes from the outline on pages 413–414.

- An introduction has been added, phrased in the first person, "I," to unify the essay.
- Transitions have been added within and between paragraphs.
- Sentences have been combined.
- Details have been added.
- General statements have been replaced by more specific ones.
- Word choice has been improved.
- A conclusion has been added. The conclusion uses one of the ideas from the lead-in, the idea that the outside and inside of National College are different. In addition, one of the other ideas in the conclusion, the point that no one seems to care about the condition of the classrooms, comes from the original list of ideas about the topic of college classrooms. It did not fit in the body paragraphs, but it works in the conclusion.

A Draft of an Essay

(Thesis and topic sentences are underlined.)

National College, which I attend, has impressive buildings of glass and concrete. It has covered walkways, paved patios, and large clusters of trees and flowers. From the outside, the college looks great. However, on the inside, National College has some problems. The most important rooms in the institution do not attract the most important people in the institution, the students. <u>The typical classroom at my college is unwelcoming because of its tiny furniture, uncomfortable temperature, and student damage.</u>

First of all, <u>child-size furniture makes it difficult to focus on adult-level classes.</u> The student chairs are tiny. They are too small for anyone over ten years old, but for large or tall people, they are torture. For example, I am six feet tall, and when I sit on one of the classroom chairs, I feel like I am crammed into a kindergarten chair. They are attached to miniature desks, which are the size of slightly enlarged armrests. As I sit in class, I cannot fit my legs under the desk. I cannot fit my textbook and a notebook on the surface of the desk. Something always slips off and makes a noise that disrupts the class. In some classrooms, the instructor has no desk and is forced to use one of the miniature student versions.

As students twist and fidget in their tiny desks, they face another problem. <u>The temperature in the classroom is anything but pleasant.</u> I have been at the college for both fall and winter terms, and I have seen both extremes of temperature. In the early fall, the rooms were hot. The air conditioner feebly pumped hot air, which, of course, made the heat worse. Meanwhile, the sun beat through the glass windows because the blinds were broken. Winter did not bring any relief because in winter we froze. On some days, we wore our winter coats during class. Two of my teachers reported the problems to the maintenance department, but nothing changed. I wish the maintenance manager understood how hard it is for students to concentrate when they are sweating or shivering.

Heat and cold create an uncomfortable learning place, but students create a shabby one. <u>Student damage to the classrooms makes them seedy and ugly.</u> Graffiti covers the desks with childish messages, slogans, and drawings. In addition, half the desks have gum stuck to their undersides. Some students even carve their initials and artwork into the plastic and wood of the desks and chairs. Others have stained the carpet with spilled coffee or soft drinks. Sometimes I have to be careful where I walk so that my shoes don't stick to the mess. It's depressing to think that my fellow students enjoy damaging the place where they come to learn.

National College is impressive outside, but no one seems to care about the problems inside. The classrooms seem to be designed without a thought for adult learners who need to sit in adult-size seats and take lecture notes at adult-size desks. The maintenance department does not maintain a comfortable temperature so that students can learn, and students do not respect their learning environment. These problems surprise me. <u>When I started college, I knew I would face many challenges, but I didn't expect them to include squeezing into the chairs, dressing for a blizzard or heat wave, and picking the gum off my desk.</u>

Exercise 11   **Identifying the Main Points in the Draft of an Essay**

Following is the draft of a four-paragraph essay. Read it, then reread it and underline the thesis and the topic sentences in each body paragraph and in the conclusion.

During my high school years, I held several part-time jobs that involved dealing with the public. I once worked as an activities director for an after-school program where ten-year-olds started giving me orders. In my senior year, I worked at a local sandwich shop and learned how to smile at hungry, impatient customers waiting for their twelve-inch submarine orders. I am now a sophomore in college and work at Cook's Place, a small but popular family restaurant. I have learned much while working at this family establishment, first as a waiter and now as the restaurant's first night manager.

The restaurant's owner, Dan Cook, hired me a year ago to be a waiter for what he humorously calls "the dinner crowd shift." I learned several essential business skills in a short time. Although the restaurant has only ten tables (each seating four), I quickly learned how to keep track of multiple orders, how to work the computerized cash register, how to verify active credit card numbers, and how to use certain abbreviations while taking orders. Dan also showed me how to fill out weekly orders for our food and beverage suppliers. Many of our customers are regulars, and I also learned that maintaining a positive attitude and friendly manner can make my job enjoyable, even on slow nights. After a few weeks, I felt confident about my skills as a waiter and looked forward to going to work.

After I had been a waiter for five months, Dan told me he'd like to start spending more time visiting his grown children who live in another state. He asked me if I would like to become the restaurant's "first official night manager." I accepted his offer immediately, and I have acquired even more business skills in this position. I now manage the restaurant three nights each week and one Saturday evening each month. I plan the dinner specials with the cook, negotiate with suppliers to get the best bulk-order prices, and make calls to customers who fill out an evaluation form Dan and I devised. I have learned that if I treat people respectfully, they will usually treat me professionally. Over the past year, I've had to interview applicants whenever a server position became available, and I've learned how important it is to be tactful and encouraging even when I've had to turn someone down. Finally, I've even met with Dan's accountant several times.

She showed me the forms various business owners have to fill out, and I've learned about the importance of accurate records for tax purposes. Dan says he's proud of my progress and jokes that I "work well with people and work the numbers well."

At Cook's Place, I was fortunate to have on-the-job training that was both educational and enjoyable. I've gained many business skills, but most importantly, I've learned the value of encouragement, teamwork, respect, and friendship. They are my ingredients for success in any relationship.

Exercise 12 **Adding Transitions to an Essay**

The essay below needs transitions. Add the transitions where indicated, and add the kind of transition—word, phrase, or sentence—indicated.

I have always liked math and done well in my math classes, so I planned to major in math once I finished my required courses in college. However, I am thinking of changing my major because of a course I signed up for almost by accident. When I registered, the course was the only one left open that would fit into my schedule. The course was Business Law, and I love it. It is a great course because the teacher makes it clear, interesting, and lively.

_____ (add a phrase) Mr. Morales, the instructor, makes the subject easy to follow. When I started the class, I knew nothing about business law; _____ (add a word or phrase) I now understand the basics. Mr. Morales has a very structured, simple plan for covering the class material. He doesn't just talk to us. _____ (add a word or phrase) he provides outlines and study guides. He uses class discussion to make sure that we understand each new concept. _____ (add a word or phrase) he gives us practice quizzes before we take any major tests.

_____

_____

(add a sentence). Business law is an interesting class because Mr. Morales constantly links the lessons to current events or current legal issues. We read and study newspaper articles on business fraud and lawsuits. _____ (add a word or phrase) we watch videos of television programs on scandals in the stock market. I never thought I'd be enjoying reading about accounting or insurance, but they're fascinating

subjects when they tell of crime in high places or billionaires gone wrong. _____

_____

_____

(add a sentence). Sometimes Mr. Morales invites guest speakers to the class. They are

people like forensic accountants, who investigate accounting fraud, or local detec-

tives, who investigate insurance crimes.

_____

_____

(add a sentence). Business law is the one class that always keeps me alert. Mr.

Morales is a very active teacher. He walks around the room, sits on his desk for a few

minutes, then jumps off and paces back and forth. He is always telling jokes. Even

though most of the jokes are corny, they vary the rhythm of the class and stimulate the

students. _____ (add a word or phrase) they put everyone at ease and make

it easy for students to ask questions. _____ (add a word) Mr. Morales

makes the students move around, putting them in small groups or splitting the class in

two so that each half can argue one side of an issue. _____ (add a

word or phrase) the class time seems to fly by.

I still like my math classes, but I love my business law class. Math is my strength,

_____ (add a word or phrase) the legal side of business intrigues me. What-

ever major I choose, I am sure of one thing. I will always remember Mr. Morales' class.

Exercise 13   **Recognizing Synonyms and Repetition
Used to Link Ideas in an Essay**

In the following essay, underline all the synonyms and repetition (of words or
phrases) that help remind the reader of the thesis sentence. (To help you, the
thesis is underlined.)

Some people have artistic talent. They become famous painters, musicians, or actors.

Others are known for their athletic abilities, and they are seen on television in tourna-

ments, matches, games, or other sports contests. My brother will never be on stage or in

a tournament, yet he has a special talent. <u>My brother Eddie has a gift for making friends.</u>

Our family has moved six times in the past ten years, and every time, Eddie was the first to get acquainted with the neighbors. There is something about his smile and cheerful attitude that draws strangers to him. On one of our moves, Eddie had met our neighbors on both sides of the house and directly across the street by the time we unloaded the van. Within a week, Eddie had made the acquaintance of almost every family on the block. Eddie's ability to connect with others helped our whole family to feel comfortable in a new place. As Eddie formed links within the area, he introduced us to the community. Thanks to my brother, we all got to know Mrs. Lopez next door, the teenagers down the street, and even the mail carrier. Soon familiarity turned into deeper friendships.

One of the most amazing examples of Eddie's talent occurred when he and I took a long bus trip. Twenty-four hours on a bus can be exhausting and depressing, but Eddie made the trip fun. He began by talking to the man seated across from us. Soon the couple behind us joined in. When Eddie passed around a bag of potato chips, he drew four more passengers into this cluster of newfound buddies. Eddie and I didn't sleep during the entire trip. We were too busy talking, laughing, and swapping life stories with the other travelers. Some of the toughest-looking passengers turned out to be the kindest, warmest companions.

Only Eddie could transform a dreary bus ride into a cheerful trip with new friends. And thanks to Eddie, our family's many moves became opportunities to meet new people. If I am with my brother, I know we will never be lonely, for Eddie's real talent is his ability to draw others to him.

POLISHING   Polishing and Proofreading: An Essay

Creating a Title

When you are satisfied with the final draft of your essay, you can begin preparing a good copy. Your essay will need a title. Try to think of a short title that is connected to your thesis. Because the title is the reader's first contact with your essay, an imaginative title can create a good first impression. If you can't think of anything clever, try using a key phrase from your essay.

The title is placed at the top of your essay, about an inch above the first paragraph. Always capitalize the first word of the title and all other words *except* "the," "an," "a," prepositions (like "of," "in", "with"), and coordinating conjunctions ("for," "and," "nor," "but," "or," "yet," "so"). *Do not* underline or put quotation marks around your title.

The Final Version of an Essay

Following is the final version of the essay on college classrooms. When you compare it to the draft on page 426, you will notice some changes:

- A title has been added.
- Transitions have been added; one is a phrase, and one is a sentence.
- The word choice has been changed so that descriptions are more precise and repetition (of the word "problems") is avoided.
- Specific details have been added.

A Final Version of an Essay

(Changes from the draft are underlined.)

A Look Inside College Classrooms

National College, which I attend, has impressive buildings of glass and concrete. It has covered walkways, paved patios, and large clusters of trees and flowers. From the outside, the college looks <u>distinguished.</u> However, on the inside, National College has some problems. The most important rooms in the institution do not <u>appeal to</u> the most important people in the institution, the students. The typical classroom at my college is unwelcoming because of its tiny furniture, uncomfortable temperature, and student damage.

First of all, child-size furniture makes it difficult to focus on adult-level classes. The student chairs are tiny. They are too small for anyone over ten years old, but for large or tall people, they are torture. For example, I am six feet tall, and when I sit on one of the classroom chairs, I feel like I am crammed into a kindergarten chair. They are attached to miniature desks, which are the size of slightly enlarged armrests. As I sit in class, I cannot fit my legs under the desk. I cannot fit my textbook and a notebook on the surface of the desk. Something always slips off and makes a noise that disrupts the class. <u>The child-friendly atmosphere even affects the instructors.</u> In some classrooms, the instructor has no desk and is forced to use one of the miniature student versions.

As students twist and fidget in their tiny desks, they face another problem. The temperature in the classrooms is anything but pleasant. I have been at the college for both fall and winter terms, and I have seen both extremes of temperature. In the early fall, the rooms were <u>sweltering</u>. The air conditioner feebly pumped hot air, which, of course, made the heat worse. Meanwhile, the sun beat through the glass windows because the blinds were broken. Winter did not bring any relief because in winter we froze. On some days, we wore our winter coats during class. <u>At different times during the semester,</u> two of my teachers reported the problems to the maintenance department, but nothing changed. I wish the maintenance manager understood how hard it is for students to concentrate when they are sweating or shivering.

Heat and cold create an uncomfortable learning place, but students create a shabby one. Student damage to the classrooms makes them seedy and ugly. Graffiti covers the desks with childish messages, slogans, and drawings. In addition, half the desks have gum stuck to their undersides. Some students even carve their initials and artwork into the plastic and wood of the desks and chairs. Others have stained the carpet with spilled coffee or soft drinks <u>and left crumbs and ground-in food behind.</u> Sometimes I have to be careful where I walk so that my shoes don't stick to the mess. It's depressing to think that my fellow students enjoy damaging the place where they come to learn.

National College is impressive outside, but no one seems to care about the <u>flaws</u> inside. The classrooms seem to be designed without a thought for adult learners who need to sit in adult-size seats and take lecture notes at adult-size desks. The maintenance department does not maintain a comfortable temperature so that students can learn, and students do not respect their learning environment. These problems surprise me. When I started college, I knew I would face many challenges, but I didn't expect them to include squeezing into the chairs, dressing for a blizzard or heat wave, and picking the gum off my desk.

Before you prepare the final copy of your essay, check your latest draft for errors in spelling and punctuation, and for any errors made in typing or recopying.

Exercise 14   Proofreading to Prepare the Final Version

Following are two essays with the kinds of errors it is easy to overlook when you prepare the final version of an assignment. Correct the errors, writing above the lines. There are twenty errors in the first essay and sixteen in the second.

"My Three Treasures"

1. My room is filled with CDs, sports equiptment, audio equipment, and a computer. I like having all these items but I could live without them. The three thing's that are most valuable to me don't take up much room. The things I value most are a photograph, a medal, and ticket.

The photograph reminds me of how lucky I am It is a photo of my girlfriend Lucy on her birthday. In the picture, she is happy and beautiful, but not as beautiful as she is on the inside. Everytime I look at this photograph, I remeber how fortunate I am to have a woman like Lucy love me. Her face reminds me of all the happiness we have shared and promises we will have more good times together. If there was a fire in my house I would run into the blaze to save my picture of Lucy.

One tresure, Lucy's photograph, reminds me of my present and future happiness, but another is a memory of the past. It is an army medal that connects me to my grandfather. He was in the Vietnam War, and when he was wounded, he got a medal. I am the onely granson in the family, so when I turned eighteen, my grandfather gave me his medal. My grandfather past away last year, so the medal is even more special to me now. I carry it in my wallet to remember my grand father, the heroe.

The last treasure is another gift. It is a ticket stub from the first professional baseball game I ever saw. The ticket represents the first time my Father took me into the world he loves so much. My father is a baseball fanatic, and even when I was a toddler, I used to set in front of the television with him and watch the games. But he never took me along to the real games; he always said I was too little. Then, on my eight birthday, he gave me a big surprise. He and I went to a professional game. The game was exciting, but the best part of it was being with my father, sharing his favorite place. I kept the ticket to prove that I had passed the little boy stage of my life.

An old ticket, a medal, and a photograph arent worth any money. However, they are worth the world to me. they all connect me to the most important people in my past, present, and future.

How my dog trained me

2. When my aunt moved to Texas, she had to leave her dog behind. I told her I would take the dog because I figured he would be no trouble. After all, he was two years old and already housebroken and trained. I did'nt know that I was the one who would receive the training.

Rocket, the dog, had very strong beliefs about walk's. He liked to go for a walk the first thing in the mourning. However, I liked to sleep late, so I just assumed Rocket would change his ways and learn to sleep longer. One day with my pet open my eyes to my new morning routine. At 7:00 a.m., Rocket began to whine softly. When I ignore him, he began licking my face. To sum up, I can only say that an early walk was better than endless licking by a dog.

Now that I had learned to take early walks, Rocket moved on to the next lessen. This one was a little, harder for me to figure out. Every night about 11:00 p m, Rocket would get up from his place on the couch and stand by the kitchen cabinets. He would first look at the cabinets and then stair at me. I didn't understand. I checked Rocket's bowls. He had clean water in his water bowl and dry food in his food bowl. But Rocket continued to stand and stare. Even when I went to bed Rocket would still be in his spot in the kitchen. Finely, I called my Aunt in Texas to see if Rocket had a problem with kitchen cabinets. My aunt informed me that Rocket was accustomed to getting a dog biscuit every night at bedtime and that he could not sleep without his biscits, which she kept in a box in a kitchen cabinet. So now I have learn to read my dog's signal and to obey it by giving him his nightly snack.

Rocket is a wonderful dog, and he's smart, too. I just never thought he'd be smart enough to teach *me* how to behave. I only hope that my dog isn't planning any new tricks for me to learn

Lines of Detail: A Walk-Through Assignment

Write a five-paragraph essay about three things in your life you would like to get rid of. These things must be tangible objects like an old car, a bicycle, a uniform, and so forth. They cannot be people or personal qualities like fear or insecurity. To write the essay, follow these steps:

Step 1: Freewrite a list of all the things you would like to get rid of in your life. To get started, think about what is in your room, car, purse, wallet, house, apartment, garage, basement, and so forth.

Step 2: Select the three items you would most like to toss out. Then prepare a list of questions you can ask yourself about these three items. You can ask questions such as the following:

> Why do I want to get rid of the following?
> Is it useless to me?
> Does it remind me of an unpleasant part of my life?
> Is it ugly? Broken? Out of style?
> Does it remind me of a habit I'd like to break?
> Can I get rid of it? If so, why don't I get rid of it? If not, why can't I get rid of it?

Answer the questions. The answers can lead you to details and topic sentences for your essay. For instance, you might hate the uniform you have to wear because it represents a job you would like to leave. However, you might not be able to get rid of the uniform because you need the job. Or maybe you'd like to toss out your cigarettes because you want to stop smoking.

Step 3: Survey your answers. Begin by listing the three things you would like to get rid of. Then list the details (the answers to your questions) beneath the item they relate to. For example, under the item "uniform," you could list the reason you hate it and the reason you cannot get rid of it.

Step 4: Once you have clustered the three items and the details related to each, you have the beginnings of a five-paragraph essay. Each item will be the focus of one of the body paragraphs, and its details will develop the paragraph.

Step 5: Focus all your clusters around one point. To find a focus, ask your-self whether the things you want to throw away have anything in common. If so, you can make that point in your thesis. For instance, you could write a thesis like one of these:

> The things I would like to get rid of in my life are all related to a _____ part of my life.

> My weaknesses are reflected in three items I would like to get rid of in my life. If I could get rid of _____, _____, and _____, I would be _____.

If the things you would like to be rid of are not related, then you can use a thesis like one of the following:

> Three items I'd like to throw out reflect different aspects of my life.

> I'd like to get rid of _____ because it _____, of _____ because it _____, and of _____ because it _____.

Step 6: Once you have a thesis and clustered details, draft your outline. Then revise your outline until it is unified, expresses the ideas in a clear order, and has enough supporting details.

Step 7: Write a draft of your essay. Revise the draft, checking it for a smooth lead-in, balanced paragraphs, relevant and specific details, a strong conclusion, and smooth transitions.

Step 8: Before you prepare the final version of your essay, check for spelling, word choice, punctuation, and formatting errors.

Writing Your Own Essay

When you write on any of these topics, be sure to work through the stages of the writing process in preparing your essay.

1. Take any paragraph you wrote for this class and develop it into an essay of four or five paragraphs. If your instructor agrees, read the paragraph to a partner or group, and ask your listener(s) to suggest points inside the paragraph that can be developed into paragraphs of their own.

Collaborate

2. Narrow down one of the following topics, and then write an essay on it.

parents	work	crime	cities
small towns	war	fashion	country life
pleasures	worries	relationships	fears
fitting in	accidents	goals	responsibilities

3. Write an essay on any one of the following topics:

My Three Favorite Places
Three People I Have Known and Loved
Three Skills I Would Like to Learn
Three Songs I Will Always Remember
Three Mistakes That Drivers Make
My Three Best/Worst Experiences Playing _____
    (name a sport)

4. Write a four-paragraph essay about a dream you had. In your first body paragraph, describe the dream in detail. In your second body paragraph, explain what you think the dream means: Does it connect to one of your fears or hopes? Is it related to a current problem in your life? Does it suggest an answer to a problem? What does the dream tell you about yourself?

5. Examine your place in your family. Are you an only child? The oldest child? The youngest? A middle child? Do you have brothers? Sisters? Both? Write an essay on the advantages (or disadvantages) of your place in the family.

6. Study Photographs A, B, C, and D. Use them to think about this topic for an essay: The three best part-time jobs for college students.

Photograph A

Photograph B

Photograph C

Photograph D

7. Write a five-paragraph essay about Photograph E. In the first body paragraph, describe one of the people in the photo. Describe what the person looks like, the expression on his or her face, and what the person is doing. In the second body paragraph, describe the other person in the photograph. In the third body paragraph, write about the relationship of the two people. Are they married? Friends? In love? Use specific details from the photograph to support your ideas about their relationship.

Photograph E

8. The cat in Photograph F seems determined to get the fish, even if it means snorkeling in a fish tank. Write an essay about three pets or people who were willing to do ridiculous things to get what they wanted.

Photograph F

Topics for a Narrative Essay

1. Write about a time when you were surprised. It can be a good or bad experience.

2. Write about the most frustrating experience of your life.

3. Write about how you met your current boyfriend, girlfriend, partner, or spouse.

4. Write about the time you lost something or someone.

5. Write about your first day in a new home, at a new job, or in a new town.

Topics for a Descriptive Essay

1. Imagine your ideal home or apartment. In a five-paragraph essay, describe the three rooms that would be most important to you. Describe their appearance and their contents, such as furniture, accessories, equipment, and appliances.

2. Describe the best social event you ever attended. It can be a wedding, a dance, a holiday party, a graduation celebration, or any other special event. Describe the people at the event, the place where it happened, the food and refreshments served, and the activity (dance, music, awards ceremony) connected to the event.

3. Write an essay describing any of the following:

    your two favorite childhood toys
    your two (or three) favorite places to relax
    three beautiful animals
    any scene at sunset

4. Go to a place you visit regularly, but on this visit, study the place carefully. You may choose to visit a supermarket, service station, coffee shop, convenience store, and so forth. As soon as you leave, take notes about what you noticed. Then write an essay describing that place.

5. Imagine that someone who has never seen you (a distant relative, someone you've been corresponding with) is coming to visit. You will be meeting this person at the airport or train station. In an essay, describe yourself to this person. You can describe your face, body, clothes, walk, voice, or any other distinguishing characteristic.

Topics for an Illustration Essay

1. Make a statement about yourself and illustrate it with examples. You can use a thesis like one of the following:

    When faced with a problem, I am a person who _____.

    Everyone who knows me thinks I am too _____.

    I have always felt satisfied with my _____.

    My greatest strength is _____.

    My greatest weakness is _____.

2. Write about a person who has been kind to you. In the body paragraphs, give examples of this person's kindness to you.

3. Here are some general statements that you may have heard:

   > The college years are the best in a person's life.
   > Teenage marriages never work out.
   > Hard work will get you where you want to be.
   > Children these days are too spoiled.
   > When their children grow up and leave home, many parents feel lost.
   > Old people have an easy life; all they do is sit around all day.

   Pick one of these statements and, in an essay, give examples (from your own experience and observation) of the truth or falseness of the statement.

4. Complete this statement:

   > The best part of living in _____ (name your city, town or
   >
   > neighborhood) is its _____.

   Then write an essay supporting this statement with examples.

5. Write a thesis that sums up your social life in high school. In an essay, support that thesis with examples.

Topics for a Process Essay

1. Think of some process you perform often. It could be something as simple as doing the laundry or setting your DVR to record a program while you are not home. Now, pretend that you must explain this process to someone who has no idea how to perform it. Write an essay explaining the process to that person.

2. Observe someone perform a task you've never looked at closely. You can watch your boss close up the store, for instance, or watch a friend braid hair. Then write an essay on how the person works through the steps of that process.

3. Interview a law enforcement officer, asking him or her what steps a person should take to protect a home from crime. Use the information you learned from the interview to write an essay on how to protect a home from crime.

4. Write an essay on a common legal or business procedure such as taking the driver's test, filling out a job application, applying for a passport or visa, applying for a loan, or establishing residency to get lower tuition rates. Write an essay about the steps of that process.

5. Write an essay about how to train for a specific sport.

Name: _____ Section: _____

Peer Review Form for an Essay

After you have completed a draft of your essay, let a writing partner read it. When your partner has completed the form below, discuss the comments. Then repeat the same process for your partner's paragraph.

The thesis of this essay is _____

_____

_____

The topic sentences for the body paragraphs are _____

_____

_____

_____

_____

The topic sentence in the conclusion is _____

_____

_____

The best part of the essay is the _____(first, second, third, etc.) paragraph.

I would like to see details added to the part about _____

_____

I would take out the part about _____

_____

Additional comments: _____

_____

_____

_____

_____

_____

Reviewer's Name: _____

CHAPTER 29

Writing from Reading

WHAT IS WRITING FROM READING?

One way to find topics for writing is to draw from your ideas, memories, and observations. Another way is to write from reading you've done. You can react to something you've read; you can agree or disagree with it. You can summarize what you've read. Many college assignments ask you to write about an assigned reading such as an essay, a chapter in a textbook, or an article in a journal. This kind of writing requires an active, involved attitude toward your reading. Such reading is done in steps:

1. Preread.
2. Read.
3. Reread with a pen or pencil.

Attitude

Before you begin the first step of this reading process, you have to have a certain attitude. That attitude involves thinking of what you read as half of a conversation. The writer has opinions and ideas; he or she makes points just as you do when you write or speak. The writer supports his or her points with specific details. If the writer were speaking to you in conversation, you would respond to his or her opinions or ideas. You would agree, disagree, or question.

You would jump into the conversation, linking or contrasting your ideas with those of the other speaker.

The right attitude toward reading demands that you read the same way you converse: you become involved. In doing this, you talk back as you read, and later, you may react in your own writing. Reacting as you read will keep you focused on what you are reading. If you are focused, you will remember more of what you read. With an active, involved attitude, you can begin the step of prereading.

Prereading

Before you actually read an assigned essay, a chapter in a textbook, or an article in a journal, magazine, or newspaper, take a few minutes to look it over, and be ready to answer the following questions.

Checklist: A Prereading Checklist

✓ How long is this reading?

✓ Will I be able to read it in one sitting, or will I have to schedule several time periods to finish it?

✓ Are there any subheadings in the reading? Do they give any hints about the reading?

✓ Are there any charts? Graphs? Is there boxed information? Are there any photographs or illustrations with captions? Do the photos or captions give any hints about the reading?

✓ Is there any introductory material about the reading or the author? Does the introductory material give me any hints about the reading?

✓ What is the title of the reading? Does the title hint at the point of the reading?

✓ Are there any parts of the reading underlined or emphasized in some other way?

✓ Do the emphasized parts hint at the point of the reading?

Why Preread?

Prereading takes very little time, but it helps you immensely. Some students believe it's a waste of time to scan an assignment; they think they should just jump right in and get the reading over with. However, spending just a few minutes on preliminaries can save hours later. And most important, prereading helps you become a focused reader.

If you scan the length of an assignment, you can pace yourself. And if you know how long a reading is, you can alert yourself to its plan. For example, a short reading has to come to its point soon. A longer essay may take more time to develop its point and may use more details and examples.

Subheadings, charts, graphs, and boxed or other highlighted materials are important enough that the author wants to emphasize them. Looking over that material before you read gives you an overview of the important points the reading will contain.

Introductory material or introductory questions also help you know what to look for as you read. Background on the author or on the subject may hint at ideas that will come up in the reading. Sometimes the title of the reading will give you the main idea.

You should preread so that you can start reading the entire assignment with as much knowledge about the writer and the subject as you can get. When you then read the entire assignment, you will be reading actively, for more knowledge.

Forming Questions Before You Read

If you want to read with a focus, it helps to ask questions before you read. Form questions by using the information you gained from prereading.

Start by noting the title and turning it into a question. If the title of your assigned reading is, "Causes of the Civil War," ask, "What were the causes of the Civil War?"

You can turn subheadings into questions. If you are reading an article about self-esteem, and one subheading is "Influence of Parents," you can ask, "How do parents influence a person's self-esteem?"

You can also form questions from graphics and illustrations. If a chapter in your economics textbook includes a photograph of Wall Street, you can ask, "What is Wall Street?" or "What is Wall Street's role in economics?" or "What happens on Wall Street?"

You can write down these questions, but it's not necessary. Just forming questions and keeping them in the back of your mind helps you read actively and stay focused.

An Example of the Prereading Step

Take a look at the article that follows. Don't read it; preread it.

Part-Time Job May Do Teenagers More Harm Than Good

Gary Klott

Gary Klott is a personal finance consultant for the National Newspaper Syndicate. In this article, he explores the effects of part-time jobs on high school students.

Words You May Need to Know (Corresponding paragraph numbers are in parentheses.)

extracurricular activities (2): activities outside the regular academic course, like clubs and sports

assume (3): suppose, take for granted

menial (4): of a low level, degrading

instant gratification (4): immediate satisfaction

Given today's high cost of auto insurance, dating, video games, music CDs and designer clothing, it shouldn't come as any surprise that a growing number of high school students are taking part-time jobs during the school year. Most parents have done little to discourage their children from working after school. In fact, many parents figure that part-time jobs can help teach their children about responsibility and the value of a dollar and better prepare them for life in the adult workaday world. But there is growing evidence to suggest that parents ought to sharply restrict the number of hours their children work during the school year.   1

2   Academic studies over the past decade have found that high school students who work—particularly those who work long hours during the school week—tend to do less well in school, miss out on the benefits of extracurricular activities and have more behavioral problems. Most recently, a study of 12th-graders by Linda P. Worley, a high school counselor in Marietta, Georgia, indicated that grades suffer when students work more than ten hours during the school week. The highest grade-point averages were found for students who worked only on weekends, 3.07, and for those who baby-sat or did yard work, 3.13. Students who didn't work at all had an average GPA of 3.02, while those who worked up to ten hours a week earned an average GPA of 2.95. Students working ten to twenty hours a week averaged 2.77, twenty to thirty hours per week 2.53 and thirty or more hours 2.10.

3   Even if a student manages to maintain good grades, parents shouldn't automatically assume that long work hours aren't harming their child's education. Several studies found that many students kept up their grades by choosing easier courses. A 1993 study of 1,800 high-school sophomores by researchers at Temple University and Stanford University found that students who worked more than twenty hours a week spent less time on homework, cut class more often, cheated more on tests and assignments, had less interest in formal education, had a higher rate of drug and alcohol use and had lower self-esteem.

4   Researchers also note that some of the perceived benefits of after-school jobs are often overrated. For example, many of the jobs high school students take on are menial and provide few skills that will prove useful after high school. And many students learn the wrong lessons about the value of a dollar since they tend to spend all of their job earnings on cars, clothes, and other purchases that provide instant gratification without saving a penny.

By prereading the article, you might notice the following:

- The title of the article is "Part-Time Job May Do Teenagers More Harm Than Good."
- The article is short and can be read in one sitting.
- The author writes about money, and he writes for newspapers.
- The introductory material says the article is about teenagers with part-time jobs.
- There are several vocabulary words you may need to know.

You might begin reading the article with these questions in mind:

- Why are part-time jobs harmful to teens?
- What are the harmful effects?
- Why is a writer who writes about money arguing that it is bad for teens to make money?
- Should teens have full-time jobs instead of part-time ones?

Reading

The first time you read, try to *get a sense of the whole piece* you are reading. Reading with questions in mind can help you do this. If you find that you are confused by a certain part of the reading selection, go back and reread that part. If you do not know the meaning of a word, check the vocabulary list to see if the word is defined for you. If it isn't defined, try to figure out the meaning from the way the word is used in the sentence.

If you find that you have to read more slowly than usual, don't worry. People vary their reading speed according to what they read and why they are reading it. If you are reading for entertainment, for example, you can read quickly; if you are reading a chapter in a textbook, you must read more slowly. The more complicated the reading selection is, the more slowly you will read it.

An Example of the Reading Step

Now read "Part-Time Job May Do Teenagers More Harm Than Good." When you've completed your first reading, you will probably have some answers to the prereading questions that you formed.

Answers to Prereading Questions:

Part-time jobs can hurt teens' grades and other areas of their lives such as their behavior and attitudes.

The writer, who writes about money, says part-time jobs give students bad spending habits.

Full-time work would be worse than part-time work.

Rereading with Pen or Pencil

The second reading is the crucial one. At this point, you begin to think on paper as you read. In this step, you make notes or write about what you read. Some students are reluctant to do this because they are not sure what to note or write. Think of *making these notes as a way of learning, thinking, reviewing, and reacting.* Reading with a pen or pencil in your hand keeps you alert. With that pen or pencil, you can

- mark the main point of the reading,
- mark other points,
- define words you don't know,
- question parts of the reading that seem confusing,
- evaluate the writer's ideas,
- react to the writer's opinions or examples,
- add ideas, opinions, or examples of your own.

There is no single system for marking or writing as you read. Some readers like to underline the main idea with two lines and to underline other important ideas with one line. Some students like to put an asterisk (a star) next to important ideas, while others like to circle key words.

Some people use the margins to write comments like "I agree!" or "Not true!" or "That's happened to me." Sometimes readers put questions in the margin; sometimes they summarize a point in the margin, next to its location in the essay. Some people list important points in the white space above the reading, while others use the space at the end of the reading.

Every reader who writes as he or she reads has a personal system; what these systems share is an attitude. *If you write as you read, you concentrate on the reading selection, get to know the writer's ideas, and develop ideas of your own.*

As you reread and write notes, don't worry too much about noticing the "right" ideas. Instead, think of rereading as the time to jump into a *conversation* with the writer.

An Example of Rereading with Pen or Pencil

For "Part-Time Job May Do Teenagers More Harm Than Good," your marked article might look like the following:

Part-Time Job May Do Teenagers More Harm Than Good

Gary Klott

I agree!

Given today's high cost of auto insurance, dating, video games, music CDs and designer clothing, it shouldn't come as any surprise that a growing number of high school students are taking part-time jobs during the school year. Most parents have done little to discourage their children

What parents believe

from working after school. In fact, many parents figure that part-time jobs can help teach their children about responsibility and the value of a dollar and bet-

What parents should do

ter prepare them for life in the adult workaday world. But there is growing evidence to suggest that parents ought to sharply restrict the number of hours their children work during the school year.

*

Academic studies over the past decade have found that high school students who work—particularly those who work long hours during the school week—tend to do less well in school, miss out on the benefits of extracurricu-

example

lar activities and have more behavioral problems. Most recently, a study of 12th-graders by Linda P. Worley, a high school counselor in Marietta, Georgia,

The more you work, the lower the grades

indicated that grades suffer when students work more than ten hours during the school week. The highest grade-point averages were found for students who worked only on weekends, 3.07, and for those who baby-sat or did yard work, 3.13. Students who didn't work at all had an average GPA of 3.02, while those who worked up to ten hours a week earned an average GPA of 2.95. Students working ten to twenty hours a week averaged 2.77, twenty to thirty hours per week 2.53 and thirty or more hours 2.10.

Even if a student manages to maintain good grades, parents shouldn't automatically assume that long work hours aren't harming their child's education. Several studies found that many students kept up their grades by choosing easier courses. A 1993 study of 1,800 high-school sophomores by researchers at Temple University and Stanford University found that students

other harm to education

who worked more than twenty hours a week spent less time on homework, cut class more often, cheated more on tests and assignments, had less interest

self-respect, pride

in formal education, had a higher rate of drug and alcohol use and had lower self-esteem.

Researchers also note that some of the perceived benefits of after-school jobs are often overrated. For example, many of the jobs high school students take on are menial and provide few skills that will prove useful after high school. And many students learn the wrong lessons about the value of a dollar since they tend to spend all of their job earnings on cars, clothes, and other purchases that provide instant gratification without saving a penny.

What the Notes Mean

In the preceding sample, much of the underlining indicates sentences or phrases that seem important. The words in the margin are often summaries of what is underlined. In the first paragraph, for example, the words "what parents believe" and "what parents should do" are like subtitles in the margin.

An asterisk in the margin signals an important idea. When "example" is written in the margin, it notes that a point is being supported by a specific example. Sometimes, what is in the margin is the reader's reaction, like "I agree!" One item in the margin is a definition. The word "self-esteem" is circled and defined in the margin as "self-respect, pride."

The marked-up article is a flexible tool. You can go back and mark it further. You may change your mind about your notes and comments and find other, better, or more important points in the article.

You write as you read to involve yourself in the reading process. Marking what you read can help you in other ways, too. If you are to be tested on the reading selection or are asked to discuss it, you can scan your markings and notations at a later time for a quick review.

Exercise 1 Reading and Making Notes for a Selection

Following is a paragraph from "Part-Time Job May Do Teenagers More Harm Than Good." First, read it. Then reread it and make notes on the following:

1. Underline the first eight words of the most specific example in the paragraph.

2. Circle the phrase "formal education" and define it in the margin.

3. At the end of the paragraph, summarize its main point.

Paragraph from "Part-Time Job May Do Teenagers More Harm Than Good"

Even if a student manages to maintain good grades, parents shouldn't automatically assume that long work hours aren't harming their child's education. Several studies found that many students kept up their grades by choosing easier courses. A 1993 study of 1,800 high-school sophomores by researchers at Temple University and Stanford University found that students who worked more than twenty hours a week spent less time on homework, cut class more often, cheated more on tests and assignments, had less interest in formal education, had a higher rate of drug and alcohol use and had lower self-esteem.

Main point of the paragraph (in your own words): _____

_____

_____

WRITING A SUMMARY OF A READING

One way to write about a reading is to write a summary. A *summary* of a reading tells the important ideas in brief form and in your own words. It includes (1) the writer's main idea, (2) the ideas used to explain the main idea, and (3) some examples or details.

PREWRITING Marking a List of Ideas: Summary

When you preread, read, and make notes on the reading selection, you have already begun the prewriting stage for a summary. You can think further, on paper, *by listing the points* (words, phrases, sentences) you've already marked on the reading selection.

To find the main idea for your summary and the ideas and examples connected to the main idea, you can *mark related ideas* on your list. For example, the list below was made from "Part-Time Job May Do Teenagers More Harm Than Good." Three symbols are used to mark the following:

S the effects of part-time jobs on **schoolwork**
O **other** effects of part-time jobs
P what **parents** think about part-time jobs

Some items on the list don't have a mark because they do not relate to any of the categories.

A Marked List of Ideas for a Summary of "Part-Time Job May Do Teenagers More Harm Than Good"

  high cost of car insurance, dating, video games, music CDs, and designer clothing
P *parents think part-time jobs teach responsibility, money, and job skills*
  parents should restrict teens' work hours
S *working students do less well in school*
S *study of 12th-graders by Linda P. Worley said grades suffer if students work more than ten hours in school week*
S *students who work long hours choose easier courses*
S *they spend less time on homework*
S *they cut class more*
S *they cheat*
S *they are less interested in school*
O *they use drugs and alcohol more*
O *they have lower self-esteem*
  some perceived benefits are overrated
O *students spend money foolishly*

The marked list could then be reorganized, like this:

the effects of part-time jobs on school work

- *working students do less well in school*
- *study of 12th-graders by Linda P. Worley said grades suffer if students work more than ten hours in the school week*
- *students who work long hours choose easier classes*
- *they spend less time on homework*
- *they cut class more*
- *they cheat*
- *they are less interested in school*

other effects of part-time jobs

- *if they work over twenty hours, they use drugs and alcohol more*
- *they have lower self-esteem*
- *working students spend money foolishly*

what many parents think about part-time jobs

- *parents think part-time jobs teach responsibility, money, and job skills*

Selecting a Main Idea

The next step in the process is to select the idea you think is the writer's main point. If you look again at the list of ideas, you see one category that has only one item: what many parents think about part-time jobs. In this category, the only item is that parents think part-time jobs teach responsibility, money, and job skills.

Is this item the main idea of the article? If it is, then all the other ideas support it. But the other ideas contradict this point.

It is not the main idea, but it *is* connected to the main idea. The author is saying that parents *think* part-time jobs are good for high school students, but they may not be, especially if students work long hours.

You can write a simpler version of this main idea:

Parents should know that working long hours at part-time jobs is not good for teens.

Once you have a main idea, check it to see if it fits with the other ideas in your organized list. *Do the ideas in the list connect to the main idea?* Yes. The ideas about the effects of jobs on schoolwork show the negative impact of part-time work. So do the ideas about the other effects. And even the part about what some parents think can be used to contrast what jobs *really* do to teens.

Now that you have a main point that fits an organized list, you can move to the *planning* stage of a summary.

Exercise 2   **Marking a List and Finding the Main Idea for a Summary**

Following is a list of ideas from an article called "Binge Nights: The Emergency on Campus" by Michael Winerip. It tells the true story of Ryan Dabbieri, a senior at the University of Virginia who nearly died from binge drinking at a tailgating party before a football game. Read the list, and then mark each item with one of these symbols:

L   **lessons learned** from the experience

P   **personal background** on the binge drinker

S   **steps** leading to the emergency

E   the life-and-death **emergency**

After you've marked all the ideas, survey them, and think of one main idea. Try to focus on a point that connects to what Ryan Dabbieri, the binge drinker, learned.

_____ Ryan Dabbieri was a 22-year-old senior at the University of Virginia.

_____ Ryan did not think he was a binge drinker.

_____ About once a week, he would drink five to seven drinks in two hours.

_____ Before one big football game, he drank five or six very big shots of bourbon in fifteen minutes at a party.

_____ At the stadium, he straightened up to get by security.

_____ Inside, he passed out.

_____ His friends carried him outside.

_____ They couldn't revive him.

_____ In the emergency room, he stopped breathing for four minutes.

_____ His friends were terrified.

_____ The doctors did a scan for brain damage.

_____ Ryan's father flew in from Atlanta.

_____ Ryan awoke the next day in intensive care.

_____ Ryan says he won't drink again.

_____ He says he is lucky to be alive.

main idea: _____

_____

_____

PLANNING   **Summary**

Following is an outline for a summary of "Part-Time Job May Do Teenagers More Harm Than Good." As you read it, you'll notice that the main idea from the prewriting stage has become the topic sentence of the outline, and most of the other ideas have become details.

Outline for a Summary of "Part-Time Job May Do Teenagers More Harm Than Good"

topic sentence:	Parents should know that working long hours at part-time jobs is not good for teens.
details: **effects on schoolwork**	Working students do less well in school. A study of 12th-graders by Linda P. Worley showed this. It showed that grades suffer if students worked more than ten hours in the school week. Students who work long hours choose easier classes. They spend less time on homework. They cut class more. They are less interested in school.
other effects	They use drugs and alcohol more. They have lower self-esteem. They spend money foolishly.

In the outline, the part about what many parents think about part-time jobs has been left out. Since it was an idea that contrasted with the topic sentence, it didn't seem to fit. That kind of selecting is what you do in the planning stage of writing a summary. In the drafting and revising stage, you may change your mind and decide to use the idea later.

DRAFTING Attributing Ideas in a Summary

The first draft of your summary paragraph is your first try at *combining* all the material into one paragraph. The draft is much like the draft of any other paragraph, with one exception: *When you summarize another person's ideas, be sure to say whose ideas you are writing.* That is, *attribute* the ideas to the writer. Let the reader of your paragraph know the following:

1. the author of the selection you are summarizing
2. the title of the selection you are summarizing

You may want to *attribute ideas by giving your summary paragraph a title,* such as

> A Summary of Gary Klott's "Part-Time Job May Do Teenagers More Harm Than Good"

Note that you put the title of Klott's article in quotation marks.

Or you may want to *put the title and author into the paragraph itself.* Below is a draft version of a summary of "Part-Time Job May Do Teenagers More Harm Than Good" with the title and the author incorporated into the paragraph.

A Draft of a Summary of "Part-Time Job May Do Teenagers More Harm Than Good"

"Part-Time Job May Do Teenagers More Harm Than Good" by Gary Klott says that parents should know that working long hours at part-time jobs is not good for teens. Working students do less well in school. A study of 12th-graders by Linda P. Worley showed that grades suffer if students work more than ten hours during the school week. Students who work long hours choose easier courses, spend less time on homework, cut class more often, and cheat. They are less interested in school. They use drugs and alcohol more and have lower self-esteem. They spend money foolishly.

When you look this draft over and read it aloud, you may notice a few problems:

- The draft is very choppy; it needs transitions.
- In some places, the word choice could be better.
- The beginning of the paragraph could use an introduction.
- Linda P. Worley did a study about grades and working students. But the other information about effects on schoolwork came from other studies. This difference should be made clear.
- The paragraph ends abruptly.

POLISHING Summary

Look carefully at the final version of the summary. Notice how the idea about what parents think has been added to an introduction and how transitions and word choice have improved the summary. Also notice how one phrase, "Other studies indicate that," clarifies the ideas in the summary and how an added conclusion clinches the paragraph.

A Final Version of a Summary of "Part-Time Job May Do Teenagers More Harm Than Good"

(Changes from the draft are underlined.)

<u>Many parents think part-time jobs teach their children responsibility, money and job skills, but they may be wrong. An article called</u> "Part-Time Job May Do Teenagers More Harm Than Good" by Gary Klott says that parents should know that working long hours at part-time jobs is not good for teens. <u>First of all,</u> working students do less well in school. A study of 12th-graders by Linda P. Worley showed that grades suffer if students work more than ten hours during the school week. <u>Other studies indicate that</u> students who work long hours choose easier courses, spend less time on their homework, <u>and are likely to cheat and cut classes. In addition, such students</u> are less interested in school. <u>Their problems extend outside of school, too, where</u> they use drugs and alcohol <u>more than other students</u> and have lower self-esteem. <u>Finally,</u> they <u>do not learn financial responsibility from their jobs since</u> they spend money foolishly. <u>Parents must consider all these drawbacks before they allow their teens to work long hours.</u>

Writing summaries is good writing practice, and it also helps you develop your reading skills. Even if your instructor does not require you to turn in a polished summary of an assigned reading, you may find it helpful to summarize what you have read. In many classes, midterms or other exams cover many assigned readings. If you make short summaries of each reading as it is assigned, you will have a helpful collection of focused, organized material to review.

WRITING A REACTION TO A READING

A summary is one kind of writing you can do after reading, but there are other kinds. Your instructor might ask you to *react* by writing about some idea you got from your reading. If you read "Part-Time Job May Do Teenagers More Harm Than Good," your instructor might have asked you to react by writing about this topic:

> Gary Klott says that parents may have the wrong idea about their children's jobs. Write about another part of teen life that parents may not understand.

You may begin to gather ideas by freewriting.

PREWRITING Reaction to a Reading: Freewriting

You can freewrite in a reading journal, if you wish. This kind of journal is a special journal in which you write about selections that you've read. To freewrite, you can

- write key points made by the author,
- write about whatever you remember from the reading selection,

- write down any of the author's ideas that you think you might want to write about someday,
- list questions raised by what you've read,
- connect the reading selection to other things you've read, heard, or experienced.

A freewriting that reacts to "Part-Time Job May Do Teenagers More Harm Than Good" might look like this:

Freewriting for a Reaction to a Reading

"Part-Time Job May Do Teenagers More Harm Than Good"—Gary Klott

Jobs can be bad for teens. Author says parents should stop teens from working too many hours. But how? Most parents are afraid of their teens. Or they don't want to interfere. They figure teens want to be independent. I know I wanted to be independent when I was in high school. Did I? I'm not so sure. I think I wanted some attention from my folks. Maybe parents don't know this. Why didn't I say anything?

Selecting a Topic, Listing and Developing Ideas

Once you have your freewriting, you can survey it for a topic. You might survey the freewriting above and decide you can write about how parents don't know that their teens want attention. To gather ideas, you begin a list:

teens want attention and parents don't know

sometimes teens look independent

they act smart

no real self-confidence

friends aren't enough

I wanted my father's approval

teens can't say what they need

to get attention, they break rules

I would have liked some praise

Next, you organize, expand, and develop this list until you have a main point, the topic sentence, and a list of details. You decide on this topic sentence:

Some parents are unaware that their teenage children need attention.

With a topic sentence and a list of details, you are ready to begin the planning stage of writing.

PLANNING **Reaction to a Reading**

An outline might look like the one following. As you read it, notice that the topic sentence and ideas are *your* opinions, not the ideas of the author of "Part-Time Job May Do Teenagers More Harm Than Good." You used his ideas to come up with your own. Also notice how it builds on the ideas on the list and organizes them in a clear order.

An Outline of a Reaction to a Reading

topic sentence:	Some parents are unaware that their teenage children need attention.
details: **what parents** **see**	Teens act independent. They act smart. They break rules. Parents think that rule-breaking means teens want to be left alone.
what teens **want**	Teens do it to get attention. Teens can't say what they need. They have no real self-confidence. Their friends aren't enough.
personal **example**	I wanted my father's approval. I would have liked some praise.

DRAFTING   Reaction to a Reading

If your outline gives you enough good ideas to develop, you are on your way to a paragraph. If you began with the ideas above, for example, you could develop them into a paragraph like this:

A Draft of a Reaction to a Reading

Some parents are unaware that their teenage children need attention. Teens act independent and smart. They break their parents' rules, so their parents think teenage rule-breaking is a sign the children want to be left alone. Teens break rules to get attention. They can't say what they need; therefore, they act out their needs. Teens have no real self-confidence. Friends aren't enough. I wanted my father's approval. I would have liked some praise.

POLISHING   Reaction to a Reading

When you read the draft version of the paragraph, you probably noticed some places where it could be revised:

- The word choice could be better.
- There is too much repetition of words like "need," "needs," "their parents," and "children."
- The paragraph needs many transitions.
- Since the ideas are reactions related to a point by Gary Klott, he needs to be mentioned.
- The ending is a little abrupt.

Following is the final version of the same paragraph. As you read it, notice how the changes make it a clearer, smoother, more developed paragraph.

A Final Version of a Reaction to a Reading

(Changes from the draft are underlined.)

<u>Gary Klott says that many parents do not understand the impact of their teenagers' part-time jobs. There is another part of teen life that parents may not understand.</u> Some parents are unaware that their teenage children need attention. Teens act independent and <u>self-assured</u>. They will break their parents' rules, so their parents think the rule-breaking is a sign the children want to be left alone. However, <u>adolescents</u> break rules to get attention. They can't say what they <u>crave</u>; therefore, they act out their needs. Teens have no real self-confidence. <u>While friends help adolescents develop self-confidence,</u> friends aren't enough. <u>My own experience is a good example of what adolescents desire.</u> I wanted my father's approval. I would have liked some praise, <u>but I couldn't ask for what I needed. My father was a parent who was unaware.</u>

WRITING ABOUT AGREEMENT OR DISAGREEMENT

PREWRITING   Agree or Disagree Paragraph

Another way to write about a reading selection is to find a point in it and *agree or disagree with that point.* To begin writing about agreement or disagreement, you can review the selection and jot down any statements that provoke a strong reaction in you. You are looking for statements with which you can agree or disagree. If you reviewed "Part-Time Job May Do Teenagers More Harm Than Good," you might list these statements as points of agreement or disagreement:

Points of Agreement or Disagreement from a Reading

"Grades suffer when students work more than ten hours during the school week."—agree
High school students who work many hours "have less interest in formal education"—disagree

Then you might *pick one of the statements and react to it in writing.* If you disagreed with the statement that high school students who work many hours "have less interest in formal education," you might begin by brainstorming.

Brainstorming for an Agree or Disagree Paragraph

Question: **Why do you disagree that high school students who work long hours "have less interest in formal education"?**

Answer: *I worked long hours. I was interested in getting a <u>good</u> education.*

Question: **If you were interested in school, why were you so focused on your job?**

Answer: *To make money.*

Question: **Then wasn't money more important than school?**

Answer: *No. I was working to make money to pay for college. Working was the only way I could afford college.*

Question:	***Do you think you <u>looked</u> as if you didn't care about education?***
Answer:	*Yes, sure.*
Question:	***Why?***
Answer:	*I used to be so tired from working I would fall asleep in class.*

Once you have some ideas from brainstorming, you can list them, group them, and add to them by more brainstorming. Your topic sentence can be a way of stating your disagreement with the original point, like this:

Although Gary Klott says that high school students who work long hours tend to lose interest in school, my experience shows the opposite.

With a topic sentence and details, you can work on the planning stage of your paragraph.

PLANNING   Agree or Disagree Paragraph

An outline might look like the following. Notice that the topic sentence is your opinion and that the details are from your experience.

An Outline for an Agree or Disagree Paragraph

topic sentence:	Although Gary Klott says that high school students who work long hours may lose interest in school, my experience shows the opposite.
details: **my experience**	While I was in high school, I worked long hours. I was very interested in getting a good education. I wanted to graduate from college. To save money for college, I was working long hours. Working was the only way I could pay for college.
why I appeared uninterested	I probably looked as if I didn't care about school. I fell asleep in class. I was tired from working.

DRAFTING   Agree or Disagree Paragraph

Once you have a good outline, you can develop it into a paragraph:

A Draft of an Agree or Disagree Paragraph

   Although Gary Klott says that high school students who work long hours lose interest in school, my experience shows the opposite. When I was in high school, I worked long hours. I endured my job and even increased my hours because I was interested in getting a good education. I wanted to graduate from college. I was working long hours to save money for college. Working was the only way I could pay tuition. I know that, to my teachers, I probably looked like I didn't care about school. I was tired from working. I fell asleep in class.

POLISHING   Agree or Disagree Paragraph

When you surveyed the draft of the paragraph, you probably noticed some places that need revision:

- The paragraph could use more specific details.
- Some sentences could be combined.
- It needs a last sentence, reinforcing the point that students who work long hours may be very interested in school.

As you read the final version of the paragraph, notice how the revisions improve the paragraph.

A Final Version of an Agree or Disagree Paragraph

(Changes from the draft are underlined.)

Although Gary Klott says that high school students who work long hours lose interest in school, my experience shows the opposite. When I was in high school, I worked long hours. Sometimes I worked twenty-five hours a week at a fast-food restaurant. I endured my job and even increased my hours because I was interested in getting a good education. I wanted to graduate from college. I was working long hours to save money for college since working was the only way I could pay tuition. I know that, to my teachers, I probably looked like I didn't care about school. I was so tired from working that I came to school in a daze. I fell asleep in class. But my long, hard hours at work made me determined to change my life through education.

WRITING FOR AN ESSAY TEST

Another kind of writing from reading involves the essay test. Most essay questions require you to write about an assigned reading. Usually, an essay test requires you to write from memory, not from an open book or notes. Such writing can be stressful, but breaking the task into steps can eliminate much of the stress.

Before the Test: The Steps of Reading

If you work through the steps of reading days before the test, you are halfway to your goal. Prereading helps to keep you focused, and your first reading gives you a sense of the whole selection. The third step, rereading with a pen or pencil, can be particularly helpful when you are preparing for a test. Most essay questions will ask you either to summarize or react to a reading selection. In either case, you must be familiar with the reading's main idea, supporting ideas, examples, and details. If you note these by marking the selection, you are teaching yourself about the main point, supporting ideas, and structure of the reading selection.

Shortly before the test, review the marked reading assignment. Your notes will help you focus on the main point and the supporting ideas.

During the Test: The Stages of Writing

Answering an essay test question may seem very different from writing at home. After all, on a test, you must rely on your memory and write within a time limit, and these restrictions can make you feel anxious. However, by following the stages of the writing process, you can meet that challenge calmly and confidently.

PREWRITING Essay Test

Before you begin to write, think about these questions: Is the instructor asking for a summary of a reading selection? Or is he or she asking you to react to a specific idea with examples or by agreeing or disagreeing? For example, in an essay question about the article, "Part-Time Job May Do Teenagers More Harm Than Good," by Gary Klott, you might be asked to (1) explain why Klott thinks a part-time job can be bad for a teenager (a summary), (2) explain what Klott means when he says that students who work long hours may keep their grades up but still miss out on the best education (a reaction, in which you develop and explain one part of the reading), or (3) agree or disagree that after-school jobs teach the wrong lesson about the value of money (a reaction, so you have to be aware of what Klott said on this point).

Once you have thought about the question, list or freewrite your first ideas. At this time, do not worry about how "right" or "wrong" your writing is; just write your first thoughts.

PLANNING Essay Test

Your writing will be clear if you follow a plan. Remember that the audience for this writing is your instructor and that he or she will be evaluating how well you stick to the subject, make a point, and support it. Your plan for making a point about the subject and supporting it can be written in a brief outline.

First, reread the question. Next, survey your list or freewriting. Does it contain a main point that answers the question? Does it contain supporting ideas and details?

Next, write a main point, and then list supporting ideas and details under the main point. Your main point will be the topic sentence of your answer. If you need more support, try brainstorming.

DRAFTING Essay Test

Write your point and supporting ideas in paragraph form. Remember to use effective transitions and to combine short sentences.

POLISHING Essay Test

You will probably not have time to copy your answer, but you can review it, proofread it, and correct any errors in spelling, punctuation, or word choice. The final check can produce a more polished answer.

Organize Your Time

Some students skip steps: without thinking or planning, they immediately begin writing their answer to an essay question. Sometimes they find themselves stuck in the middle of a paragraph, panicked because they have no more ideas. At other times, they find themselves writing in a circle, repeating the same point over and over. Occasionally, they even forget to include a main idea.

You can avoid these hazards by spending time on each of the stages. Planning is as important as writing. For example, if you have half an hour to write an essay, you can divide your time like this:

5 minutes thinking, freewriting, listing
10 minutes planning, outlining
10 minutes drafting
5 minutes reviewing, proofreading

Writing from Reading: A Summary of Options

Reading can give you many opportunities for your own writing. You can summarize a writer's work, use it as a springboard for your own related writing, or agree or disagree with it. However you decide to write from reading, you must still work through the same writing process. Following the steps of prewriting, planning, drafting, and polishing will help you develop your work into a successful paragraph.

Lines of Detail: A Walk-Through Assignment

Here are three ideas from "Part-Time Job May Do Teenagers More Harm Than Good":

 a. Students who work long hours miss out on extracurricular activities at school.

 b. Parents should prevent their teenage children from working long hours.

 c. Teens who work spend their money foolishly.

Pick *one* of these ideas with which you agree or disagree. Write a paragraph explaining why you agree or disagree. To write your paragraph, follow these steps:

Step 1: Begin by listing at least three reasons or examples why you agree or disagree. Make your reasons or examples as specific as you can, using your experiences or the experiences of friends and family.

Step 2: Read your list to a partner or group. With the help of your listener(s), add reasons, examples, and details.

Step 3: Once you have enough ideas, transform the statement you agreed or disagreed with into a topic sentence.

Step 4: Write an outline by listing your reasons, examples, and details below the topic sentence. Check that your list is in a clear and logical order.

Step 5: Write a draft of your paragraph. Check that you have attributed Gary Klott's statement, you have enough specific details, you have combined any choppy sentences, and you have used good transitions. Revise your draft until the paragraph is smooth and clear.

Step 6: Before you prepare the final copy, check your draft for errors in spelling, punctuation, and word choice.

WRITING YOUR OWN PARAGRAPH

Writing from Reading "Part-Time Job May Do Teenagers More Harm Than Good"

When you write on any of these topics, be sure to work through the stages of the writing process in preparing your paragraph.

 1. Klott talks about high school students who work to pay for car insurance, dates, video games, music, and designer clothes. However, students might not have to work so hard if they learned to do without things they don't really need: the latest clothes, the newest CD, their own car, and so on. Write a paragraph about the many things high school students buy that they don't really need.

2. Work can interfere with high school. Write about something else that interferes with high school. You can write about social life, extracurricular activities, sports, family responsibilities, or any other part of a student's life that can prevent him or her from focusing on school.

   As you plan this paragraph, think about details that could fit these categories:

   Why students choose this activity/responsibility over school
   The effects on students' schoolwork
   How to balance school and other activities or responsibilities

Collaborate

3. Many parents believe that a part-time job is good for high school students, but the job can be harmful. Write a one-paragraph letter to parents, warning them about some other part of teen life (not jobs) that parents may think is good but that may be harmful. You can write about the dangers of their child being popular, or having a steady boyfriend or girlfriend, or always being number one in academics.

   Once you've chosen the topic, brainstorm with a partner or group: ask questions, answer them, add details. After you've brainstormed, work by yourself and proceed through the stages of preparing your letter to parents.

4. Some parents have misconceptions (incorrect ideas) about their teenage children; for instance, they may believe the teen with a part-time job is automatically learning how to handle money. On the other hand, teenage children have misconceptions about their parents. Write about some misconception that teens have about their parents. You might, for instance, write about some teens' mistaken belief that (1) the best parents are the ones who give their children the most freedom, or (2) parents who love you give you everything you want, or (3) parents do not remember what it is like to be young.

   To begin, freewrite on one mistaken idea that teens might have about their parents. Focus on your own experiences, memories, and so forth— as a teen or as a parent of teenagers. Use your freewriting to find details and a focus for your paragraph.

5. Klott writes about parents' need to restrict teens' work hours. This restriction might be a difficult rule for some working students to accept. Write about a family rule that you hated when you were a child or teen. Include your feelings about that rule today.

Writing from Reading

To practice the skills you've learned in this chapter, follow the steps of prereading, reading, and rereading with a pencil as you read the following selection.

New Directions

Maya Angelou

Maya Angelou was born Marguerite Johnson in St. Louis, Missouri, in 1928. She survived many hardships to become one of the most famous and beloved writers in America. Although she is best known for her autobiographical books, Angelou is also a political activist, singer, and performer on stage and screen. Her achievements include best-selling books, literary awards, and the reciting of her poetry at the inauguration of President William Jefferson Clinton. In this essay, Angelou tells the story of a woman who cut a new path for her life.

Words You May Need to Know (Corresponding paragraph numbers are in parentheses.)

burdensome (1): troublesome, heavy

conceded (2): admitted

domestic (3): a household worker

meticulously (4): very carefully

cotton gin (4): a factory with a machine for separating cotton fibers from seeds

brazier (6): a container that holds live coals covered by a grill, used for cooking

savors (6): food that smells and tastes good

lint (6): cotton fibers

specters (6): ghosts

balmy (9): mild and soothing

hives of industry (9): places swarming with busy workers

looms (11): rises in front of us

ominous (11): threatening

resolve (11): determination

unpalatable (11): not acceptable

In 1903 the late Mrs. Annie Johnson of Arkansas found herself with two toddling sons, very little money, a slight ability to read and add simple numbers. To this picture add a disastrous marriage and the burdensome fact that Mrs. Johnson was a Negro. 1

When she told her husband, Mr. William Johnson, of her dissatisfaction with their marriage, he conceded that he too found it to be less than he expected, and had been secretly hoping to leave and study religion. He added that he thought God was calling him not only to preach but to do so in Enid, Oklahoma. He did not tell her that he knew a minister in Enid with whom he could study and who had a friendly, unmarried daughter. They parted amicably, Annie keeping the one-room house and William taking most of the cash to carry himself to Oklahoma. 2

Annie, over six feet tall, big-boned, decided that she would not go to work as a domestic and leave her "precious babes" to anyone else's care. There was no possibility of being hired at the town's cotton gin or lumber mill, but maybe there was a way to make the two factories work for her. In other words, "I looked up the road I was going and back the way I come, and since I wasn't satisfied, I decided to step off the road and cut me a new path." She told herself that she wasn't a fancy cook but that she could "mix groceries well enough to scare hungry away from starving a man." 3

She made her plans meticulously and in secret. One early evening to see if she was ready, she placed stones in two five-gallon pails and carried them three miles to the cotton gin. She rested a little, and then, discarding some rocks, she walked to the sawmill five miles farther along the dirt road. On her way back to her house and her babies, she dumped the remaining rocks along the path. 4

That same night she worked into the early hours boiling chicken and frying ham. She made dough and filled the rolled-out pastry with meat. At last she went to sleep. 5

The next morning she left her house carrying the meat pies, lard, an iron brazier, and coal for a fire. Just before lunch she appeared in an empty lot behind the cotton gin. As the dinner noon bell rang, she dropped the savors into 6 boiling fat, and the aroma rose and floated over the workers who spilled out of the gin, covered with white lint, looking like specters.

7   Most workers had brought their lunches of pinto beans and biscuits or crackers, onions, and cans of sardines, but they were tempted by the hot meat pies which Annie ladled out of the fat. She wrapped them in newspapers, which soaked up the grease, and offered them for sale at a nickel each. Although business was slow, those first days Annie was determined. She balanced her appearances between the two hours of activity.

8   So, on Monday if she offered hot fresh pies at the cotton gin and sold the remaining cooled-down pies at the lumber mill for three cents, then on Tuesday she went first to the lumber mill presenting fresh, just-cooked pies as the lumbermen covered in sawdust emerged from the mill.

9   For the next few years, on balmy spring days, blistering summer noons, and cold, wet, and wintry middays, Annie never disappointed her customers, who could count on seeing the tall, brown-skin woman bent over her brazier, carefully turning the meat pies. When she felt certain the workers had become dependent on her, she built a stall between the two hives of industry and let the men run to her for their lunchtime provisions.

10   She had indeed stepped from the road which seemed to have been chosen for her and cut herself a brand-new path. In years that stall became a store where customers could buy cheese, meat, syrup, cookies, candy, writing tablets, pickles, canned goods, fresh fruit, soft drinks, coal, oil, and leather soles for worn-out shoes.

11   Each of us has the right and responsibility to assess the roads which lie ahead, and those over which we have traveled, and if the future road looms ominous or unpromising, and the roads back uninviting, then we need to gather our resolve and, carrying only the necessary baggage, step off that road into another direction. If the new choice is also unpalatable, without embarrassment, we must be ready to change that as well.

Writing from Reading: "New Directions"

When you write on any of the following topics, be sure to work through the stages of the writing process in preparing your paragraph.

1. Using the ideas and examples you gathered by prereading, reading, and, with a pen or pencil, rereading "New Directions," write a summary of Maya Angelou's essay.

2. Write about someone who had many strikes against him or her but who succeeded. Be sure that you include some of the difficulties this person faced.

Collaborate

3. Maya Angelou says, "Each of us has the right and responsibility to assess the roads which lie ahead, and those over which we have traveled," and if an old road or a future road looks dark, we must "step off that road into another direction."

   Write a paragraph that agrees or disagrees with that statement.
   Begin by working with a group. First, discuss what you think the

statement means. Then ask at least six questions about the statement. You may ask such questions as, "Does everyone have the courage or talent to choose a new road?" or "What keeps some people from choosing a new direction?" or "Do you know anyone who has done what Angelou advises?"

Use the questions and answers to decide whether you want to agree or disagree with Angelou's statement.

4. There is an old saying, "When the going gets tough, the tough get going," and Mrs. Annie Johnson's story seems to prove the saying is true. She was faced with poverty, lack of job opportunities, raising two children alone, and yet through hard work, creativity, and determination, she triumphed.

Write a paragraph that tells a story and proves the truth of another old saying. You can use a saying like, "Take time to stop and smell the roses," or "You never know what you can do until you try," or any other saying.

Begin by freewriting about old sayings and what they mean to you. Then pick one that connects to your experience or the experience of someone you know. Use that saying as the focus of your paragraph.

Name :_____ Section : _____

Peer Review Form for Writing from Reading

After you have written a draft version of your paragraph, let a writing partner read it. When your partner has completed the following form, discuss the comments. Then repeat the same process for your partner's paragraph.

This paragraph (circle one) (1) summarizes, (2) agrees or disagrees, (3) reacts to an idea connected to a reading selection.

I think this paragraph should include (circle one) (1) both the title and author of the reading selection, (2) the author of the reading selection, (3) neither the title nor the author of the reading selection.

The topic sentence of this paragraph is _____

_____

_____

The most effective part of this paragraph starts with the words _____

_____

One suggestion to improve this paragraph is to _____

_____

_____

Other comments on the paragraph: _____

_____

_____

_____

_____

_____

_____

Reviewer's Name: _____

WRITING A PARAGRAPH

When Fame Falls Short

Sally Loftis

Sally Loftis is a community columnist at the Charlotte, North Carolina Observer, a full-time wife and mother, and a former bank executive. Writing soon after the 2007 tragedy of wrestling celebrity Chris Benoit and his family, Loftis' essay links teens' daydreams of fame to their hunger to belong.

Words You May Need to Know (Corresponding paragraph numbers are in parentheses.)

horrific (1): dreadful, horrible
gruesome (2): horribly repulsive
engaging (6): interacting
modeling (6): imitating

momentary (7): very short
legacies (7): what is left behind after a person's death

Chris Benoit, a World Wrestling Entertainment star, killed his wife and seven-year-old son before killing himself last month. Fans have been shocked by this horrific event, especially as details of Benoit's personal life unfold and involve drug use, domestic violence, and possible child abuse. 1

When completing the autopsy on Benoit's son, medical examiners found needle marks in his arm and traces of a growth hormone in his body—probably administered by one of his own parents. Here is yet another tragic ending to a celebrity life, where we find out the gruesome details of living life in the spotlight. Fame has been an attraction for humans since the beginning of time. We each have a deep need to belong, and in many people's views, fame seems to answer that need by giving us approval by crowds and instant "friends" by our status. But is fame all it is cracked up to be? Look at the tragic deaths of celebrities such as Princess Diana or Anna Nicole Smith, and you begin to question the value of being famous. In his book, *Fame Junkies: The Hidden Truths Behind America's Favorite Addiction*, Jake Halpern describes the widespread attraction of fame in our society. 2

Fame Trumps Achievement

Working with Boston College and Babson College, Halpern surveyed hundreds of middle school students about fame. The results are fascinating—and depressing. Asked to choose from a list of famous people with whom they could dine for one evening, the Number 1 answer was Jennifer Lopez. Jesus Christ came in second, and Paris Hilton and Rapper 50 Cent tied for third. Who was at the bottom of the list? You guessed it—George W. Bush and Albert Einstein. 3

4   In another question, students were asked to choose one job, out of a list of five, that they would most like to have. Here's how the five options were ranked, highest to lowest: personal assistant to a very famous singer or movie star, president of a great university like Harvard or Yale, a U.S. senator, a Navy Seal, and chief of a major company such as General Motors. It seems more teens are dreaming about becoming famous than how to use their education and talents in the real world.

Teen Daydreaming Is Normal

5   Let me cut teens some slack for a minute. Do you remember some of your daydreams about famous people? I vividly remember crying the day Jon Bon Jovi got married. At age twelve, I was devastated by the news, because in my mind this famous rock star was going to marry me (even though he lived in New Jersey and was fourteen years older). Now in my heart of hearts, I knew this was a fantasy, but daydreaming about it helped me form an individual identity from my family. I was exploring life as an adult within a safe environment.

6   While daydreaming about being famous is a normal part of development, the danger comes when the daydreams become our reality. Most experts agree people will enter into shallow relationships that focus on being admired versus authentically engaging with other people—modeling what they see as the celebrity lifestyle. In the 2005 Youth Risk Behavior Survey of Mecklenburg County High School students, more than fifteen percent of teens reported they felt all alone in their lives. Combine these shallow relationships with loneliness, and you have a recipe for life disaster.

We All Want Our Fifteen Minutes

7   With the popularity of reality shows, it seems anyone can have his or her fifteen minutes of fame and profit from it. Why wouldn't being famous seem like reality to us? Yet, as adults, we know most brushes with fame are momentary and cannot support us financially, or even emotionally, for a lifetime. The legacies of many famous people have shown lives full of intense loneliness, pain, and suffering.

8   Based on reports to date, police investigators have stated that the motive for the Benoit killings was a combination of family health issues, marital problems, work stress, and financial worries. Those are things each of us battles every day, whether we are famous or not. We can learn a lesson from this tragedy, the Virginia Tech shootings, and many others. Fame isn't the solution to the loneliness all of us feel at certain points in our lives. The only lasting way to battle loneliness is to stay connected in authentic relationships with our friends, family, and community.

Writing from Reading: "When Fame Falls Short"

When you write on any of the following topics, be sure to work through the stages of the writing process in preparing your paragraph.

1. Would you like to be famous? If your answer is yes, write a paragraph explaining what you would like to be famous for. If your answer is no, write a paragraph to explain.

2. Would a famous person be more likely to form authentic relationships than a less well-known person would? In a paragraph, explain your answer to this question.

Computer

3. Sally Loftis notes that the success of reality shows has made it seem that "anyone can have his or her fifteen minutes of fame and profit." If you watch any reality shows, remember someone who became "famous" on a reality show several years ago and who has been out of the spotlight recently. Do a little research on Google or another search engine to discover what that once-famous person has been doing lately. Use that information to discuss whether the former reality show "star" has benefited from a brief period of fame.

4. If you could have dinner with any famous person from the present or past, who would it be? Write a paragraph explaining your choice.

Collaborate

5. Can a person become famous but neither admired nor liked? Working with a partner or group, make a list of people, living today, who are well-known yet disliked, ridiculed, or scorned. Once you have the list, work alone and write an individual paragraph about one person on the list. You might think about how this person became famous, why he or she is disliked (or worse), and whether being well-known benefits this person in some way.

6. Sometimes cartoon characters become role models for children. Working with a group, make a list of cartoon characters whom children love and admire. Then work alone and write an individual paragraph that focuses on one character from the list. Write about the character's values, actions, and special appeal to children.

NARRATION

Only Daughter

Sandra Cisneros

Sandra Cisneros, the child of a Mexican father and a Mexican-American mother, grew up in Chicago. She has worked as a teacher to high school dropouts and in other areas of education and the arts. A widely published writer of poetry and short stories, she has won many awards, but in this narrative, first published in 1990, she writes about a time when she craved a different kind of recognition: her father's approval.

Words You May Need to Know (Corresponding paragraph numbers are in parentheses.)

anthology (1): a collection of writing by various authors
mi'ja **(4):** my daughter
in retrospect (5): looking back
putter about (5): get busy in an ineffectual manner
philandering (7): unfaithful
woo (8): seek the affection of
bouts (9): periods
nostalgia (9): homesickness
flat (9): apartment

short-order cook (11): a cook specializing in food cooked quickly, on request, as in diners
fellowship (15): a grant of money for further study
Fellini (16): an Italian movie director who focused on strange characters and grotesque events
Chicano (17): an American of Mexican descent
colonia **(19):** neighborhood

1   Once, several years ago, when I was just starting out my writing career, I was asked to write my own contributor's note for an anthology I was part of. I wrote: "I am the only daughter in a family of six sons. *That* explains everything."

2   Well, I've thought about that ever since, and yes, it explains a lot to me, but for the reader's sake I should have written: "I am the only daughter in a *Mexican* family of six sons." Or even: "I am the only daughter of a Mexican father and a Mexican-American mother." Or: "I am the only daughter of a working-class family of nine." All of these had everything to do with who I am today.

3   I was/am the only daughter and *only* a daughter. Being an only daughter in a family of six sons forced me by circumstance to spend a lot of time by myself because my brothers felt it beneath them to play with a *girl* in public. But that aloneness, that loneliness, was good for a would-be writer—it allowed me time to think and think, to imagine, to read and prepare myself.

4   Being only a daughter for my father meant my destiny would lead me to becoming someone's wife. That's what he believed. But when I was in the fifth grade and shared my plans for college with him, I was sure he understood. I remember my father saying, "*Que bueno, mi'ja,* that's good." That meant a lot to me, especially since my brothers thought the idea hilarious. What I didn't realize was that my father thought college was good for girls—good for finding a husband. After four years in college and two more in graduate school, and

still no husband, my father shakes his head even now and says I wasted all that education.

In retrospect, I'm lucky my father believed daughters were meant for husbands. It meant it didn't matter if I majored in something silly like English. After all, I'd find a nice professional eventually, right? This allowed me to putter about embroidering my little poems and stories without my father interrupting with so much as a "What's that you're writing?"

But the truth is, I wanted him to interrupt. I wanted my father to understand what it was I was scribbling, to introduce me as "My only daughter, the writer." Not as "This is my only daughter. She teaches." *Es maestra*—teacher. Not even *profesora*.

In a sense, everything I have ever written has been for him, to win his approval even though I know my father can't read English words, even though my father's only reading includes the brown-ink *Esto* sports magazines from Mexico City and the bloody *!Alarma!* magazines that feature yet another sighting of *La Virgen of Guadalupe* on a tortilla or a wife's revenge on her philandering husband by bashing his skull in with a *molcajete* (a kitchen mortar made of volcanic rock). Or the *fotonovelas*, the little picture paperbacks with tragedy and trauma erupting from the characters' mouths in bubbles.

My father represents, then, the public majority. A public who is uninterested in reading, and yet one whom I am writing about and for, and privately trying to woo.

When we were growing up in Chicago, we moved a lot because of my father. He suffered bouts of nostalgia. Then we'd have to let go our flat, store the furniture with mother's relatives, load the station wagon with baggage and bologna sandwiches, and head south. To Mexico City.

We came back, of course. To yet another Chicago flat, another Chicago neighborhood, another Catholic school. Each time, my father would seek out the parish priest in order to get a tuition break, and complain or boast: "I have seven sons."

He meant *siente hijos*, seven children, but he translated it as "sons." "I have seven sons." To anyone who would listen. The Sears Roebuck employee who sold us the washing machine. The short-order cook where my father ate his ham-and-eggs breakfasts. "I have seven sons." As if he deserved a medal from the state.

My papa. He didn't mean anything by that mistranslation, I'm sure. But somehow I could feel myself being erased. I'd tug my father's sleeve and whisper, "Not seven sons. Six! and one *daughter.*"

When my oldest brother graduated from medical school, he fulfilled my father's dream that we study hard and use this—our heads, instead of this—our hands. Even now my father's hands are thick and yellow, stubbed by a history of hammer and nails and twine and coils and springs. "Use this," my father said, tapping his head, "and not this," showing us those hands. He always looked tired when he said it.

14   Wasn't college an investment? And hadn't I spent all those years in college? And if I didn't marry, what was it all for? Why would anyone go to college and then choose to be poor? Especially someone who had always been poor.

15   Last year, after ten years of writing professionally, the financial rewards started to trickle in. My second National Endowment for the Arts Fellowship. A guest professorship at the University of California, Berkeley. My book, which sold to a major New York publishing house.

16   At Christmas, I flew home to Chicago. The house was throbbing, same as always; hot *tamales* and sweet *tamales* hissing in my mother's pressure cooker, and everybody—my mother, six brothers, wives, babies, aunts, cousins—talking too loud and at the same time, like in a Fellini film, because that's just how we are.

17   I went upstairs to my father's room. One of my stories had just been translated into Spanish and published in an anthology of Chicano writing, and I wanted to show it to him. Ever since he'd recovered from a stroke two years ago, my father likes to spend his leisure hours horizontally. And that's how I found him, watching a Pedro Infante movie on Galavision and eating rice pudding.

18   There was a glass filmed with milk on the bedside table. There were several vials of pills and balled Kleenex. And on the floor, one black sock and a plastic urinal that I didn't want to look at but looked at anyway. Pedro Infante was about to burst into song, and my father was laughing.

19   I'm not sure if it was because my story was translated into Spanish, or because it was published in Mexico, or perhaps because the story dealt with Tepeyac, the *colonia* my father was raised in and the house he grew up in, but at any rate, my father punched the mute button on his remote control and read my story.

20   I sat on the bed next to my father and waited. He read it very slowly. As if he were reading each line over and over. He laughed at all the right places and read lines he liked out loud. He pointed and asked questions: "Is this so-and-so?" "Yes," I said. He kept reading.

21   When he was finally finished, after what seemed like hours, my father looked up and asked: "Where can we get copies of this for the relatives?"

22   Of all the wonderful things that happened to me last year, that was the most wonderful.

Writing from Reading: "Only Daughter"

When you write on any of the following topics, be sure to work through the stages of the writing process in preparing your paragraph.

1. Have you ever wanted a parent's approval? If so, write about a time when you received or were denied that approval.

2. Write a narrative paragraph about a time when your place in your family (such as an only son, the oldest child, the youngest, one of three daughters, and so forth) gave you an advantage or put you at a disadvantage.

3. Cisneros writes of times when her father would say, "I have seven sons," even though he had six sons and one daughter. At such times, she says, "I could feel myself being erased." Working with a partner or a group, discuss what she meant by that comment. After your discussion, write individual paragraphs about a time when you felt as if you were "being erased."

4. Sandra Cisneros' father expected that his daughter would marry, and he believed that her college education was useful as a way for her to meet and marry "a nice professional." Have you ever imposed your own expectations on another person? For example, have you expressed disappointment when your child didn't make the best grades or wasn't interested in your favorite sport? Or have you (subtly) pressured a boyfriend or girlfriend to change goals or beliefs because they did not match yours? Write about a time when you tried to make someone what he or she is not.

5. Sandra Cisneros' essay includes many details about her life in opposing worlds: Spanish versus English, working-class background versus college-educated future, the traditionally male world of her father and six brothers versus a world with wider choices for women. Write your own story about an incident that placed you in a conflict between two worlds.

NARRATION

The Seamier Side of Life

Michale Mohr

When Michale Mohr's adult son disappeared, she entered a dark and dirty world to find him. Her story is about danger, courage, strength, and love.

Words You May Need to Know (Corresponding paragraph numbers are in parentheses.)

ominous (1): threatening
domain (1): territory
denizens (2): inhabitants
ceased (3): ended
sought (4): the past tense of *seek*
rude (4): rough
criteria (4): standards necessary for a search

constitute (4): make up
means (5): financial resources
rivaled (6): could compete with
depiction (6): portrayal
communes (9): small communities with shared resources
wealth (10): abundance, great amount

1   The dim, flickering street lamp cast an ominous shadow on the tall, well-built man standing beneath it. Not moving, staring into my eyes, never blinking or altering his gaze, he waited there silently, not allowing his eyes to reveal the thoughts below the surface. In the search for my son, walking the streets among drug pushers and addicts, I'd become used to the look. With minimal movement, he slowly pulled back his jacket enough to expose the butt of a gun peeking out above his left belt. His message was clear: this area of Oceanside, California, was his domain. I was not welcome here.

2   For the past three years, I've found myself standing toe-to-toe with the denizens of the drug underworld. My son, Jeff, vanished from his home in Phoenix, Arizona, just before his twenty-fifth birthday. He was a drug user, and I went looking for him.

3   Jeff worked from his home as a computer technician after moving to Arizona in 1990. When his weekly phone calls ceased and his phone and pager were shut off, I started writing him letters. He didn't answer. Then one came back stamped by the post office HOUSE VACANT. I phoned Jeff's friends. They, too, had lost touch with him because, as they sadly revealed, he had begun taking drugs. I was stunned. Jeff had not done them as a teen, so I'd never even considered the idea. His drug of choice, I was told, was crystal meth.

4   I immediately sought out authorities who I believed would, should, and could help. I was in for a rude awakening. The Phoenix police wouldn't file a missing persons report on Jeff because they said he didn't fit the criteria. The FBI refused to help me. Even *Unsolved Mysteries* wouldn't do a story. A drug addict walking out of his home didn't constitute a mystery.

5   Private detectives were above my means, but I picked their brains for ways to locate people who've gone missing. One investigator told me Jeff was probably living on the street. "To find him, you have to get out there, kick some

ass, and take some names." I am a small woman, 5 feet 3, weighing about 113 pounds. I couldn't kick my own ass, but I went anyway.

Not even sure he was still in Arizona, I didn't know where to start. A friend   6 guided me to a psychic who felt Jeff had traveled to the San Diego area. That's where I began. Armed with photos of Jeff, my cell phone, and my very brave best friend Vickie, I left my home in Portland, Oregon, and took my first trip to the streets. First stop: the Oceanside police station, to find out where the heaviest crystal-meth users could be found. The search took us to neighborhoods that rivaled any movie depiction of the drug world. Rundown houses stood sadly with broken windows and torn shades. Yards were piled with trash, toys, and car parts. The poverty was humbling.

One step led to the next. Each person would expand our search by suggesting new places to look. Those who trusted us gave us addresses of crack houses. Others would either clam up or show us their weapons. We never tested the threats. We would quietly say "Thanks" and leave.

One pool hall in El Cajon, California, fronted for a shooting gallery. Filth   8 seemed to ooze from the walls. Stale cigarette smells coupled with the longtime unwashed bodies of the inhabitants assaulted us as we walked in. I spoke with a young girl who thought she'd seen Jeff the week before. As we talked, she began to weep. Putting her arms around me, she said, "I wish my mom would look for me. I really hope you find him." With that, she straightened her shoulders and walked through the door, disappearing into the darkness.

I took seven trips in all. Vickie came with me on three. I moved as far into   9 the drug underworld as I could, even dressing as a bag lady to search for Jeff in homeless communes. I'd work, save money, take a trip, return home, and start the process all over again.

Finally my efforts paid off. Years of searching the streets taught me well.   10 Besides questioning addicts and pushers, I'd stop in at retail stores, showing Jeff's picture to see if they recognized him. Slowly I learned there was a wealth of information on those stores' computers. Birth dates, Social Security numbers, addresses are all available, depending on the establishment.

When Jeff left his house in Phoenix, he'd had a roommate. I'd never been   11 able to locate or find any information on her. No one I talked to seemed to know her whereabouts. I knew her name, but what I didn't know was that I had the incorrect spelling.

Returning to Phoenix in June, I tried my newfound technique of using   12 store computers. A video store close to Jeff's house turned out to be a gold mine. The clerk tried various spellings of the name and surprised us both by finding an old account for her. It had been closed for two years, but it provided me with her Social Security number and birth date.

Once back in Portland, I used this information to run an address check.   13 The last listing was from May of '95. I called a Phoenix real estate agent who used a reverse street directory to come up with a phone number. I called and reached the woman's parents.

14   Jeff was buried deep in the drug life, but through them I eventually managed to get a message to my son. I had no money, so my friends raised funds for me to leave for Phoenix the next day. I checked into a hotel, left my number with the ex-roommate's parents, and waited.

15   Jeff rode ten miles on his bike in 106-degree heat to reach me. He was thin, he had recently been beaten up, and his teeth badly needed repair, but he was alive. He had been trying to leave the drug life for about a year. His silence had been about protecting me. My search had been about protecting him.

16   Jeff is now back home with me, clean, working, attending Narcotics Anonymous, and hoping to help others walk out of the darkness of the life he worked so hard to leave behind. We've both learned a lot through this. For me, it's simple. Enough love can move mountains and create miracles.

Writing from Reading: "The Seamier Side of Life"

When you write on any of the following topics, be sure to work through the stages of the writing process in preparing your paragraph.

1. Michale Mohr writes about the time she entered a new world: she walked "among drug pushers and addicts" in search of her son. Write about your first trip into a new world. It might have been the world of college, great wealth, great poverty, crime, illness, peace, safety, or some other new environment. Write about your experiences and their effects on you.

2. Write about your search for someone (a person or even a pet) you loved. Include the outcome of the search.

3. Write about a time when the support of friends helped you accomplish a goal. Be sure to include an explanation of your goal, the obstacles you faced, and the way(s) the support of others helped you.

4. Write about a time when you were in danger. Include the outcome of the situation.

5. Write a narrative about you or someone you know whose experience proves the truth of what Michale Mohr said she learned for her search for her son: "Enough love can move mountains and create miracles."

DESCRIPTION

The War Within

David C. Botti

David C. Botti joined the Marine reserves while he was in college. Shortly after the September 11, 2001, attack on the World Trade Center, Botti's Marine unit was mobilized. After nearly a year of duty in the United States, Botti's unit was sent home, and he began a new life in New York City. However, after just a few weeks in the city, he was called to duty in Iraq. In this excerpt from his New York Times *article, Botti describes the day he was given his orders.*

Words You May Need to Know (Corresponding paragraph numbers are in parentheses.)

mobilize (1): to become prepared for war

contemplate (1): to consider carefully and thoughtfully

deployment (1): the time a soldier spends in action

infantry (3): the combat arm of units trained to fight on foot

After just one month of city living, the call to mobilize came. I was given the necessary information. And in an even tone, I replied that I understood, closing my eyes in my cubicle to contemplate the new phase of life I was entering. Word traveled quickly through the office that day. Friends and strangers approached me with words of encouragement and admiration. I left the office hours later, carrying a small flag signed by my coworkers that I would carry in the top flap of my pack throughout my deployment. 1

The city was beautiful my last night on the street, the chill making me appreciate the inviting warmth in a corner café or the familiar rock of a heated subway car. I headed south on Park Avenue, February numbing my hand as I held the cell phone to my ear. There was a marathon of calls through chattering teeth. Friends and family were confused, wanted to know more than I knew myself. Then I found a park bench and sat alone for the first time since the news came. I tried to remember everything I could, collecting memories for the times ahead. 2

I watched the day end, the people returning home or preparing for a night out. When it got late, I headed home, wishing I could line up every person in the city, shake each one's hand, say, "Good-bye, I've had a good time, maybe I can come back again some day." I spent the bus ride home that night consoling my mother by cell phone, telling her lies as I tried to persuade her they would never send a reserve infantry company into Iraq; we would only be asked to guard the supply lines throughout Kuwait. She didn't believe me, but pretended to. 3

After I hung up, a woman sitting in front of me turned and said she had heard my whole conversation. She promised to pray for me. 4

Writing from Reading: "The War Within"

When you write on any of the following topics, be sure to work through the stages of the writing process in preparing your paragraph.

Collaborate

1. Write about a time when you received surprising news (bad or good), and describe your immediate actions and reactions. If your instructor agrees, work with a partner to gather details. Once you have selected an incident, ask your partner to interview you. Your partner can ask questions such as the following:

   What exactly was the news?
   How was it delivered to you?
   Do you remember any sensations as you received the news?

   Your partner can write down your answers. Once you have been interviewed, trade places with your partner. Each partner should be prepared with five or more questions before the interview process begins.

   After both interviews, exchange the notes from the interviews so that each person can use the details to develop his or her paragraph.

2. On a life-changing day, Botti walks alone through New York City, noting how beautiful it is. Describe a time when you walked somewhere, alone or with others, and suddenly felt the beauty of the place. Use the details of the place to explain your reaction.

3. Botti's description includes many references to telephones. For example, the orders to mobilize come on the phone at his office; later, he deals with "a marathon of calls" from friends and family as he walks in the city, his cell phone to his ear. Also, he consoles his mother by cell phone as he sits on a bus. Describe a dramatic moment in your life in which a phone or phones played a significant role.

4. An emotional moment in this description came when a stranger overheard Botti's conversation with his mother (in which he tries to comfort her about his deployment). The stranger promised to pray for him. Write about a time when you received unexpected sympathy or kindness from a stranger. Describe the circumstances, the act of kindness, and your reaction.

5. On the day Botti describes, he is saying goodbye to people, a place, and a new life he had barely begun. Describe a significant time in your life when you said goodbye. You may have been leaving a place, ending a relationship, giving up a dream, or breaking a dangerous addiction.

DESCRIPTION

Deep Cold

Verlyn Klinkenborg

Verlyn Klinkenborg writes a column called "The Rural Life" for The New York Times. *His regular descriptions of nature, its beauty and harshness, rely on exact details and sense descriptions. As you read "Deep Cold," note how the author's language draws the reader into the world of an icy day.*

Words You May Need to Know (Corresponding paragraph numbers are in parentheses.)

gnashing (1): grinding or grating
muted (1): softened, made less ringing or resonant
rime (2): white frost
reservoirs (3): a place where water is stored for future use

brood (3): think deeply and with gloom
current (3): stream of water
paradox (3): a situation or statement seemingly impossible but also true
trepidation (3): agitation or fear

If deep cold made a sound, it would be the scissoring and gnashing of a   1
skater's blades against hard gray ice, or the screeching the snow sets up when you walk across it in the blue light of afternoon. The sound may be the stamping of feet at bus stops and train stations, or the way the almost perfect clarity of the audible world on an icy day is muted by scarves and mufflers pulled up over the face and around the ears.

But the true sound of deep cold is the sound of the wind. Monday morning,   2
on the streets of Cambridge, Massachusetts, the wind chill approached fifty below zero. A stiff northwest wind rocked in the trees and snatched at cars as they idled at the curb. A rough rime had settled over that old-brick city the day before, and now the wind was sanding it smooth. It was cold of Siberian or Arctic intensity, and I could feel a kind of claustrophobia settling in all over Boston. People went about their errands, only to cut them short instantly, turning backs to the gust and fleeing for cover.

It has been just slightly milder in New York. Furnace repairmen and oil-   3
truck drivers are working on the memory of two hours' sleep. Swans in the smaller reservoirs brood on the ice, and in the swamps that line the railroad tracks in Dutchess County, you can see how the current was moving when the cold snap brought it to a halt. The soil in windblown fields looks—and is—iron hard. It's all a paradox, a cold that feels absolutely rigid but which nonetheless seeps through ill-fitting windows, between clapboards, and along uninsulated pipe chases. People listen superstitiously to the sounds in their heating ducts, to the banging of their radiators, afraid of silence. They turn the keys in their cars with trepidation. It's an old world this week.

Writing from Reading: "Deep Cold"

When you write on any of the following topics, be sure to work through the stages of the writing process in preparing your paragraph.

1. Write about heat. You can call the heat "extreme heat," or "deep heat," or use another term to sum up the heat you are describing. Concentrate on using sense words to explain the power and impact of this heat.

2. Klinkenborg describes the negative effects of deep cold. Write a description of the positive effects and the beauty of deep cold.

3. If your earliest years were spent in a warm climate, write about your first experience of cold weather.

4. Describe your experience of some type of extreme weather: a flood, a tornado, a hurricane, a forest fire, a sandstorm, and so forth.

5. Describe some element of nature (such as snow or surf) to someone who has never experienced it.

ILLUSTRATION

A Different Mirror

Ronald Takaki

Ronald Takaki, born in Honolulu, is a historian known for his books on history, race, and multiculturalism. The following excerpt is from his book A Different Mirror. *In the book, Takaki argues that in studying America's history, we must study all the groups who have created America so that we "see ourselves in a different mirror." This excerpt focuses on specific details that support the idea of America's diversity.*

Words You May Need to Know

ethnic diversity: variety of people, races, and cultures
discerned: recognized, perceived
Ellis Island: an island off the shore of New York City, where many immigrants first landed in America
Angel Island: an island off San Francisco

Chinatown, Harlem, South Boston, the Lower East Side (of New York City): places associated with a variety of ethnic groups and races
derived: originated from
Forty-Niners: People who joined the Gold Rush of 1849, when gold was discovered in California
vaqueros: cowboys

The signs of America's ethnic diversity can be discerned across the continent: Ellis Island, Angel Island, Chinatown, Harlem, South Boston, the Lower East Side, places with Spanish names like Los Angeles and San Antonio or Indian names like Massachusetts and Iowa. Much of what is familiar in America's cultural landscape actually has ethnic origins. The Bing cherry was developed by an early Chinese immigrant named Ah Bing. American Indians were cultivating corn, tomatoes, and tobacco long before the arrival of Columbus. The term *okay* was derived from the Choctaw word *oke*, meaning "it is so." There is evidence indicating that the name *Yankee* came from Indian terms for the English—from *eankke* in Cherokee and *Yankwis* in Delaware. Jazz and blues as well as rock and roll have African-American origins. The "Forty-Niners" of the Gold Rush learned mining techniques from the Mexicans; American cowboys acquired herding skills from Mexican *vaqueros* and adopted their range terms—such as *lariat* from *la reata*, *lasso* from *lazo*, and *stampede* from *estampida*. Songs like "God Bless America," "Easter Parade," and "White Christmas" were written by a Russian-Jewish immigrant named Israel Baline, more popularly known as Irving Berlin.

Writing from Reading: "A Different Mirror"

When you write on any of the following topics, be sure to work through the stages of the writing process in preparing your paragraph.

1. Interview three people in your class. Ask each to tell you about his or her family background. Before you begin, prepare a list of at least six questions such as "Were you born in this country?" and "Do you know

Collaborate

how long your family has been in America?" Use the answers as the basis for a paragraph on diversity in your classroom. You may discover a wide range of backgrounds or a similarity of backgrounds. In either case, you have details for a paragraph about your classmates and their origins.

2. Write a paragraph about the many foods that are considered American but that really originated in another country or culture. Give specific examples.

Computer

3. Takaki gives examples of words Americans use, like *Yankee*, that originated in another language. Write a paragraph on words or expressions that Americans use that originated in another language. You can visit *http://en.wikipedia.org/wiki/Lists_of_English_ loanwords_by_ country_or_language_of_origin*. Here you will find lists of words from such origins as African, Chinese, Hawaiian, Indian, Native American, Italian, and Korean languages. In your own words, give examples of at least three American words that have interesting origins. Be sure to click on each word in the list for interesting information about the word's original meaning, history, and present-day meaning.

4. Write a paragraph on the place names in America that came from one or more other languages. You might write about only Spanish place names, for example, and group them into states and cities. Or you could write about names from several languages and group them into Spanish names, Indian names, French names, and so forth.

5. Write a paragraph about what one ethnic group has contributed to American life and culture. You can use specific examples of contributions to language, music, dance, food, clothing, customs, and so forth.

ILLUSTRATION

Why Not Real Awards for Real Achievements?

Ben Stein

Ben Stein is a writer, attorney, and actor. He is also known as the host of the television quiz show Win Ben Stein's Money. *In this essay, Stein talks about a different kind of awards show.*

Words You May Need to Know (Corresponding paragraph numbers are in parentheses.)

Evian (1): a brand of bottled water
Winnebago (1): a make of recreational vehicle
Ron Howard (2): the director of *Backdraft*, a movie about firefighters
garner (2): collect

apathy (3): lack of interest or concern
wrenched (4): painfully strained or twisted
casting illusions (6): creating what is not real

1   Strange. We have an Oscars ceremony to tell wildly pampered people (the kind who demand and get Evian water for their Winnebago showers while on location) how great they are for daring to stand in front of a camera for thousands of dollars per day, playing the role of, say, a brave cop. Yet we have no TV award show that gives recognition to real cops who really do risk their lives year in and out to keep other people safe. Why not have a nationally broadcast presentation of prizes for officers who deserve some thanks from society?

2   Or maybe firefighters. Ron Howard and others have made fine movies about firefighters, and these sometimes garner Oscars. But we have hundreds of thousands of real firefighters who day in and night out risk their lives in the most dangerous job in America. Why not have a show that recognizes these brave men and women for the lives they save?

3   Michelle Pfeiffer starred in a fine movie about teaching kids in the inner city, but she was just acting. In real life, there are men and women who struggle against danger, apathy, and shortages of material and money to teach children and give them hope. Sometimes these teachers are even injured in their classrooms, as recently happened here in Los Angeles. Why not acknowledge this?

4   Movie-viewers and TV-watchers are used to seeing heroics and tears in emergency rooms. But those scenes are just pretend, staged by people paid thousands of dollars a week to do it. In America, actual nurses and doctors get exposed to HIV and spat upon and wrenched emotionally while trying to save the lives of people they don't even know. They often make the difference between life and death. Why don't they have an award? Why aren't they ever called before national cameras?

5   We have a million military men and women living in bitter cold in Korea, mud in Bosnia, wrenched heat in Cuba and Haiti, separated from their families for six months at a time while on submarines, landing jets on aircraft carriers at

for six months at a time while on submarines, landing jets on aircraft carriers at night—as frightening an exercise as exists on earth—all in order to protect us and keep us free. We have Marines at Parris Island, sailors on the water, and pilots flying over Iraq who live modestly, train, fight, and sometimes die with no day-to-day TV recognition. Why not fix that?

6   Why not put before America the best real men and women we produce, instead of only showing the folks who are good at casting illusions? I'm an actor myself and am happy to give actors their due. But actors are not true heroes or stars. Why not give a stage to the real thing once a year? That would be an awards ceremony worth watching.

Writing from Reading: "Why Not Real Awards for Real Achievement?"

When you write on any of the following topics, be sure to work through the stages of the writing process in preparing your paragraph.

Collaborate

1. Working with a partner or group, brainstorm all the television awards shows you can remember. Then discuss which one was the worst. It may have been the worst because it was too long, gave the awards to the wrong people, seemed phony, and so forth. After your group work, write individual paragraphs on the worst awards show you have seen. Be sure to include many specific examples of its defects.

2. Think of a film you saw that was meant to be a realistic picture of some group such as police, soldiers, sailors, nurses, teachers, students, or gangs, or of some issue such as drug abuse, poverty, terrorism, or crime. Write a paragraph about how realistic or unrealistic this film was. Be sure to use many specific examples.

3. Write a paragraph that gives specific examples of people you know (not celebrities) who deserve recognition for one of these qualities:

   bravery
   compassion
   kindness
   sacrifice for others

4. Write a paragraph with one of the following topic sentences:

   The most unappreciated group in America is _____.
   My childhood heroes had several common characteristics.
   Three people have become heroes for today's teens.

   Be sure to develop and explain your thesis with specific examples.

5. Interview a teacher, police officer, medical worker, firefighter, or member of the armed forces. Before the interview, prepare a list of at least ten questions to ask about the person's job. You can include questions about the stresses, dangers, and rewards of the job. Write and/or tape the answers during the interview and ask follow-up questions. Finally, ask the person to add any comments he or she would like to make. Use this information to write a paragraph about the good and bad aspects of this work.

PROCESS

Coming Over

Russell Freedman

In this selection from Russell Freedman's book, Immigrant Kids, *he describes the difficult and often frightening process European immigrants of the 1880s to the 1920s endured when they looked for a better life in America. From the dark conditions of the Atlantic crossing to the terror of the examinations at Ellis Island, the immigrants found strength in their dreams and in their first glimpse of the Statue of Liberty.*

Words You May Need to Know (Corresponding paragraph numbers are in parentheses.)

impoverished (1): poor
fervent (1): passionate
penniless (2): without any money
foul-smelling (3): having an offensive odor
lounges (3): public sitting rooms
New World (5): The Western Hemisphere
the Narrows (5): a narrow channel of water between Brooklyn and Staten Island in New York City
foredeck (6): the forward part of the deck of a ship
jabbered conversation (6): rapid talk that can't be understood

din (6): loud noise
veered (7): swerved
scowling (7): frowning
maze (10): a confusing network of interconnecting pathways
nationality (12): the country a person belongs to
flustered (12): nervous and upset
rigorous (13): harsh, severe
momentarily (13): for a minute
indomitable (13): not able to be overcome
teeming (14): crowded, filled to overflowing

In the years around the turn of the twentieth century, immigration to America reached an all-time high. Between 1880 and 1920, twenty-three million immigrants arrived in the United States. They came mainly from countries of Europe, especially from impoverished towns and villages in southern and eastern Europe. The one thing they had in common was a fervent belief that in America life would be better.   1

Most of these immigrants were poor. Somehow they managed to scrape together enough money to pay for their passage to America. Many immigrant families arrived penniless. Others had to make the journey in stages. Often the father came first, found work, and sent for his family later. Immigrants usually crossed the Atlantic as steerage passengers. Reached by steep, slippery stairways, the steerage lay deep down in the hold of the ship. It was occupied by passengers paying the lowest fare.   2

Men, women, and children were packed into dark, foul-smelling compartments. They slept in narrow bunks stacked three high. They had no showers, no lounges, and no dining rooms. Food served from huge kettles was dished into dinner pails provided by the steamship company. Because steerage conditions were crowded and uncomfortable, passengers spent as much time as possible up on deck.   3

4   The voyage was an ordeal, but it was worth it. They were on their way to America. The great majority of immigrants landed in New York City at America's biggest port. They never forgot their first glimpse of the Statue of Liberty. Edward Corsi, who later became United States Commissioner of Immigration, was a ten-year-old Italian immigrant when he sailed into New York Harbor in 1907. Here is how he later described the experience:

5   My first impression of the New World will always remain etched in my memory, particularly that hazy October morning when I first saw Ellis Island. The steamer *Florida*, fourteen days out of Naples, filled to capacity with 1600 natives of Italy, had weathered one of the worst storms in our captain's memory, and glad we were, both children and grown-ups, to leave the open sea and come at last through the Narrows into the bay.

6   My mother, my stepfather, my brother Giuseppe, and my two sisters, Liberta and Helvetia, all of us together, happy that we had come through the storm safely, clustered on the foredeck for fear of separation and looked with wonder on this miraculous land of our dreams. Giuseppe and I held tight to Stepfather's hands while Liberta and Helvetia clung to Mother. Passengers all about us were crowding against the rail. Jabbered conversation, sharp cries, laughs, and cheers—a steadily rising din filled the air. Mothers and fathers lifted up babies so that they too could see, off to the left, the Statue of Liberty.

7   Finally, the *Florida* veered to the left, turning northward into the Hudson River, and now the incredible buildings of lower Manhattan came very close to us. The officers of the ship went striding up and down the decks shouting orders and directions and driving the immigrants before them. Scowling and gesturing, they pushed and pulled the passengers, herding us into separate groups as though we were animals. A few moments later, we came to our dock, and the long journey was over.

8   But the journey was not yet over. Before they could be admitted to the United States, immigrants had to pass through Ellis Island, which became the nation's chief immigrant processing center. There they would be questioned and examined. Those who could not pass all the exams would be detained; some would be sent back to Europe. And so their arrival in America was filled with great anxiety. Among the immigrants, Ellis Island was known as "Heartbreak Island."

9   When their ship docked at a Hudson River pier, the immigrants had numbered identity tags pinned to their clothing. Then they were herded onto special ferryboats that carried them to Ellis Island. Officials hurried them along, shouting "Quick! Run! Hurry!" in half a dozen languages.

10   Filing into an enormous inspection hall, the immigrants formed long lines separated by iron railings that made the hall look like a great maze. Now the

examinations began. First the immigrants were examined by two doctors of the United States Health Service. One doctor looked for physical and mental abnormalities. When a case aroused suspicion, the immigrant received a chalk mark on the right shoulder for further inspection: L for lameness, H for heart, X for mental defects, and so on.

The second doctor watched for contagious and infectious diseases. He looked especially for infections of the scalp and at the eyelids for symptoms of trachoma, a blinding disease. Since trachoma caused more than half of all medical detentions, this doctor was greatly feared. He stood directly in the immigrant's path. With a swift movement, he would grab the immigrant's eyelid, pull it up, and peer beneath it. If all was well, the immigrant was passed on.

11

Those who failed to get past both doctors had to undergo a more thorough medical exam. The others moved on to the registration clerk, who questioned them with the aid of an interpreter: What is your name? Your nationality? Your occupation? Can you read and write? Have you ever been in prison? How much money do you have with you? Where are you going? Some immigrants were so flustered that they could not answer. They were allowed to sit and rest and try again. About one immigrant out of every five or six was detained for additional examinations or questioning. The writer Angelo Pellegrini recalled his own family's detention at Ellis Island:

12

> We lived there for three days—Mother and we five children, the youngest of whom was three years old. Because of the rigorous physical examination that we had to submit to, particularly of the eyes, there was this terrible anxiety that one of us might be rejected. And if one of us was, what would the rest of the family do? My sister was indeed momentarily rejected; she had been so ill and had cried so much that her eyes were absolutely bloodshot, and mother was told, "Well, we can't let her in." But fortunately, Mother was an indomitable spirit and finally made them understand that if her child had a few hours' rest and a little bite to eat, she would be all right. In the end, we did get through.

13

Most immigrants passed through Ellis Island in about one day. Carrying all their worldly possessions, they left the examination hall and waited on the dock for the ferry that would take them to Manhattan, a mile away. Some of them still faced journeys overland before they reached their final destination. Others would head directly for the teeming immigrant neighborhoods of New York City.

14

Writing from Reading: "Coming Over"

When you write on any of the following topics, be sure to follow the stages of the writing process in preparing your paragraph.

1. Travel involves a number of processes. One of the most common today is the process of the security check at the airport. Using clear

steps and specific details, describe this process to a reader who has never experienced it.

2. Write about the steps involved in another process that involves some local, state, or national agency. For example, you can write about the steps involved in obtaining a driver's license, paying for a traffic ticket, getting a marriage license, applying for a green card, or obtaining a passport.

3. Write about a process that was new for you. You might write about the first time you registered for college classes, went through Customs in a foreign country, were prepared for surgery, or took a medical test that required local or general anesthesia.

4. As it was in the late nineteenth and early twentieth centuries, America today is filled with immigrants. If you began your life in another country, trace the steps of your first entry into (and first glimpse of) America.

Computer

5. Using Russell Freedman's steps as a guideline, write your own version of the journey of the immigrants from Southern and Eastern Europe to New York City. Make this version your own by adding details about Ellis Island you find in research. For such details, try these sources:

http://www.nps.gov/elis/ (This address uses "elis" instead of "ellis.")

http://www.history.com/minisites/ellisisland/

Your details can include two or more photographs of different stages of the journey. For selected images of Ellis Island and of immigration, see this source:

http://www.loc.gov/rr/print/list/070_immi.html

Grammar Practice for Nonnative Speakers

NOUNS AND ARTICLES

A **noun** names a person, place, or thing. There are *count nouns* and *noncount nouns*.

> **Count nouns** refer to people, places, or things that can be counted.
> three *cookies*, two *dogs*, five *suitcases*

> **Noncount nouns** refer to things that can't be counted.
> *luggage, employment, attention*

Here are some more examples of count and noncount nouns.

count	noncount
joke	humor
movie	entertainment
dream	inspiration
automobile	transportation

One way to remember the difference between count and noncount nouns is to put the word *much* in front of the noun. For example, if you can say *much entertainment*, then *entertainment* is a noncount noun.

Exercise 1 Identifying Count and Noncount Nouns

Put *count* or *noncount* next to each word below.

1. _____ grandchild
2. _____ gas
3. _____ support
4. _____ coin
5. _____ money

6. _____ sympathy
7. _____ electricity
8. _____ animal
9. _____ interference
10. _____ idea

Using Articles with Nouns

Articles point out nouns. Articles are either **indefinite** (*a, an*) or **definite** (*the*). There are several rules for using these articles.

1. Use *a* in front of consonant sounds; use *an* before vowel sounds.

a filter	an orphan
a room	an apple
a bench	an event
a thought	an issue
a necklace	an umbrella

2. Use *a* or *an* in front of singular count nouns. *A* or *an* means *any one*.

   I saw *an* owl.
   She rode *a* horse.

3. Do not use *a* or *an* with noncount nouns.

   not this: I need a money.
   but this: I need money.

   not this: Selena is passing an arithmetic.
   but this: Selena is passing arithmetic.

4. Use *the* before both singular and plural count nouns whose specific identity is known to the reader.

   The dress with the sequins on it is my party dress.
   Most of *the* movies I rent are science fiction films.

5. Use *the* before noncount nouns only when they are specifically identified.

   not this: He wants the sympathy. (Whose sympathy? What sympathy? The noncount noun *sympathy* is not specifically identified.)
   but this: I need *the sympathy* of a good friend. (Now *sympathy* is specifically identified.)

   not this: Generosity of the family who paid for my education was remarkable. (The noncount noun *generosity* is specifically identified, so you need *the*.)
   but this: *The generosity* of the family who paid for my education was remarkable.

Exercise 2   Using *a* or *an*

Put *a* or *an* in the spaces where it is needed. Some sentences are correct as they are.

1. Once she started her new job, Elisa was filled with _____ enthusiasm.

2. Tommy offered me _____ cup of green tea.

3. On summer nights, _____ soft breeze cooled the backyard.

4. The neglected child was desperate for _____ affection.

5. There was nothing in the refrigerator except _____ apple and _____ box of stale crackers.

6. After listening to my girlfriend's obvious lies, I lost _____ control.

7. Mr. Stein has _____ allergy to _____ dust, and he avoids dusty rooms and objects.

8. _____ sense of _____ humor can break the tension at _____ interview.

9. _____ fuel can be expensive for anyone who needs _____ car to get to work or school.

10. I needed to see _____ counselor yesterday, but the counseling office was so busy that I had to make _____ appointment for Friday.

Exercise 3   Using *the*

Put *the* in the spaces where it is needed. Some sentences are correct as they are.

1. When Kevin gets a little older, he will have _____ physical strength of his father.

2. My mother never let me play near _____ canal behind my house.

3. Hank has _____ ability to meet a customer once and remember _____ person's name forever.

4. _____ city commission of _____ Forest Park met to discuss _____ possibility of building more low-cost housing.

5. _____ movies I prefer focus on _____ action rather than on _____ romance.

6. My father was _____ first person in his family to make _____ money in _____ real estate business.

7. With _____ help from his father, Matthew converted an old barn into an attractive house.

8. Tanisha is overcome by _____ anxiety every time she stands at _____ edge of a bridge or dock.

9. When my father died, my friends offered me _____ comfort I needed.

10. Sometimes Callie behaves foolishly because she wants _____ attention.

Connect

Exercise 4 **Correcting a Paragraph with Errors in Articles**

Correct the eleven errors with *a*, *an*, or *the* in the following paragraph. You may need to add, change, or eliminate articles. Write the corrections in the space above the errors.

The traveling can be a frustrating experience. Last week, I spent four hours at airport, waiting for plane that would take me to Atlanta. The person at the check-in counter did not announce an delay until one hour after the plane was supposed to take off. One hour later, we finally boarded the plane, only to sit for another two hours. During those two hours, the air conditioning was turned off, and no one offered me the drink or the snack. Pilot kept coming on the loudspeaker to say he had a news of bad weather ahead and had to wait. Sitting in the tiny seat, sweltering in the heat, I felt the anger and an impatience. I experienced bad side of travel.

NOUNS OR PRONOUNS USED AS SUBJECTS

A noun or a **pronoun** (a word that takes the place of a noun) is the subject of each sentence or dependent clause. Be sure that all sentences or dependent clauses have a subject.

> **not this:** Cooks breakfast on weekends.
> **but this:** *He* cooks breakfast on weekends.

> **not this:** My cousin was hurt when fell down the stairs.
> **but this:** My cousin was hurt when *he* fell down the stairs.

Be careful not to *repeat* the subject.

> **not this:** The lieutenant ~~she~~ said I was brave.
> **but this:** The lieutenant said I was brave.

> **not this:** The cat that bit me ~~it~~ was a Siamese.
> **but this:** The cat that bit me was a Siamese.

Exercise 5 **Correcting Errors with Subjects**

Correct any errors with subjects in the sentences below. Write your corrections in the space above the errors.

1. The ugliest part of my apartment it was the kitchen.

2. After finishes his work, he takes a train back to his house.

3. Likes to go shopping as a way to relieve tension.

4. Yesterday the copy machine at the office it didn't work.

5. My sister Isabella she has friends in the neighborhood.

6. A day at an amusement park is getting more expensive every day; can cost me a week's salary.

7. On Tuesday, got an email from an old friend in Albuquerque.

8. Extra pillows on a bed they are essential for a good night's sleep.

9. When my little boy started crying, my dog she started crying, too.

10. Makes a mess in the garage whenever he works on his car.

VERBS

Necessary Verbs

Be sure that a main verb isn't missing from your sentences or dependent clauses.

> **not this:** Carlos extremely talented.
> **but this:** Carlos *is* extremely talented.

> **not this:** Bill called the police when saw the robbery.
> **but this:** Bill called the police when *he* saw the robbery.

-s Endings

Be sure to put the -s on present tense verbs in the third person singular.

> **not this:** She ~~take~~ a break in the afternoon.
> **but this:** She *takes* a break in the afternoon.

> **not this:** The plane ~~arrive~~ at 7:00 p.m.
> **but this:** The plane *arrives* at 7:00 p.m.

-ed Endings

Be sure to put -ed endings on the past participle form of a verb. There are three main forms of a verb:

> **present:** Today I walk.
> **past:** Yesterday I walked.
> **past participle:** I *have* walked. He *has* talked.

The past participle form is also used after *were, was, had,* and *has.*

> **not this:** We had ~~talk~~ about this plan for several weeks.
> **but this:** We had *talked* about this plan for several weeks.

> **not this:** The baby was ~~amuse~~ by the new toy.
> **but this:** The baby was *amused* by the new toy.

Do not add -ed endings to infinitives. An infinitive is the verb form that uses *to* plus the present form of the verb:

> to suggest

> **not this:** My husband wanted me to ~~suggested~~ a family party.
> **but this:** My husband wanted me to *suggest* a family party.

> to revise

> **not this:** I finally learned how to ~~revised~~ a draft.
> **but this:** I finally learned how to *revise* a draft.

> **Exercise 6**   **Correcting Errors in Verbs: Necessary Verbs, Third Person Present Tense, Past Participles, and Infinitives**

Correct any errors in verbs in the sentences below. Write your corrections in the space above the line. Some sentences do not need any correcting.

1. Every time I drive for more than one hundred miles, my mother feel anxious.

2. Over the weekend, I was determine to finish my psychology assignment.

3. The cough syrup smell terrible, but I need something for my cold.

4. On Saturday mornings, my roommate wakes up at dawn so he can go to the gym.

5. My father was so sick that he was not expected to recovered.

6. By the time George arrived at the restaurant, the staff had lock the doors for the night.

7. A romantic setting for a wedding is the rose garden at Hamilton Park.

8. This semester, Emily will get better grades because she has learn about managing her time.

9. You can spend a day at the lake when get some vacation time.

10. A few months ago, Sammy and I were trick into buying an old, creaky table.

Exercise 7 **Correcting a Paragraph with Errors in Necessary Verbs, Third Person Present Tense, Past Participles, and Infinitives**

Correct the nine verb errors in the following paragraph. Write your corrections in the space above the errors.

Eileen is the most popular person in her department because she give so much to her fellow employees. Whenever she greets her office mates with a smile or a silly joke, Eileen has the power to turned a dull day into a happier one. Even when Eileen herself is feeling low, manages to make others laugh. She is also a good listener. She offer her total attention and does not judge those who confide in her. She been known to spend hours on the phone with someone in trouble. Everyone feel comfortable talking to Eileen, for she genuinely care about others. She is well-liked because she knows how to responded to others and to brightened their lives.

Two-Word Verbs

Many verbs called **two-word verbs** contain a verb plus another word, a preposition or adverb. The meaning of each word by itself is different from the meaning the two words have when they are together. Look at this example:

I ran across an old friend at the ballgame.

You might check *run* in the dictionary and find that it means *to move quickly*. *Across* means *from one side to the other*. But *run across* means something different:

not this: I ~~moved quickly from one side to the other of~~ an old friend at
the ballgame.

but this: I *encountered* an old friend at the ballgame.

Sometimes a word or words come between the words of a two-word verb:

Yesterday I *took* my brother *out* to dinner.

Here are some common two-word verbs:

ask out:	I hope Steve will *ask* me *out* tomorrow.
break down:	If you drive too far, the car will *break down*.
call off:	I will *call* the game *off*.
call on:	He may *call on* you for advice
call up:	Neil *calls* Marsha *up* on weekends.
come across:	Sometimes Joe *comes across* Nick at work.
drop in:	We can *drop in* on the neighbors.
drop off:	I can *drop* you *off* on my way to school.
fill in:	For this test, just *fill in* the blanks.
fill out:	You must *fill out* an application.
hand in:	Harry has to *hand in* his lab report.
hand out:	Marcy will *hand out* the tickets.
keep on:	We can *keep on* rehearsing our music.
look into:	The police want to *look into* the matter.
look over:	Tom intends to *look* the place *over*.
look up:	I can *look* the number *up* in the phone book.
pick up:	Tom went to *pick up* his dry cleaning.
quiet down:	The neighbors asked us to *quiet down*.
run into:	Maybe I will *run into* you at the park.
run out:	We have *run out* of coffee.
think over:	Thank you for the offer; I will *think* it *over*.
try on:	I like that dress; I will *try* it *on*.
try out:	Jack needs to *try* the drill *out*.
turn on:	*Turn* the radio *on*.
turn down:	Lucy wants to *turn* the proposal *down*.
turn up:	The lost keys will *turn up* somwehere.

Exercise 8   Writing Sentences with Two-Word Verbs

Write a sentence for each of the following two-word verbs. Use the examples
above as a guide, but consult a dictionary if you are not sure what the verbs
mean.

1. quiet down   _____

2. try out   _____

3. fill in   _____

4. run into   _____

5. come across   _____

6. turn up _____

7. hand in _____

8. drop off _____

9. keep on _____

10. look up _____

Contractions and Verbs

Contractions often contain verbs you may not recognize in their shortened forms.

contraction: *I'm* making cookies.
long form: *I am* making cookies.

contraction: *He's* been out of town for two weeks.
long form: *He has* been out of town for two weeks.

contraction: *He's* studying German.
long form: *He is* studying German.

contraction: *They'll* meet us at the beach.
long form: *They will* meet us at the beach.

contraction: The *cat's* in the basement.
long form: The *cat is* in the basement.

Exercise 9 **Contractions and Verbs**

In the space above each contraction, write its long form. The first one is done for you.

1. *She would*
   She'd make a fine manager of a large department store.

2. Jimmie's making a mess in the kitchen.

3. Jimmie's made a mess in the kitchen.

4. My supervisor won't accept any excuses for lateness.

5. Next week they'll perform at the Crystal Springs auditorium.

6. I was sure he'd want some time alone.

7. You're never home when I call.

8. After a tough day at work, I'm too tired to study.

9. Your truck's in better condition than my car.

10. My neighbors were great; by the time I regained consciousness, they'd already called an ambulance.

Text Credits

Page 6: Excerpt from "The Tell-Tale Heart" by Edgar Allan Poe. Reprinted with the permission of Simon & Schuster, Inc., from *Great Tales and Poems of Edgar Allan Poe* by Edgar Allan Poe. Copyright © 1960 by Washington Square Press, Inc. Copyright renewed 1988 by Simon & Schuster, Inc. All rights reserved.

Page 81: Excerpt from John F. Kennedy's Inaugural Address. Found in *The Oxford History of the American People*. Samuel Eliot Morison. New York: Oxford University Press, 1965.

Page 81: Excerpt from Martin Luther King, Jr. "I Have a Dream" speech. Reprinted by arrangement with the Estate of Martin Luther King, Jr., c/o Writer's House as agent for the proprietor. New York, NY. Copyright renewed 1991 by Coretta Scott King.

Page 98: Excerpt from "Remembering Lobo" by Pat Mora. Copyright 1993 by Pat Mora. First appeared in *NAPANTLA: Essays from the Land in the Middle*, published by the University of New Mexico Press. Reprinted by permission of Curtis Brown, Ltd.

Page 156: Excerpt from "The World's Most Dangerous Profession." From *The Corpse Had a Familiar Face* by Edna Buchanan. Copyright © 1987 by Edna Buchanan. Used by permission of Random House, Inc.

Page 262: Winston Churchill, excerpt from "Dunkirk," speech from *The World's Greatest Speeches* by Lewis Copeland and Lawrence Lamm, eds. Dover Publications, 1973.

Page 443: "Part-Time Job May Do Teenagers More Harm Than Good" by Gary Klott. *South Florida Sun-Sentinel*. September 1, 1996.

Page 460: "New Directions," from *Wouldn't Take Nothing for My Journey Now* by Maya Angelou. Copyright © 1993 by Maya Angelou. Used by permission of Random House, Inc.

Page 465: "When Fame Falls Short—Benoit Tragedy Shows How 'Celebrity' Doesn't Equal a Happy Life," by Sally Loftis. *The Charlotte Observer*, July 18, 2007.

Page 468: "Only Daughter," by Sandra Cisneros. First published in *Glamour*, November 1990. "Reprinted by permission of Susan Bergholz Literary Services," New York.

Page 472: "The Seamier Side of Life," by Michale Mohr. "My Turn" column in *Newsweek*, August 18, 1997. Reprinted by permission.

Page 475: "The War Within," by David C. Botti, from *New York Stories: The Best of the City Section of the New York Times*. Copyright © 2003 by the New York Times Co. Reprinted by permission.

Page 477: "Deep Cold," by Verlyn Klinkenborg, from *A Rural Life* by Verlyn Klinkenborg. Copyright © 2003 by Verlyn Klinkenborg. By permission of Little, Brown and Co.

Page 479: "A Different Mirror," by Ronald Takaki. Copyright © 1993 by Ronald Takaki. Reprinted by permission of Little, Brown and Co., Inc.

Page 481: "Why Not Real Awards for Real Achievements?" By Ben Stein. From *The American Enterprise* magazine, September/October 1997.

Page 483: "Coming Over," from *Immigrant Kids* by Russell Freedman. Copyright © 1995 by Russell Freedman. Used by permission of Penguin Putnam, Inc.

Photo Credits

Cover: Michelle Marsan/ Shutterstock; **Pages 1, 22, 38, 47, 56, 65, 76, 85, 97, 107, 129, 140, 150, 167, 179, 190, 224, 236, 253, 264, 265, 282, 292, 298:** Photos.com; **Page 305 (top):** Bill Aron/PhotoEdit Inc.; **Page 305 (bottom):** Graham Monro/Photolibrary.com; **Page 307:** Photos.com; **Page 335 (top):** Bob Daemmrich/The Image Works; **Page 335 (bottom):** Paul Edmondson/Getty Images Inc.–Stone Allstock; **Page 337:** Photos.com; **Page 360 (left):** Getty Images–Stockbyte, Royalty Free; **Page 360 (right):** Michael Newman/PhotoEdit Inc.; **Pages 361, 363, 380, 381, 383:** Photos.com; **Page 399:** Jack Star/Getty Images, Inc.–PhotoDisc; **Pages 400, 402, 436 (all), 437 (top):** Photos.com; **Page 437 (center):** Arthur Tilley/Getty Images, Inc.–Taxi; **Page 437 (bottom):** Hart, G. K. & Vikki/Getty Images Inc.–Image Bank; **Pages 441, 484:** Photos.com

Note: Readings are listed under "reading selections" on page 500.

Notes

Notes

Notes

Notes

Notes

Notes